PEASANT POLITICS OF THE TWENTY-FIRST CENTURY

A volume in the series

Cornell Series on Land: New Perspectives on Territory, Development, and Environment

Edited by Wendy Wolford, Nancy Lee Peluso, and Michael Goldman

A list of titles in this series is available at cornellpress.cornell.edu.

PEASANT POLITICS OF THE TWENTY-FIRST CENTURY

Transnational Social Movements and Agrarian Change

Marc Edelman

CORNELL UNIVERSITY PRESS   ITHACA AND LONDON

First published 2024 by Cornell University Press

Library of Congress Cataloging-in-Publication Data

Names: Edelman, Marc, author.
Title: Peasant politics of the twenty-first century : transnational social
    movements and agrarian change / Marc Edelman.
Description: Ithaca [New York] : Cornell University Press, 2024. | Series: Cornell
    series on land: new perspectives on territory, development, and environment |
    Includes bibliographical references and index.
Identifiers: LCCN 2023011463 (print) | LCCN 2023011464 (ebook) |
    ISBN 9781501773440 (hardcover) | ISBN 9781501773945 (paperback) |
    ISBN 9781501773457 (epub) | ISBN 9781501773464 (pdf)
Subjects: LCSH: Land tenure—History—21st century. | Peasants—History—
    21st century. | Agriculture—Social aspects—History—21st century. |
    Social movements—History—21st century.
Classification: LCC HD1251 .E345 2024 (print) | LCC HD1251 (ebook) |
    DDC 333.3—dc23/eng/20230908
LC record available at https://lccn.loc.gov/2023011463
LC ebook record available at https://lccn.loc.gov/2023011464

For Alexandra, who sustains me with light, brilliance, warmth, and inexhaustible joie de vivre

La resurrección de los estudios campesinos en la segunda mitad del siglo XX se debe, ante todo, a los campesinos mismos. Ellos continuaron ignorando las profecías de los científicos sociales y de los marxistas sobre su inminente extinción, y siguieron resistiendo los esfuerzos del complejo urbano-industrial capitalista (privado y estatal) para destruirlos. Desde México hasta la Unión Soviética, desde Argel, China y Vietnam hasta los Estados Unidos y Polonia, el campesino ha hecho sentir su fuerte y continua presencia política y económica. Resulta evidente que en lugar de las hipótesis y las prácticas de su desaparición, se necesita una teoría de su continuidad y una praxis derivada de su permanencia histórica.

The revival of peasant studies in the second half of the twentieth century was due, above all, to the peasants themselves. They continued to ignore the predictions of social scientists and Marxists about their imminent extinction, and they continued resisting the efforts of the urban-industrial capitalist complex (private and state-owned) to destroy them. From Mexico to the Soviet Union, from Algeria, China and Vietnam to the United States and Poland, the peasants have made felt their strong and continuous political and economic presence. In place of the hypotheses about and practices aimed at their disappearance, what is needed is a theory of their continuity and a praxis based on their historical permanence.

—Ángel Palerm, *Antropología y marxismo*

Et si le monde paysan, réputé archaïque et conservateur, commençait à incarner la vraie modernité?

And if the peasant world, supposedly archaic and conservative, began to incarnate true modernity?

—José Bové and François Dufour, *Le monde n'est pas une marchandise*

Los antropólogos tenemos más dificultades para entrar en la modernidad que los grupos sociales que estudiamos.

We anthropologists have more difficulties entering modernity than the social groups that we study.

—Néstor García Canclini, *Culturas híbridas*

Contents

Acknowledgments

Most of the peasants, farmers, organizers, militants, and civil society activists I met during this research (apart from the diplomats in chapter 8) rejected anonymity and wanted me to mention their names in whatever I wrote. My profoundest thanks go to them. Their names appear throughout the pages to come.

I am grateful for support from the American Philosophical Society, National Endowment for the Humanities, National Science Foundation, Wenner-Gren Foundation, and PSC-CUNY Research Program, as well as the Advanced Research Collaborative, the Center on Philanthropy and Civil Society, and the Center for Place, Culture, and Politics, all at the City University of New York Graduate Center. Hunter College's Presidential Faculty Advancement Fund supported the indexing of this book.

It was a delight to work with talented research assistants, many of whom have gone on to successful professional careers. Many thanks to León Arredondo, Elvira Basevich, Brenda Biddle, Carwil Bjork-James, Priya Chandrasekaran, Mauricio Claudio, Alcira Forero-Peña, Kate Goff, Néstor Hincapié, Víctor Ortiz, Christian Pacheco, Jane Rubio, and Nara Roberta Silva.

For incisive comments on one or more draft chapters, I thank Helmut Anheier, Tony Bebbington, Brenda Biddle, Kees Biekhart, Jutta Blauert, Jun Borras, Philippe Bourgois, Jeff Boyer, Priscilla Claeys, John Clark, Annette Desmarais, Michael Dorsey, Jonathan Fox, Lesley Gill, Marlies Glasius, Christophe Golay, Linda Grasso, Charlie Hale, Jack Hammond, Angelique Haugerud, Dominick Jenkins, Jeff Rubin, Jane Schneider, Jim Scott, and Simon Zadek. More colleagues too numerous to name provided useful insights during the give-and-take of conference presentations and university seminars, as did anonymous reviewers.

I am especially indebted to two people who reinvigorated and inspired me in a period when I needed a new start. Jun Borras invited me to the International Institute of Social Studies in 2006, beginning a long-term collaboration and dialogue around scholar-activism and agrarian struggles and connecting me to a vast network of like-minded comrades on every continent except Antarctica. In 2008, Wendy Wolford broached the idea of codirecting a Social Science Research Council workshop on dissertation proposal development in critical agrarian studies. This proved affirming beyond my expectations. Years later, Wendy hinted at the idea for this book, and I am honored that it finally appears as part of the series she coedits with Nancy Lee Peluso and Michael Goldman. Clare

Jones and the Cornell University Press team have moved it from manuscript to book with wonderful professionalism.

Alexandra Neuber came into my life in 2007 and became a wonderful inspiration of a different sort, tearing me away from work, upending my seriousness with humor, and pressing me to put my life where my research had always been and move to a rural area. *Obrigado, meu amor.* My children—Daniel, Ariel, Oskar, and David—have also filled my life to overflowing. Alexandra, together with Daniel and Ariel, provided last-minute graphics expertise.

Various publishers provided permission to reprint the following material, which has been lightly edited for stylistic consistency: Chapter 1 first appeared in *Global Civil Society 2003*, edited by Mary Kaldor, Helmut Anheier, and Marlies Glasius, published by Oxford University Press; chapter 2 was in *Dialectical Anthropology* 33, no. 2 (2009); chapter 4 was in *Latin American Research Review* 33, no. 3 (1998); chapter 5 was in *Social Movements: An Anthropological Reader*, edited by June C. Nash, published by Blackwell in 2005; chapter 6 appeared in *American Anthropologist* 107, no. 3 (2005); chapter 7 was in the *Journal of Peasant Studies* 41, no. 6 (2014); and chapter 10 appeared in the *Journal of Peasant Studies* 36, no. 1 (2009). The introduction, conclusion, and other chapters appear here for the first time.

Abbreviations

AAM	American Agriculture Movement
AbL	Working Community on Peasant Agriculture (Arbeitsgemeinschaft bäuerliche Landwirtschaft) (Germany)
ACWW	Associated Country Women of the World
ADC	Democratic Peasant Alliance (Alianza Democrática Campesina) (El Salvador)
AMIHAN	National Federation of Peasant Women in the Philippines
ANAP	National Association of Small Agriculturalists (Asociación Nacional de Agricultores Pequeños) (Cuba)
AoA	Agreement on Agriculture (WTO)
APEMEP	Association of Small and Medium Producers of Panama (Asociación de Pequeños y Medianos Productores de Panamá)
APM-Afrique	Agriculture Peasant and Modernization Network—Africa (Réseau Agricultures Paysannes et Modernisation Afrique)
APM Mondial	Agriculture Peasant and Modernization Network-World (Réseau Agricultures Paysannes et Modernisation Mondial)
APRODEV	Association of Development Agencies, World Council of Churches (Asociación de Agencias de Desarrollo ligadas al Consejo Mundial de Iglesias) (Belgium)
ASOCODE	Association of Central American Peasant Organizations for Cooperation and Development (Asociación Centroamericana de Organizaciones Campesinas para la Cooperación y el Desarrollo)
ATC	Association of Rural Workers (Asociación de Trabajadores del Campo) (Nicaragua)
ATTAC	Association for the Taxation of Financial Transactions to Aid the Citizenry (Association pour la Taxation des Transactions Financières pour l'Aide aux Citoyens)
BAPO	Belize Association of Producers' Organizations
BAYAN	New Patriotic Alliance (Bagong Alyansang Makabayan) (Philippines)

BFAC	Belize Federation of Agricultural Cooperatives
CADESCA	Support Committee for the Economic and Social Development of Central America (Comité de Apoyo al Desarrollo Económico y Social de Centroamérica)
CAN	Ethnic and People's Agrarian Summit (Cumbre Agraria Étnica y Popular) (Colombia)
CAP	Common Agricultural Policy (EU)
CARICOM	Caribbean Common Market
CAS	critical agrarian studies
CCC-B	Confederation of Cooperatives and Credit Unions of Belize
CCC-CA	Confederation of Cooperatives of the Caribbean and Central America (Confederación de Cooperativas del Caribe y Centroamérica)
CCJYD	Justice and Development Peasant Council (Consejo Campesino Justicia y Desarrollo) (Costa Rica)
CCOD	Coalition of Central American Development Organizations (Concertación Centroamericana de Organismos de Desarrollo)
CENCAP	Cooperative Training Center (Centro de Capacitación Cooperativista) (El Salvador)
CETIM	Third World Center (Centre Europe-Tiers Monde) (Switzerland)
CICA	Central American Indigenous Council (Consejo Indígena Centroamericano)
CICAFOC	Indigenous and Peasant Community Agroforestry Coordinator (Coordinadora Indígena y Campesina de Agroforestería Comunitaria) (Central America)
CIFCA	Copenhagen Initiative for Central America
CLOC	Latin American Coordinator of Rural Organizations (Coordinadora Latinoamericana de Organizaciones del Campo)
CNA	National Agrarian Coordinator (Coordinadora Nacional Agraria) (Costa Rica)
CNC	National Peasant Council (Consejo Nacional Campesino) (Honduras)
CNOC	National Coordinator of Peasant Organizations (Coordinadora Nacional de Organizaciones Campesinas) (Guatemala)
CNP	National Production Council (Consejo Nacional de Producción) (Costa Rica)

CNSTP	National Confederation of Worker-Peasant Unions (Confédération Nationale des Syndicats Travailleurs-Paysans) (France)
CNTC	National Central of Rural Workers (Central Nacional de Trabajadores del Campo) (Honduras)
COAG	Coordination of Agriculturalists' and Livestock Producers' Organizations (Coordinadora de Organizaciones de Agricultores y Ganaderos) (Spain)
COATI	Collective for the Self-Management of Interpretation Technologies (Colectivo para la Autogestión de las Tecnologías de la Interpretación) (Spain)
COCENTRA	Central American Workers Coordination (Coordinación Centroamericana de Trabajadores)
COCICA	Peasant Confederation of the Central American Isthmus (Confederación Campesina del Istmo Centroamericano)
COCOCH	Coordinating Council of Peasant Organizations of Honduras (Concejo Coordinador de Organizaciones Campesinas de Honduras)
CONAC	National Confederation of Peasant Settlements (Confederación Nacional de Asentamientos Campesinos) (Panama)
CONAIE	Confederation of Indigenous Nationalities of Ecuador (Confederación de Nacionalidades Indígenas del Ecuador)
CONAMPRO	National Coordinator of Small and Medium Producers (Coordinadora Nacional de Pequeños y Medianos Productores) (Guatemala)
CONFRAS	Confederation of Federations of Cooperatives of the Salvadoran Agrarian Reform (Confederación de Federaciones de Cooperativas de la Reforma Agraria Salvadoreña)
CONIC	National Indigenous and Peasant Coordination (Coordinadora Nacional Indígena y Campesina) (Guatemala)
COPA	Committee of Professional Agricultural Organizations (Comité des Organisations Professionelles Agricoles) (EU)
CRC	Combahee River Collective
CUC	Committee of Peasant Unity (Comité de Unidad Campesina) (Guatemala)
CUT	Central Única dos Trabalhadores (Unified Workers' Central) (Brazil)
DSU	Dispute Settlement Understanding (WTO)

EC	European Community (after 1993, EU)
ECM	Mesoamerican Peasant Meeting (Encuentro Campesino Mesoamericano)
ECOSOC	Economic and Social Council of the United Nations
EEC	European Economic Community
EFC	European Farmers Coordination
EHNE	Basque Agriculturalists Union (Euskal Herriko Nekazarien Elkartasuna)
ENABAS	Nicaraguan Basic Products Enterprise (Empresa Nicaragüense de Productos Básicos)
ERP	Revolutionary People's Army (Ejército Revolucionario del Pueblo, after 1994, Expresión Renovadora del Pueblo) (El Salvador)
ERPI	Emancipatory Rural Politics Initiative
ETC Group	Action Group on Erosion, Technology and Concentration (formerly RAFI)
EU	European Union
FAO	Food and Agriculture Organization (UN)
FARC-EP	Revolutionary Armed Forces of Colombia-People's Army (Fuerzas Armadas Revolucionarias de Colombia-Ejército del Pueblo)
FDC	Democratic Peasant Front (Frente Democrático Campesino) (Mexico)
FEDEPRICAP	Federation of Private Entities of Central America and Panama (Federación de Entidades Privadas de Centroamérica y Panamá)
FENACOOP	National Federation of Cooperatives (Federación Nacional de Cooperativas) (Nicaragua)
FENOC	National Federation of Peasant Organizations (Federación Nacional de Organizaciones Campesinas) (Ecuador)
FESACORA	Salvadoran Federation of Agrarian Reform Cooperatives (Federación Salvadoreña de Cooperativas de la Reforma Agraria)
FESACORASAL	Federation of Agrarian Reform Cooperatives of the Western Region (Federación de Cooperativas de la Reforma Agraria de la Región Occidental) (El Salvador)
FIAN	Food First Information and Action Network
FIDH	International Human Rights Federation (Federación Internacional de Derechos Humanos)

FIMARC	International Federation of Rural Adult Catholic Movements (Fédération Internationale des Mouvements d'Adultes Ruraux Catholiques)
FIPA	International Federation of Agricultural Producers (Federación Internacional de Productores Agropecuarios) (see also IFAP)
FLOC	Farm Labor Organizing Committee (United States)
FMLN	Farabundo Martí National Liberation Front (Frente Farabundo Martí de Liberación Nacional) (El Salvador)
FNSEA	National Federation of Agricultural Enterprises (Fédération Nationale de Exploitations Agricoles) (France)
FNSP	National Federation of Peasant Unions (Fédération Nationale des Syndicats Paysans) (France)
FPH	Charles Léopold Mayer Foundation for Human Progress (Fondation Charles Léopold Mayer pour le Progres de l'Homme) (Switzerland)
FPL	Popular Forces of Liberation (Fuerzas Populares de Liberación) (El Salvador)
FSLN	Sandinista National Liberation Front (Frente Sandinista de Liberación Nacional) (Nicaragua)
FTAA	Free Trade Area of the Americas
FUNDESCA	Foundation for the Economic and Social Development of Central America (Fundación para el Desarrollo Económico y Social de Centroamérica) (Panama)
G7	Group of Seven
G8	Group of Eight
GABRIELA	General Assembly Binding Women for Reforms, Integrity, Equality, Leadership, and Action (Philippines)
GATT	General Agreement on Tariffs and Trade
GM	genetically modified
IALA	Latin American University Institute of Agroecology "Paulo Freire" (Instituto Universitario Latinoamericano de Agroecología "Paulo Freire")
IATP	Institute for Agriculture and Trade Policy (United States)
ICIC	Civil Initiative for Central American Integration (Iniciativa Civil para la Integración Centroamericana)
ICW	International Council of Women
IFAP	International Federation of Agricultural Producers (see also FIPA)

IIA	International Institute of Agriculture
IITC	International Indian Treaty Council
IMF	International Monetary Fund
Iniciativa CID	Mesoamerican Initiative for Trade, Integration, and Sustainable Development (Iniciativa Mesoamericana de Comercio, Integración y Desarrollo Sostenible)
IPA	International People's Assembly
IRA	Supplies Regulation Institute (Instituto Regulador de Abastecimientos) (El Salvador)
IRAM	Research Institute on Applied Development Methods (Institut de Recherches et d'Applications de Methodes de Developpement) (France)
IUF	International Union of Food, Agricultural, Hotel, Restaurant, Catering, Tobacco, and Allied Workers' Associations
KMP	Peasant Movement in the Philippines (Kilusang Magbubukid ng Pilipinas)
KRRS	Karnataka State Farmers Association (Karnataka Rajya Ryota Sangha) (India)
LVC	La Via Campesina
MAI	Multilateral Agreement on Investment
MNC	National Peasant Coalition (Mesa Nacional Campesina) (Costa Rica)
MNCI	National Peasant Indigenous Movement (Movimiento Nacional Campesino Indígena) (Argentina)
MST	Landless Rural Workers Movement (Movimento dos Trabalhadores Rurais sem Terra) (Brazil)
N30	November 30, 1999 (Seattle anti-WTO protests)
NAFA	North American Farm Alliance
NAFTA	North American Free Trade Agreement
NFU	National Farmers Union (Canada)
NGO	nongovernmental organization
OECD	Organization for Economic Cooperation and Development
OHCHR	Office of the High Commissioner for Human Rights, United Nations
PAC	Action Plan for Central American Agriculture (Plan de Acción para la Agricultura Centroamericana)
PARLACEN	Central American Parliament (Parlamento Centroamericano)

PFS	Paulo Freire Foundation (Paulo Freire Stichting) (Netherlands)
PFSA	Food Security Training Program (Programa de Formación en Seguridad Alimentaria)
PIDHDD	International Human Rights Platform (Plataforma Interamericana de Derechos Humanos) (Ecuador)
PPP	Plan Puebla-Panamá
PSA	Food Security Program (Programa de Seguridad Alimentaria) (Central America)
RAFI	Rural Advancement Foundation International (since 2001 called ETC Group)
REDIJ	Ibero-American Network of Judges (Red Iberoamericana de Jueces)
RIAD	Interamerican Network on Agricultures and Democracy (Red Interamericana de Agriculturas y Democracia)
RMALC	Mexican Action Network on Free Trade (Red Mexicana de Acción Frente al Libre Comercio)
ROPPA	Network of Peasant and Agricultural Producers Organizations of West Africa (Réseau des Organisations Paysannes et des Producteurs Agricoles de L'Afrique de L'Ouest)
SELA	Latin American Economic System (Sistema Económico Latinoamericano)
SICA	Central American Integration System (Sistema de Integración Centroamericana)
SnB	People's Centennial of the Philippine Revolution of 1896 (Sentenaryo ng Bayan)
SNTOAC	National Union of Rural Wage Workers (Sindicato Nacional de Trabajadores y Obreros Asalariados del Campo) (Mexico)
SOCRA	Society of Agrarian Reform Coffee Cooperatives (Sociedad de Cooperativas Cafetaleras de la Reforma Agraria) (El Salvador)
SRI	System of Rice Intensification
TAMs	transnational agrarian movements
TRIPS	Agreement on Trade-Related Aspects of Intellectual Property Rights (WTO)
UCADEGUA	Peasant Union of Guatuso (Unión Campesina de Guatuso) (Costa Rica)

UCS	Salvadoran Communal Union (Unión Comunal Salvadoreña)
UFW	United Farm Workers (United States)
UNAG	National Union of Agriculturalists and Livestock Producers (Unión Nacional de Agricultores y Ganaderos) (Nicaragua)
UNC	National Peasant Union (Unión Nacional Campesina) (Honduras)
UNCTAD	United Nations Conference on Trade and Development
UNDROP	United Nations Declaration on the Rights of Peasants and Other People Working in Rural Areas
UNORCA	National Union of Autonomous Regional Peasant Organizations (Unión Nacional de Organizaciones Regionales Campesinas Autónomas) (Mexico)
UPAGRA	Atlantic Region Small Agriculturalists Union (Unión de Pequeños Agricultores de la Región Atlántica) (Costa Rica)
UPANACIONAL	National Union of Small and Medium Agricultural Producers (Unión Nacional de Pequeños y Medianos Productores Agropecuarios) (Costa Rica)
UPROCAFE	Union of Small Coffee Producers of Central America, Mexico, and the Caribbean (Unión de Pequeños Productores de Café de Centroamérica, México y el Caribe)
USAID	United States Agency for International Development
USFA	US Farmers Association
UTAF	Union of Border Agricultural Workers (Unión de Trabajadores Agrícolas Fronterizos) (United States)
WAMIP	World Alliance of Mobile Indigenous People
WFF	World Forum of Fish Harvesters and Fish Workers
WFFP	World Forum of Fisher Peoples
WI	Women's Institute
WINFA	Windward Islands Farmers Association
WTO	World Trade Organization

PEASANT POLITICS OF THE TWENTY-FIRST CENTURY

THE LONG TWENTY-FIRST CENTURY

The seeds of this book on transnational peasant politics sprouted in the late 1980s in the hills and savannas of Costa Rica's Nicoya Peninsula. Costa Rica was among the first places in the Americas where rural people experienced the shock of neo-liberal globalization, and I was studying how they fought back (Edelman 1999). The country had an advanced social welfare system and a developmental state that provided most rural dwellers with adequate living standards and that structural adjustment threatened to hollow out. As my research progressed, however, I realized that my single-country focus sidelined significant broader processes.

Small annoyances of ethnographic fieldwork in the days before mobile phones, email, and the internet triggered my interest in *transnational* peasant organizing. In the early 1990s, the only way to reach someone in many rural communities was to call that community's single telephone—typically installed in a tiny grocery—and wait while the storeowner sent a child to run and find the person, who might not be easily located. On several occasions, unable to reach someone, I showed up at their yard or front door only to find that the person "is taking a course in Panama," "went to Mexico for a meeting of coffee cooperatives," or "is coming back from a workshop in Honduras." At first, I experienced these absences as lost time, a source of frustration, setbacks in my work. Then, suddenly and belatedly, it dawned on me that these trips abroad and embryonic networks of cross-border solidarity meant that rural activists were on the move and that this was a significant "social fact."

In the mid-1990s, research brought me to every country in the Central American isthmus, from Panama in the south to Belize and Guatemala in the north, based sometimes in Costa Rica and other times in Honduras (see chapters 4 and 5). This required being a fast study, given the different realities of Central American countries and the complexities of their peasant politics. In El Salvador, I ran into what George Orwell (1952, 47)—in another revolutionary situation, Catalonia in 1936—had lamented as a "plague of initials." Each of the five guerrilla factions in the recently concluded civil war, as well as the Christian Democrats and other parties, had sponsored a peasant federation in each of the country's four regions, and every organization had its own long acronym that rolled off people's tongues and that I had to at least recognize, if not master. Each country had lexical peculiarities, and this, too, required mindfulness. Once, on a small Nicaraguan farm, the owner proudly showed me his field of *trigo*, which was clearly not wheat but sorghum. In Guatemala, I spoke with Indigenous peasants of limited means who referred to their many *coches*, a standard if peninsular-sounding Spanish term for automobile, which in Guatemala means "pigs."

Fieldwork across Central America admittedly involved some sacrifice of depth for breadth. It was hardly, however, the "hit-and-run ethnography" that Clifford Geertz lambasted in his grumpy polemic against cultural studies and multisited research (2000, 141). I moved around so much because it was the only way to develop depth on the regional, transnational dynamics of peasant organizing. A mixed methods approach also made greater depth possible. Unlike earlier agrarian movements, which generally left scant paper trails, the Central American peasant organizations employed *técnicos*—agronomists, communications specialists, lawyers—and were prolific creators of newsletters and reports that, if read with a critical and sometimes skeptical eye, helped offset the loss of depth that occurred with greater breadth. Some of these were manuals about agronomy, popular education, and cooperative organization, with whimsical titles like "The Velvet Bean, Maize's Companion" (*El chinapopo, compañero del maíz*), "The Indian Abacus: A Proposal for Teaching and Learning Mathematics with Adults" (*El ábaco hindú: una propuesta para la enseñanza-aprendizaje de matemáticas con adultos*), or "The Peasants Will Know How to Organize Themselves" (*El campesino va a saber organizarse*) (Salomón 1993; CNTC 1992; UNAG 1988). Others were internal summaries of activities that donors required and that not infrequently became objects of the "document fetishism" that Annelise Riles (2000) savaged in her scathing critique of the NGOization of women's movements in Asia and the Pacific. While social movements and their academic allies frequently attack nongovernmental organizations (NGOs) and NGOization, I point out that lines between social movements and NGOs are often blurry (chapter 5), that "NGOs" is a very heterogeneous category, and that strategic and respectful alliances with select donor and grassroots NGOs can advance movement objectives (chapter 8).[1]

In these first years of fieldwork, conversations with rural activists made clear that transnational alliances increasingly transcended the Central American region. I met Honduran and Salvadoran agrarian reform beneficiaries who had taken courses on cooperative administration in Canada, Israel, Germany, and Puerto Rico, and Belizeans who studied beekeeping in Mexico. Several Nicaraguans told me that farmers from India had given them seeds from the neem tree (*Azadirachta indica*), a plant with extraordinary insecticidal, antibiotic, and medicinal properties, which they had planted on their farms. Three friends from Costa Rica told of traveling to the Netherlands and Belgium for meetings that led to the formation of a global network, La Via Campesina. Nicaraguan, Costa Rican, and Guatemalan activists stayed in my New York apartment while they visited United Nations agencies, foundations, universities, and radio stations (see chapter 10).

Networks of peasant solidarity were expanding before my eyes and out of my sight. They were too extensive for a single researcher or even a team to study if the researchers had positivist pretensions of comprehensiveness and, particularly, if they had other work and family obligations, finite resources, or were trained in and partial to slow, artisanal ethnographic methods.[2] In the ensuing years, I visited many network nodes, including in Canada, Indonesia, Mexico, Cuba, Honduras, Ecuador, India, several countries in Europe (the Netherlands, Belgium, Germany, France, and Switzerland), and Washington, DC. Each site involved specific questions and challenges. It became unremarkable to see in Jakarta or Schwäbisch Hall somebody I had encountered years earlier in Managua, Saskatoon, Pondicherry, Washington, DC, or Brussels. Over time, I noticed that many of the peasants and small farmers I met were in production lines that required only intermittent attention—beekeeping, raising goats, growing olive trees or tubers—and that this sporadic work, along with belonging to cooperatives and having household or hired labor and NGO backing, was what made their international travels possible.

This research began as a multisited project years before multisitedness became a thing in anthropology. Starting from the commonsense premise that one had to base research on questions and that one had to go to the places where the answers might be found, I became so drawn into the process that I neglected to name what I was doing, as George Marcus eventually did (1995) and as others reformulated it under the rubrics of "mobile" or "itinerant" ethnography (Novoa 2015; Schein 2002; Muzzopappa and Ramos 2017). Like Michael Burawoy's team, I "had to rethink the meaning of fieldwork, releasing it from solitary confinement, from being bound to a single place and time" (Burawoy 2000, 4). And, like Vinay Gidwani and K. Sivaramakrishnan, I found that "to produce ethnographies of people on the move is to unsettle the certitudes of Modernity" (2003, 342).

Even in a research project that relied mainly on interviews with key inter-locutors, documentary sources, and attendance at small and large public events where political performances were on display, it was essential to retain an ethnographic sensibility. It is not just that ethnographically perceivable processes were "cases" (or "extended cases") of larger phenomena. A weak point of civil society and social movement studies is the tendency of sympathetic researchers to take at face value political performances and the assertions of spokespeople and organizations' publications and websites. Early on in my work, I noticed the gatekeeping that characterizes almost all collective projects. Grassroots organizers told of doors barred, promised invitations or airplane tickets that intentionally arrived late or not at all, and fights over the "juridical personality" and resources of organizations. In some countries, particularly in the 1980s and 1990s, women—sick and tired of patriarchy and pervasive machismo—left male-dominated movements and formed their own organizations (Stephen 1997; Rubin and Sokoloff-Rubin 2013). Spokespeople or key interlocutors rarely, if ever, mention this, and the documents the organizations produce elide discussions of their border maintenance practices. Yet movements sometimes exclude, expel, or marginalize certain individuals or organizations, and they usually fail to recruit a large proportion of those they claim to represent. As I suggest in chapter 10, among the most useful contributions that academics can make to the social movements they study is to convey patterns in the testimony of people in the movement's target group who are sympathetic to movement objectives but feel alienated by the movement's practices.

Cultivating an ethnographic sensibility also was crucial for making sense of "fictitious" organizations that look good on paper—groups that have a leader, letterhead, and maybe a website and office but lack any substantial constituency. In Panama, I once spent hours in the office of a national peasant movement where the telephone rang only once, alerting me to the possibility—subsequently corroborated though other sources—that the organization had little base in the countryside and was largely a "paper" one, set up mainly to garner European Union grants. In studies of agrarian movements, as Saturnino Borras and I suggested, "'representation' may be understood in two senses: as a claim about *representativeness*, or having a constituency or social base, and . . . as a practice of *representing* a movement and its leaders as authentically incarnating a peasant political project" (Edelman and Borras 2016, 95). Both are key to how movements attain legitimacy and build momentum.

Peasant Politics of the Twenty-First Century analyzes transnational agrarian movements (TAMs) that seek to remake the world's food and agriculture systems and—more broadly—changes in rural areas that are reshaping social struggles of all kinds. It charts the historical roots of TAMs, their objectives and campaigns, and how they converged with environmental, human rights, labor, women's, and food justice movements. Geographically, the book moves from farmers' fields in Central America, Canada, Indonesia, and Switzerland to massive protests in Seattle, Western Europe, and India to heated debates over peasants' rights and the very category of "peasant" in the United Nations. It scrutinizes biographies of first-generation charismatic activists in La Via Campesina, such as José Bové, who dismantled a McDonald's restaurant in France; the late professor M. D. Nanjundaswamy, who looted files from Cargill's office in Bangalore and brought the World Trade Organization's (WTO) agreement on Trade-Related Aspects of Intellectual Property Rights (TRIPS) to international attention; Saskatchewan farmer Nettie Wiebe, who celebrates the Canadian prairies' legacy of agrarian feminism; and Basque farmer Paul Nicholson, who in his youth worked on an Israeli kibbutz and in middle age joined Yasser Arafat inside the Palestine Liberation Organization (PLO) compound during the Israeli siege of Ramallah. A younger generation of lesser-known militants, including migrant women in Europe, are among the "rooted cosmopolitans" who are taking up the once seemingly quixotic struggles initiated by the older activists (chapter 3). The book examines the forgotten genealogies and policy implications of foundational analytical frameworks like "moral economy," increasingly popular programmatic concepts such as "food sovereignty," and long-standing categories of international governance, such as "civil society" (chapters 5, 6, and 7). It acknowledges the dilemmas of politically engaged research while arguing for its necessity in studies of social movements, drawing on experiences in Central America and in the UN Human Rights Council.

What's in a Title?

Aspects of the book's title may cry out for explanation. "Peasant" (and its equivalents in other languages) has a troubling history, with implications ranging from pejorative to romantic, and a complicated politics in rural places, national histories, and international governance institutions. The reader who listens to Nettie Wiebe in chapter 1 or who peruses chapter 9 will, I hope, be persuaded that the term "peasant" can be eminently contemporary and is not just an anachronism. Today, it is a label of self-ascription and a badge of pride for millions of small agriculturalists, rural workers, and country dwellers. This is particularly true for participants in the organizations that form transnational agrarian movements, notably La Via Campesina, the most emblematic TAM, but also lesser-known regional and global networks, such as the Asian Peasant Coalition. Scholars who study transnational social movements accorded scant attention to transnational *agrarian* movements, even though they have become some of the largest social movements in recent history.

Historian Eric Hobsbawm—echoing orthodox Marxists that anthropologist Ángel Palerm decries in this book's epigraph—famously declared: "The most dramatic and far-reaching social change of the second half of this [twentieth] century, and the one which cuts us off for ever from the world of the past, is the death of the peasantry" (Hobsbawm 1994, 289).

Hobsbawm cited the decline in the *relative* proportion of people working in agriculture in developed countries and in the global population, which he rightly ascribed to urbanization and industrialization.[3] But what Hobsbawm and "modernizers" of the left and right fail to acknowledge is that peasants' *absolute* numbers now surpass what they were in those earlier periods when they were the vast majority of humankind (Van der Ploeg 2008). Even allowing for imprecision in category boundaries, peasants still constitute one-third or more of humanity. They include poor and well-to-do small-scale agriculturalists producing for subsistence or for the market, "part-lifetime" and "semi-proletarian" rural dwellers who combine waged work with agriculture, pastoralists and nomads, and multifunctional or pluriactive rural households that mix diverse occupations in the struggle for a better life.[4]

And what about the "twenty-first century"? This century has hardly begun, so to the literal-minded among us, it might seem presumptuous to include it in the book's title. The rhythms of history have never followed the numerical grids that people impose on them. "Periodization," as Perry Anderson remarked, "always involves arbitrary simplifications" (2002, 6). When I refer to the "twenty-first century," I nod to the interconnectedness of the uncertain future and the proximate and knowable past. Peter Waterman put it aptly when he observed that "the 21st century began at Seattle" (2001, vii) in the 1999 demonstrations against the WTO and its neoliberal agenda, which many consider the spark that lit the antiglobalization movement and involved many peasant militants (see chapter 2). Today's peasant politics have roots in the late twentieth century, especially in its last two decades, that coincide with the rise of neoliberalism, a new and cutthroat version of capitalism that had especially deleterious impacts on rural zones and people. Chapter 1, however, documents the emergence of transnational peasant politics in the late nineteenth and early twentieth centuries, such as the Women's Institute movement in Canada, the United States, and Britain. So I use "twenty-first century" in the spirit of nonviolent activist Gene Sharp, as an uncertain future filled with potential, or following Fernand Braudel and Immanuel Wallerstein, who invoked "the long sixteenth century," or Giovanni Arrighi's "the long twentieth century" to cover an extended range of slowly unfolding processes (Sharp and Paulson 2005; Braudel 1972; Wallerstein 1974; Arrighi 2010).

For some readers, the title may sound like an echo of *Peasant Wars of the Twentieth Century*, Eric Wolf's (1969) monumental study of revolutions in Mexico, Russia, China, Vietnam, Algeria, and Cuba. As Wolf made clear, peasants were major historical protagonists for the three-quarters of the twentieth century that culminated, not long after his book came out, in the 1975 defeat of the United States at the hands of the South Vietnam National Liberation Front and its North Vietnamese allies. Also in 1975, independence fighters in Angola and Mozambique expelled the Portuguese from their main African colonies. A few years later—in 1979—the Sandinistas, a revolutionary movement with significant rural support, triumphed in Nicaragua. In 1980, largely rural guerrilla movements liberated Zimbabwe from white supremacist rule. Brutal civil wars that pitted peasant and other revolutionaries against intransigent elites sputtered to inconclusive finales in El Salvador and Guatemala in the 1990s.

From Peasant Studies to Critical Agrarian Studies

Despite these anticolonial and revolutionary advances, this grand scale of peasant protagonism waned in the twentieth century's last two decades (Gill, Binford, and Striffler 2020). As chapter 6 indicates, the diminished impact of late-twentieth-century peasantries on world historical transformations resulted not only from urbanization and industrialization but also from growing peasant involvement in unattractive predatory wars, frequently over natural resources or drugs, though sometimes also with millenarian ambitions, such as those waged by Shining Path in Peru, the Lord's Resistance Army in Central and East Africa, Charles Taylor in West Africa, the gangs of Central America's Northern Triangle, and the ethno-nationalist insurgencies in Myanmar. The end of the Cold War and the spread of neoliberalism played key roles in this shift. University-based intellectuals, enamored of the new pro-market vogue or poststructuralist theoretical "turns," downplayed or abandoned political-economic analysis despite their institutions being hammered by austerity. With the unraveling of the Soviet Union, the West no longer had a geopolitical competitor that backed revolutionary movements and governments. Neoliberalism unleashed market forces that led national and multinational capital to target resource-rich territories previously beyond their reach, often employing peasant mercenaries as cannon fodder. It fueled rural–urban and international migration, undermining webs of community and kin and territorially based struggles. The free-market "revolution" exacerbated individualism in myriad ways, complicating collective projects, especially progressive ones.

If the peasant studies of the 1960s and 1970s at times idealized the rural revolutionary (Huizer 1973), shifts in the 1980s and 1990s transformed both peasant collective action and academic approaches to studying it. In many countries, peasant organizations previously subordinated to political parties of the left, center, and right broke with their erstwhile tutors and articulated new discourses of "autonomy." Frequently, they replaced "vertical" party ties with dependency on international NGOs, but they nonetheless provided platforms for genuinely peasant voices and programs and established horizontal relations on their own terms with diverse agrarian and non-agrarian movements. For the most part, the left-wing movements shunned revolutionary violence, acknowledging that the human costs of the previous decades had been too great, although in some countries in South and Southeast Asia, militant peasants—often from racialized and socially excluded minorities—continued guerrilla struggles in remote areas (Edelman and Borras 2016).

Intellectuals' disillusion with disappearing rural revolutionaries was not their only disappointment. In the 1960s and 1970s, state-led agrarian reforms in developing countries sometimes provided genuine benefits. Peasants and rural people achieved greater economic security and, occasionally, modest prosperity. Greater access to education, literacy, and healthcare had synergetic effects with redistributive land reform, giving rise to a peasantry that was well informed, more outward looking, and better equipped for political struggle. But the global metastasis of a ruthless neoliberal capitalism in the 1980s and after brought "counter agrarian reform" and "market-led agrarian reform," cutting short these promising developments and the hopes of millions (Edelman and León 2013; Lahiff, Borras, and Kay 2007).

This changing panorama on-the-ground constituted the backdrop for emerging scholarly frameworks. By the turn of the twenty-first century, social scientists concerned with rural realities increasingly eschewed the term "peasant studies" in favor of "agrarian change" or "critical agrarian studies."[5] This was less a paradigm shift than a recognition of the complexity they had documented for a long time: Rural zones included not only peasants but diverse other actors, among them large and small landowners, plantation and farmworkers, artisanal fishers, ranchers and pastoralists, Indigenous and other ethnic groups, industrialists, professionals, and merchants. A *critical* agrarian studies lens placed the field alongside others—critical legal studies, critical development studies, critical race theory, and science and technology studies—that analyzed and combated the biases and forms of representing and legitimizing knowledge that characterized the conventional wisdom. For critical agrarian studies, this meant confronting understandings emanating from multilateral development institutions, particularly the World Bank, and from private-sector agribusiness and its allies in philanthropy and university programs in agronomy and economics (Edelman 2016; Chang 2009). It also meant deepening engagement with activists in agrarian, environmentalist, agroecology, food, feminist, Indigenous, and human rights movements. I initiated this research before critical agrarian studies (CAS) had a name. But *Peasant Politics of the Twenty-First Century* evolved alongside CAS and is very much a product of it.

Lacunae and Interpretative Challenges

This book collects essays on transnational agrarian movements written over more than two decades of research and reflection. Each is the product of different historical conjunctures and moments in the research. Over the years, and with the evolution of my own thinking, there are, naturally, aspects that could have been modified. I have nonetheless resisted the temptation to update the texts, since this would have meant artificially extracting them from the historical and intellectual contexts that shaped them in the first place.

There also are lessons to be learned from maintaining the original versions. It is not just the author's thinking that evolves over time but also the "historical subjects." Who could have known, for example, that the robust transnational Central American peasant networks analyzed in chapter 4 would implode and disappear (as chapter 5 describes)? And the circumstances in which the "historical subjects" arise and develop also change. A collection of essays like this—both retrospective and forward-looking—is an opportunity to reflect on how all three things shift over time: the researcher's perspective and intellectual and academic context; the transnational agrarian movements and peasant politics and economy; and the larger socioeconomic, political, and environmental contexts that shaped both.

There are several crucial topics that this collection does not reflect on or analyze (at least not sufficiently). While chapters 4 and 5 examine how peasants and Indigenous people engage with modernity and communications technology, the prominent role of native people in some movements was something I witnessed but also came to see as unremarkable. In 1994, a Kuna shaman chanted the invocation opening a Central America–wide meeting of peasant activists in Panama. One morning at the same event, I had breakfast with a half dozen Indians from Central America, including Guatemalan Cachiquels, Panamanian Kunas, a Costa Rican Bribri, and a Tawahka from Honduras. Like me, several of them had university degrees. As we finished our eggs, coffee, and *arepas*, the tiny corn cakes that are Panama's equivalent of tortillas, they began to tell "Indian" stories, mocking and doing impressions of whites and mestizos who had a hard time believing that Indigenous people could use computers, run broadcasting equipment, or debate complex issues comfortably and articulately with cabinet ministers and presidents of the republic. "'How can you be an Indian with that laptop?'" one mimicked, provoking peals of laughter. "'If you're an Indian, why do you have on a suit and tie?'" another quipped, quoting a government minister and reporting that he had retorted that everyone else in the office except the female secretary also had on a suit and tie. It was not a surprise to me that downtrodden peoples often delight in inversion tales that accentuate their wit and intelligence in exchanges with oppressors who believe them to be dense but who, in the anecdotes, figure as the actual dullards and the butt of the jokes. The elite skepticism these sophisticated Indians experienced epitomized a style of invective long characteristic of Central America's dominant groups, and that extended to peasants in general. As Jeffrey Gould described early twentieth-century Nicaragua: "When Indians achieved education but still desired an indigenous identity, lands, and organization, they were dubbed ersatz, artificial creations" (1998, 71).

Many years later, in 2014, in Geneva's august Palais des Nations, I attended a UN event on a proposed treaty on the human rights obligations of transnational corporations. A speaker from Mexico began his intervention in Zapotec before switching to Spanish, and another from Paraguay opened in Guaraní. These heartfelt performances of indigeneity, like those in Panama, occurred in the context of struggles that linked the demands of native peoples to those of the larger agrarian and human rights movements I was studying. In reflecting on the continuous presence of Indigenous activists in these groups, I believe I sought to normalize it and to move beyond the exoticizing gaze that anthropologists have long turned on their traditional objects of study.

The growing centrality of agroecology in the agronomic and political practice of agrarian organizations is another area deserving of more in-depth treatment (Rosset and Altieri 2017). Chapter 4 mentions the rise of Central America's *Campesino a Campesino* or peasant-to-peasant participatory extension movement (Holt-Giménez 2006; J. Boyer 2007). Beyond these initial efforts, in recent years, La Via Campesina (LVC) and allied organizations established numerous large and small agroecology institutes in the Americas, Africa, and Asia (Lima et al. 2015; Rosset et al. 2019; Val et al. 2019; LVC 2021).[6] Some are one-time training events, but others are thoroughly institutionalized, with research, extension, and educational agendas like those of conventional universities (Bringel and Vieira 2015; McCune, Reardon, and Rosset 2014). The System of Rice Intensification (SRI) predates LVC and has diffused mainly through other channels. An agroecological method that generates vastly higher yields, albeit with greater labor inputs, SRI was pioneered in Madagascar and spread widely in Asia and to some places in the Americas, notably Cuba (Uphoff 2003). Yet another example of agroecological approaches comes from South India, where tens of millions of smallholders responded to the neoliberal onslaught by adopting "Zero Budget Natural Farming," an ideologically problematical movement with sympathies for the Hindu right that nonetheless minimizes farmers' indebtedness and maximizes self-reliance and autonomy from markets (Münster 2016; Khadse and Rosset 2019). In Mexico and Central America, peasants have long used a zero-budget slash-mulch system (*tapado*) to grow beans, sometimes with outstanding yields (Thurston et al. 1994).

These are *intensive* systems, capable of feeding large numbers of people with few or no external inputs and—most importantly—few or no destructive "externalities," such as chemical contamination, erosion, and greenhouse gas emissions (Stone 2022a). Even the most conservative estimates, by scientists beholden to industrial agriculture interests, concede that farms under two hectares produce 30 percent of the world's food. Critics claim that these producers (together with slightly larger ones) feed up to 70 percent of the global population and that much of the "food" industrial farms produce is wasted or becomes feed concentrates and biofuels (ETC Group 2022). They also point out that, especially but not only in developing countries, many sources of food security—gathered plants, gleaning, backyard gardens, fishing, and hunting—escape measurement, which artificially inflates macro-level estimates of industrial agriculture's contribution to feeding the planet. Grassroots efforts to extend productive smallholder farming systems have gained growing traction in international policymaking, such as the UN Food and Agriculture Organization's "Scaling Up Agroecology Initiative" and the International Assessment of Agricultural Knowledge, Science and Technology for Development, a consortium of the World Bank and several UN agencies (FAO 2018; IAASTD 2009; Herren, Haerlin, and IAASTD+10 Advisory Group 2020).

The urgency of the agroecology agenda is not only about conserving biodiversity, soil, and water or ensuring higher incomes, greater autonomy, and improved nutrition. With a looming climate catastrophe, it is essential to consider that high-input industrial agriculture produces around one-quarter of greenhouse gas emissions, and much more if habitat destruction and production and transport of fertilizer and other inputs and equipment are considered (Toensmeier et al. 2020; Li et al. 2022). La Via Campesina has long argued that the diversified peasant farm is a carbon sink and contributes to cooling the planet (LVC 2009b); increasingly, it joins climate justice initiatives with non-agrarian organizations. Moreover, during the COVID-19 pandemic, the roles of habitat destruction and industrial monocultures, particularly large-scale pig and poultry farms, in propagating zoonoses and future pandemics has raised increasing alarm (Wallace 2016; Wallace et al. 2020).

"The Largest Protest in Human History"

Ecuador and India, among many other places, underscore the *continuing relevance of peasant politics in the twenty-first century*, even after COVID-19 complicated transnational activism. In 2019 and 2022, Ecuador's Indigenous movement, labor unions, and students spearheaded massive anti-austerity protests that paralyzed the entire country. Fuel subsidies, tax hikes, cost of living, indebtedness, mining, and worsening inequality were the major issues, but in both 2019 and 2022, Indigenous peasants from the Andes and the Amazon—organized in CONAIE (Confederation of Indigenous Nationalities of Ecuador)—took the lead in demonstrations and negotiations with the government (see figure I.1). Long the largest social movement in a country where nearly half the population is Indigenous, CONAIE stages intermittent "uprisings," ousted three governments between 1997 and 2005, demanded and achieved a more inclusive constitution in 2008, and remains an ever-present nightmare for Ecuador's dominant groups. Since its founding in 1986, CONAIE has backed transnational struggles, hosting Indigenous congresses and demonstrations against free-trade treaties. While several smaller Ecuadorian peasant organizations participate in global movements like La Via Campesina and often collaborate with CONAIE, the latter's formal alliances abroad are with native rather than agrarian networks.

Ecuador was only one place where the ravages of neoliberalism detonated an explosion. In India in late 2020, some 300,000 farmers from forty or so organizations drove their tractors, bullock carts, and motorcycles to the outskirts of Delhi and laid siege to the capital, protesting three laws that opened markets to corporate agribusiness, reduced public procurement of food staples at guaranteed prices, and encouraged contract farming with little state oversight. In November 2020, upwards of 250 million people around the subcontinent joined them in a twenty-four-hour solidarity strike, which some observers called "the largest single protest in human history" (Pahwa 2020). The protests spread to at least eighteen Indian states, despite sporadic state repression, and generated unprecedented alliances across caste, religious, and class lines (Lerche 2021). For a year, the farmers camped on the outskirts of Delhi, making this also "the lon-

FIGURE I.1. Indigenous protesters sing outside Congress, Quito, Ecuador, 2016. Photo by the author.

gest lasting and most significant peasant mobilization in postcolonial India" (Singh 2021, 70). Then, in November 2021, the autocratic government of Narendra Modi unexpectedly yielded and repealed the disputed laws.

Few of the largely Sikh farmers who launched the protests were agroecology enthusiasts or allies of La Via Campesina (though LVC's member organization Bharatiya Kisan Union had a prominent role). On the contrary, most were the children and grandchildren of the 1960s Green Revolution, which used high-yielding seeds, bore wells, and copious fertilizer and pesticide applications—as well as price supports and subsidized credit, fuel, and electricity—to turn the Punjab and Haryana into India's breadbasket and to produce a class of prosperous agriculturalists. While the Green Revolution famously exacerbated social class divisions and depleted and contaminated aquifers, these farmers were, at least temporarily, the winners in that differentiation and modernization process. The free-market measures that began in the early 1990s and have accelerated since, however, threatened to remove the protective cushion of subsidies and minimum price supports, subordinating many of the farmers to giant corporations via lopsided contract farming arrangements. Drowning in unpayable debts and despair, growing numbers of farmers committed suicide (Dhanagare 2016). When the farmers marched on Delhi, they were demanding dignity and recognition, but their targets were the same types of neoliberal "reforms" that impoverish those who produce our food and that agriculturalists around the world have protested and will continue to confront as the long twenty-first century unfolds.

Part 1
ORIGINS

TRANSNATIONAL PEASANT AND FARMER MOVEMENTS AND NETWORKS

This chapter, based on research in Central America, Canada, and Europe, analyzes a plethora of historical and contemporary transnational agrarian movements and documents their early organizing experiences that heretofore had received little, if any, attention. The focus is largely on the activities and histories of formally constituted organizations. For further analysis of how many of these organizations developed in the succeeding decades, see Edelman and Borras 2016.

In 1999, thousands of protesters—many dressed as monarch butterflies and sea turtles—disrupted the Seattle meeting of the World Trade Organization (WTO) and helped to shine a spotlight on controversial global development issues. A less flamboyant and fashionable part of the crowd consisted of peasant and small farmer organizers, from dozens of countries, who proclaimed that worldwide economic liberalization endangered their livelihoods. Sporting green baseball caps and bandannas, these activists have been a significant presence outside post-Seattle meetings of international financial, trade, and governance institutions in Washington, DC, Prague, Cancún, Quebec, Genoa, Barcelona, and elsewhere, as well as in the civil society delegations to the Food and Agriculture Organization summit (Rome+5), the Porto Alegre World Social Forums, and the World Summit on Sustainable Development (Rio+10). The voices of small agriculturalists are having a growing impact in global arenas. Farmers in India were among the first sector anywhere to object to the controversial Agreement on Trade-Related Aspects of Intellectual Property Rights (TRIPS), which empowers the WTO to enforce global rules on patents, copyrights, and trademarks. The French Confédération Paysanne, which grabbed headlines worldwide when its supporters dismantled a half-built McDonald's restaurant, played a key role in having the European Union (EU) declare a moratorium on commercial planting of genetically modified (GM) crops. The success of the Brazilian Landless Rural Workers Movement (MST) in pressing for agrarian reform influenced peasant organizations throughout the Americas and as far away as South Africa. Much of this rural effervescence developed from cross-border links that peasant and small farmer organizations from many parts of the world forged with each other and with nongovernmental organizations (NGOs) concerned with agrarian reform, food security, trade, biotechnology, and environmental and human rights issues.

This chapter first examines early and mid-twentieth-century attempts to link agriculturalists' organizations in different countries. It then analyses how the farm crisis, market openings, and regional integration projects of the 1980s galvanized new movements and cross- border linkages among farmers in Latin America, North America, Europe, and India. This "globalization from below" allowed agriculturalists' organizations to develop common agendas and more creative protest repertoires as well as to have tangible impacts in areas as diverse as trade policy and human rights advocacy. In the past two decades, farmers achieved a prominence in international arenas that they rarely enjoyed in their own countries, where they were often among the most economically and culturally marginalized sectors of the population. The networks that make up global civil society, including those of agriculturalists, nonetheless raise delicate questions about representation: Who speaks for the peasant and farmer (see box 1.1), and through what political processes are those claims to legitimacy established?

Historic Organizations
Associated Country Women of the World

Transnational networking among small farmer organizations accelerated during the 1980s and 1990s, but its roots lie in the late nineteenth and early twentieth centuries. This suggests that cross-border organizing is neither a new phenomenon nor simply an outcome of recent revolutions in communications technology, the emergence of supranational governance institutions, or a weakening of the contemporary state system under globalization. Early transnational farmers' organizations manifested eclectic amalgams of elite-led reformism and noblesse oblige, pacifism, Christian missionary zeal, first-wave feminism, and agrarian populism.

The genealogy of Associated Country Women of the World (ACWW) exemplifies these diverse origins. ACWW, "the largest international organization for rural women," claims a membership of nine million in 365 participating societies in over seventy countries (ACWW 2002). It developed in the late 1920s through encounters between leaders of the International Council of Women (ICW)—founded in Washington, DC, in 1888—and the Women's Institute movement, which began in Canada in the 1890s and spread to the United States, England, and many British colonies.

The ICW was founded by US activists (and delegates from eight other countries) who had participated in the abolitionist, women's suffrage, and temperance movements (Rupp 1997, 15). The Women's Institutes (WI) were initiated by leaders of ICW's Canadian affiliate as auxiliaries to the farmers' institutes, a provincial extension program. In 1913, Canadian WI activist Madge Watt moved to Britain, where she helped found several hundred local WI organizations and interested long-time ICW President Ishbel Gordon Aberdeen in starting an international federation. Watt and Lady Aberdeen, an aristocratic feminist whose husband had served as the British governor general of Canada, called a meeting in London in 1929 with women from twenty-three countries who established an ICW committee on rural women (Drage 1961). The committee published a yearbook and circulated leaflets in three languages to recruit new national associations (Meier 1958). In 1933, in Stockholm, it became the Associated Country Women of the World.

In ACWW's early years, women from the English, Belgian, Romanian, German, and Swedish nobility played key roles. The association set up speakers' schools for organizers and researched issues such as midwifery services and nutrition. In the prewar period, it worked with the League of Nations, and following World War II, it attained consultative status with several United Nations agencies. More recently, ACWW has supported development and income-generating programs and advocated in international forums for women's rights. Despite growing participation by women from less developed countries and an increasingly sophisticated approach to gender issues, ACWW never transcended its elite British origins. Its conventions are still held in English, without translation services, which limits participation from outside the English-speaking world primarily to educated middle- and upper-class women, most of whom are NGO personnel rather than rural producers (Storey 2002).

Agricultural Missions

Agricultural Missions, a multidenominational Christian organization founded in 1930 by US religious leaders and deans of agricultural colleges, originally assisted churches in sending rural missionaries to some fifty countries. Supported by the US National Council of Churches (NCC), it emphasized technical assistance and a gospel of rural life and worship. In the 1970s, influenced by liberation theology's "preferential option for the poor" and by nationalist and anticolonial struggles, the organization established relations with grassroots movements. In 1979, as Agricultural Missions neared its fiftieth anniversary, it sponsored a "consultation" in Jayuya, Puerto Rico, that brought together religious and farmer activists from the Caribbean, Central America, Micronesia, Africa, Korea, and the Philippines, as well as Mexican Americans, Native American, and African Americans (Matejka 1979). "We discovered, sometimes only after confrontation," J. Benton Rhoades, the Missions' executive secretary wrote, "that technical expertise was not enough."

> It was useless to speak of mini-tractors, hybrid seeds or breeding techniques with the rural poor, if those small farmers were unsure of their land ownership, or trapped between tenancy and loan sharks. It was ridiculous to push new varieties when a farmer's biggest problem was not seedlings, but a place to plant them. It was difficult to bring people together when military rule had soldiers in every village and land-grabbers fast behind them. (Rhoades quoted in Matejka 1979, 3)

This shift in the orientation of the Agricultural Missions facilitated transnational collaboration by peasant and farmer activists. In 2002, Agricultural Missions organized a three-week "Education for Rural Justice Tour" in ten US states, which featured peasant movement representatives from Mexico, Brazil, and Venezuela who spoke on conditions in their countries to audiences of farmers, church members, students, and environmentalists (NCC 2002).

International Federation of Agricultural Producers

The International Federation of Agricultural Producers (IFAP) was founded amid post–World War II optimism about global cooperation and fears of impending food shortages and a recurrence of agricultural depression like that of the 1930s. In 1946, the British National Farmers Union convoked a meeting in London of agriculturalists' representatives from thirty countries, with the objective of supporting the newly formed UN Food and Agriculture Organization (FAO) and overcoming differences between commodity-based interest groups— grain farmers and feed-lot livestock producers, for example—within the agricultural sector (London Times 1946a, 1946b).

The northern European groups that dominated IFAP already had a decades-long history of international congresses, many involving cooperative societies and Christian farmers' organizations created in the early twentieth century (ICA and IFAP 1967; IFAP 1957, 5). Despite a certain ambivalence about market liberalism, these forces often backed center-right political parties. They worked with the Rome-based International Institute of Agriculture (IIA), which was established with Rockefeller Foundation support in 1905, which engaged in agronomic research, campaigned for uniform systems of statistical reporting, and cooperated with the League of Nations in the interwar period. The FAO, founded in 1945, was explicitly modeled on this earlier experience, and IFAP was intended as the FAO's private-sector ally.

The postwar food crisis led IFAP to emphasize raising production, even though some delegations, such as the Canadians, called for international marketing mechanisms that "would distribute abundance efficiently and in such a way that surpluses would not spell disaster to the producers" (London Times 1946b). IFAP leaders served in government delegations to FAO conferences, sometimes exercising substantial influence on FAO policies (IFAP 1952). IFAP subsequently joined ACWW in publicizing World Rural Women's Day, which has been celebrated each year since the 1995 Beijing Women's Conference on October 15.

Box 1.1. "Peasant" and "farmer"—What's in a name?

In the 1960s and 1970s, scholars devoted a great deal of attention to defining the term "peasant." Teodor Shanin, dean of the new field of "peasant studies," suggested that "peasants" everywhere shared four main characteristics: (1) a livelihood based on subsistence and also perhaps on commodity production, but not usually involving profit maximization as an objective; (2) a reliance on family labor and on the household as a unit of production, consumption, reproduction, and risk-spreading; (3) political, economic, and cultural subordination to dominant classes and state authorities; and (4) traditional village relations of solidarity and reciprocity (Shanin 1971, 14–15). "Farmers," in contrast, primarily produced for the market, and they did so with advanced technology, hired labor, and formal credit. In the popular imagination, "farmers" were emblematic of modernity; "peasants" represented backwardness.

(continued)

Box 1.1. continued

Bounding the "peasant" category permitted certain kinds of analysis, but it foreclosed others. Some rural people who considered themselves peasants—agricultural laborers, for example— were not usually included in the definition, even if they acted politically in concert with others who were. Urbanites or members of elites sometimes claimed to be peasants in order to marshal support for revolutionary or clientelistic political programs. Rigid definitions also tended to obscure the complexity of rural social relations in places where an individual might labor for wages, till a small plot of land for food, produce export crops under contract to a foreign corporation, and engage in a nonagricultural income-producing activity such as fishing or repairing machinery. Equivalent terms in other languages—*campesino* or *paysan*—had different and usually broader connotations, often implying simply "people from the countryside." And some widely used terms— the Spanish *agricultor*, for example—were scale-neutral, including those who in English would be both peasants and farmers.

By the 1990s, academic specialists had largely discarded "peasant studies" in favor of "agrarian change" or "agrarian studies," a conceptual field that more easily covered relations between the rural poor and a variety of other actors, such as large landowners, banks and agribusiness corporations, and urban politicians and social movements (Bernstein and Byres 2001). A few scholars maintained that the term "peasant" was so imprecise or so laden with pejorative meanings and cultural freight that it ought to be discarded (Kearney 1996). This position, however, ignored the efforts of contemporary activists to reappropriate the term "peasant" and infuse it with new and positive content, including a celebration of peasants as sophisticated bearers of modern values and political projects. This rethinking leads today's rural activists to insist on the commonalities of peasants and farmers and often to use the two words interchangeably—in conversation, in written analyses, and in their movements' names (the European Farmers Coordination and the Coordination Paysanne Européenne, for example, are the same organization). As Nettie Wiebe, a Via Campesina activist and past president of the National Farmers Union of Canada, remarked in an interview,

> If you actually look at what "peasant" means, it means "people of the land." Are we Canadian farmers "people of the land"? Well, yes, of course. And it's important to take that language back. . . . We too are peasants, and it's the land and our relationship to the land and food production that distinguishes us. . . . We're not part of the industrial machine. We're much more closely linked to the places where we grow food and how we grow food, and what the weather is there. . . . The language around this matters. It begins to make us understand that "people of the land"—peasantry *everywhere*, the millions of small subsistence peasants with whom we think we have so little in common—identifies them, and it identifies us. They're being evicted from their land, and that decimates their identity and their community. And we're also being relocated in our society—it's as undermining for us as it is for them. The language? As long as you keep us in separate categories, and we're the highly industrialized farmers who are sort of quasi-business entrepreneurs and they're the subsistence peasants, then we can't see how closely we and all our issues are linked. (Wiebe 2002)

The 1980s Farm Crisis

The upsurge in transnational agriculturalists' movements during the past two decades is a direct result of a massive, worldwide farm crisis. The origins of the crisis in the 1970s included skyrocketing prices for petroleum and fossil-fuel-based inputs, particularly fertilizer and pesticides; sharply higher interest rates, resulting from oil-price shocks and monetary policies intended to slow inflation; and the breakdown of the Bretton Woods system of capital controls and fixed exchange rates, which set the stage for a rapid expansion and liberalization of global food trade (Greider 2000; Helleiner 1994; McMichael 1998). At the same time, growing ownership concentration among input, machinery, and credit suppliers and in the processing, storage, brokering, and exporting stages of key commodity chains allowed a handful of giant corporations to garner a rising share of the total value added along the way from field to dinner plate (Morgan 1980; Kneen 2002).

Since the 1960s, high subsidies in the United States and in Europe had generated vast food surpluses. Excess grain had been dumped in the countries of the South, often through aid agreements rather than trade. By the late 1960s, huge European markets opened up for France, the continent's largest agricultural economy, and the Soviets began to purchase enormous quantities of US wheat. This new demand led to sudden shortages and climbing prices. From 1970 to 1980, US farm exports jumped 150 percent, and France's doubled, making it the world's second largest exporter of agricultural products after the United States (Sheingate 2001). The response was a worldwide credit-based expansion of production by commercial farmers. By the late 1970s, surpluses returned, a problem that worsened when the United States and Canada cut off grain sales to the Soviets following the invasion of Afghanistan. Commodity and land prices plummeted, and interest rates soared (Friedmann 1992) (see figure 1.1). Many US and Canadian producers defaulted on loans and lost their land, spurring the rise of militant farmers' movements and reviving antiforeclosure tactics such as "farm gate defenses" not seen since the "penny auctions" of the Great Depression in the 1930s (Mooney and Majka 1995; NFU 1985c; Wilford 1985).

In poorer countries, particularly in Latin America, the debt crisis of the early 1980s, also rooted in part in rising interest rates and oil import bills, brought neoliberal reforms that often devastated small agricultural producers accustomed to guaranteed prices, low-interest loans, and state-sponsored extension services (Edelman 1998). Ironically, these reforms, encouraged by the Bretton Woods institutions, dismantled the commodities boards and the systems of subsidies for inputs, machinery, fuel, water, and credit that the World Bank had helped to set up in country after country in the 1950s and 1960s in order to make capital-intensive agriculture possible in conditions of poverty (Shiva 2001).

While the main focus of this chapter is on agriculturalists' participation in global civil society, it is important to acknowledge that the farm crisis generated a tremendous range of political responses, from great enthusiasm for transnational solidarity to extreme hostility toward producers in other countries. Economic liberalization and the growing export orientation of highly subsidized farm sectors in the European Union and the United States tended to enlarge markets and force down prices for key internationally traded commodities such as

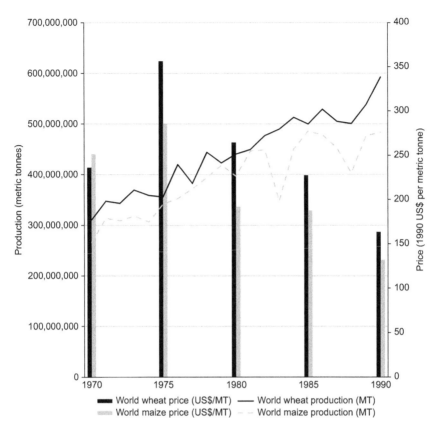

FIGURE 1.1.   The farm crisis: world production and prices of wheat and maize, 1970–1990.

grains, oilseeds, and cotton. Falling commodity prices boosted the profitability of, and encouraged mergers among, the giant agribusiness corporations that dominated input sales, postharvest processing, and export trade (and, with increased consolidation and vertical integration, they could readily engage in noncompetitive pricing practices). Farmers sometimes reacted to intensifying competitive pressures with organized transnational efforts to directly affect the supranational governance structures that pushed for and administered the newly liberalized global economic system. In some countries, in contrast, they chose to influence supranational institutions primarily through pressuring national governments that participated in them. At times, the changed economic environment led them to view their counterparts elsewhere as a threat, especially when influxes of inexpensive foreign products collapsed prices. In Europe, during the 1992–1997 period, for example, farmers' protests that had a transnational dimension were much more likely to have nationalist and protectionist objectives than cooperative ones (Bush and Simi 2001).

Regional Integration: Latin America

The rise of regional integration and supranational governance institutions in the 1980s and early 1990s fueled the rise of cross-border organizing by farmers—a movement that was already occurring in response to the farm crisis. In Latin America, North America, and Europe, in particular, new free-trade accords and supranational governance institutions became the focus of an increasingly internationalist peasant and farmer activism and fostered new alliances between agriculturalists in different countries and between them and social movements and NGOs from other sectors.

Central American Origins

Within Latin America, the Central America region proved especially significant as a fount of innovative transnational peasant organizing. More rural and, for the most part, poorer than the rest of Latin America, the Central American countries were small and had long seen intraregional migrations of peasants and agricultural laborers. Some peasant movements in the region, notably in Honduras, were historically among the best organized in the hemisphere and had won significant agrarian reforms in the 1970s (Posas 1985), while others, in Costa Rica, were among the first to develop detailed analyses of the impact of neoliberal reforms on small-scale agriculturalists (Edelman 1999). The 1979 Sandinista revolution made Nicaragua an important reference point for radical social movements throughout the area, a top priority for European cooperation agencies, and a key champion of new forms of internationalism (Blokland 1995, 161; Freres 1998, 23). In the early 1980s, European governments reacted with alarm to attempts by President Ronald Reagan's administration to overthrow the Sandinistas in Nicaragua and roll back leftist guerrillas in El Salvador and Guatemala. This anxiety—based on fears of a major regional war and an analysis that stressed inequality and injustice rather than communism as causes of the conflicts—brought large increases in European cooperation expenditures and extensive backing for the Contadora peace process, initiated in 1983 by Mexico, Colombia, Venezuela, and Panama (and later for the efforts of Costa Rican President Oscar Arias that led to the 1987 Esquipulas Peace Accords).

In El Salvador, Guatemala, and Nicaragua in the 1980s, peasants often joined armed movements, and hundreds of thousands of them became refugees, frequently elsewhere on the isthmus. In Panama, Honduras, and Costa Rica, organizations of the rural poor engaged in bitter struggles over structural adjustment programs that had slashed extension services and credit, reduced price supports and subsidies for loans and inputs, reversed hard-won agrarian reforms, and facilitated the penetration of transnational capital in agriculture (Fallas 1993; Stein and Arias Peñate 1992). In the late 1980s and early 1990s, governments and business groups moved rapidly toward regional integration as the civil wars ended or ebbed. The 1991 Tegucigalpa Protocol created the Central American Integration System that institutionalized periodic meetings of presidents and ministers and incorporated the Central American Parliament founded as part of the 1987 Esquipulas Peace Accords, as well as the existing regional economic integration institutions (importantly, it also established a consultative committee for regionally organized civil society groups). Also in 1991, the Presidents' Summit in San Salvador promulgated an "Action Plan for Central American Agriculture," which had as one of its main objectives the establishment of intraregional free trade in basic grains and the linking of regional prices to international ones (Segovia 1993).

In 1990, the European-funded Support Committee for the Economic and Social Development of Central America (CADESCA), based in Panama, started a Food Security Training Program (PFSA) directed at government functionaries and peasant leaders. This concern with training leaders of popular organizations reflected a view of civil society and democratization that stressed grassroots participation in policymaking, a conception that contrasted with the US emphasis on free elections and elite-led reforms (Macdonald 1994). The creation of PFSA coincided as well with a shift in European cooperation strategies in the late 1980s and early 1990s as multilateral, bilateral, and NGO donors began to support projects with a Central American regional, as opposed to a national or local, focus (Biekart 1999, 204–206; Edelman 1998).

The PFSA brought peasant leaders from Panama, Costa Rica, Nicaragua, Honduras, and El Salvador to two seminars in late 1990 and early 1991 for intensive minicourses in credit, marketing, land reform, technology, and environmental issues. In the first seminar, several organization leaders demanded, as a condition of their participation, that the PFSA provide time so that peasant groups from different countries could discuss common problems. By the end of the second seminar, peasant leaders had formed a provisional commission—coordinated by the Costa Rican delegation—with a view to forming a Central America–wide association (see box 1.2). The Association of Central American Peasant Organizations for Cooperation and Development (ASOCODE), founded in 1991 and headquartered in Nicaragua, came to have member coalitions in all seven countries of the isthmus. During its brief heyday, it was widely viewed in and beyond the Central American region as a quintessentially successful model of transnational small farmer organizing.

Box 1.2. Central America—The rise and fall of the ASOCODE network

For a half dozen years in the 1990s, the Association of Central American Peasant Organizations for Cooperation and Development (ASOCODE) achieved an extraordinarily high profile in regional and hemispheric politics, attending numerous presidential and ministerial summits, sending frequent delegations to Europe and North America, publishing numerous position papers and a bimonthly newsletter in Spanish and English, sponsoring meetings and courses for peasant activists, and attracting a copious flow of cooperation funds that reached an annual peak in 1996 at US$1.5 million, largely from the Dutch agency HIVOS, Ibis-Denmark, Oxfam, and other NGOs in the Copenhagen Initiative for Central America (Biekart 1999, 280) (see table 1.1). Led initially by a charismatic young Costa Rican, Wilson Campos, ASOCODE spawned several other Central American networks: the Indigenous and Peasant Community Agroforestry Coordinator (CICAFOC); the Central American Indigenous Council (CICA), and the Civil Initiative for Central American Integration (ICIC), an umbrella group for diverse movements aimed at participating in the consultative committee of the Central American Integration System (and, not incidentally, at securing additional funding and employment for ASOCODE leaders).

From 1994 to 1997, according to an internal ASOCODE report, "cooperation resources were so abundant that they exceeded the capacity of the headquarters" to administer them (ASOCODE 1999, 24). "Overfunding" contributed to struggles for resources that exacerbated already existing factionalism and ultimately led funding agencies to cut off support (Biekart 1999, 286–93). In 2000, ASOCODE closed its Managua office, and in 2001, representatives of its member coalitions from five countries agreed to reorganize it as a decentralized network of issue-specific working groups that would communicate virtually or meet on an ad hoc basis, with a nominal headquarters in the office of one of the main Honduran peasant confederations (ASOCODE 2001). Most of ASOCODE's network "offspring" were never able to shake their image as creations of EU cooperation agencies.

The "crisis and rupture" in ASOCODE raises questions for scholars, supporters, and activists of transnational civil society networks that have only begun to be addressed (ASOCODE 1999, 25). Conservative and left-wing theorists (Ronfeldt and Arquilla 2001; Castells 1996) coincide in highlighting the potency and durability of network forms of organization and in giving scant attention to how civil society networks may rise and fall, much as individual social movements manifest a periodicity linked to broader "cycles of protest" (Tarrow 1994). Only rarely is the possibility considered that the "network" may become "a form that supersedes analysis and reality" and that its "'failure' is endemic, indeed, . . . [an] effect of the Network form" (Riles 2000, 174, 6). In ASOCODE's case, a top-heavy organization, a preponderance of activities that responded to donor rather than peasant priorities, and incessant internecine squabbling brought the association to a point where it still exists in name but enjoys little of its earlier support, dynamism, or prestige. Cooperation agencies, having identified similar problems in other Central American regional civil society networks, tempered their enthusiasm for cross-border initiatives, even though several donors that supported ASOCODE have backed other networks—generally leaner and less centralized—which it or its erstwhile activists helped to establish.

Legacy of ASOCODE: CLOC and La Via Campesina

Although ASOCODE entered into a marked decline several years after its founding, its accomplishments—training a generation of sophisticated activists, attracting funding for cross-border organizing, and gaining peasants access to the powerful—inspired the formation of two Latin America–wide networks that still have a visible presence. In 1992 in Nicaragua, two years after the Sandinistas' electoral defeat, the National Union of Agriculturalists and Livestock Producers (UNAG), then ASOCODE's Nicaraguan affiliate, invited leaders of farmers' movements from Central America, the Caribbean, Canada, the United States, and Europe to its second congress (Desmarais 2002, 95). While UNAG had sought international ties virtually since its inception (see box 1.3), this invitation arose from an ASOCODE call to begin drafting development alternatives born from the experience of peasant and farmer movements and from the efforts of Dutch cooperators in Nicaragua who, together with a small Dutch foundation, the Paulo Freire Stichting (PFS), assisted UNAG in identifying foreign contacts (Blokland 1995, 161). The "Managua Declaration," signed by representatives of the Central American, Caribbean, North American, and European organizations, condemned the inclusion of agriculture in General Agreement on Tariffs and Trade (GATT) negotiations and the impact of foreign debt on poor countries, demanded direct participation in the upcoming Rio Environmental Conference, and called on "sister farm organizations from around the world" to join in constructing an alternative development model (LVC 1996, 67–69). Over the following year, the PFS coordinated plans for the founding congress of a global network, La Via Campesina (Peasant Road), which took place in Belgium in 1993.

In early 1994, in Lima, Peru, representatives of eighty-four organizations from twenty-one countries formed the Latin American Coordinator of Rural Organizations (Coordinadora Latinoamericana de Organizaciones del Campo, or CLOC). International solidarity efforts since the mid-1980s by the Brazilian MST and the Ecuadorian National Federation of Peasant Organizations (FENOC) were important antecedents to the formation of the CLOC, in addition to the work of ASOCODE and the Nicaraguan Association of Rural Workers (ATC). The network's proximate origins were in the 1992 continental Indigenous campaign against official celebrations of the Columbian quincentenary. CLOC and its affiliates express militant opposition to neoliberalism and to the US embargo on trade with Cuba. Closely allied with Via Campesina, CLOC campaigns for food sovereignty, agrarian reform, and Indigenous rights (CLOC 1997, 2001; Petras 1998; Welch 2000). Almost all Via Campesina member organizations in Latin America participate in CLOC, and many CLOC organizations participate in Via Campesina (see figure 1.2). Both contributed to the formation of other Latin American networks, including the Grito de los Excluidos/Cry of the Excluded and the Forum for Biological and Cultural Diversity (Bell 2002).

FIGURE 1.2. Meeting of CLOC-LVC, Tlalpan, Mexico City, 2001. Photo by the author.

Box 1.3. Latin America peasant movements: Expanding cross-border links

1970

Guatemala: Campesino a Campesino, a peasant-led extension program that spread to Mexico in the 1970s and Nicaragua in 1986, is founded.

1980

Central America and Caribbean: Confederation of Cooperatives of the Caribbean and Central America (CCC-CA), which came to include many rural producer groups, is founded.

1981

Panama: Nicaragua's newly formed National Union of Agriculturalists and Livestock Producers (UNAG) convenes a meeting of a short-lived Continental Coordinating Group of Agricultural Workers and Peasants of Latin America.

(continued)

Box 1.3. continued

1984

Mexico: Latin American meeting of peasant organizations with delegates from Mexico, Brazil, Nicaragua, Peru, Ecuador, and the Dominican Republic, as well as observers from France.

1985

Brazil: The first congress of the Landless Rural Workers Movement (MST) hosts an international meeting of Latin American peasant organizations.

1986

Ecuador: The National Federation of Peasant Organizations (FENOC) sponsors a meeting of Latin American peasant organizations.

1987

Panama: Interamerican Cooperative Institute invites fifty women representatives of rural organizations from fourteen Latin American and Caribbean countries to a workshop on women and grassroots development.

Ecuador: First Annual Andean Workshop and Exchange of Experiences, Education, and Communication for Indigenous and Rural Organizations, with delegates from Peru, Bolivia, Colombia, and Ecuador.

Central America: Founding of the Central American Workers Coordination (COCENTRA) group, which included rural workers' unions.

1988

Brazil: The fourth national meeting of the MST discusses struggles for land with peasant organization representatives from Chile, Paraguay, and El Salvador.

Colombia: Encounter of Rural and Indigenous Women in Latin America and the Caribbean, with delegations from Brazil, Chile, Colombia, Costa Rica, Honduras, Mexico, Nicaragua, Panama, and Peru. Italian trade union representatives also attend.

Costa Rica: Peasant activists seek funds from the European Economic Community to organize a meeting of agriculturalists from El Salvador, Nicaragua, and Honduras.

1989

Mexico: First International Forum on the Human Rights of Indian Peoples prepares for a campaign against the Columbian quincentenary and for justice for Indigenous peoples.

Colombia: Latin American Meeting of Rural and Indigenous Organizations inaugurates campaign entitled "500 Years of Popular and Indigenous Resistance."

1990

Panama: The Support Committee for the Economic and Social Development of Central America (CADESCA) begins a food security research and training program for peasant movement leaders.

Mexico: Coffee producers from Mexico, the Dominican Republic, Honduras Guatemala, Nicaragua, Costa Rica, and Panama establish the Union of Small and Medium-Size Coffee Producers of Central America, Mexico and the Caribbean to address the crisis caused by the collapse of the supply quota system of the International Coffee Agreement.

Ecuador: The first issue of the *Boletín Campesino-Indígena de Intercambio Informativo* is published; in 1994, the newsletter becomes an organ of the Latin American Coordinator of Rural Organizations (CLOC).

Costa Rica: Peasant activists participate in the parallel forum that coincides with the annual meeting in Washington, DC, of the World Bank and International Monetary Fund.

(continued)

Box 1.3. continued

1991

Guatemala: A meeting of the Continental Campaign for 500 Years of Indigenous, Black, and Popular Resistance attracts representatives from twenty-four countries.

Nicaragua: Founding congress of the Association of Central American Peasant Organizations for Cooperation and Development (ASOCODE), a seven-country coalition.

1992

Nicaragua: UNAG invites leaders of farm organizations from Central America, North America, and Europe to its congress. They issue the "Managua Declaration," which becomes the founding document of the Via Campesina network.

Nicaragua: Participants in a meeting of the Continental Campaign for 500 Years of Indigenous, Black, and Popular Resistance agree to hold a founding congress of the Latin American Coordinator of Rural Organizations (CLOC). Two hundred women delegates form a Continental Women's Commission to promote women's participation at all levels of the participating movements.

1993

Guatemala: Second Congress of ASOCODE, attended by President Ramiro de León Carpio.

1994

Peru: First congress of the CLOC, attended by representatives of eighty-four organizations from twenty-one countries.

1996

Mexico: Second International Conference of the Via Campesina, attended by representatives of sixty-nine organizations from thirty-seven countries. During the event, nineteen peasants, supporters of the MST are massacred by gunmen in Eldorado de Carajás, Brazil.

Mexico: Thousands of foreign activists in diverse social movements attend the Zapatista-sponsored First International Encounter for Humanity and against Neoliberalism, held in a remote jungle in Chiapas.

1997

Brazil: First Assembly of Latin American Rural Women, attended by 125 delegates from twenty-three countries, is held in conjunction with the second congress of the CLOC. The CLOC congress resolves that women will be allocated one-half of all leadership and decision-making positions in its constituent organizations.

1998

El Salvador: Peasant organizations from throughout Latin America, many of them affiliated with ASOCODE, CLOC, and Via Campesina, participate in an International Forum on Communication and Citizenship held to celebrate the fiftieth anniversary of the Universal Declaration of Human Rights.

1999

Washington, DC: A South–North encounter to construct alternatives to neoliberalism is held under the auspices of the Convergence of Movements of Peoples of the Americas (COMPA), with representatives of organized peasants and other sectors from Brazil, Cuba, El Salvador, Haiti, Honduras, Mexico, and Nicaragua.

2000

Nicaragua: Foreign donors end all support for ASOCODE, which closes its regional headquarters.

Honduras: International Landless Meeting, sponsored by Via Campesina's Global Campaign for Agrarian Reform, attracts eighty-four participants from twenty-four countries in Africa, Asia, Europe, and Latin America.

(continued)

Box 1.3. continued

Mexico: The second South–North exchange takes place in Chiapas with 222 representatives of 128 peasant, Indigenous, and other civil society organizations from sixteen countries of the Americas.

2001

Brazil: Over 1,000 Brazilian peasants from the MST, joined by Via Campesina activists attending the first World Social Forum, occupy a biotechnology facility and experimental farm owned by Monsanto and uproot genetically modified corn and soybean plants from test plots.

Mexico: More than 500 delegates from 171 organizations in fifteen countries gather in Chiapas at the first meeting of the Forum for Biological and Cultural Diversity, which aims to defend native medicinal and crop plant varieties against threats posed by free trade, genetic engineering, biopiracy, and corporate agriculture.

Mexico: The third congress of the CLOC is followed by an International Meeting of Social Movements, sponsored by Via Campesina, Focus on the Global South, the anti-globalization movement ATTAC-France, and the Brazilian labor federation CUT, called to plan participation in the second Porto Alegre Social Forum and other upcoming events.

Cuba: World Forum on Food Sovereignty supported by CLOC, Via Campesina, APM-Mondial, and various other farm organization networks and NGOs.

2002

Mexico: Via Campesina organizations participate in the NGO Forum at the UN International Conference on Financing for Development.

Mexico: The first Mesoamerican Peasant Meeting (ECM) attracts more than 250 delegates from Central America and Mexico who condemn Mexican President Vicente Fox's Plan Puebla-Panamá

(PPP) as a "savage project of colonization that will destroy our lands, our cultures, biodiversity, and natural resources."

New York and Washington, DC: Representatives of the Meso-american Initiative for Trade, Integration, and Sustainable Development (Iniciativa CID) meet with US labor, church, and development organizations to discuss the proposed hemispheric and Central American free-trade treaties.

Ecuador: The Continental Campaign against the Free Trade Area of the Americas (FTAA) holds a meeting of fourteen networks, including CLOC and the Hemispheric Social Alliance, to plan for a hemispheric referendum on the proposed Free Trade Area of the Americas. Protesters from CLOC and Via Campesina organizations, along with other social movements in the Hemispheric Social Alliance, disrupt the FTAA trade negotiation committee and ministerial meeting.

New forms of communications facilitated the expansion of networks of Latin American peasant and other movements, although adoption of new technologies was slow until the late 1990s, when computer skills had spread and internet and telephone services in the region became more reliable. In 1997, however, only twenty-six of the forty-six movements attending the second CLOC congress in Brasilia had electronic mail (León, Burch, and Tamayo 2001, 102), and the digital divide between national- and local-level organizations remained significant. A Latin American social movements portal, www.movimientos.org, which launched in 2000, has solidified information flows and simplified the organization of protests, training programs, and meetings.

Regional Integration: North America
National Mobilization in the 1980s

The farm crisis and the rapid advance of trade liberalization and regional integration in North America spurred new forms of cross-border collaboration among farmers and between farmers and other sectors. In 1984, the election of

Brian Mulroney, whose Conservative Party won the largest number of parliamentary seats in Canadian history, and the reelection of Ronald Reagan in the United States created an opportunity for advocates of free trade in both countries to advance a common agenda. Until just before the 1993 signing of the North American Free Trade Agreement (NAFTA) and GATT, however, farmers in each country engaged mainly in national politics as a way of expressing opposition to economic integration and liberalization, and sometimes they looked askance at the possibility of building solidarity with counterparts across the border.

Many farmers' movements in the United States espoused right-wing conspiracy theories about the 1980s crisis and championed ultranationalist and, at times, violent responses, such as the formation of armed "militias" (Berlet and Lyons 2000; Diamond 1995). Other movements, such as the US Farmers Association (USFA), included members who had been expelled as communists from the US National Farmers Union during the 1950s McCarthy period, as well as more recent migrants to rural areas who had new left, countercultural perspectives. Some organizations combined right- and left-wing influences, notably the American Agriculture Movement (AAM), which worked closely with country singer Willie Nelson in producing a series of high-profile Farm Aid concerts to benefit indebted farmers. In 1978, AAM vaulted to prominence with a massive "tractor-cade" demonstration in Washington, DC, for higher price supports (Mooney and Majka 1995).

In Canada, the National Farmers Union (NFU) had an active program of international exchanges almost since its formation in 1969 (see box 1.4). An amalgamation of several provincial unions, the founding of the NFU was part of a wave of sectoral coalition building that occurred across Canada during the 1970s as diverse kinds of policymaking increasingly shifted from the provinces to Ottawa (Ayres 1998, 50). Strongly influenced by farmers' historic successes in winning preferential rail freight rates, creating cooperatively owned grain-handling pools, and establishing a national wheat board, the NFU and its predecessor organizations were fervent advocates of orderly marketing and supply management policies that permitted producers to receive adequate prices for their harvests (Qualman and Wiebe 2002). Like many other Canadians, small farmers feared that closer economic integration with the United States would not only worsen the agricultural crisis but would also dilute an already-fragile national identity by undermining the strong, interventionist state and social welfare system (Ayres 1998, 22).

The Canadians also highlighted women's issues within the emerging transnational farmers' networks, in North America, and elsewhere. Many of the

Box 1.4. National Farmers Union of Canada: Growing international involvement, 1971–1994

1971

The National Farmers Union (NFU) President and Women's President travel to China.

NFU Vice President attends the UN Food and Agriculture Organization (FAO) conference in Rome.

1977

Nine NFU representatives attend the Fifteenth Triennial Conference of the ACCW.

1978

NFU leader joins representatives of farm organizations from major wheat-exporting countries in London.

1980

Four NFU representatives visit the eastern Caribbean to participate in the founding convention of the St. Vincent National Farmers Union.

1981

NFU delegation visits Cuba and meets with members and officials of ANAP, the association of small agricultural producers.

NFU representative lobbies at FAO conference in Rome in favor of conserving plant genetic resources.

1982

NFU member participates in trade union tour of Nicaragua and meets with small farmers and representatives of the National Union of Agriculturalists and Livestock Producers (UNAG).

(continued)

Box 1.4. continued

1983

Farmers from nearly fifty countries attend the First International Farm Crisis Summit in Ottawa, sponsored by the North American Farm Alliance (NAFA).

NFU President accompanies a government delegation to the Rome FAO conference and expresses opposition to plant breeders rights legislation and in favor of continuing public-sector crop research.

1984

NFU Women's President is an official delegate to the World Food Assembly in Rome.

NFU members participate in Canadian Farmers Technical Brigade to Nicaragua.

NFU and WINFA (Windward Islands Farmers Association) initiate a Canada–Caribbean farmer exchange, with young agriculturalists from each region spending four to six weeks in the other region.

NFU sends representatives to Washington, DC, to lobby the US Congress against the Garrison Diversion Project, which would shift the course of the headwaters of the Missouri River in North Dakota.

1985

NFU Women's President is a delegate to the "End of Decade" Women's Conference in Nairobi, Kenya, where she chairs a panel on rural women.

A representative of the recently founded Peasant Movement in the Philippines (KMP) tours Canada, meeting with the NFU and other organizations and denouncing the Marcos dictatorship's repression.

1986

NFU members participate in Oxfam Farmers Brigade Project, which aids Nicaraguan farmers with machinery maintenance and repair.

Farmers from ten countries attend the Second International Farm Crisis Summit in St. Louis, Missouri, sponsored by NAFA.

1987

NFU President tours Europe to gain firsthand knowledge of the European Economic Community's Common Agricultural Policy.

NFU representative attends the International Conference in Solidarity with the Filipino Peasantry, sponsored by the KMP.

1988

NFU representatives participate in a General Agreement on Tariffs and Trade (GATT) counter-conference in Montreal.

1989

NFU initiates a campaign to educate Canadians about negative consequences of the North American Free Trade Agreement (NAFTA).

NFU representatives meet with three North Dakota farm organizations to discuss binational trade issues.

NFU women's delegation tours Nicaragua.

1990

NFU President, together with Canadian labor leaders, tours maquiladora free-trade zone along Mexico's northern border.

Farmers from Jilin, China, and Saskatchewan, Canada, participate in a lengthy work exchange program.

1991

Three NFU women visit Nicaragua on a ten-day working tour sponsored by the UNAG women's section. UNAG women later visit Saskatchewan.

Philippine farm leaders tour Canada, seeking international support for their agrarian reform campaign.

(continued)

Box 1.4. continued

1992

NFU Women's President attends conference in Honduras on how free trade and structural adjustment affect rural communities.

NFU delegates to the ACCW convention in The Hague persuade ACCW to take a stand against GATT.

1993

NFU Women's Vice President joins GATT protests in Geneva, speaks to 5,000 farmers from across Europe.

NFU Youth President travels to Mexico on a labor exchange.

NFU President demands that government use free-trade agreement provisions to prohibit US export subsidies aimed at traditional Canadian wheat markets, particularly Mexico.

NFU representative attends founding conference of the Via Campesina in Belgium.

1994

NFU representative attends congress in Guatemala City of the Association of Central American Peasant Organizations for Cooperation and Development (ASOCODE).

ASOCODE leaders undertake a speaking tour, with NFU support, to four Canadian cities.

NFU leadership meets with Northern Plains Resource Council from the United States to discuss joint wheat-marketing strategies.

NFU President meets in Austin, Texas, with US and Mexican farm and labor organizations.

Representatives of Nicaragua's UNAG visit Saskatchewan to meet with NFU members.

NFU Women's President travels to New York for the Women, Food, and Agriculture Working Group, comprising a hundred people from forty countries.

Sources: Ayres 1998; Ritchie 1996, 495; Wilford 1985; and various issues of *Union Farmer*.

provincial groups that coalesced in the NFU had, since their inception, reserved specific leadership posts for women, a practice rooted in the parallel structure of the early twentieth-century Women's and Farmers' Institutes. The NFU preserved this system, with a Women's President and Vice President responsible for defending the specific interests of farm women within and outside the organization (Gleave 1991, 212–122).

One early cross-border initiative to confront the farm crisis was the North American Farm Alliance (NAFA), formed in 1983 by activists from twenty-three US states and two Canadian provinces who convened at a USFA-sponsored assembly in Iowa. NAFA drew its members largely from the USFA, the left-wing of the AAM, and a small AAM offshoot called the Canadian Farmers' Survival Association (Mooney and Majka 1995; Wilford 1985). In 1985, the Canadian NFU presented a brief to Parliament arguing that free trade would undermine orderly marketing for grain; a few months later, it became affiliated with NAFA (NFU 1985a, 1985b).

In 1983, NAFA hosted the First International Farm Crisis Summit in Ottawa, which attracted peasants, farmworkers, the landless, and family farm organization leaders from nearly fifty countries. Delegates from different regions and varied economic circumstances pointed to strikingly similar concerns, particularly the push by export-oriented agribusiness corporations to boost international competitiveness at the expense of small farmers (Ritchie 1996; Wilford 1985). NAFA was unusual among US farm organizations in the 1980s in its advocacy of environmentalism and less capital-intensive agriculture, which some of its spokespeople argued was a form of supply management, a traditional demand of farmers' movements (Mooney and Majka 1995). NAFA distributed a monthly newspaper on both sides of the border. It also coordinated the drafting of debt-restructuring legislation introduced in the US Congress and advanced the slogan "Farms, Not Arms" to call attention to how the Pentagon competed with family farms for government support. In 1986, a second NAFA Farm Crisis Summit in St. Louis, Missouri, drew delegates from eight countries, as well as representatives from the European Parliament and the United Nations (Ballantine 1986). By the late 1980s, many US organizations left NAFA for the new National Family Farm Coalition (Mooney and Majka 1995; NFU 1988). The Canadian NFU withdrew as well, as key NAFA member groups, particularly the AAM, took protectionist stances and protested along the border to keep Canadian wheat and meat out of the US market. NFU members too protested along the US border against imports of cheap corn and, on one occasion in 1988, blocked the bridge linking Windsor and Detroit with tractors (NFU 2001).

Farmers, the US–Canada Free Trade Agreement, and NAFTA

Prime Minister Mulroney's announcement in 1985 that he intended to negotiate a free-trade treaty with the United States galvanized opposition from farmers and other sectors and led to the formation of several Canadian civil society networks, notably the Coalition against Free Trade, the Council of Canadians, and the Pro-Canada Network. At first, these groups devoted most of their efforts to lobbying, organizing, and protesting within Canada. The Canadian economy depended heavily on export production, and the vast majority of exports went to the United States. Free-trade proponents argued that a free-trade treaty would gain Canada greater access to US markets and thwart any US attempts to impose protectionist measures. The protracted treaty negotiations provided an ample period in which both sides could organize, and in 1988, with free trade the principal election issue, Mulroney won reelection. The treaty went into effect in 1989, and the US and Canadian governments announced their intention to broaden it to Mexico. This double setback for free-trade opponents in Canada led to a greater willingness to seek allies in the United States and Mexico (Ayres 1998, 121–123).

With the US–Canada Free Trade Agreement a fait accompli, the attention of transnational activists turned to Mexico and especially to its northern border region. Much of the bilateral and trilateral coalition building of the early 1990s involved joint action around the proposed NAFTA or sectoral alliances around environmental, occupational safety and health, or other issues. US agricultural workers' unions, with Mexican members, had already established cross-border links and, in the early 1990s, encouraged the AFL-CIO to modify its traditionally protectionist position toward foreign labor. In 1987, the Farm Labor Organizing Committee (FLOC) developed joint bargaining strategies with a Mexican counterpart, the National Union of Rural Wage Workers (SNTOAC), when Campbell Soup threatened to move an Ohio canning plant to Mexico, where it had contracts with SNTOAC (IRC 1992).

The US-based Rural Coalition began to oppose NAFTA on both sides of the border in 1992 with an assembly in El Paso and Chihuahua, and it more than doubled the number of its affiliated organizations in 1993. Chaired by Carlos Marentes, director of the Union of Border Agricultural Workers (UTAF) in El Paso, Texas, the Rural Coalition helped sponsor a reception in Washington for new congressional representatives from rural areas, who would soon have to vote on NAFTA, and hosted several who visited northern Mexico. On November 16, 1993, the day before the US House of Representatives was to vote on NAFTA, a US UTAF delegation marched to the Santa Fe International Bridge to meet Mexican supporters coming from the south. On their return, the Mexican demonstrators were attacked by police. "We deeply regret that NAFTA has been passed by the House," peasant leader Víctor Quintana wrote two days later to US Representative Bernard Sanders.

> But every one of us fought from his trench: you in the House, we in the street or the bridge. . . . This battle against NAFTA brought something we hadn't even imagined: the closeness, cooperation, [and] solidarity between the people who love and struggle for democracy on both sides of the border. (Rural Coalition 1994, 21)

In 1990, a Canada–Mexico meeting of anti-NAFTA labor, farm, environmental, church, and human rights groups led to the formation of the Mexican Action Network on Free Trade (RMALC) (IRC 1992). RMALC became an important source of analysis on trade issues for Mexican peasant movements. These were almost universally opposed to NAFTA, although the official National Peasant Confederation argued that "liberalization was already a given" and that the important question was that peasants be represented in the negotiations and have access to US markets. Among the many cross-border farmers' exchanges in this period, one of the most significant was the Trinational Meeting on Agriculture, Environment, and the Free Trade Treaty in November 1991, which included National Union of Autonomous Regional Peasant Organizations (UNORCA), the US Institute for Trade and Development Policy, and the Canadian Centre for Policy Alternatives (L. Hernández 1992, 257).

The movements of farmers and others around NAFTA reconfigured traditional alliances and oppositions along non-national lines. While once US, Canadian, or Mexican actors stood opposed to each other in discussions of trade, environment, or migration, NAFTA opened social cleavages that blurred domestic and foreign policy concerns in all three countries, generating new forms of contention that required transnational action and that increasingly divided or united people less along national lines than in relation to shared class, issue-based, or sectoral interests. The common preoccupation with continental free trade also paved the way for new kinds of cross-sector collaboration, between agriculturalists and environmentalists, for example, and between NGOs and popular movements. More broadly, it contributed to transcending the parochial, identity-based politics that were characteristic of the "new social movements" of the previous two decades.

The New Zapatistas and Global Civil Society

The Zapatista uprising in the southern Mexican state of Chiapas began on January 1, 1994, the day NAFTA went into effect, dramatically highlighting the multiple crises affecting rural and Indigenous Mexicans and calling attention to the devastating impact on the peasantry of the 1992 constitutional reforms that permitted privatization of agrarian reform lands and, more generally, of neoliberalism. As the first post–Cold War peasant and Indigenous insurrection in Latin America, the Chiapas rebellion sparked enormous hopes in Mexico and generated enormous sympathy in much of the rest of the world. Although the Zapatistas initially had no international allies, their dissemination of email communiques and their poetic disdain for the status quo provided a platform for democratizing Mexico and for imagining new alliances and alternatives to the dominant economic model. Not surprisingly, the Zapatista-sponsored First International Encounter for Humanity and against Neoliberalism, which brought thousands of Mexican and foreign activists to a remote Chiapas jungle in 1996, is sometimes considered the "genesis" of today's global justice movement (Seoane and Taddei 2001b, 108). But while the Zapatistas established ties to diverse, largely urban movements in Mexico and abroad, their connections to Mexican and transnational networks of peasant and Indigenous organizations remained tenuous. On January 1, 2003, when Mexico lifted tariffs on all agricultural imports from NAFTA countries except corn, beans, and powdered milk, peasants staged widespread demonstrations and hunger strikes under the banner of a coalition called "the Countryside Can't Take Any More" (*El Campo no Aguanta Más*). Yet the same day, when 20,000 machete-wielding native Mexicans converged on San Cristóbal, Chiapas, to mark the ninth anniversary of the Zapatista uprising, their leaders voiced a range of Indigenous and international solidarity concerns but said little about the country's broader agrarian crisis (Bellinghausen 2003).

European Integration and Anti-GATT Protest

Europe experienced an earlier and more profound process of regional integration than any other part of the world, and this conditioned the character of the organizing efforts of farmers (see box 1.5). In the Americas, supranational governance institutions were quite new, and transnational activism emerged in response to perceived threats to rural livelihoods and the shared belief that organizing was needed to deter government repression. In Europe, in contrast, regional policymaking bodies had been significant for decades.

The Common Agricultural Policy (CAP), established as part of the 1957 treaty that created the then-six-member European Community (EC), was only phased in during the 1960s, the same year that the EC customs union went into effect.

Box 1.5. European farmers and new forms of protest and solidarity

1970s

France: Dissidents in the mainstream National Federation of Agricultural Enterprises (FNSEA) and its youth wing organize a minority tendency, Interpaysanne, which leads protests against agricultural taxes, overproduction of commodities, and corporate agribusiness.

1981

France: Founding of the National Confederation of Worker-Peasant Unions (CNSTP) by groups that left the FNSEA.

Austria: The first of four annual meetings that precedes the formal creation of a European peasant coordinating group. Participating organizations come from Germany, Austria, France, the Netherlands, and Switzerland.

1985

The European Farmers Coordination (EFC) is founded.

1986

Madrid: The EFC holds a meeting with representatives of twenty-seven organizations from eleven countries on the theme of "European Peasants: Competitors or Partners?"

1987

Geneva: Over fifty farm activists from Europe, North America, and Japan meet to discuss the GATT negotiations. A statement of principles, emphasizing measures to restore world prices and the necessity of market share negotiations, is drafted for distribution to farm organizations around the world.

1989

Brussels: The EFC opens a headquarters office.

(continued)

Box 1.5. continued

1990

Brussels: Thousands of farmers from around the world protest against the GATT talks. The EFC attributes the GATT adjournment "primarily" to "the successful farmers' resistance" and calls "for public GATT negotiations under UN control."

France: Elizabeth Lepetitcolin, a veterinarian in the sheep-farming region of Larzac, a center of Confédération Paysanne support, travels to the Middle East and establishes ties with a group of Palestinians in the occupied territories.

1991

Brussels: The EFC and the US National Family Farm Coalition issue a joint communique warning that proposed reforms to the European Common Agricultural Policy (CAP) are modeled on the US Farm Bill that contributed to the demise of one-fifth of all US farms during the 1980s.

1992

France: Protests against reforms to CAP include a FNSEA-led demonstration with over three hundred tractors around Euro-Disney, highway blockades, and dumping of manure and rotten vegetables in front of government buildings.

Geneva and Strasbourg: Ten thousand demonstrators from Europe, Japan, South Korea, Latin America, and Canada protest against the GATT talks.

Strasbourg: The FNSEA brings tens of thousands of demonstrators to a protest against the EU-US Oilseeds Agreement (also called the Blair House Agreement), which limits the area eligible for support payments.

1993

France: Farmers protesting against the French government's stance on oilseed production in the GATT talks smear the office of Foreign Minister Alain Juppé (who became prime minister in 1995) with yellow paint (the color of canola seed). Other demonstrators dump manure outside government offices in Normandy and stage a new blockade of Euro-Disney.

Geneva: Farmers from Europe, Canada, the United States, Japan, and India demonstrate against the signing of the GATT.

Mons, Belgium: Representatives of fifty-five peasant and farmer organizations from thirty-six countries found a world network called La Via Campesina (or Peasant Road).

1994

Austria, Luxembourg, Netherlands: The EFC launches a campaign to continue a ban on the bovine growth hormone manufactured by Monsanto, citing widespread anxiety among consumers, farmers, and environmental and animal welfare organizations. The EFC asks the European Commission to ban meat flour consumption by ruminants, noting that bovine spongiform encephalopathy (BSE), or mad cow disease, is an example of "the shortsightedness to which intensive farming can lead."

Austrian and Norwegian farm organizations issue a joint declaration charging that their countries' entrance into the EU single market will spell disaster for small grain and dairy farmers and the environment.

France: Larzac region civic associations host a farm visit from two Palestinians, representatives of the Palestinian Agricultural Relief Committee and the International Family Planning Committee.

1995

Netherlands: Farmers dump manure at the entrance to the Ministry of Agriculture in The Hague to protest EU regulations about processing animal waste.

(continued)

Box 1.5. continued

France: Larzac farm militants travel to French Polynesia and, in collaboration with Greenpeace, protest French underground nuclear weapons tests.

1996

Rome: Dozens of peasant and farmer activists attend the FAO Food Security Summit.

Greece: Thousands of farmers block the country's main north–south highway for over two weeks to protest trade liberalization, cuts in subsidies, and growing indebtedness. They declare that "Farmers can't go to Brussels to protest. That's the government's job."

Britain: In March, the government reverses its position and reveals that the death of a young man was caused by exposure to BSE. British farmers launch beef giveaways and other protests against the EU-imposed international ban on exports of British beef.

The EFC calls on the EU to stand firm in the face of a US complaint in the WTO against the European ban on hormone-treated beef.

1997

The EFC calls on the EU to block US efforts in the Codex Alimentarius to ban trade in raw milk-based cheeses. This would "impose an industrialized production model and, as a result, rob food of its originality, as has happened in the USA."

The EFC condemns the marketing of false Roquefort, feta, and Parmesan cheeses and suggests that "the agri-food multinationals now want to plunder the riches that have been preserved in the regions of the 'South' [of Europe] and use their images of high-quality local produce to deceive consumers."

Basel: The EFC protests in front of the offices of Novartis, the agribusiness and pharmaceutical firm, against imports of genetically modified maize. The demonstration is part of an international action week against genetic engineering in agriculture.

1998

The EFC is granted rights to attend the European Commission's advisory committees, which provide a small subsidy to civil society organizations that participate in their deliberations.

France: Confédération Paysanne supporters enter a warehouse belonging to Novartis and spray genetically modified (GM) corn seed with fire extinguishers in order to protest the dangers of GM food. José Bové receives an eight-month suspended sentence.

France: The Confédération Paysanne participates in the founding of ATTAC (Association for the Taxation of Financial Transactions to Aid the Citizenry), an international network that advocates the Tobin tax, a small levy on speculative currency transactions that would be used to "tame" volatile capital movements and generate funds for development.

1999

The EFC coordinates a multicountry caravan of farmers from India who came to Europe to protest against corporate control of seeds, particularly by Monsanto, and the WTO's forced liberalization of agricultural trade.

France: Confédération Paysanne activists and visiting Indian farmers enter a greenhouse in Montpellier and uproot GM rice plants before they could be replanted in a nearby nature preserve. José Bové receives a six-month prison sentence.

France: José Bové and Confédération Paysanne supporters "symbolically dismantle" a McDonald's restaurant under construction in Millau.

2000

France: Tens of thousands of demonstrators gather in Millau during José Bové's trial for the McDonald's action. Bové receives a sentence of three months in prison for criminal vandalism.

(continued)

Box 1.5. continued

Dresden: The EFC, together with Thai and Philippine peasant groups and Via Campesina, presented a proposal for a new concept of farmer-driven agricultural research at a parallel conference to the Global Forum on Agricultural Research, part of the Consultative Group on International Agricultural Research (CGIAR), which coordinates the world's principal centers of crop plant genetic research.

2001

France: José Bové sentenced to fourteen months in prison for participation in direct action protests against GM crops.

Rome: Via Campesina brings approximately a hundred supporters to the NGO parallel forum at the FAO World Food Summit (Rome+5). The farm activists constitute about one-sixth of all delegates at the parallel forum. At a University of Rome campus, EFC supporters sheath GM olive trees in plastic as a symbolic prophylactic measure.

2002

Austria, Belgium, France, Netherlands, and Spain: On April 17, the International Day of Peasant Struggles, farmer and environmentalist organizations stage coordinated protest actions against the testing of GM crops. In the Netherlands, visiting farmers from Via Campesina member groups in Indonesia and Bangladesh join the actions.

Madrid: A May meeting of women in Via Campesina organizations resolves that quotas must be established to ensure greater representation of women in leadership positions.

Madrid: The Third World Congress of Rural Women is held in October, presided by Queen Sofía. The plenaries and workshops are dominated by government representatives, leaving little space for interventions by grassroots activists.

Two EFC leaders, José Bové and Paul Nicholson, join Via Campesina activists Doris Gutiérrez (Honduras) and Mario Lill (Brazil) and other members of an international delegation in Ramallah to protest the Israeli blockade of the city.

The CAP provided incentives to farmers that were intended to guarantee food supplies, stabilize prices, modernize production, and ensure that farmers earn adequate incomes. In practice, however, CAP subsidies generated huge surpluses of commodities and absorbed a rising share of the EC budget. France—and the large wheat farmers of the Paris Basin, in particular—was the main beneficiary of the CAP, contributing in its first year less than one-quarter of contributions to the Guarantee Fund but receiving over three-quarters of all monies paid out (Sheingate 2001, 175). Within Europe, France was (and still is) the most important national actor in the contentious area of agricultural politics. While less than 8 percent of the economically active population works in agriculture, the centrality of fresh, artisanal foods and wines in conceptions of quality, local distinctiveness, and national identity has contributed to a strong identification with farmers among urban dwellers (Trubek 2000).

French farmers also have greater representation in the political system than their counterparts in most other developed countries. Nearly one-third of French mayors are farmers, most parliamentarians represent rural districts, and many National Assembly deputies and senators sit on communal and departmental councils (Bush and Simi 2001, 113). Elected local, departmental, and national Chambres d'Agriculture have, since the 1920s, served as forums of consultation between the farm sector and the state, which is also their main source of funds. In the 1960s, Chambres d'Agriculture became the primary provider of technical extension for farmers and a significant source of rural development funds. The importance of the Chambres d'Agriculture in French rural life has made them a barometer of support for different agrarian organizations.

The Chambres d'Agriculture are one element in a corporatist arrangement that links the French state to mainstream agriculturalists' organizations, particularly the National Federation of Agricultural Enterprises (FNSEA). As the FNSEA won control and came to dominate the Chambres d'Agriculture, it gave supporters privileged access to employment and services. FNSEA domination of the Chambres was also consonant with the French state's emphasis on capital-intensive agriculture (Gorneg 2001; Sheingate 2001, 172–176).

The French state's corporatist pact with the FNSEA mirrored the relation at the European level between the EC and the Committee of Professional Agricultural

Organizations (COPA) (Roederer-Rynning 2002). The FNSEA's and COPA's emphasis on technological modernization met with skepticism and resistance in mountain and smallholding regions, where greater mechanization was often not practical. In 1981, farm activists from Austria, France, Germany, the Netherlands, and Switzerland held the first of several annual meetings that led to the founding of the European Farmers Coordination (EFC) in 1985 (see box 1.5).

European Protests against CAP Reform and GATT

The 1986 inauguration of the Uruguay Round of GATT and the efforts the following year of the EC's Council of Ministers to reform the Common Agricultural Policy brought the discontent of many European farmers into sharp relief (E. A. Santos 1988). Reform of the CAP was required by budgetary constraints and to bring it into compliance with GATT. Farmers' organizations, particularly those in the EFC, called for the CAP to establish a per-farm ceiling on price supports so that large enterprises would not be the main beneficiaries of CAP subsidies. Improved supply management, they argued, was necessary to prevent the production of huge surpluses, which had to be stored at public expense, as well as to limit overintensification, ownership concentration, and emigration from rural areas. The EFC further charged that unchecked production of surpluses, together with export subsidies, led to dumping in poor countries that undermined peasant livelihoods. The linkage of CAP reform and GATT also caused concern, especially in France, that European officials were caving into US pressure to liberalize agricultural trade at farmers' expense (Sheingate 2001, 214–222).

Some accounts of the GATT process, which culminated in 1994 with the establishment of the WTO, suggest that elite disagreements over export subsidies and market access accounted for the delay in concluding the Uruguay Round. Pressure from small farmers, however, was also a conspicuous factor. The GATT ministerial session in Brussels in 1990 was supposed to complete the round, but protests from a multinational coalition of small farmer, consumer, and environmentalist groups helped stall the talks, in part because massive protests made some developing-country GATT delegates feel sufficiently empowered to raise objections to provisions in the draft agreement that would harm their countries' economies. Among the estimated 30,000 farmers who joined the 1990 protests were a hundred from North America, two hundred from Japan, and others from Korea, Africa, and Latin America (Brecher 1993; Kidder and McGinn 1995; Ritchie 1996). These protests—"far bigger than Seattle [1999], but less violent" (Ritchie 2001, 4)—followed on related anti-GATT farmers' demonstrations in the United States and Canada.

The first round of CAP reforms, however, went forward in 1992, in conjunction with the Maastricht Treaty that established the European Union (a second round would occur in 2000, and a third in 2003, tied to the planned enlarge-ment of the EU). It provided retirement incentives for older farmers, extended the dairy quota system, and cut livestock and cereal support prices while pro-viding for compensatory payments contingent on producers' taking some land out of cultivation. Critics in the EFC and other organizations argued that the failure to impose a ceiling on payments did little to address the problem of farm ownership concentration and that the land set-aside provisions, while intended as a conservation measure, would bring intensified production, with detrimen-tal environmental impacts, in areas not left fallow.

Protests became increasingly dramatic in the two years before the signing of the GATT accord in 1993. FNSEA supporters used hundreds of tractors to block-ade Euro-Disney, suggesting that US pressure was behind the French govern-ment's concessions on oilseeds subsidies in the GATT talks. Elsewhere, protesters sprayed defoliants around the home of European Commissioner Jacques Delors, staged highway blockades, and dumped manure and rotten vegetables in gov-ernment buildings (see box 1.5).

India: Farmers Mobilize against GATT and TRIPS

Small farmer opposition to GATT burgeoned in India toward the end of the Uru-guay Round (Gupta 1998, 291–292). The lightning rod for peasant anger was the proposed Trade-Related Intellectual Property Rights (TRIPS) agreement, which would empower the WTO to enforce global rules on patents, copyrights, and trademarks. This was a sensitive issue, since W. R. Grace and other companies had acquired US patents for active ingredients in the seeds of the neem tree (*Aza-dirachta indica*), which South Asians had used since ancient times as an insec-ticide, toothpaste substitute, and medicine (Shiva and Holla-Bhar 1996). With the prospect of a TRIPS agreement in the early 1990s, W. R. Grace sought to be-gin production of neem-derived products in India, threatening both national manufacturers and local users of the tree. Many peasants viewed the neem "theft" as a harbinger of future corporate attempts to monopolize crop genetic mate-rial that they and their ancestors had developed over generations.

In December 1992, some seventy-five members of the Karnataka State Farm-ers Association (KRRS) raided the Bangalore offices of Cargill, the multina-tional grain giant, smashing furniture and tossing files out the window to a large crowd, which set the papers on fire. The action drew a formal protest from Wash-ington and is widely credited with bringing the proposed TRIPS agreement to world attention (Gupta 1998, 322). In the following months, giant rallies of several hundred thousand peasants in Bangalore and New Delhi demanded that the Indian government reject the TRIPS draft and that all international agreements be approved by both houses of parliament and at least half the state legislatures.

While this ambitious agenda remained unrealized, the KRRS won new allies by helping to reframe the TRIPS discussion. Critics asserted that TRIPS was a form of protectionism that shielded developed-country seed and pharmaceutical monopolies and that it contradicted the Convention on Biological Diversity developed at the 1992 Rio Earth Summit. Even Columbia University economist and WTO adviser Jagdish Bhagwati, normally an enthusiast of global trade liberalization, came to argue that protection for intellectual property should not fall within the WTO's purview and that "the IP leg of the WTO [ought] to be sawn off" (Ramanujam and Sangeetha 2001).

Via Campesina/Peasant Road
Emergence of a Radical Transnational Network

The anti-GATT campaign by farmers in the Americas, Europe, and Asia was the main impetus for founding the Via Campesina or Peasant Road, a network that sought to coordinate peasant and farmer struggles worldwide. The group's initial nucleus consisted of a small number of Central American, Canadian, and European activists who met at the 1992 congress of UNAG, the Nicaraguan union of small farmers and livestock producers (discussed previously). Via Campesina's founding convention in Belgium, in 1993, coincided with anti-GATT protests and with a meeting of European NGOs concerned with agriculture. From the beginning, Via Campesina was marked by disagreements between the Paulo Freire Foundation, which had helped to plan the convention, and farm organization leaders, especially those in the EFC, who opposed the participation of conservative groups affiliated with the International Federation of Agricultural Producers (IFAP) (Desmarais 2002). Few IFAP members were in attendance, however. The US National Farmers Union, an IFAP member, had endorsed the 1992 Managua Declaration but did not come to Belgium or affiliate with Via Campesina. Several other organizations, including Nicaragua's UNAG, which—despite its Sandinista roots—was an IFAP affiliate, participated in the founding congress but did not stay in Via Campesina. Nevertheless, the fifty-five peasant and farmer organizations from thirty-six countries that joined the network represented an unprecedented unity of a considerable range of political positions and productive situations (PFS 1993).

For its first three years, Via Campesina's structure was that of an international coordinating committee (ICC), with representatives of organizations from different regions, each of which was responsible for overseeing activities in their respective areas of the world. Basque activist Paul Nicholson Solano was chosen as the network's first coordinator. In 1996, an international operational secretariat was established to oversee day-to-day functioning of the entire network and complement the work of the ICC. Because of the Central Americans' extensive experience in cross-border work, responsibility for the secretariat was entrusted to ASOCODE, which in turn assigned its Honduran member coalition responsibility for the Via Campesina. Rafael Alegría, an energetic peasant activist who had managed to complete a law degree, became executive secretary and installed the Via Campesina in a small one-room office in a house rented by one of the principal Honduran peasant coalitions. As a youth, in 1975, Alegría had been a peasant organization promoter in the Department of Olancho when the Honduran military and local landowners massacred fourteen activists who had intended to lead a hunger march on the capital (Posas 1985, 59–60).

The Via Campesina first emerged as a significant international actor at the 1995 Global Assembly on Food Security, held in Quebec City. The Canadian National Farmers Union, part of the assembly's steering committee, succeeded in having numerous Via Campesina representatives invited as panelists and plenary speakers (Desmarais 2002, 103). In a hastily typed press release faxed to news media and signed by Canadian, Honduran, Brazilian, Spanish, Polish, and Philippine activists, the Via Campesina condemned "the coexistence in the world of food surpluses and hunger" and "the large-scale dislocation of farmers," and it called for "respect for the food sovereignty of every country" and "the inclusion in the price of foodstuffs of all the real costs of production—social, ecological, and economic" (LVC 1995).

In 1996, the Via Campesina held its second congress in Tlaxcala, Mexico, which was attended by representatives from thirty-seven countries and funded by NGOs from Europe, Canada, and the United States. Many delegates, particularly from Asia and Africa, belonged to organizations that were not officially part of the Via Campesina; nearly three dozen were denied visas and could not attend. During the congress, news arrived that Brazilian military police had massacred nineteen peasants in Eldorado dos Carajás, where supporters of the MST, the landless workers movement, had blocked a highway to pressure the government to negotiate an agrarian conflict (LVC 1996, 49; Fernandes 2000, 209). Television reporters stuck in traffic nearby caught the action on film, which created a public uproar (Cadji 2000, 30). In Mexico, the Via Campesina condemned the murders and declared that April 17 would henceforth be commemorated as an International Day of Peasant Struggles. Later that year, dozens of peasant and farmer organization leaders attended the Rome World Food Summit, some invited and accredited by the FAO and others by IFAP, Via Campesina, and the NGOs that sponsored a parallel forum. Via Campesina supporters advanced the position that the summit's emphasis on "food security" ought to be replaced with a commitment to "food sovereignty," reflecting a view of food as a human right rather than primarily as a commodity.

Media-Savvy Protests and Via Campesina's Rising Profile

In 1999, some seventy-five Via Campesina supporters from more than a dozen countries converged on Seattle to join protests at the WTO ministerial and to take part in press conferences, workshops, and strategy meetings. Their activities included a symbolic tree planting and visits to a farmers' market. They distributed Roquefort sandwiches to passersby in front of a McDonald's restaurant in an effort to explain European farmers' opposition to US sanctions imposed on their products in retaliation for the EU's ban on imports of hormone-treated US beef (LVC 1999a). In the giant demonstrations that ultimately contributed to derailing the Seattle WTO negotiations, Via Campesina activists adopted a practice employed by the Brazilian MST and its allies (and earlier by the American Agriculture Movement), where the symbolic politics of wearing bandannas and flying flags symbolizing the movements built a mystique among militants and generated media photo opportunities (MAB 2001). Donning green bandannas and baseball caps and distributing more to sympathizers in the crowd, Via Campesina supporters attracted considerable attention from other activists and the many journalists covering the protests.

This high-profile participation in international protests and civil society gatherings continues to be a hallmark of Via Campesina activity. Its supporters played prominent roles at the World Social Forums in Porto Alegre, Brazil, and at the 2002 Rome+5 FAO World Food Summit. Following the violence outside the 2001 G8 summit in Genoa, *Newsweek* singled out the Via Campesina as one of eight "kinder, gentler globalist" groups behind the anti-G8 protests (Newsweek 2001, 17).

Much of the Via Campesina's organizing is carried out by its constituent groups, often with funds from European NGOs (see table 1.1). In 2003, the Via Campesina itself had a tiny staff: the executive secretary, a part-time bilingual "technical secretary" and a regular secretary in the operational secretariat in Honduras; a part-time consultant in Nicaragua who works with the Via Campesina's global agrarian reform campaign; and a multilingual "technical assistant" based in Europe who handles the network's internal communications and media relations. It relied on Yahoo Listserves for distributing position papers and announcements, which circulated in English, Spanish, and occasionally in other languages.

TABLE 1.1. NGO collaboration with peasant and small farmer networks

ORGANIZATION	HEADQUARTERS AND OFFICES	ACTIVITIES AND POSITIONS
Action Group on Erosion, Technology and Concentration (formerly Rural Advancement Foundation International, RAFI) http://www.etcgroup.org	Canada	Mobilizes public opinion against patenting of life forms, especially crop genetic material.
Agriterra http://www.agriterra.org	Netherlands	Formerly the Paulo Freire Foundation (PFS), which played a key role in founding Via Campesina. Specializes in agricultural credit and technology issues and works closely with the International Federation of Agricultural Producers (IFAP) and with some organizations in Via Campesina.
ARnet (Popular Coalition Agrarian Reform Network)	Italy	Promotes land reform and related initiatives in areas such as water rights, common property resources, inheritance rights for women, and Indigenous rights. Part of the Popular Coalition to Eradicate Hunger and Poverty, a consortium of governmental organizations and NGOs established by the International Fund for Agricultural Development.
Asia-Pacific Research Network (APRNet) http://www.aprnet.org	Philippines	Sponsors capacity advocacy training and strategy workshops around WTO-related issues. Collaborates with the Pesticide Action Network and Via Campesina.
Brot Für die Welt (Bread for the World)	Germany	Funds meetings and development projects of local-level and transnational farmers organizations.
Farmers Link	United Kingdom	Promotes awareness of sustainable agriculture, food production and distribution, and rural development issues; works on fair trade campaigns; sponsored farmer exchanges between England and Nicaragua, France, Zimbabwe, India, Chile, the United States, and Cuba.
Focus on the Global South http://www.focusweb.org	Thailand, Philippines, Switzerland	Conducts research and reporting on trade negotiations; accompanies small farmer organizations at protests and parallel forums; criticizes free-trade accords.
Food First Information and Action Network (FIAN) http://www.fian.org	Germany, with sections in 18 other countries	Advocates agrarian reform and founded an urgent action network to alert participants about land conflicts, human rights violations, and food emergencies.

(continued)

TABLE 1.1. continued

ORGANIZATION	HEADQUARTERS AND OFFICES	ACTIVITIES AND POSITIONS
Food First (Institute for Food and Development Policy) http://www.foodfirst.org	United States	Conducts research and analysis on agronomic, trade, and food sovereignty issues; accompanies small farmer movements at protests and parallel forums; strongly opposes free-trade treaties and biotechnology.
Genetic Resources Action International (GRAIN) http://www.grain.org	Spain	Promotes sustainable management and agricultural biodiversity based on people's control over genetic resources and local knowledge.
HIVOS (Humanistisch Instituut voor Ontwikkelingssamenwerking, Humanist Institute for Development Cooperation) http://www.hivos.nl	Netherlands	Works with organizations of the poor and marginalized in the countries of the South; facilitates access to fair trade markets and small-scale credit; and supports arts, gender equity, human rights, HIV/AIDS, information access, and sustainable development programs.
Institut de Recherches et d'Applications de Methodes de Developpement (Research Institute on Applied Development Methods, IRAM) http://www.iram-fr.org	France	Supports programs in agricultural credit and microfinance, food security, local development, rural organization, and microenterprises.
Institute for Agriculture and Trade Policy http://iatp.org	United States, Switzerland	Works on behalf of family farms, rural communities, and ecosystems through research and education, science and technology, and advocacy; provides analysis to farmers organizations involved in anti-neoliberal movements.
Instituto Brasileiro de Análises Sociais e Econômicas (Brazilian Institute of Social and Economic Analysis) https://ibase.br	Brazil	Conducts research on social and economic conditions, which it makes available to peasant organizations and other grassroots sectors.

Organization	Location/Scope	Description
Oxfam International http://www.oxfam.org	National organizations (12 total), including United Kingdom, Belgium, Canada, Germany, Ireland, United States, Netherlands, and Spain	Supports famine relief, grassroots development, international farm movement meetings, and public education around food, agriculture, and development issues. Oxfam's 2002 "Make Trade Fair" campaign, while critical of unfair trade practices, produced skepticism among radical peasant and farmer organizations.
Pesticide Action Network International http://www.pan-international.org	Five regional centers, with several hundred participating NGOs	Holds training workshops and protests; member groups campaign against corporate agribusiness and for low-input agriculture.
Red Interamericana de Agriculturas y Democracia (Interamerican Network on Agricultures and Democracy, RIAD)	Mexico	Provides an information clearinghouse and source of analysis for peasant organizations and NGOs working on agricultural issues.
Servicio, Desarrollo y Paz, A.C. (Service, Development and Peace, SEDEPAC) http://sedepac.org	Mexico	Promotes organizational development, labor rights, and sustainable production practices; cosponsored international meetings of the Programa Campesino a Campesino in the 1980s and 1990s.
Solidarités Agroalimentaires (Agro-Food Solidarities, SOLAGRAL)	France	Seeks to support citizens' networks and to influence global trade and environmental policies by strengthening the negotiating capacity of delegates from poor countries to international governance institutions.

The Revival of Agrarian Reform

In the early 1990s, agrarian reform had largely dropped off the agenda of policy-makers. In Latin America in particular, diverse reform programs had been stymied by elite intransigence, privatization measures and "counter-reforms," or failure to provide the complementary resources—credit, titling, irrigation, technical assistance, and transport, processing, and marketing facilities—required for the success of peasant enterprises (Dorner 1992). At the 1995 FAO conference, several member nations called for eliminating land reform from the program. However, at the following year's FAO conference, the issue of agrarian reform reemerged with force in discussions over food security and at the insistence of the dozens of peasant and farmer activists present there. The same countries that asked the FAO to cut support for land reform were, within a few years, requesting FAO aid for new reform projects. Citing land invasions in Brazil, Malawi, and Zimbabwe, a FAO specialist acknowledged in 1998 that "first and foremost land reform is back on the agenda because rural populations have put it there" (Riddell 1998).

In 1999, Via Campesina and the German-based Food First Information and Action Network (FIAN) launched a global campaign on agrarian reform intended to take advantage of this growing momentum and to counter the World Bank's promotion of "market-assisted land reform," in which public- and private-sector credits are provided to beneficiaries who individually negotiate land purchases with willing sellers. Via Campesina and FIAN believe that the World Bank approach will not solve the problem of access to land for the poorest farmers or for those in places where property ownership is highly skewed and the supply of land is inelastic (FIAN 2000). The campaign briefly brought the Via Campesina into dialogue with the World Bank. Rafael Alegría spoke at a 1999 bank forum on "Strengthening Producer Organizations," which was also attended by an IFAP representative (LVC 1999c). Not long after, Via Campesina and FIAN presented a petition to World Bank officials in Washington, DC, and Mexico City, arguing that "land is much more than a commodity" and that state-sponsored agrarian reforms are a human right (FIAN 2000). In early 2001, the World Bank's director of rural development responded by changing the program's name from "market-assisted" to "community-managed" and by suggesting that the bank's approach was complementary "and not a substitute" for laws allowing governments to expropriate land for distribution to peasants. Alegría and FIAN director Michael Windfuhr wrote another letter to World Bank President James Wolfensohn reiterating their concerns, but they found few grounds for believing that continued negotiations would be productive (R. L. Thompson 2001; Windfuhr and Alegría 2002).

An Emergency Human Rights Network and Widening Political Engagement

The "emergency network" established as part of the Via Campesina–FIAN agrarian reform campaign has likely had more impact than the discussions with the World Bank. Modeled on the urgent action campaigns of Amnesty International and other human rights organizations, the emergency network seeks to apply rapid pressure to state authorities in situations where peasants have suffered or are threatened with violent repression. When peasants involved in land conflicts were in danger, the network circulated electronic communiques with instructions about how to contact government officials and peasant organizations. In 2001, Via Campesina sponsored an "international seminar on agrarian reform for peace in Colombia" that drew three hundred participants from Colombia and beyond, including French activist José Bové, Bolivian parliamentary deputy (and later president) Evo Morales, and the president of the European Parliament's Development Commission, Joaquim Miranda (LVC 2000a; Via Campesina, ANUC, and FENSUAGRO 2001). Similar missions to the Philippines, Brazil, and Honduras generated media coverage and increased government efforts to resolve agrarian disputes. The global campaign for agrarian reform also sponsored training seminars in eight countries, as well as radio campaigns and protest actions (LVC 2000a).

Concern with peasants' human rights and increased experience in international protest actions led the Via Campesina to a dramatic engagement with the Palestinian–Israeli conflict in 2002. Ties between Palestinian peasants and French agriculturalists in the Larzac region, home base of the peripatetic José Bové, dated to 1990, and had included visits and other intermittent contacts (Alland and Alland 2001, 176). In January 2002, Palestinian olive farmers came to the Porto Alegre World Social Forum, where they contacted the large Via Campesina delegation and spoke of the difficulties they faced under Israeli occupation. A few months later, four Via Campesina leaders traveled to the West Bank, where they visited bedouins whose olive trees had been sprayed with herbicides by the Israeli military. Three of the four Via Campesina leaders were among the activists who accompanied Yasir Arafat inside the compound of the Palestine Liberation Organization during the Israeli siege of Ramallah. José Bové was deported after a few days, but Paul Nicholson from Spain and Mario Lill from Brazil remained in Arafat's compound for three weeks (LVC 2002b).

The Via Campesina's involvement with the Palestinian–Israeli conflict is illustrative of how cross-border networking and the increasingly global and complex character of agricultural policy itself have broadened the alliances and concerns of peasant and farmer movements. Trade, phytosanitary measures, intellectual property rights, animal and human health, environment, human rights, biotech-nology, gender equity, and food sovereignty have, in everyday political conten-tion, become inextricably bound up with one another. Protest repertoires too have converged, as political campaigns are carried out in transnational contexts and as movements from different sectors and countries exchange experiences.

The multiple foci and theatricality of agriculturalists' public actions need to be understood in relation to these processes. The much-heralded 1999 symbolic "dismantling" of an "incredibly flimsy," half-built McDonald's restaurant by José Bové and his Confédération Paysanne neighbors in the French town of Millau was a carnivalesque protest against US tariffs imposed on Roquefort cheese in retaliation for the EU ban on US hormone-treated beef (Bové and Dufour 2001, 3–31; Herman and Boisgontier 2001, 68). More generally, it was a response to a series of food safety crises in Europe—namely, dioxin-tainted poultry and mad cow and foot-and-mouth diseases. It also tapped fears about the potential dan-gers of GM crops, which farmers' movements saw as part of the economic and ecological logic of intensive agriculture and a US- and corporate-dominated food system that threatened to undermine health, environment, and cultural speci-ficity. The Millau "McDo" episode could also be read in part as a reprise of the 1996 attack on a Kentucky Fried Chicken (KFC) outlet in Bangalore, India, by a hundred and fifty members of the Karnataka State Farmers Association, who accused KFC of selling "carcinogenic junk food" (Gupta 1998, 331). The 1999 In-dian farmers' caravan to Europe, which had brought together many of the pro-tagonists in both actions, ended barely two months before the incident that catapulted Millau to world attention. And the Via Campesina's third congress (and its first international women's meeting) in Bangalore in 2000 brought them together once more.

A Profusion of Networks

The geographical coverage of the transnational networks is decidedly uneven. Via Campesina, for example, had significant backing in most of the Spanish-speaking world and virtually no affiliates in Africa, a region where IFAP has a number of member groups. IFAP, in turn, has little presence in Mexico or Chile and counts among its members only a handful of nonelite groups in the rest of Latin America or in Europe. China has the largest number of peasants, and despite widespread rural unrest there attributable, in many cases, to market-driven dislocations of the rural population (Walker 2002), neither Via Campe-sina nor IFAP has a presence there (perhaps not surprising, given the political system).

IFAP's close collaboration with governments and multilateral agencies, as well as its large-producer orientation, gives it access to resources and makes it a centrist or even conservative voice within the spectrum of global agriculturalists' movements. Operating primarily behind the scenes as a traditional lobby, however, its public profile has been lower than that of Via Campesina, even though it enrolls more participating organizations. Although IFAP affirms its commitment to family farms as the basis of a sustainable agricultural system (PROSI 1996), many of its constituent organizations represent elites and corporate producers. This is particularly evident in Argentina, Brazil, Canada, Colombia, France, the Philippines, and the United States, where IFAP affiliates enroll large farmers and more radical Via Campesina organizations represent peasant, Indigenous, and small family farmers. IFAP leaders, in contrast to those of less conservative groups, are frequently skeptical of, or even hostile to, environmentalists and critics of industrial agriculture. In 2001, some charged that "lunatic eco-terrorists" might have deliberately caused epidemics of foot-and-mouth disease and swine fever in Britain in order to "scare" the public and "destroy meat consumption" (Byrnes 2001).

In 1983, the Swiss-based Charles Léopold Mayer Foundation for Human Progress (FPH) initiated a program for agriculturalists' organizations in Senegal, Tanzania, and a few other African countries. Within a few years, the FPH decided that the problems peasants faced in Africa—glutted markets, dismantling of state commodity boards, liberalization of agricultural trade—required an international response. In 1993, in Cameroon, twenty peasant and NGO activists started a regional network called APM-Afrique (Agriculture Peasant and Modernization Network–Africa). In contrast to Via Campesina, which favored pressure tactics and protests, APM-Afrique sought principally to "rediscover the intellectual capacity" of its peasant participants—largely from Francophone Africa—with a view to "resolving concrete problems" (Berthomé and Mercoiret 1993, 67). By 1995, APM-Afrique had created working groups on the WTO and the coffee and cotton sectors, a magazine, and an "itinerant" African Peasants' Academy (Université Paysanne Africaine), which offered courses in Senegal and Cameroon. Simultaneously with the creation of APM-Afrique, the FPH initiated a parallel project in Eastern Europe and sponsored international meetings of peasant organizations in the Larzac region of France in 1993, in Cameroon in 1996, in Brazil in 1998, and again in the Larzac in 2000. By 1996, these events had given rise to APM-Mondial, which helped to create the Inter-American Network on Agricultures and Democracy (RIAD) and also maintained links with NGOs close to Via Campesina, such as the US-based Institute for Trade and Agricultural Policy (APM-Mondial 2001; "APM-Afrique" 2001). The APM networks' analysis of the WTO is similar to that of the Via Campesina, and the two networks eventually collaborated on projects such as the 2001 World Forum on Food Sovereignty in Havana.

In 2002, APM-Mondial assembled a hundred thirty peasant and Indigenous leaders from thirty-six countries at a World Peasant Meeting in Cameroon. Some of the Asian and Latin American organizations that attended belonged to Via Campesina, but most of the participating groups were in other networks. The meeting's Yaoundé Declaration condemned "the negative impacts of neoliberal globalization" in terms very similar to those employed by the Via Campesina and, echoing the slogan of the World Social Forum, declared that "another world is possible." APM-Mondial has also had set up an APM network in China (Réseau APM Chine) and convened conferences there, although the individuals and institutions involved are designated by the Chinese government (APM-Mondial 2001, 2002).

To what extent does the proliferation of networks with similar agendas—Via Campesina and APM-Mondial, among others (see boxes 1.3 and 1.5)—represent a force for synergy, a territorial division of labor, or alternatively, a kind of organizational competition or redundancy? The balance between these possibilities is likely to be constantly shifting and rather delicate. The Via Campesina tried on a number of occasions to make inroads in Africa, hosting African organizations at its 1996 congress and holding a 1998 coordinating committee meeting in Senegal at the same time as a convention of African peasant groups (LVC 1996; LVC 1998). These efforts bore little fruit, however, in terms of building durable ties to what was, as Via Campesina leader Rafael Alegría put it in a 2001 interview in Tegucigalpa, a largely "blank" region (Alegría 2001). Around the time of the 2002 World Summit on Sustainable Development in Johannesburg, the Via Campesina joined African organizations in an acerbic exchange of letters about land reform with the World Bank and issued joint statements with the National Land Committee, backing its demands for negotiations with the South African government, but these efforts were hard to sustain once the summit ended and did not lead to the formal incorporation of African organizations, many of which were part of APM-Afrique, into Via Campesina (Mngxitama 2002; NLC and LPM 2002). APM and Via Campesina were, in effect, territorially specialized, but while this helped each by not spreading scarce resources too thinly, it also undercut the claims of both networks to truly global reach.

Contradictions and Future Prospects

In little more than a decade of intensive transnational networking and political action, peasant and small farmer movements have contributed to stalling the

Uruguay and Millennium rounds of world trade talks, to achieving at least temporary bans in several countries and regions on commercial planting of GM crops promoted by giant agribusiness corporations, and to returning agrarian reform to the global agenda in an era of privatization and paeans to the magic of the marketplace. They have also attempted to shift the terms of discussion in international arenas around fundamental development and ethical issues, arguing, for example, that quantitative measures of "food security" need to be replaced with an understanding of "food sovereignty," which prioritizes a multidimensional commitment to human well-being and insists that food and land are not simply commodities. Importantly, small farmers have reinforced alliances with and heightened the legitimacy of movements around trade, biotechnology, corporate accountability, environment, health, and human rights issues. Participants in the peasant and farmer networks have also come to have a dynamic sense of themselves as political actors empowered with new knowledge, conceptions of solidarity, and tools of struggle, and surprisingly, unlike the unsophisticated rustics that urban elites often imagine them to be.

These are formidable accomplishments for movements that not long ago often barely knew of one another's existence, but they exist alongside opposing trends that are hardly auspicious. Relations between NGOs and the peasant and farmer networks have frequently been fraught with tension. At times, this tension has involved questions of representation—who may speak in the name of the peasantry—and on other occasions accountability to constituencies and to those who provide funds for network activities. The imposition of donor-driven agendas has contributed to the decline or demise of more than one civil society initiative.

Network activists, like other overworked professionals, feel the tug of disparate demands from regional, national, and local organizations in which they take part and, in the case of farmers, from the imperatives of agricultural production, in which they usually must participate as a livelihood and to sustain their legitimacy vis-à-vis supporters and antagonists. Concretely, the same individuals who mobilize for international conferences may also have to assemble a legal team to defend contested property titles, follow up on orders for a cooperative's rubber boots, and harvest a field of cabbages before the rains arrive. Tensions between transnational and national activism may become more acute as democratization advances in previously authoritarian societies, since possibilities of affecting transnational processes through national action may improve and traditional political forms—parties, unions, and lobbies—may assume many demands initially articulated through transnational civil society initiatives. In Central America, for example, several organizations that pioneered cross-border linkages in the 1980s have largely withdrawn from time-consuming transnational activism.

An added contradiction is what one critic terms network activity's "dual quality as both a means to an end and an end in itself" (Riles 2000, 51). Networks appear, formally, to link organizations, but they also are based on personal ties between activists (and between activists and funders). These issues, together with the "verticalist" tendencies of some organizations, may produce instances of exclusion that limit network members' political imagination, effectiveness, and credibility. Network practices of representation—submitting proposals, organizing meetings, publishing newsletters or websites, drafting "action platforms"—sometimes seek to demonstrate the effectiveness of a network with reference to its own self-description and activities rather than its tangible impact on targeted constituencies, policies, and institutions. The difficulty is compounded for organizations that participate in various transnational networks of differing geographical scope or purpose. Movements of poor rural people, with few skilled leaders, can usually ill afford the cost in separation from their constituencies that intense transnational activism implies.

The major obstacle facing the peasant and small farmer networks, however, continues to be the sheer force of ongoing worldwide economic liberalization and ever-greater corporate power. No society has ever entirely resolved the tension between agriculture and industry over terms of trade, over fair prices for farmers versus cheap food for urban people or cheap raw materials for food and fiber manufacturers. Many societies in the past, however, did achieve a decent, stable balance between the interests of farmers and those of large and small consumers through political compromises or stalemates. Farmers in many places sought and achieved a degree of vertical integration, through cooperatives and other noncorporate ownership forms, that provided them with more value-added and constituted a check on the agribusiness monopolies. These hard-won gains, however, are everywhere disappearing in the face of heightened competition at the farm level and decreased competition and ever-larger mergers among the corporations that buy, process, and transport what farms produce. As societies throughout the world urbanize, rural areas and rural people often lose political clout.

The regional and global free-trade pacts targeted by the peasant and farmer networks—such as NAFTA, WTO, and the proposed Free Trade Area of the Americas—generally aim to legislate the behavior of national governments but only secondarily that of corporations. Today's conflicts over farming and food pit some of the most powerful global institutions against incipient transnational movements of some of the most marginalized and destitute people on earth. The peasants and small farmers of the twenty-first century—still almost half of the world's economically active population—have, in the past decade, risen to the challenge, found new means of struggle, and scored an occasional victory, but it is still too early to call the match.

PEASANT-FARMER MOVEMENTS, THIRD WORLD PEOPLES, AND THE SEATTLE PROTESTS AGAINST THE WORLD TRADE ORGANIZATION, 1999

This chapter was part of a special *Dialectical Anthropology* issue commemorating the tenth anniversary of the Seattle protests against the World Trade Organization (WTO), which many consider a formative moment in the global justice or alter-globalization movement. Agrarian activists in the Seattle protests saw them not just as an opportunity for developing alliances and solidarity but also for deepening their knowledge and strategic visions.

In a much-debated 2000 essay in *Colorlines*, Elizabeth Betita Martínez asked, "Where was the color in Seattle?" She lamented that the anti-WTO "demonstrators were overwhelmingly Anglo" and that there was a "low turnout of people of color" (2000a).[1] Jennifer Hadden and Sidney Tarrow similarly suggest that "insignificant numbers traveled to Seattle from the global South" (2007, 211).[2] This chapter, based on interviews and documentary sources, seeks to nuance these claims and to examine the events of November 30, 1999 (N30) and the participation of peasants and farmers.[3] It argues (1) that N30 in Seattle was more diverse than is usually appreciated, both in terms of the provenance of the participants and the activities in which they engaged; (2) that Seattle was a transformative moment not just for global civil society as a whole but for agrarian movements in particular and for many individual rural activists; (3) that the emphasis of Martínez and others on color and origin relies on a politically unproductive essentialism, obscures the emergence of new actors, notably transnational peasant and farmer organizations, and distracts attention from fundamental gains, especially the derailing of global trade talks, which derived in significant measure from the participation in N30 of third world peoples; and (4) that these successes grew out of "street heat" that swayed developing-country WTO delegates to the demonstrators' positions and led them to stand up to pressures from more powerful governments. This "street heat" dynamic is quite different from the "boomerang effect" or global grassroots pressure on governments to respect international norms that is frequently invoked to explain the success of transnational social movements (Keck and Sikkink 1998).

Some eyewitnesses maintain, pace Martínez, that considerable numbers of "people of color" *were* present in Seattle. Jeffrey St. Clair mentions "a robust international contingent on the streets Tuesday morning [November 30, 1999]: French farmers, Korean greens, Canadian wheat growers, Mexican environmentalists, Chinese dissidents, Ecuadorian anti-dam organizers, U'wa tribespeople from the Colombian rainforest and British campaigners against genetically modified foods" (Cockburn and St. Clair 2000, 28). Luis Hernández Navarro, similarly, lists "people from the United States, Canada, Europe, Latin America, Europe and Asia—all unleashed a peaceful protest against the new Babylon" (2000, 41). Susan George refers to "many foreign delegations, the two largest being those from France and Canada" (2000, 55). According to Jackie Smith, "Southern activists and scholars comprised 30 to 40 percent of the panelists at the largest protest rallies" and "the Battle of Seattle" involved "extensive transnational mobilizing structures" (2002, 211, 221). Contemporaneous reports point to considerable participation by Philippine activists and Filipino Americans who, along with many from elsewhere, attended an International People's Assembly during the Seattle protests (BAYAN 1999; Mora, Soto, and Bello 1999). Kuna young people from Panama were among those drafting the Indigenous Peoples' Seattle Declaration (Indigenous Peoples' Caucus 2000). Activists from Mexico, Malaysia, the Philippines, Trinidad, Pakistan, and Ghana addressed the "People's Tribunal" on "The Human Face of Trade: Health and the Environment" (J. Smith 2002, 224). French activist José Bové estimated that there were "between 800 and 1000" N30 participants from outside the United States (Alland and Alland 2001, 200). Gilles Luneau reports that the demonstrators included "farmers from eighty different countries" (2001, xi). Even if the latter assertions may be somewhat exaggerated, these contrasting perceptions require posing a different question: Can the significance of N30 for people in the Global South be reduced simply to the supposedly "insignificant numbers" who were present in Seattle? It is also worth asking a related, albeit by now rhetorical, question of Martínez: Has the global justice movement remained (or was it ever) "overwhelmingly Anglo," with little participation by "people of color"?

Many N30 participants, and peasants and farmers in particular, came to Seattle not only to march in the streets but to network and attend political education forums. These less visible and dramatic aspects of the Seattle events deserve attention, if only because they contributed to building an ongoing movement and to convincing developing-country WTO delegates to resist the unfettered free-trade agenda of the more powerful developed-country governments. Street heat, like the less dramatic forums and assemblies, also played a role in the collapse of the WTO negotiating round. Most fundamentally, however, the significance of N30 has less to do with the proportion of demonstrators who came from the Global South (or of those "of color") than with the impact that the Seattle events had on those who did come, on developing-country WTO delegates, and on other sympathizers who stayed home but nonetheless followed the situation closely.

Peasants and Farmers, Global Protests, and the WTO

N30 in Seattle in 1999 (together with the Zapatistas' 1996 International Encounter for Humanity and against Neoliberalism in Chiapas, Mexico) is frequently described as a key foundational moment in what became the global justice movement or global civil society.[4] Importantly, however, the Seattle protests against the WTO marked the culmination of a movement against the globalization of trade and against the GATT (General Agreement on Tariffs and Trade, the predecessor to the WTO) that had been building since the mid-1980s.[5] GATT-WTO trade rules had been one important target in a broader upsurge against neoliberalism. Others included the stabilization and economic structural adjustment programs of the International Monetary Fund (IMF) and the World Bank and the proposed Multilateral Agreement on Investment (MAI), which took shape in the Organization for Economic Cooperation and Development (OECD). The MAI succumbed at the end of 1998 to an international campaign aided by sympathetic governments (notably France) that brought the previously secret treaty negotiations to public light (Desai and Said 2001, 60–61).[6]

One of the big surprises of the era of neoliberalism was that peasants and farmers—and not organized labor—were often in the forefront in opposing free-market, pro-corporate policies. The privatization and deindustrialization that frequently formed part of neoliberal projects tended to undermine labor organizations. Also, one legacy of Cold War ideology was that organized labor, especially in the United States but also elsewhere, was historically "more supportive of the WTO's trade liberalization project than other elements of the social movement community" (O'Brien et al. 2000, 67). Trade unionists were, of course, an important presence in the N30 Seattle protests, accounting for perhaps as much as half the participants, even though their presence, like that of the international contingents, was consistently underreported (Waterman 2001, viii–ix).[7] The big worker turnout for protests with such a pronounced counter-cultural dimension ("Teamsters and Turtles, Together at Last!") inspired considerable euphoria among global justice activists about new kinds of solidarity that transcended narrow, nationalist economic self-interest. As part of the anti-WTO protest, the International Longshore and Warehouse Union, a uniquely internationalist US union, shut down the ports on the entire West Coast of the United States. After N30, the involvement of mainstream American unions in internationalist actions did not sustain the (inflated?) hopes of activists from other sectors, despite ongoing involvement with non-US labor federations in the World Social Forums and in lobbying the International Labor Organization (Waterman and Timms 2005; De Armond 2001).

Farmer protests, on the other hand, were particularly pronounced in Western Europe, India, and Latin America in the period leading up to N30, largely because of a deepening global agricultural crisis (and they have remained so in the post-Seattle period) (Edelman 2003). Since the mid-1980s and the conclusion of the Uruguay Round of GATT, agriculture has been subject to global trade rules. As commodity markets globalized, farmgate prices plummeted and small agriculturalists experienced increasing difficulty. Developed countries engaged in various forms of dumping at the same time that they protected their own agricultural sectors (particularly in the United States, the European Union, and Japan). Emboldened by global trade liberalization, a handful of giant corporations tightened their control over markets for staple foods and diverse kinds of farming technology.

The WTO is unusual among global governance institutions in that it is supposed to operate on a consensus basis.[8] In contrast to the Bretton Woods institutions (the World Bank and the IMF), where each country's vote is in proportion to its capital contribution, in the WTO, each country theoretically has one vote. In practice, however, votes are rarely taken and trade- and investment-related issues are governed by a series of accords, the most important of which, for this discussion, are the Agreement on Agriculture (AoA), the Trade-Related Intellectual Property Rights (TRIPS) agreement, anti-dumping (article VI of GATT 1994), and the Dispute Settlement Understanding (DSU). Importantly, all of these accords limit the policy options of national governments (Sandbrook et al. 2007, 215–219). The AoA details concessions and commitments that WTO member countries are supposed to make in relation to market access, nontariff barriers, subsidy reduction, and increasing their exposure to international trade and competition. TRIPS attempts to establish uniform standards for protecting and enforcing intellectual property rights, including such controversial practices as patenting seeds and other life forms. WTO's anti-dumping agreement seeks to protect member countries' economies against imports of products that are sold below the "normal" price in the producing country and that might injure the importing country. While some countries seek to reduce their surpluses or gain market share by dumping their subsidized products in the markets of less developed countries, much dumping occurs in disguised form as food "aid," a problem that is difficult to address in the WTO Committee on Anti-Dumping Practices. The DSU rules on trade-related disagreements between WTO members. Its decisions are adopted unless a consensus forms to reject a ruling. A country that seeks to block a ruling must persuade all other WTO members, including its adversary in the case, to vote to reject. The consensus-based model can thus be an obstacle for any country that tries to use the WTO framework to defend its interests against the most powerful actors in the global economy. Moreover, many important WTO negotiations only involve a few of the most economically powerful countries. These "mini-ministerials" and "green room" negotiations—the name comes from the color of the WTO Director-General's Office in Geneva—typically exclude small and less developed countries and attempt to arrive at policy prescriptions that are then imposed on the less developed WTO member countries, which sometimes lack the technical expertise or resources to evaluate the measures that they are being pressured to approve (Wijkman 2003; Rosset 2006).

Peasants and farmers, especially but not only in the developing world, thus had ample reason for seeing the GATT and, beginning in 1995, the WTO as a threat to their livelihoods and as an affront to their sense of justice (see figure 2.1). The Seattle anti-WTO protests occurred during the formative years of what became important transnational agrarian movements, such as La Via Campesina (LVC), an international umbrella group founded in 1993 that now includes peasant and farmer organizations from almost sixty countries. LVC (or "Peasant Way"), which is always referred to by its Spanish name, has been in the forefront of struggles against neoliberal globalization and in particular the WTO (and its predecessor, the GATT). Its activities and those of its affiliated national-level organizations include mass mobilizations at meetings of global governance institutions, direct actions against agribusiness corporations that produce genetically modified crops, and campaigns for agrarian reform and for "food sovereignty" based on smallholding production and national- or local-level control of food systems (Borras 2004, 2008c, 2008d; Desmarais 2002, 2007b; Edelman 2003; Borras, Edelman, and Kay 2008). Peasant and farmer activists who went to Seattle were mostly from abroad, some from the Global South and some not, and some were "of color" and some not. Most were supporters of LVC member organizations. Few participated in any fighting in the streets. They did use the

FIGURE 2.1. Cover of a Via Campesina pamphlet from 2000. The photo portrays peasant and farmer demonstrators in Seattle on N30.

Seattle demonstrations as an opportunity to strengthen alliances, make contacts, organize workshops, refine analyses, draft declarations, and stage political theater.

The "First Shot"

The "first shot in the battle for Seattle," according to Jeffrey St. Clair, grew directly out of a farmers' protest, the November 29 demonstration led by French

FIGURE 2.2. In the 1990s, this cow appeared on press releases of the European campaign against rBST (recombinant bovine somatotropin or bovine growth hormone).

activist José Bové in front of a McDonald's restaurant (Cockburn and St. Clair 2000, 21). McDonald's—in Seattle and in France—was a symbol of both beef consumption and what Bové called *la malbouffe* (junk food). Bové and other farmers targeted it to protest US tariffs on Roquefort cheese and other luxury goods that were instituted six months earlier in retaliation for a European ban on imports of US beef produced with growth hormones (see figure 2.2).[9]

Roquefort—made from raw ewe's milk, aged in caves, and widely regarded as "the king of cheeses"—was among the approximately one hundred European products affected by the punitive tariffs. The Larzac region of France, where Roquefort is produced, was a stronghold of the Confédération Paysanne, a militant farmers union. As a protest against the US retaliatory tariffs and the WTO ruling that France had to import hormone-tainted beef, Bové, a local Confédération Paysanne activist, led a group of demonstrators in the town of Millau in August 1999 in dismantling a McDonald's outlet that was still under construction. This largely symbolic action vaulted Bové to international fame (and briefly landed him in jail).[10] The November protest at a Seattle McDonald's was thus a natural continuation of an ongoing struggle. Bové arrived in the United States on the way to N30 having smuggled in 200 kilograms of Roquefort, much of which he distributed to passersby in front of that Seattle McDonald's on the first day of the protests. The rest of the cheese, as Chaia Heller reports,

> circulated through the streets and press conferences all that week, toted around in duffle bags by Bové and the other farmers in its sparkling black and gold foil. The Roquefort's charisma moved NGO leaders to assist the farmers in setting up tables and platters full of thick bread and cheese. Creating an ambiance of sharing and cultural awe, it inspired reporters to run out to local markets to buy wine as accompaniment. Riddled with blue pockets of bacterial culture, Roquefort was a

visual and olfactory reminder of the stakes that had brought activists
to confront globalization in both Millau and Seattle: Roquefort stood
for culture against transnational capital. (Heller 2002, 30)

When Bové spoke from the roof of a van in front of that Seattle McDonald's,
peasant and farmer activists from around the world—Canadians, Indians, Central Americans, and Mexicans, among others—were part of a crowd that
quickly grew to several thousand. LVC, which briefly reported on the protest in
stilted English on its Honduran website, noted that the demonstration was
against "hormoned meat" and "transgenics" and "for healthier food for everyone." Earlier on the same day, LVC members, led by the US National Family Farm
Coalition, planted trees in a Seattle park "to demonstrate that we are struggling
pacifically for a healthier environment for everyone and that we have faith and
hope in a fairer and more human future" (LVC 1999a).

As the tree-planting activity suggests, much of the activity around N30 involved political theater, teach-ins, and meetings rather than marches or clashes
with the police. LVC organized "a big workshop over several days on the issue
of globalization, attended by seventy delegates from thirty countries" (Bové and
Dufour 2001, 157). The Latin American peasant organizers present in Seattle
used the occasion to have an extraordinary session of one of the continent's main
transnational agrarian movements, the CLOC (Hernández Cascante 2002).[11] On
December 1, "Agriculture Day" for the WTO, thousands of peasants, farmers,
environmentalists and young people gathered at a farmers' market in order to
support fair trade and organic agriculture. US farmers distributed organic apples to the crowd that then marched to protest in front of the headquarters of
Cargill, the multinational grain giant (LVC 1999a). Peasant and farmer activists also participated in daily press conferences; forums on "food sovereignty"
organized by the US National Family Farm Coalition; the International People's
Assembly, which was organized by several Asian groups (discussed further below); and an event on "agriculture and the WTO" sponsored by the NGO parallel forum (LVC 1999a). LVC women activists, declaring that "you cannot put
sugar coating on a rotten pie," issued a statement pointing to the particularly
adverse effects of WTO and of neoliberal policies more generally on women, including the feminization of poverty and diminished access to land, whether
through the market or state-led agrarian reforms that favored male beneficiaries.[12] They concluded by thanking "the WTO for helping to unify small farmers worldwide. During the week-long work in Seattle, we have now succeeded in
globalizing the struggle and globalizing our hopes" (LVC 1999b).

Peasants and Farmers in Seattle

Peasants and farmers in Seattle also joined the big marches, and many felt the sting of pepper spray or tear gas. LVC supporters sported green baseball caps and kerchiefs and paraded with a huge green banner saying "¡Fuera la agricultura de la OMC!" ("Agriculture out of the WTO!"), with the WTO portrayed as a bright red and evil-looking octopus. Environmentalist Paul Hawken recalled the scene as follows:

> Ten Koreans came around the corner carrying a 10-foot banner protesting genetically modified foods. They were impeccable in white robes, sashes, and headbands. One was a priest. They played flutes and drums and marched straight toward the police and behind the seated demonstrators. Everyone cheered at the sight and chanted "The whole world is watching." (Hawken 2000, 21)

Jorge Hernández Cascante, an activist in the politically moderate Costa Rican organization UPANACIONAL and a participant in the founding of LVC, recalled in a 2002 interview that "Seattle was a very intense experience, very, very intense. It's something that can't be repeated.[13]

> That we could be in the same place with North American farmers groups, with groups from Canada, who had a large presence and very clear positions, very belligerent positions, with peasant groups from Africa, Asia, Japan. The Japanese had a very large presence, very clear positions with clear data about how their government's agrarian policy was eliminating any possibility for the reproduction of peasant families. The Koreans, of course, and peasant groups from Europe [were also present]. We had strong arguments in order to agree on things that for us are key, such as subsidies, since the strong countries support their agricultures.... To have that unique opportunity to share a struggle and the same slogans. To be able to discuss, for example, the thesis that agriculture should be taken out of the WTO, which was a position that at first appeared quite radical. To be able to hear all the opinions, the analysis of José Bové and the French compañeros of the French Confédération Paysanne—it was all extremely important.... [We learned of] the situation of fisherfolk in the Arctic, in Russia, Japan, the United States, and Canada, who are experiencing serious problems, of the situation of Indigenous peoples in different parts of the world, of the situation in Africa. This was something incredible, very new, very unexpected, to be able to

sit down and hear all the arguments about excluding agriculture from the WTO and about the search for alternative forms of agricultural development in the midst of this very exclusionary model. . . . For us, Seattle is historic. Because it opened up hope for humanity that, yes, there are other voices. Yes, there are other ways of conceiving the world. Yes, there are other ways of thinking. It's a hope, a symbol, in that sense a very beautiful sacrament. (Hernández Cascante 2002)

For Hernández, US and European agricultural subsidies had been a particular sore point and a potential source of division between farmers in developing and developed countries.

But then it was discussed how these protections are divided up inside the European countries and countries such as the United States. And it's evident that the benefits are highly concentrated. As a Spaniard there said, in Europe, the biggest beneficiary of agricultural subsidies is the Queen of England, because the English Crown has vast properties registered as agricultural lands and because it's agricultural land, it's necessary to subsidize it. That was the same argument as the North American small farmers who, in some cases, owed so much on their lands that they had to defend them with arms. They explained to us that they wouldn't let public functionaries come on their lands or anything. They were holding onto the land that used to be theirs and that now belonged to the banks. (Hernández Cascante 2002)

Terry Boehm, a young farmer from Saskatchewan, went to Seattle with a group of about a dozen activists from the National Farmers Union of Canada and "got arrested or detained or whatever it is." He described in a 2002 interview how he had long been interested in GATT and the Uruguay Round.

But with Seattle and the meeting of people in Seattle in 1999, I started serious participation on the international front. I saw the list of workshops and topics and was very interested. At home, I had often found myself in a position of expressing positions and analysis that were generally seen as outside conventional wisdom. What I found from going to Seattle and listening to people speak and participating in talks and meeting people from other farm organizations from different parts of the world, was that the perspective that I had was shared by many [and] by people of diverse circumstances. Perhaps the scale [of their farms] varied somewhat, but the situation and ultimate effects of extremely liberalized trade and neoliberal economics were being felt by all of them. (Boehm 2002)

For Boehm, like Hernández, the opportunity to learn was at least as important as the opportunity to protest:

> What was discussed there was everything from the ramifications of the WTO [to] the commodification of nature, of genetics, the appropriation by corporations of these things. There was talk about trade policies, the nasty effects of structural adjustment programs by the International Monetary Fund and the World Bank, the pressures to produce export crops and the environmental and economic damage that resulted from those pressures, the loss of certain environmental and nutritionally important production regions for export purposes. And how farmers, workers, all kinds of societies were feeling the ill effects of this. . . . Another thing I enjoyed very much was one evening, in a church amphitheater, there was a call for interested parties to put together a statement on agriculture. It was an interesting meeting because it was almost anarchist; the organization of it verged on anarchy, [with] all these diverse people coming together to make their statements . . . and then this attempt, very loosely moderated by Mark Ritchie and IATP, to try to put some sort of statement together.[14] I was intrigued by this attempt at this horizontal process. I became very interested in intellectual property rights in terms of knowing more, which I knew about and was interested in before, but the information was expanded there. And just speaking with people there and meeting people there with ATTAC I found interesting.[15]

Finally, Boehm had a comment on the contrast between media portrayals of N30 and what he had witnessed:

> The immediate presentation of Seattle and the reality of Seattle were polar opposites. I watched guys in their black handkerchiefs kicking in windows, and I watched the police watch these guys do this. I was standing there with other peaceful protesters. They watched this happen and then they gassed the peaceful people, and of course, there was mayhem and people running around, and then it was presented as wholesale violence on the part of protesters, but that's not what I saw. (Boehm 2002)

The International People's Assembly

At the International People's Assembly held in Seattle's Filipino-American Community Center on Martin Luther King, Jr. Way, representatives from GABRIELA and AMIHAN, two Philippine women's organizations, together with the KMP peasant organization and the pro-democracy alliance BAYAN, issued a joint declaration.[16]

> We, the impoverished producers of Asia, await with much apprehension the outcome of the 3rd WTO Ministerial Meeting, one of which main agenda [sic] is a review of the Agreement on Agriculture [AoA]. . . . Most of our governments are gearing to further open up our markets for agricultural products and our lands and other resources to corporate plunder. . . . We, who toil daily under the scorching sun to produce 91% of the world's rice, barely have enough rice to eat. We, who work in the plantations of bananas, pineapples, rubber and palm oil, barely have enough cash to send our children to school and buy medicine when we get sick. . . . We have never benefited from our governments' commitments to the AoA and the rest of the WTO agreements. The market access provision of the AoA, which provides for tariff reduction, is skewed to the advantage of industrialized countries which start off with high tariff rate bases and therefore end up still being able to protect their local markets. The developing countries are left with their local markets wide open for imports thus displacing their local products. (GABRIELA 1999)

The International People's Assembly (IPA) lasted for three days, from November 28 to November 30, with a schedule of speakers, musical groups, film screenings, cultural programs, and celebrations. Filipino and Asian groups were the main participants, but others included Canadian activist Maude Barlow (who had spearheaded the successful campaign to derail the MAI), US environmental justice activist Richard Moore, and LVC coordinator Rafael Alegría from Honduras. Ace Saturay, a founder of SnB, a four-year-old Filipino community organization and coordinator of the IPA, described it as the "highest expression of international solidarity against the World Trade Organization where people of color were not only visible, but clearly in leadership" (SIPA 2000).[17]

The IPA not only provided a forum for speakers from the Philippines, Taiwan, Japan, Malaysia, and Thailand, it served in addition as an informal venue for bilateral consultations between Korean and Japanese farmer organizations and for a pan-Asian celebration of rice culture. Other presentations discussed Yugoslavia, Cuba, and the situations of women and immigrants in the United States and Canada. The one break in the program came on November 30, when the IPA participants planned to march from the Filipino-American Community Center to the main anti-WTO rally downtown. The mayor of Seattle denied the group's request for a permit, but "this did not stop international delegations and several hundred militant Filipino and other youth-student and women activists of color from marching on [the] planned route and joining over 50,000 protestors coming from many cities throughout the US, Canada and worldwide to condemn the WTO" (IPA 1999).[18]

Social Energy after Seattle

Scholars of social movements, as well as activists themselves, have long recognized that participation in one struggle or movement, even one that fails or fades away, commonly engenders new rounds of participation in collective action. Albert Hirschman termed this the "conservation and mutation of social energy" and spoke of "a special kind of sequence" characteristic of most activists' biographies that, in contrast to many leading theorists of social movements, he considered an important methodological focus (1983, 4). Sidney Tarrow, similarly, suggests that "the best predictor of activism is past activism" (2005, 47).

Numerous observers emphasized that the anti-WTO protests engendered optimism and gave new energy to diverse movements, some of which were closely allied with or echoed or expressed the demands of peasants and farmers. The momentum of the diverse strands of the global justice movement in the year 2000 was extraordinary, both in the United States and elsewhere (Seoane and Taddei 2001a).[19] The movement against genetically engineered foods, for example, turned out more than a thousand people in Oakland in December 1999 to protest Food and Drug Administration hearings on genetic engineering technology. The organizers' slogan was "Last week Seattle, this week Oakland" (Mittal 1999). One activist remarked,

> Seattle made people feel as if they had some power once again. As the Battle of Seattle showed, the entire World Trade Organization is now being undermined by a growing international alliance of Civil Society— consumers, farmers, workers, environmentalists, and young people. The most important lesson of Seattle is that there is now a global New Democracy Movement being built, from the grassroots up. Food safety and genetic engineering are clearly proving to be one of the strategic pressure points or weak spots of global corporate power. (Cockburn and St. Clair 2000, 7)

Notably, this comment included "farmers" as key coalition participants and also stressed the international character of the anti-WTO activities in Seattle.

In February 2000, the United Nations Conference on Trade and Development (UNCTAD) held its tenth quadrennial meeting in Bangkok (Glassman 2002).

Since the creation of the WTO, the major developed countries had attempted to delink trade from development issues and to relegate the latter to the UNCTAD, which, unlike WTO, was not empowered to make decisions that would be binding on member states. Anti-WTO activists employed the networks that came out of N30 to organize an UNCTAD counter-summit with two main events, the "Post-Seattle Forum on Trade and Agriculture: Advancing the Call to Take Agriculture out of the WTO" and the "Forum on Trade, Finance Liberalization, and Implications of the Debt Crisis." Hosted by the Thai Assembly of the Poor and the Bangkok affiliate of the research and advocacy NGO International South Group Network, the forums were attended by activists from the Americas, Asia, Africa, and Europe. "The aftershock from Seattle is bound to shape the outcome of UNCTAD X," the organizers wrote. "It will be worthwhile to observe and explore possibilities of pushing developing nations into firming up a collective position in support of people's demands in Seattle" (International South Group Network 2000).

The formation and proliferation of Independent Media Centers (Indymedia) was another significant outcome of the N30 events. Established by progressive journalists to provide insiders' perspectives on the anti-WTO protests, Indymedia Seattle provided breaking news as well as audio and video clips on its website, published and distributed a newsletter, and sent news feeds to diverse mainstream media. In the years following N30, Indymedia centers were created in other US and Canadian cities, as well as in Europe, Latin America, Asia, South Africa, and elsewhere. With minimal resources but maximal "social energy," Indymedia became an important source of news and information about issues that the corporate media often distorted or failed to cover at all.

The activists were not the only ones to gain knowledge from the experience of Seattle. The WTO learned some lessons as well. Its first ministerial meeting after Seattle was held in 2001 in Doha, in the Persian Gulf emirate of Qatar, located on a small peninsula. In addition to the meeting being physically inaccessible, the Qatar government let it be known that it would carefully screen visa applicants and would ensure that the WTO meeting could transpire uninterrupted. The anti-WTO movement, largely unable to travel to the Persian Gulf, organized demonstrations in over 150 cities worldwide to coincide with the WTO conclave.[20] "It was," wrote Lesley Wood, "possibly the largest globally coordinated protest ever held to that date" (2004, 83).

What, then, of Elizabeth Betita Martínez's claim that the N30 protests included few "people of color"? Or Hadden and Tarrow's assertion that "insignificant numbers traveled to Seattle from the global South"? The category "people of color" is, of course, vague and protean, but even so, it ought to be clear that the number of such people participating in N30 was far from negligible.[21] Martínez estimates that "the overall turnout of color from the U.S. remained around five percent of the total" (2000b, 143). In the 2000 census, Seattle was 70 percent white and only 8 percent black and 5 percent Hispanic, so massive local participation of "people of color" would have been unlikely in any case (Seattle Government 2001). The number of people who came to Seattle from the Global South was also greater than Hadden and Tarrow indicate. Moreover, while the Seattle anti-WTO protests were taking place, simultaneous actions occurred in some twenty countries, including India, Pakistan, the Philippines, and Colombia, among others, in the Global South (J. Smith 2002, 215). The worldwide momentum that Seattle and these other activities generated was undeniably very substantial, as the upsurge in protests throughout 2000 suggests.

N30 was also successful in derailing the WTO Millennium Round and at least delaying further liberalization of global trade—no small victory considering the vastly lopsided forces arrayed against each other.[22] Indeed, for both the activists and social control theorists on the opposing side, the Seattle events have become a prototypical case of asymmetrical conflict, with the protesters' tactics sometimes dubbed "netwar" or "swarming" (De Armond 2001). Understanding how the N30 protests contributed to bringing the trade talks to a standstill, however, requires examining not just the tactical dimension, the media attention given to the police riot, or anything else that occurred in the streets. Rather, the impact on developing-country WTO delegates of what some pundits called "street heat" requires analysis as well.

One of the most influential theories about the political potency of global civil society centers on what Margaret Keck and Kathryn Sikkink (1998, 12–13) called "the boomerang effect" and others have termed "scale jumping" (N. Smith 1993; Glassman 2002), "venue shifting" (Van Rooy 2004, 20) or "leap-frogging" (O'Brien et al. 2000, 61). Essentially, movements that are unable to attain their objectives in domestic politics seek out international allies in order to pressure governments to conform to international norms. Keck and Sikkink's model focused on human rights and environmental campaigns. Yet, as Paul Nelson (2004) has argued, other issue areas, particularly trade and financial policies, have been less susceptible to "boomerang" strategies. This is because trade and financial policies are more central to powerful G8 governments than, say, World Bank project lending, human rights, or debt relief for poor and mostly small countries.[23] International financial and trade organizations, such as the World Bank, IMF, and WTO, are less vulnerable to grassroots pressure and lobbying than is usually the case with national governments. In part, this is because NGOs that attained considerable legitimacy as critics of development and aid policies have been slower to achieve similar levels of credibility as critics of macroeconomic and financial policies and institutional reforms. Furthermore, in the case of the WTO, with its by-invitation-only "mini-ministerials" and "green room" sessions, all but the most powerful or largest member states are frequently excluded from key decision-making venues, so it is harder to exert pressure on national states and then have them influence the WTO. Finally, civil society responses to global trade and financial issues frequently call for strengthening—rather than "boomeranging"—national governments in areas as varied as labor and environmental regulations, trade protections, intellectual property, or the "food sovereignty" that is a key demand of LVC.

Several factors internal to the WTO accounted for the collapse of the Seattle Millennium negotiating round. Developed countries failed to agree on the contentious issue of agricultural support, with France and Japan, in particular, tenaciously defending their own levels of protectionism. Conflicts over biotechnology between the United States and the EU countries were also heated and failed to reach even a minimal consensus. Many developing-country delegations, especially from Africa and Asia, expressed concerns about possible negative impacts of uncontrolled foreign investment and the dumping of farm products, as well as about their own lack of technical capacity for defending themselves in the discussions. Less developed countries often lacked sufficient specialized personnel (lawyers, economists, interpreters, diplomats) who could participate in the many highly technical and often simultaneous small meetings that were part of the trade negotiations. Some developing-country representatives were also appalled that Charlene Barshefsky, the US Trade Representative, chaired the main WTO negotiations and appeared to be manipulating the agenda in accord with US interests. Not surprisingly, in the final two days of the trade talks, various delegations from the Global South held joint press conferences with the Third World Center and other NGOs identified with the anti-WTO protesters in the streets.

N30 in Seattle was less a boomerang effect that used an intergovernmental body to pressure a state than a street heat effect that supported state representatives with arguments for derailing a global governance institution. The commonality of views and objectives between the anti-WTO demonstrators, on the one hand, and many developing-country WTO delegations, on the other, was ultimately the most significant ingredient in the success of the N30 protests and the failure of the Millennium Round of trade negotiations. Certainly, the demonstrators physically prevented many delegates from reaching the meeting site, and police violence against peaceful protesters cast the WTO in an unfavorable light. But more importantly, developing-country delegates felt empowered and validated by the viewpoints and activities of the protesters and decided, in many cases, that scuttling the negotiations would be the best outcome, especially given the arrogance and intransigence of the more powerful players in the WTO. The voices and actions of the protesters from the Global South played a major role in influencing these developing-country delegates, something that would have been far more difficult, and most likely impossible, if the "street heat" had come only from masses of disaffected white Americans.

ROOTED, RURAL, AND SUBALTERN COSMOPOLITANS IN TRANSNATIONAL PEASANT AND FARMER MOVEMENTS

How did peasants and farmers from different countries, cultures, and language groups build solidarity across borders? This chapter unpacks the figures of the "rooted cosmopolitan," the "rural cosmopolitan," and the "subaltern cosmopolitan" by scrutinizing these concepts alongside activists' complicated biographies. Media pundits, politicians, and urbanites often question the authenticity of peasant activists whenever they manifest worldliness. The chapter outlines forces that produced contemporary peasant intellectuals, critiques the facile application of Gramsci's notion of "organic intellectuals," and suggests why agrarian movements sometimes downplay the impressive accomplishments and trajectories of their leaders and spokespeople. Migration, exile, and complex political involvements mark the biographies of peasant activists. The peasant sector has always been heterogeneous across multiple dimensions, and this has increased with the rise of transnational activism.

Around the turn of the twenty-first century, scholars embraced a renewed interest in "cosmopolitanism" (Hannerz 2007). This revival grew out of intellectuals' fear of and skepticism about rising nationalism and ethnocentrism (Nussbaum 1994) as well as a search for "a unifying vision for global democracy and governance" (Harvey 2009, 11). A distinctive feature of this literature is the effort to locate cosmopolitanism in places and philosophical traditions outside its supposed historical source in the Athenian Stoics, Kant, and Enlightenment Western Europe (Humphrey 2004; Mignolo 2002; Rapport 2006; Werbner 2008). These are the very places that Merton (1949, 458), in an earlier effort to theorize the concept, had viewed as "local" rather than "cosmopolitan." This looking outside necessarily involved rethinking the idea of cosmopolitanism as elite cultural project.

Cosmopolitanism and "internationalism" have a fraught political history. In some Marxist traditions, they are opposed principles (Humphrey 2004). At least one analysis warns that cosmopolitanism, if viewed simply as universalism or global citizenship, may undermine solidarity and impede "efforts to defend the achievements of previous social struggles against neoliberal capitalism, or to ground new political action" (Calhoun 2002, 871). An examination of transnational agrarian movements (TAMs), and specifically La Via Campesina (LVC), indicates instead that new cosmopolitanisms may facilitate solidarity, internationalism, and counterhegemonic struggles.

Rooted, Rural, and Subaltern Cosmopolitans

How have scholars characterized these new cosmopolitans with origins in "local" and "outside" places and groups? Sidney Tarrow called them "rooted cosmopolitans" (2005). Vinay Gidwani and K. Sivaramakrishnan analyze "rural cosmopolitans" (2003). Boaventura de Sousa Santos speaks of "subaltern cosmopolitans" (2009). These are not mutually exclusive concepts. Rather, one might think of a Venn diagram that reveals areas of overlap and differing analytical emphases. This chapter will not belabor which concept is a more generative descriptor for the subject at hand—activists in transnational agrarian movements. Perhaps the element that most distinguishes one from another is the degree to which they are imbued with class or counterhegemonic content. This in turn indicates that the "rooted," "rural," or "subaltern" cosmopolitan categories may be applicable to different rural and agrarian sectors and classes of labor.

The term "rooted cosmopolitanism" has a peculiar genealogy (Anderson 2002, 11; Tarrow 2005, 5, 42). Mitchell Cohen (1992) coined the term but only employed it once—and then just in the last sentence—in his essay of the same name. Cohen used it to argue for a universalism that accepts plural identities and loyalties and against the particularism that he saw as characteristic of both post-Soviet ethno-nationalist chauvinism and US left-wing multiculturalism with its associated cultural nationalisms. In a 1994 essay of the same name (which did not acknowledge Cohen and only employed the term in the last section of a lengthy text), Bruce Ackerman (1994) similarly inveighed against the troubling rise of communitarian identities while asserting the impossibility of a cosmopolitan politics among peoples in the grip of historically particular cultural codes and values. Kwame Anthony Appiah followed up with an identically titled chapter in *The Ethics of Identity*, which sought to defend the possibility of overlapping loyalties and "a form of universalism that is sensitive to the ways in which the historical context may shape the significance of a practice" (2005, 256). He also emphasized that nationalism and cosmopolitanism, usually assumed to be antagonistic, are similar inasmuch as both require "a loftily abstract level of allegiance—a vast, encompassing project that extends far beyond ourselves and our families" (2005, 239).

Sidney Tarrow, a leading US social movement theorist, adapted "rooted cosmopolitans" to the study of transnational activism. For Tarrow, rooted cosmopolitans are "individuals and groups who mobilize domestic and international resources and opportunities to advance claims on behalf of external actors, against external opponents, or in favor of goals they hold in common with transnational allies" (2005, 29).

"Transnational activists," according to Tarrow, as a "subset" of rooted cosmopolitans, are "people and groups who are rooted in specific national contexts, but who engage in contentious political activities that involve them in transnational networks of contacts and conflicts" (2005, 29).

Injecting a class dimension into Tarrow's formulation, Boaventura de Sousa Santos pointed to "subaltern cosmopolitanism" or the "cosmopolitanism of the oppressed" as emerging from emancipatory projects, counterhegemonic globalization, and struggles against social exclusion: "Who needs cosmopolitanism? The answer is simple: whoever might be a victim of intolerance and discrimination needs tolerance; whoever might be denied basic human dignity needs a community of human beings; whoever might be a non-citizen needs world citizenship in any community or nation. In sum, those who are socially excluded, victims of the hegemonic conception of cosmopolitanism, need a different type of cosmopolitanism" (2009, 567–568).

Subalterns are supposedly members of subordinate groups who are unable to speak, a characterization that frequently fails to conform to historical or observable reality. In agrarian studies and in the historiography of South Asia, "subalternity" has come to be synonymous with subordination based on class, caste, region, and racialized or language group status. Subaltern and postcolonial studies enthusiasts often forget, however, that the term originally referenced the military rank of "junior patriarchs" in "warrior clans," hardly the most subordinated segment of Indian society (Ludden 2008, 103). While Santos accepts the by now prevailing identification of subalternity with subordination, his discussion of the "subaltern cosmopolitan" emphatically breaks with the dubious perception of subalterns as lacking voice and agency. Despite Santos's involvement in activist projects such as the World Social Forum, the phrase he coined gained less traction and is less widely used than "rooted cosmopolitan," very likely an indication of the broader evisceration of class analysis from mainstream social movement theory (Hetland and Goodwin 2014; B. de S. Santos 2008).

For Gidwani and Sivaramakrishnan, "Rural cosmopolitans . . . are those who originate in rural areas and who, having become bearers of cultural versatility, turn this to some advantage in either their rural source areas and/or their non-rural destinations" (2003, 345). These authors "do not view [rural cosmopolitanism] as necessarily defiant or oppositional," largely because their empirical referents range widely, from prosperous tech workers in India who maintain connections in their villages of origin to "plebeian cosmopolitan" teenage girls who circulate between rural and urban areas in search of menial labor. In contradistinction to Santos, who focuses on counterhegemonic movements, Gidwani and Sivaramakrishnan see the cultural versatility gained in this circulation from countryside to city and back as having "indeterminate" and not necessarily politically progressive effects (2003, 344–345).

While Tarrow, Santos, and Gidwani and Sivaramakrishnan treat new cosmopolitans in a way that is suggestive, they do little to explain the presence of this social group in *agrarian* movements. As I suggest elsewhere, scrutiny of activists' biographies is an essential resource for illuminating these processes (Edelman 1999, 195–196). Another infrequently examined dimension is the area of communicative practices and skills, especially in processes of forming transnational linkages between speakers of different languages and in multilingual assemblies (Archibugi 2008; Doerr 2007).[1]

Organic Intellectuals, Provincial Narrow-Mindedness, and Middle Peasants

Little is gained by belaboring whether "rooted," "subaltern," "rural," or even "plebeian" is a more fertile descriptor for understanding TAMs activists. I view these as complementary and overlapping categories distinguished by applicability to different rural sectors and agrarian classes of labor. While LVC is a counterhegemonic movement, its class composition is heterogeneous, and its internal politics sometimes reflect profound class divides, especially between organizations of small agriculturalists who employ wage labor and other groups that advocate for the landless and rural workers (Edelman and Borras 2016). This suggests that in some cases, the "rooted" and "rural" labels might fit while the "subaltern" and certainly the "plebeian" labels might not. If, on the other hand, we see "subaltern cosmopolitan" among Santos's terms, all participants in a counterhegemonic movement might be under its umbrella. A related historical

and biographical question concerns how particular individuals came to transcend "the local" and participate in transnational counterhegemonic projects.

Gramsci's concept of the organic intellectual was a political effort to address
this kind of processual question, if not about specific individuals, then about activists' social-class origins. Writing in a fascist prison with censors looking over
his shoulder, Gramsci used cryptic language and rarely, if ever, specified how
he understood the notion of "organic." It probably had a dual meaning for him,
signifying both an origin at the grassroots and organizational ties to the revolutionary party of the working class. This generated ambivalence about the politics of the peasantry. While Gramsci asserted that "every organic development
of the peasant masses . . . is linked to and depends on movements among the intellectuals" (1972, 15), he was convinced that "the mass of the peasantry . . .
does not elaborate its own 'organic' intellectuals" (1972, 6). Instead, the many
intellectuals of peasant origin were, for Gramsci, "traditional"—priests, lawyers,
notaries, teachers, and doctors—and incapable of "assimilating" to their class
of origin (1972, 6, 14). For him, the peasantry was unlikely to become a significant historical protagonist.

Gramsci's skepticism about the peasantry's intellectuals reflects a long-
standing current in Marxist thought. Frederick Engels, for example, referred to
the "local and provincial narrow-mindedness" that fragmented early modern
German agrarian struggles (1926, 88). Ranajit Guha points to "an historiograph-
ical tradition going back to Engels" that sees localism as "a limiting factor of
peasant insurgency" (1999, 279). By the mid- to late twentieth century, however,
the panorama changed. Increasingly, the grassroots peasant and Indigenous intellectuals, which some termed "organic" because of their formation in local
communities and their unambiguous rural and lower-class origins, were part
of a continuum that linked them to high-profile intellectuals with university credentials who also arose from the movements.

Eric Wolf (1969) famously insisted on the importance in peasant revolutions
of leaders of "middle peasant" extraction, and Neil Webster (2004) argued that
rural teachers occupy strategic positions linking local and nonlocal domains.
These sectors had the vision, social capital, and material or cognitive resources
to imagine new forms of struggle, in contrast to the very poor, who were over-
whelmed by day-to-day survival imperatives. Today's rooted, rural, and subaltern cosmopolitans in TAMs share crucial characteristics with the social bases
of the mid-nineteenth-century First Workingmen's International. As Perry Anderson described the latter, "They did not lie in any factory proletariat, but overwhelmingly in a pre-industrial artisanate. This was a class in possession of its
own means of production—tools and skills; which enjoyed high levels of literacy; was typically located close to the centre of capital cities; and, last but not

least, was geographically mobile—a mobility symbolized by the famous tours of young apprentices within or beyond their own countries" (2002, 11).

Considering these long-ago labor radicals alongside today's peasantry of rooted and subaltern cosmopolitans also connects our focus here to the classic agrarian question and its concern for the ways in which capitalism has failed to completely penetrate rural zones (Hussain and Tribe 1981; Akram-Lodhi and Kay 2010; Patnaik 2011). If possessing—even if tenuously—their own means of production and high-level literacy skills equip people for a life of struggle, we may also imagine that the threat capital poses to rural livelihoods might spur such people to take action and defend their autonomy (Van der Ploeg 2008).

Today's Peasantry Is Not the Urbanite's Imagined Peasantry

The "dearth of analysis of the dynamics of interconnectivity" is a notable "silence" in literature on transnational agrarian movements (Borras, Edelman, and Kay 2008, 180). TAMs activists frequently impressed me with their analytical, oratorical, and organizing skills and strategic acumen. I also came to recognize the complex life trajectories that produced these remarkable individuals and gave them the cultural and linguistic capital that facilitated transnational organizing. Some were of peasant origin and through perseverance, extraordinary intelligence, or good fortune managed to obtain advanced educations. Others attribute their intellectual formation not so much to formal education but to a long curriculum of movement trainings and workshops—in cooperative administration, communications, economic policy, market analysis, agronomy, phytosanitary measures, seed selection, and other topics (see chapter 4). Still others threw in their lot with farming and with the agriculturalists' movements later in life, motivated by commitments to projects of political transformation that saw rural people as important historical actors or a life on the land as a desirable, ethical, or practical choice.

The cosmopolitan experiences and substantial cultural capital of these leaders have at least facilitated and have perhaps even been essential ingredients in forging transnational peasant and farmer alliances. This was especially true in the early phases of transnational networks, when participating organizations had limited resources and help from professional staffs.[2] Recognizing this complexity and ambiguity is preferable—in terms of analytical rigor, intellectual candor, and political efficacy—to propounding a unidimensional picture of peasants or of how TAMs gained such a high profile since the 1980s and 1990s.

Connecting across Difference

"Professor M. D. Nanjundaswamy." "Basque farmer Paul Nicholson." The very names of these prominent early leaders of La Via Campesina hint at cosmopolitanism or cultural hybridity.[3] What did it mean that the late Indian peasant leader was a "professor" (and that as an activist he frequently used this honorific)? Why didn't a Basque farmer named Belausteguigoitia (or something similar) become an LVC leader rather than one named Nicholson? Cases like these are abundant among the ranks of the leadership of TAMs. Several founders or early leaders of LVC either had or went on to earn doctoral degrees at major universities. Others had or eventually obtained masters or professional degrees, and still others had backgrounds in student activism. Several were multilingual and, through diverse circumstances, including exile and migration, had international experience. Studies of contemporary TAMs have paid scant attention to how these factors facilitate cross-border alliances. This raises four questions (not all of which will be addressed at length here). (1) Why the scholarly and activist silence about these aspects of leadership? (2) How might these features and their deployment in activist politics be analyzed? (3) Are there other categories of persons central to the development of TAMs that have also been rendered invisible?[4] and (4) How are the challenges of TAMs and their leadership similar to or different from those facing activists who theorists have termed "rooted" or "subaltern cosmopolitans" or "organic intellectuals"?

TAMs and their constituent organizations engage in a complicated project of representation and claims-making to establish "legitimacy" and "authenticity." This has frequently led "rooted" or "subaltern" cosmopolitans who work with TAMs to minimize their own importance and elements of their biographies that might upset simplistic societal expectations about peasants and farmers. Sympathetic academics are often similarly silent. Nonetheless, rooted and subaltern cosmopolitan militants have been central factors in the emergence and consolidation of TAMs since the early 1990s.

It is rarely acknowledged sufficiently that nongovernmental organization (NGO) allies and organization staff members who were not peasants or farmers played important roles in maintaining international linkages in the early years of LVC. Two key figures hailed from the Netherlands. The context for Dutch interest in transnational networking included the extremely high levels of organization among Dutch farmers (Klandermans et al. 1999), a long tradition of critical agrarian studies at Wageningen University and other institutions, and—more generally—a social democratic sensibility that made the Netherlands, along with other northern European countries, a world leader in per capita expenditures on foreign cooperation (Edelman and Borras 2016).

Kees Blokland, a University of Amsterdam graduate active in Central American solidarity (who later received a doctorate at Leiden), worked closely during the 1980s with the pro-Sandinista National Union of Agriculturalists and Livestock Producers (UNAG) in Nicaragua. In the early 1990s, he returned to the Netherlands and directed the Paulo Freire Foundation (PFS), a small NGO concerned with agricultural development. Blokland, who speaks English and excellent Nicaraguan-accented Spanish, helped to coordinate the founding meeting of the LVC in Mons, Belgium, in 1993. The PFS published multilingual newsletters in advance of the meeting, secured funding for participants' travel, and facilitated discussions about the creation of the new organization (Blokland 1998). "For me," Blokland recalled in a 1998 interview, "La Via Campesina was a kind of dream, to see the rise of a platform of peasant organizations from different countries, and because of the nature of the organizations that were meeting there, many . . . were very popular organizations, with long trajectories and very big memberships."

At the Mons meeting, several peasant activists challenged Blokland's vision of the new organization and his interest in maintaining ties to the International Federation of Agricultural Producers (IFAP), a more conservative coalition that large farm interests dominated (Desmarais 2007, chap. 3).[5] This conflict, which eventually became part of the nascent LVC's origin story, led it to sever ties with Blokland and the PFS.

Nico Verhagen, a Dutch LVC staff member based first in Belgium (and later in Germany) and who speaks English, Spanish, French, and German, also played a key role in these early international linkages. At the Mons meeting, he sided with the anti-IFAP majority and assumed an increasingly central role in day-to-day LVC communications.[6] In particular, he was the key person who generated documentation for and maintained LVC's multilingual email listservs. A graduate of Wageningen University, Verhagen was able to control movement communications, which eventually generated political tensions, in part because he was not and never pretended to be a peasant or farmer activist (Verhagen 1998). Verhagen continued to work for the LVC secretariat's technical support staff.

The cosmopolitan backgrounds of these staff members were shared by peasant and farmer leaders active in the early years of La Via Campesina. At the beginning of this section, I referred to two prominent LVC leaders (one now deceased), whose very names are emblematic of the hybridity or cosmopolitanism that is frequently an essential, though too often unremarked, ingredient in the formation of transnational agrarian movements. Earlier (in the introduction and in chapter 1), I mentioned Nettie Wiebe, another key LVC founder from Canada. Using interviews and publicly available biographical material, I will now briefly sketch some elements of the lives of each of these three individuals and indicate how each drew on previous experiences and exceptional endowments of cultural capital as tools for organizing.

Professor M. D. Nanjundaswamy (1935–2004) was a founder and longtime leader of the Karnataka State Farmers Association (KRRS) in India, one of the first Asian organizations to affiliate with LVC. He was a farmer's son who became a lawyer and a socialist parliamentarian. After studying science and law at Mysore and Karnataka universities, Nanjundaswamy went to The Hague Academy of International Law. After additional studies in constitutional law in West Germany and France, he returned to India in 1964 and became a law professor at Mysore and Bangalore universities (Vidal 2004). According to one sympathetic account, it was only then, when Najundaswamy was twenty-nine years old, that he became a farmer (Assunta 1996). Nanjundaswamy left academia in 1979 and established KRRS the following year.[7] From 1989 to 1994, he served as a non-party member of the Karnataka State Parliament (Custers 2004). He led KRRS in several dramatic protests against multinational corporations and the General Agreement on Tariffs and Trade (GATT) and World Trade Organization (Gupta 1998). These actions—which targeted Monsanto, Kentucky Fried Chicken, and Cargill—helped bring Nanjundaswamy to international attention. There was also a behind-the-scenes effort to raise his profile, detailed in a rejoinder that Indian environmentalist Vandana Shiva directed to Nanjundaswamy after he criticized her for mistakenly assuming that a political split within KRRS had been healed:

> My role has been to support the grassroots and make local activists visible. That is why I worked with you to organise the 1993 Bangalore rally with Third World Network. That is why I took you with me to France in 1993 for an anti-GATT rally so you could meet the European farmers. That is why, when via Campesina asked me for names from India, I sent them yours and Mahendra Singh Tikaits [*sic*]. In spite of being the national leader of independent farmers unions, Tikait is unable to travel because of his inability to speak English but you have made major impact through via Campesina. In 1996, I gave your name to the organisers of the Leipzig NGO conference because I wanted you to meet the top activists working on Plant Genetic resources such as Pat Mooney from RAFI and Henk Hobbelink from GRAIN. (Shiva 1998)[8]

While Shiva's role in Nanjundaswamy's rise to international prominence is perhaps not as central as she suggests, the passage above does raise questions about his high profile. First is Shiva's curious assertion that a leader such as Mahendra Singh Tikait "is unable to travel because of his inability to speak English."[9] Surely, non-English speakers can travel and participate in global civil society, but Shiva is clearly right that a South Asian who speaks at least three European languages (English, German, and French) is especially adapted for international activities.[10] Second, Shiva's version, even if self-aggrandizing, indicates how network formation often occurs simply as a process of asking existing contacts to identify potential collaborators and counterparts (Borras, Edelman, and Kay 2008, 187).[11] Third, Nanjundaswamy's extensive academic training and international experience were foundational pieces of his worldview, as was a more homegrown Gandhian approach to direct action and mass organization. Like many upper-caste professional Indians, he found meaning in supporting struggles of his home community and its less affluent or educated members.

Paul Nicholson, a founder of the Basque farmers' organization EHNE, as well as the European Farmers Coordination (later renamed the European Coordination of La Via Campesina) and LVC itself, comes from a multinational family "marked by war and exile" (EHNE 2002). Born in London to a Basque mother and an English father, whose mother was also Basque, Nicholson returned with his family to the Basque Country and to Franco's Spain when he was five years old. Later, he received an agriculture degree in Scotland and labored on a livestock farm there. He also worked briefly on a kibbutz in Israel. In the early 1980s, he returned to the Basque Country, started a dairy farm, and later became involved in forestry and fruit and vegetable production. As an activist, Nicholson participated in numerous actions, from land occupations with the Brazilian Landless Rural Workers Movement (MST) to serving as part of the LVC delegation that accompanied Yasir Arafat inside the Palestine Liberation Organization (PLO) compound during the 2002 Israeli siege of Ramallah (see chapter 1). A speaker of four languages (Euskera or Basque, English, French, and Spanish), Nicholson has been an effective cultural broker in the formation of peasant organization and other alliances at the national, European regional, and international levels, in addition to drawing on his diverse experience to make cogent theoretical contributions to the movements.[12] Nicholson has played an especially important role as a linguistic and cultural broker between LVC's constituent movements in the Americas and Europe, although his multilingualism, political commitment, and extensive international experience have also involved him in a wide range of activities beyond these two key regions (EHNE 2002).

Nettie Wiebe grew up on a farm in a small Mennonite community on the western prairie in Saskatchewan, Canada, speaking what she describes as "a dialect of German." Her involvement in activism came early, when her community divided over plans to site a uranium treatment facility there. She left to go to university, where she studied philosophy and eventually became a professor. "People thought that was completely impractical," she remarked in a 2002 interview, "but actually it's very useful." Then, she continued, "I married a guy who was straight city but wanted to farm, so we bought a farm."

The Canadian Prairies—like the US Great Plains—were home to a rich tradition of populist agrarian and feminist struggles dating to the late nineteenth century, not long after white settlers began to displace First Nations peoples (Carter 2016; Gleave 1991; Laycock 1990; McMath 1995). Wiebe locates herself squarely within this history, pointing to the Saskatchewan provincial farmers' unions of the 1930s and 1940s, when "agrarian feminists were active and acquired status and participation in the executive structures" (2002, 2017). In the late 1960s, when unions from Canada's provinces formed the National Farmers Union (NFU), Saskatchewan farmers were among those who insisted on affirmative action executive positions for women. Wiebe commented in a 2002 interview:

> In farm organizations, if you don't conscientiously say "the family farm includes women, men, and children, and the family farm organizations have to reflect that"—if you're not conscious about that, they don't do that at all. They only reflect the patriarchal nature of agriculture. We were very adamant about that. . . . In some ways, I was lucky. I came into an organization, the best organization, where it was understood that there would be always women around the decision-making table. And that's the position I initially got elected to—women's vice president.

By the late 1980s, Canadian farmers increasingly recognized that "what happened in Geneva and New York was really what mattered in terms of how we were going to be able to farm in Saskatchewan or Prince Edward Island." Influenced by solidarity movements with Central America, the NFU established links with UNAG in Nicaragua, initiating a wider network that eventually led to founding La Via Campesina. In Wiebe's view,

> women were in a much better position to make those initial and very useful contacts and work together because much of the ground is common ground. Domestic labor, childcare, status in society—a range of things that, no matter where you are in terms of industrial development, the position of women is remarkably similar, no matter which society. And that was a real point of strength in terms of understanding and working in solidarity with—not as a development project—but working in solidarity with women there. (Wiebe 2002)

When elected NFU president in 1995, Wiebe was among the activists at La Via Campesina's 1996 conference in Tlaxcala, Mexico, who insisted on institutionalizing gender equity at all levels of the global movement (Wiebe 2013; Wolfwood 2009). Another dimension that Wiebe brought to discussions within LVC was a clear understanding of who the real winners are. Because it's very easy for peasants from developing countries and their leadership to think that North American and European farmers are the winners and they're the losers. And it's very useful for me to say, "look what's happened to us as farmers." They're always surprised at what a big farm we have.[13] Well, in terms of capitalization, technology, size of machinery, land base, education, export-oriented cash-cropping—by all the standards of successful competitive behavior, we should be real winners. But I must tell them that, for our little family, we always have to have off-farm income because we can't make enough on that farm to feed ourselves. And it just puts all the advice they get around their own failure and their own strategies to succeed in the global marketplace—it just gives it another perspective, a reality check. You have to be really conscious about how this script is going because it's true, but it's so unbelievable to them. (Wiebe 2002)

Numerous other examples of rooted cosmopolitans with complicated life histories could be brought to discussion. The peripatetic French farm activist José Bové, for example, a child of university professors, spent four years of his childhood in Berkeley, which left him with a near-native command of English.[14] Annette Aurélie Desmarais, a founder of La Via Campesina, activist in the National Farmers Union of Canada and author of one of the most thorough accounts of the LVC's history (2007) hails from a Francophone family in an English-speaking region of Canada, speaks a very serviceable Spanish, and like Wiebe, eventually became a university professor. Rafael Alegría, LVC coordinator from 1996 to 2004 and one of the historic leaders of the Honduran campesino movement, was born in humble circumstances in remote Olancho Department but nonetheless obtained a law degree and served as a congressional deputy (Alegría 1997, 2001). Henry Saragih, LVC coordinator from 2004 to 2013, speaks sufficient English to participate in international activities (Saragih 2009) and was part of "a network of NGOs founded and run by middle-class student activists" to support the Indonesian peasant movement (Borras 2008a, 205; Bachriadi 2010, 240). João Pedro Stédile, a leader of the Brazilian MST and LVC, won a scholarship to the National Autonomous University of Mexico (UNAM) in the mid-1970s, where he perfected a Mexican-inflected Spanish and met some of Latin America's most prominent political exiles and progressive intellectuals, including fellow Brazilians Rui Mauro Marini, Teotônio dos Santos, and Vânia Bambirra and Chileans Pedro Vuskovic and Jacques Chonchol (Stédile 2002, 78–79).[15] Diamantino Nhampossa, a lawyer who became a leader of National Peasants Union (UNAC) in Mozambique and was the only African member of LVC's International Coordinating

Committee from 2004 to 2008, speaks fluent English (Second European Forum 2007; Schachet 2009). Ibrahima Coulibaly, the president of a key LVC organization in Francophone Africa, the National Coordination of Peasant Organizations of Mali, trained as an agronomist and speaks very good English (Paget-Clarke 2008). Nhampossa and Coulibaly have been able to forge important links between Lusophone, Francophone, and Anglophone movements in Africa and beyond.

Among the younger generation of LVC leaders in Europe, multilingual migrant women are prominent, such as Sandra Moreno in Spain (originally from Colombia) and Paula Gioia in Germany (originally from Brazil). Both came from urban backgrounds and had university educations before opting to migrate and become agricultural producers.[16] Both have been powerful advocates for women within and outside of LVC, and Gioia has pushed to advance an LGBTQ+ rights agenda within the peasant movements (Gioia 2019).

There are several ways that biographies such as these might be read. An elitist, uncongenial reading would stress the impossibility of anyone being simultaneously "peasant" and "sophisticated" or impugn the authenticity of peasant and farm activists whose social class or geographical origins or life experience transcend the narrow bounds of the imagined, "simple" country folk (Edelman 1999, 191–196). Such simplistic and hostile interpretations are a staple of mainstream media editorial writers and cartoonists throughout Latin America and elsewhere. They have deep historical-cultural roots in the dominant classes' views of peasants as backward, ignorant, and resistant to development (Handy 2009). More complex readings might ask about what Albert Hirschman (1983) called the "social energy" of activists—the propensity of activists to engage in activism over their entire lifetimes—or what Pierre Bourdieu (1986) might have called their "cultural capital," the accumulated knowledge and experience that facilitates their social and geographic mobility and access to wider social fields. These life trajectories could also be understood as reflections of the heterogeneous composition of contemporary (and historical) peasantries and farmers, as stories about the ubiquity and the necessity—everywhere in the world—of off-farm employment, as examples of the upward mobility that is at least occasionally available to gifted or fortunate individuals, or as demonstrations of the inadequacy of interpretations that rely on rigid essentialisms and taxonomies of social types rather than on exploring contested boundaries (outside versus inside, peasant versus non-peasant, and so on). What is perhaps more difficult to explain is why these phenomena have received so little scholarly attention and why they are so infrequently acknowledged by agrarian activists themselves.

Cosmopolitan Invisibility and Contested Authenticity

Ron Aminzade, Jack Goldstone, and Elizabeth Perry observe that scholars who are optimistic about the impacts of social movements tend to be "more diffident about the role of individuals as leaders. . . . In this view, leaders are essentially servants of their followers, or their historical situation. . . . [They] play a critical, but subordinate role, helping their followers steer through the shoals of history to reach their destined goals" (Aminzade, Goldstone, and Perry 2001, 127).[17]

The sources of this diffidence are not difficult to discern. Leaders often efface or minimize their own importance. Scholars and activists produce linear, simplified accounts of what are often complicated, nonlinear processes of individual and organizational political development. Sometimes, for activists (and for scholars who sympathize with them—or *are* them, because this boundary too is often blurry), this is because they see the linear, simplified account as the best way of advancing their political project. At other times, for scholars, the linear account reflects a desire to enact solidarity or else an ingenuousness about or insufficient scrutiny of activists' claims. Only very occasionally have scholars and activists (or scholar-activists) examined the assumption that the best way to "serve" a movement is to uncritically accept and propagate its claims.[18]

When social movements make demands on those in power, they engage in a complicated process of claims-making, which is in turn made possible in part by their own processes of internal political education and more broadly by the formal educational systems of their societies. As I indicated in this book's introduction, much of a movement's credibility relates to "representation," understood here in two interrelated senses: both as a claim about *representativeness* or having a social base and as a practice of *representing itself* and its leaders as authentic and legitimate.[19] This contest goes beyond the "framing" of issues and movements' efforts to seize favorable conjunctures or "political opportunities," both familiar concepts to social movements scholars (Benford 1997). Instead, it speaks to a certain kind of self-fashioning and presentation of that self, individual and collective, which potentially translates into political efficacy. As Rebecca Tarlau suggests, social scientists' focus on "'framing' has overshadowed a deeper understanding of educational processes within social movements" (2014, 391).

Peasants and small farmers face more daunting obstacles in these interlinked processes of claims-making and self-fashioning than is the case with other, non-agrarian struggles. Virtually everywhere, the dominant groups disdain the rural poor, typically—in private, at least—employing a rich lexicon of pejoratives to impugn peasants' intelligence, honesty, physical appearance, and—incredibly—capacity for hard labor (Handy 2009). At the same time, romanticized images of the peasant figure prominently in nationalist narratives as emblematic of historically remote roots, ethnic purity, spiritual values, and selfless sacrifice. While these contrasting visions could be construed as upper-class cognitive dissonance, what unites them is that they both hold peasants to a high standard of "purity." The pejorative vision is, after all, a critique of a failure to live up to the romanticized vision.

When the dominant groups—large landowners, urban elites, politicians, media pundits—encounter peasant movements, they may express shock and feign disappointment that the simple and heretofore "loyal" "sons of the soil" have chosen to express grievances and make demands. The very elements that may dynamize the peasants' discourse—rhetorical fluency, legal or economic knowledge, recourse to abstract notions of justice—disqualify them in the eyes of elites, who imagine these features to be incompatible with the true, rustic, or atavistic nature of "genuine" peasants. Overcoming this elite resistance may require peasants and small farmers to employ especially dramatic or forceful protest repertoires and to engage in extra efforts to establish their authenticity in the eyes of the broader public.

It would be an error, however, to view these extra efforts primarily through the prism of "performance." While peasant and farmer activists, like other activists, undoubtedly "perform" identities as a tool of struggle, the capacity to "perform" a recognizable identity and simultaneously engage in a sophisticated politics is much more a reflection—in most cases, at least—of the heterogeneity of contemporary peasantries and the complex life trajectories of the activists. Indigenous Andean women, for example, who appear at international meetings and demonstrations dressed in their traditional bowler hats and petticoats could be making a statement about who they are or performing an identity. But when they articulate demands or confront powerful institutions, they are implicitly (and occasionally explicitly) making a statement about their participation in modernity (or their aspiration to participate in it) and about the heterogeneity of today's rural population.

International alliances between peasant and farmer organizations in different countries inevitably widen the gap between elite expectations about humble rustics and the urbane bearing, extensive travel experience, and political savvy of many peasant activists. Contemporary transnational agrarian movements have had to acquire highly specialized knowledge to engage issues such as global trade, intellectual property, genetically modified organisms, fiscal and subsidy policies, environmental and health aspects of agriculture, and new communications technologies. They have confronted powerful transnational corporations and global governance institutions, notably the World Trade Organization. Some of these issues are central in *national*-level contention as well; yet, especially when organized peasants and small farmers deploy specialized knowledge in international arenas, they appear distant from the dominant groups' image of "true" peasant-ness.[20]

Added to this, is the frequent confusion of the TAMs activists themselves over who is a peasant and what is a movement.[21] One of the TAMs' limitations in terms of extending their geographical reach has been the tendency to define "peasant" or "farmer" in a restricted sense that excludes significant sectors of the rural poor, such as migrants, pastoralists, and fisherfolk (Borras, Edelman, and Kay 2008, 185–187). Similarly, the TAMs may "not see" movements in other regions because these are not recognizable according to their restricted criteria of what constitutes a "movement" or because peasant activism, particularly under repressive regimes, exists in that less organizationally coherent zone of "everyday," "rightful" or "covert" resistance (Scott 1985; O'Brien and Li 2006; Malseed 2008).

The theorists of "rooted cosmopolitanism" mentioned above (Cohen and Appiah, in particular) emphasize that nested identities and loyalties of varying spatial reach likely inhere to many individuals. This is related to, but distinct from, the hackneyed insistence of poststructuralist scholars on individuals' "multiple social positions" (e.g., national or ethnic origin, gender, class, sexual orientation, religion, and so on). Concretely, "rooted" or "subaltern cosmopolitans" may be grounded in a locale, identify with a larger region or nation, and simultaneously embody profound solidarity with broader categories of people (or even all of humanity) across much wider spaces. While intellectuals (and perhaps especially anthropologists) typically feel no difficulty embodying such complexity themselves, they sometimes become troubled when "Others" manifest it.

Scholars, like the elites and media pundits mentioned earlier, often had an investment in the peasants' purity and even in their exoticism.[22] "The founding moment of peasant studies" in the late 1960s and early 1970s, as Henry Bernstein and Terence Byres point out, was strongly inflected by a "peasant essentialism" that sought to define "generic characteristics" of peasants and that pervaded analyses of distinct political orientations (2001, 7). This taxonomic obsession was probably always of limited analytical usefulness, as I have suggested elsewhere (Edelman 1999), although as chapters 8 and 9 suggest, I have also had to return to it in studying and advocating for the peasants' rights agenda in the United Nations. In the current era of increasingly "pluriactive" rural populations and "multifunctional" farms, transnational activism, accelerating migration within and across borders, and growing urban–rural ties, the expectation that "peasants" or "farmers" would conform to generic models or eschew participation in modernity or deployment of sophisticated knowledge (when they are able to control it) borders on the absurd.[23] But like many other features of contemporary political life, patent absurdity alone is not sufficient to defeat an argument or buttress an opposing claim. The questioning of the authenticity of the rooted or subaltern cosmopolitans in today's peasant and farmer movements, domestic and transnational, is ongoing, a product not of logic or reasoned debate but of contention and power politics.

Many (though again, not all) of the leaders and founders of transnational agrarian movements, such as La Via Campesina, have complex biographies, formidable foreign-language skills, impressive accumulations of cultural capital, and high levels of formal education. This chapter has suggested that these characteristics, which agrarian activists and scholars often minimize, ought to be accorded a more central place in efforts to understand the rise of TAMs in the early 1990s. The reluctance to do this is probably connected to political imperatives related to representation and authenticity claims in contexts where the stakes are high, and where elites disparage peasant movements and leaders for failing to conform to age-old essentialist images of the rural rustic. Acknowledging the cosmopolitan backgrounds of some of today's peasant and farm leaders opens a window onto other important areas of policy, political practice, and debate. These include: (1) the varied origins and heterogeneous composition of those received and still insufficiently problematized categories, "peasant" and "farmer"; (2) the growing role of off-farm sources of livelihood; and (3) need of the movements to embrace diversity and heterogeneity to expand their social base and geographical reach. Movements are poorly served by an activist or scholarly practice that effaces the rooted and subaltern cosmopolitans in their midst or represents them as less impressive than they really are. Movement claims increasingly depend on deploying specialized knowledge in venues where such knowledge is struggled over and debated, such as United Nations bodies and agencies (see chapter 8). Non-agriculturalist allies can be key in such situations. But establishing the legitimacy, authenticity, and expertise of the movements' own rooted and subaltern cosmopolitans is likely to carry even greater weight and authority in those all-important contests.

Part 2
CENTRAL AMERICA

TRANSNATIONAL PEASANT POLITICS IN CENTRAL AMERICA

This chapter, based on fieldwork in the 1990s and internal organization docu-ments, called attention to transnational agrarian movements, the funding streams underpinning the emerging global civil society, and the vulnerabilities, frictions, and donor-driven agendas that these sometimes implied. In retrospect, the analysis focuses perhaps too much on formally constituted organizations and manifests a somewhat ingenuous attitude toward activists' claims. Much of the rich experien-tial and interview material—including descriptions of peasants' computer use be-fore the World Wide Web arrived in Central America—was consigned to lengthy endnotes, a literary and analytical strategy that I later came to regret. This chapter is best read alongside chapter 5, which provides a more sober analysis of transna-tional peasant organizing in Central America and particularly of the funding issue.

Since the late 1980s, peasants throughout Central America have begun to coor-dinate political and economic strategy. Agriculturalists from the five republics that constituted *la patria grande* of Spanish Central America (Guatemala, El Sal-vador, Honduras, Nicaragua, and Costa Rica) as well as representatives from Panama and Belize have founded regional organizations that meet to compare experiences with free-market policies, share new technologies, develop sources of finance, and create channels for marketing their products abroad. They have also established a presence in the increasingly distant arenas where decisions are made that affect their livelihood. Organizations representing small farmers now lobby at the United Nations, the World Bank, the International Monetary Fund, the European Union, and regional summit meetings. Central American *campesinos* have attended numerous regional gatherings of agriculture ministers and presidents, as well as events like the 1992 Earth Summit in Rio de Janeiro, the 1995 Western Hemisphere Presidents' Summit in Miami, the 1995 World Summit for Social Development in Copenhagen, and the 1996 Food Security Summit in Rome.

Scholars of "transnationalism," collective action, and agrarian issues have barely kept pace with the rapid internationalization of peasant politics. The anthropology of globalization and transnationalism has emphasized migration, "deterritorialization," and "cultural hybridity" rather than new forms of supranational politics (Appadurai 1990; Schiller, Basch, and Szanton 1992; Kearney 1995, 1996). Recent anthologies on collective action research (Laraña, Johnston, and Gusfield 1994; Morris and Mueller 1992) and Latin American social movements (Eckstein 1989; Escobar and Alvarez 1992; Sinclair 1995) have not mentioned any processes of internationalization. The "globalization from below" and "networks" literatures on the growing transnational ties among grassroots organizations have generally ignored peasants (Alger 1988; Brecher 1993; Clark 1995; Falk 1987; Keck and Sikkink 1998; Laxer 1995; Risse-Kappen 1995; Tarrow 1994, 1995). Instead, they have focused on Indigenous groups (Brysk 1996), human rights (Sikkink 1993), women (Elshtain 1995; Palley 1991), labor (Kidder and McGinn 1995), and environmentalist groups (Keck 1995)—even though the new transnational peasant organizations sometimes have close links to these other efforts. Finally, cutting-edge analyses of agrarian studies (Roseberry 1993) have rightly underscored the importance of historicizing rural identities and resistance but have said nothing about how these goals might be achieved in the transnational peasant organizations that sprang up in the 1980s and 1990s. The few works that analyze the new transnational peasant movement have been written largely by intellectuals from European institutions that fund it or by Latin American researchers who work for it. These studies have tended to be overly sanguine about the movement's prospects, although lately they have become more critical (Biekart and Jelsma 1994; Biekart 1996; Morales Gamboa and Cranshaw 1997; A. Smith 1997; Tangermann and Ríos Valdés 1994).

The inattention of scholars of transnationalism, collective action, and agrarian issues to cross-border peasant politics is not related to any fundamental incompatibility of vision between researchers operating in these different traditions (or to any divergence between them and the author). Rather, proponents of these and related approaches have tended to labor in separate but parallel intellectual universes, often at such high levels of abstraction that certain objects of study have largely escaped their attention. I will suggest here that contemporary transnational peasant activists share the material or class-based passions of "old social movements" as well as a concern with seeking changes in the policies of individual states. At the same time, they embrace much of the focus of the "new social movements" on identity and cultural specificity (Calhoun 1993; Hellman 1995). Similarly, while these activists constitute dense personal "networks of trust" and mobilize domestic constituencies, characteristics that some view as essential features of "social movements," they also engage in the global "information politics" and "accountability politics" said to be more typical of transnational "advocacy networks" (Keck and Sikkink 1998; Tarrow 1994, chap. 11).

If transnational peasant politics seem to fall between the cracks of existing theoretical paradigms, the concept of "peasant" has for too long been viewed as intellectually "awkward" (Shanin 1972). In an astute reconceptualization of peasant studies, Michael Kearney (1996) termed it "disruptive" and indicated that this "troublesomeness" results from the confrontation of an ambiguous analytical construct—"the peasant"—with the complex realities of migrating deterritorialized peoples engaged in multiple occupations and depending on diverse income streams.[1] This chapter suggests instead that the real challenge may well be to confront abstruse "postpeasant," "postdevelopment," and "new social movements" frameworks with a group of troublesome empirical referents that stubbornly assert "peasant identities" as well as aspirations for improved economic and social well-being, which they happen to call "development" (Warman 1988, 657–658). One need not share Teodor Shanin's preoccupation with defining generic peasant attributes to recognize the validity of his assertion that peasants "are not only an analytical construct, not only 'bearers' of characteristics . . . but a social group which exists in the collective consciousness and political deeds of its members" (1990a, 69). This chapter has three basic objectives: (1) to analyze the formation, practice, and discourse of the principal regional peasant organization in Central America, the Asociación Centroamericana de Organizaciones Campesinas para la Cooperación y el Desarrollo (ASOCODE), which has member coalitions in all seven countries of the isthmus; (2) to consider what cross-border peasant organizing suggests about the representation of peasant identity in contemporary Central America; and (3) to examine the extent to which this regional campesino association has transcended traditional sources of weakness and division that afflict peasant organizations in Central America and elsewhere.[2]

Roots of Internationalization

In Central America in the 1980s, peasants often joined armed opposition movements (as in El Salvador, Guatemala, and Nicaragua) or engaged in bitter struggles with governments over economic adjustment programs (as in Panama, Honduras, and Costa Rica). But as the civil wars of the 1980s ebbed or ended and free-market policies began to appear inexorable, smallholding agriculturalists in different countries increasingly recognized that they faced similar problems. These interrelated difficulties were numerous. First, steps by governments and entrepreneurial groups toward regional political and economic integration had created new loci of decision making above the national states and threatened to leave grassroots sectors behind.[3] Second, economic structural adjustment programs slashed social services (like agricultural extension) and credit, reduced farm price supports and other subsidies (such as those for loans and inputs), reversed hard-won agrarian reforms, and facilitated the penetration of transnational capital in agriculture (Fallas 1993; FONDAD 1993; Pino and Thorpe 1992; Stahler-Sholk 1990; Thorpe et al. 1995). Third, lowered extra-regional tariffs required grain producers to compete with foreign farmers. Fourth, the liberalization of grain trade within Central America exacerbated sectoral and regional inequalities (Fallas 1993, 87–99; Solórzano 1994). Fifth, US food aid glutted cereal markets and led consumers to substitute imported wheat for domestically grown maize (Garst and Barry 1990). Sixth, coffee prices collapsed following the termination of the International Coffee Agreement.[4] Seventh, a severe environmental crisis worsened, marked by growing agrochemical contamination of soil and water and a vicious process of deforestation, erosion, and declining fertility. Eighth, nongovernmental organizations (NGOs) were proliferating, often supported by "social compensation" funds from bilateral aid and multilateral lending agencies, which peasant organizations often viewed as interlopers or competitors (CCOD 1990; Edelman 1991; Kruijt 1992). Finally, the long-standing lack of access to transport, storage, and processing facilities and to market information heightened peasants' vulnerability to and dependence on intermediaries and large-scale agroindustries and thereby lowered their incomes.

Internationalization also resulted from efforts by a young generation of movement leaders who hoped to propagate a new collective identity for Central American peasants. These activists—products of two decades of upheaval, war, and crisis—constitute a type of "peasant intellectual" that has received little attention from social scientists.[5] Like other peasants, they have had to adapt to major technological changes in agriculture (first "green revolution" input "packages" and then high-risk nontraditional export crops) and to interact with complex financial, marketing, extension, cooperative-sector, and land-tenure institutions. Urban and rural culture have also converged—and not just because of rural–urban migration or electronic media reaching into the countryside. In much of Central America, a significant proportion of the economically active population in agriculture now resides in urban areas, and a growing portion of the economically active rural population is engaged in nonagricultural activities (Ortega 1992). In some countries—particularly Costa Rica but also Panama under Omar Torrijos and later Sandinista Nicaragua—higher education significantly expanded the horizons of the younger generation, including some from low-income rural families. Many more peasant activists participated in courses offered by the cooperative movement, church and government institutions, political parties, guerrilla movements, NGOs, and campesino organizations.[6] Many activists who have little formal education are well traveled, computer-literate, and conversant in macroeconomic policy, national and international politics, and the latest developments in agronomy and forestry.[7] They have joined forces with a committed corps of "peasantized" or "pro-peasant" intellectuals and technicians working with their organizations who were also caught up in the turmoil of the 1970s and 1980s and sometimes spent years in the countryside. Together, they aim to replace the image of peasants as atavistic rustics with that of peasants as politically savvy, dignified, and efficient small producers.[8] Adept at appropriating and refashioning discourses about democracy and civil society, these peasant intellectuals claim to articulate an alternative and more just model of development. Increasingly, they have forged ties with non-peasant groups and small farmer organizations outside Central America.[9] And they adamantly affirm their "peasant-ness," delighting all the while in challenging the dominant groups' and social scientists' "binary semiotics of identity" (D. M. Nelson 1996), which assumes that an individual cannot be both a peasant and sophisticated or modern at the same time.

Early International Contacts

In Central America, which is a region of small states and permeable frontiers, migration and participation in social movements abroad are not new to the rural poor (Acuña Ortega 1993). For example, thousands of Nicaraguans participated in the 1934 strike against the United Fruit Company in Costa Rica (Bourgois 1989, 203). Twenty years later in Honduras, hundreds of Salvadoran banana workers joined their local counterparts in a massive walkout against the United Fruit–owned Tela Railroad Company (V. González 1978). "Transnationalism"—the circulation across borders of persons, technology, money, images, and ideas that has lately fascinated anthropologists (Appadurai 1990; Kearney 1995)—has been well known to Central Americans for decades, if not centuries.

The 1970s and 1980s, nonetheless, witnessed an intensification of these transnational flows. In the 1978–1979 period, as the Sandinista campaign against the Somoza dictatorship gathered steam, young people throughout the region (and beyond) swelled guerrilla ranks or collaborated from the Honduran and Costa Rican rear guards. With the triumph of the Frente Sandinista de Liberación Nacional (FSLN), numerous "internationalists" (many of them political exiles) obtained positions in the government, party, media, and pro-Sandinista research institutes and mass organizations. With the escalation in 1980 of armed conflicts in El Salvador and Guatemala (and renewed warfare in Nicaragua beginning in 1981 and 1982), hundreds of thousands of refugees—most of them peasants—fled their homes to seek safety abroad, often elsewhere on the isthmus.

These movements of Central Americans—often spontaneous, usually prolonged, and sometimes traumatic—brought activists from different countries into contact. Members of Guatemala's Comité de Unidad Campesina (CUC), exiled in Costa Rica, sought contacts with Costa Rican campesino organizations. When Nicaraguan refugees began to pour across Costa Rica's northern border, Costa Rican campesinos who had backed the Sandinistas began to develop doubts about the revolutionary government's sometimes arbitrary land confiscations and the indiscriminate violence directed at communities suspected of harboring Contras.[10] Leaders of agricultural cooperatives from throughout the isthmus met in events sponsored by the CCC-CA (Confederación de Cooperativas del Caribe y Centroamérica). Representatives of rural workers' unions encountered each other in meetings of the Coordinación Centroamericana de Trabajadores (COCENTRA), founded following the 1987 Esquipulas Peace Accords. Many participants in the CCC-CA and COCENTRA had links to organizations that represented campesinos outside the cooperative or union sectors.[11]

The "internationalism" of Nicaragua, promoted by a revolutionary party and state, provided an impetus for more frequent encounters. In the polarized Central America of the mid-1980s, revolutionary movements and campesino activists alike viewed allies elsewhere in the region as crucial for political success and even physical survival. The main clearinghouse for these contacts was the Nicaraguan Unión Nacional de Agricultores y Ganaderos (UNAG). It was founded in 1981 by smallholders, cooperative members, and medium-sized landowners who felt unrepresented in the Sandinista-dominated rural workers' union, the Asociación de Trabajadores del Campo (ATC). Despite its status as a "mass organization," UNAG had a sometimes rocky relationship with the FSLN.[12] Leaders of left-leaning Costa Rican and Honduran organizations passed through UNAG offices and toured rural cooperatives and commercialization projects, but these visits remained at the level of "exchanges of experiences." Salvadoran and Guatemalan leaders also called, but at home they were often living clandestinely and had more urgent concerns than thinking about the shape of their postwar agricultural sectors.

In addition to receiving visitors from outside Nicaragua, UNAG assumed a central role in the Campesino a Campesino program. This effort at technology transfer trained peasant extensionists in sustainable cultivation practices (e.g., cover crops, mulches, and zero-tillage techniques) and then had them provide technical assistance in and around their communities. Initiated by foreign NGOs in Guatemala in the early 1980s, this loosely organized movement eventually led to exchanges between peasants from throughout Central America and Mexico (Bunch 1982; Eric Holt-Giménez 1996).[13] UNAG member Sinforiano Cáceres recalled in an interview:

> The Mexicans helped us systematize our knowledge [on] how to make organic fertilizer. We knew that already, but they helped us to perfect it, giving us the quantities of each component. How to make live fences, wind breaks, dikes, how to convert an ox yoke so that a mule or horse could pull it. And there we met Guatemalans, Ticos [Costa Ricans], Panamanians, Central Americans. . . . From the Hondurans we learned about [nitrogen fixing] velvet beans. From the Ticos we learned more about crop rotation. And they in turn learned something from us, too. (Cáceres Baca 1994)

The European Connection

To understand how these intermittent contacts gave rise to a Central American association of peasant organizations, it is necessary to examine briefly European policies. In the early 1980s, European governments looked on with alarm as the administration of US President Ronald Reagan tried to topple the Sandinistas in Nicaragua and roll back the revolutionary movements in El Salvador and Guatemala. This apprehension, which was based on fears of a major regional war and an interpretation that stressed inequality and injustice rather than communism as causes of the conflicts, led to extensive European backing for the Contadora peace process initiated in 1983 by Mexico, Colombia, Venezuela, and Panama. European leaders also endorsed the subsequent efforts of Costa Rican President Oscar Arias that culminated in the 1987 Esquipulas Peace Accords.[14]

In the 1983–1984 period, as part of Contadora, European governments provided funds to the Sistema Económico Latinoamericano (SELA), the consultative body of economics ministers, to set up the Comité de Apoyo al Desarrollo Económico y Social de Centroamérica (CADESCA). Headquartered in Panama, CADESCA became a channel for peace-oriented initiatives that other regional bodies could not easily handle and an alternative to the United States' near monopoly on aid to the region.[15] Initially, its programs focused on microenterprises, energy, the environment, and regional economic integration. But as its director, Guatemalan economist Eduardo Stein, recognized, "There was a political aim in our technical efforts, which was maintaining places where dialogue could take place among Central Americans" (Stein 1994).[16]

Within a few years, CADESCA was asked by the Central American ministries of agriculture and planning to start a major research program on food security, the Programa de Seguridad Alimentaria (PSA). The ministers' concern grew out of their recognition that the region's dependence on imports for more than a fifth of its cereal consumption (Arias Peñate 1989, 67) made it vulnerable to fluctuating world prices; the region was also threatened by free-market policies that discouraged grain production. Funded by the European Economic Community (EEC), the PSA also reflected European criticism of free trade in agricultural commodities, one of the main sticking points in the Uruguay Round of negotiations of the General Agreement on Tariffs and Trade (GATT) (E. A. Santos 1988, 642–644). Because the Europeans had the most highly protected agriculture in the world (with the exception of Japan) and politically influential peasant sectors in key countries, they tended to view self-sufficiency in basic foods as a matter of national security and cultural survival for French, Spanish, or other peasants. Many attributed the stalling of the GATT negotiations in part to popular pressure, such as a December 1990 demonstration in Brussels by thirty thousand farmers, including a hundred from North America, two hundred from Japan, and others from Korea, Africa, and Latin America (Brecher 1993, 10; Kidder and McGinn 1995, 18; Risse-Kappen 1995, 12). These European apprehensions contrasted with US efforts in the GATT talks to gain access to European (and other) grain markets and with the US aid strategy in Central America, which involved huge shipments of PL-480 surplus food and aggressive advocacy of liberal trade and pricing policies.[17]

The PSA's main activities were analyzing macroeconomic policies and gathering data on the agricultural sectors in the various Central American countries. Apart from some national-level seminars with peasant leaders, it worked largely with government functionaries. The PSA produced a series of technical studies that demonstrated the important role of smallholding grain producers in maintaining food security and "food sovereignty" (Arias Peñate 1989; CADESCA 1990; Calderón and San Sebastián 1991; Dévé 1989; Martínez 1990; Torres and Alvarado 1990). It also developed a macroeconomic model that (in contrast to most mainstream models) was concerned primarily with measuring the impact of adjustment policies on a broad range of income and sectoral groups (Arias Peñate, Jované, and Ng 1993).

As the PSA wound down in 1990, CADESCA started a food-security education program, the Programa de Formación en Seguridad Alimentaria (PFSA) to make the PSA's findings available to government functionaries, who would then be better able to formulate policy, and to peasant leaders, who could then participate in the debate over food security.[18] This concern with training leaders of popular organizations reflected a view of democratization shared by CADESCA and the Europeans that stressed the participation of civil society in policymaking, a conception that contrasted with the US emphasis on free elections, legal reforms, and formal institutions (Cohen and Arato 1992). Directed by Salvador Arias, a European-trained economist and former minister of agriculture in El Salvador, the PFSA hired consultants to direct key program *ejes* (areas): credit, marketing, land reform, technology, and the environment.[19] Most consultants came from outside Panama and also served as liaisons with campesino organizations in their countries. Generally economists and sociologists with considerable field experience, they became strategic figures in articulating PFSA objectives and identifying which organizations to invite to seminars.[20]

Although campesino PFSA participants differ regarding the program's usefulness, they concur in describing the seminars as having important side effects that were to some degree unintended. Sinforiano Cáceres recalled:

> In the first meeting, we discussed our problems and found that many were the same, that we had more in common than we had differences. The *corte de chaleco* ["vest cut"] that structural adjustment had done on us left us all in the same condition. . . .[21] They screw us in different ways, but in the end they're the same. . . . [Various state commodities boards including] the IRA in El Salvador, ENABAS in Nicaragua, the CNP in Costa Rica, all now play the same role: cheap food for consumers, low prices for us. . . . The "agricultural modernization law" in Honduras is the same as the plan to destroy the asentamientos campesinos [land-reform projects] in Panama. . . . And [in Nicaragua], through the market, a process of agrarian counter-reform is also taking place. (Cáceres Baca 1994)

In the first PFSA seminar in November 1990, several organization leaders demanded, as a condition of their participation, that the program provide extra time so that peasant groups from different countries could discuss common problems. This demand as well as the overly academic tone of program documents and specialists' presentations caused friction and misunderstandings at times between peasant leaders and CADESCA.[22] But as sociologist Rubén Pasos, who was present at this first encounter, pointed out:

Once the leaders met and got to know each other, many for the first time, they realized they've all always been more or less in the same situation. . . . Well, as always in these things, the whole is more than the sum of the parts, and the people began to elaborate their own agenda. The program's agenda had another rhythm. Our agenda turned out to be too rigid for the needs and expectations of a movement that was just beginning to find its identity. We had to reorganize the program several times, and adjust it and adjust it. They were telling us what themes to cover, what things they wanted to know more about. But this turned out to be precisely the virtue of the program. It wasn't easy, because when you're managing a program, you're the contracted technical personnel, [and] you understand that things have to follow a certain schedule. But that doesn't always coincide with the rhythms of the people. So there were a lot of difficulties. But the vision that prevailed was to take a chance on them, to accommodate their process. (Pasos 1994)

By the end of the second PFSA seminar in February 1991, representatives of peasant organizations had formed a provisional commission with a view to forming a regional association (ASOCODE 1991b, 4). The process took on urgency because of the Central American presidents' plans to hold a summit in mid-1991 to make major decisions about agricultural trade. The support of PFSA specialists and the prospect of continued European funding, through CADESCA and other agencies, clearly conditioned the pace of organization as well. In April, the provisional commission sent a lengthy letter to the Central American presidents on the eve of their summit. It opened by condemning "economic structural adjustment, which even the international financial institutions recognize directly attacks the interests of the majorities of our peoples." The letter called on the presidents "to promote the ongoing processes of political opening and *concertación* [reconciliation]" and reminded them "that we have already elaborated alternative and integral development proposals, which we believe are possible to execute . . ." such as "vertically integrated production, which will permit us to break out of our historical situation of producing only raw materials and to obtain the profits that are generated by the agro-industrial processing of our production." Finally, the letter cautioned that "if our rights are not respected, the process of peace, so precarious and difficult to achieve, will escape from our hands and then, with the deepening of our *miseria* and marginality, social confrontation and war will continue, frustrating our peoples' desire to live in harmony, in a stable and peaceful social climate, with justice and real democracy" (Consejo Nacional 1991).

Another summit communiqué (Comisión Centroamericana 1991) employed the novel rhetorical strategy of appropriating discourses of incontrovertible legitimacy: the Latin American bishops' condemnation in Puebla in 1979 of "economic, social, and political structures [that cause] inhuman poverty"; the Central American presidents' own call at Esquipulas for "egalitarian societies, free of misery"; and UN economists' ideas about "economic adjustment with a human face" (Bustelo et al. 1987). The authors of the communiqué declared that since beginning "the slow process of regional coordination in 1988," they had manifested "mature and responsible attitudes," a phrase that in the Central American context could be understood to mean that they eschewed guerrilla violence. They pointed out that in Costa Rica, Nicaragua, and Honduras, they had negotiated with ministers of agriculture and presidents. Finally, the authors noted that the international financial institutions and "the governments and dominant sectors in the different countries and the international solidarity cooperation agencies themselves" were beginning to operate at the regional level and that campesino organizations must now do the same to influence policies affecting them (and presumably gain access to "cooperation funds").

Nations in the Region

The creation of a Central American peasant association grew out of shared problems, but it nonetheless raised issues related to national particularities. The political situations in the different countries varied greatly, from openness in Costa Rica to continuing repression in Guatemala. Economic stabilization and structural adjustment, which began in Costa Rica in 1983, were just starting in Honduras and El Salvador. Nicaragua and El Salvador were emerging from wars and Panama from the US invasion. Belize, which is largely English-speaking, related more to the Caribbean than to Central America. Honduras had the oldest and largest peasant movement, while Panama, with its canal- and service-based economy, had neither numerous peasants nor strong campesino organizations.[23] Peasant leaders had different backgrounds, constituencies, aspirations, political loyalties, and levels of sophistication.

From the beginning, the Costa Ricans and Nicaraguans played key roles, although for different reasons. The Nicaraguans had in the UNAG the most consolidated organization in the region. They also maintained ties to a revolutionary party that, at the beginning of the 1990s, appeared to retain the possibility of returning to power. And early on, Nicaraguans had seized the initiative in meeting with organizations from elsewhere in the isthmus. At least some Nicaraguan

leaders believed that UNAG, by virtue of its size and position, ought to dominate any Central American association.

The Costa Rican movement was smaller and more heterogeneous. It consisted
of several large but resolutely apolitical cooperative-sector organizations, some
independent local groups, a centrist small producers' union based in highland
coffee- and vegetable-growing zones (the Unión Nacional de Pequeños y Medianos Productores Agrícolas, or UPANACIONAL), and a left-leaning coalition
called the Consejo Campesino Justicia y Desarrollo (CCJYD), which included
diverse small organizations and cooperatives. In 1991, UPANACIONAL and
Justicia y Desarrollo, previously distant from one another, united in a single
coordinating body, the Coordinadora Nacional Agraria (CNA), to carry out joint
negotiations with the Costa Rican government (Román Vega 1994; Voz Campesina 1995).[24] The Costa Rican organizations had the longest experience with
structural adjustment programs and the most developed analysis of them. In particular, some leaders of Justicia y Desarrollo, which in the mid-1980s had taken a
belligerent stance against Costa Rican neoliberalism, felt that they were in a privileged position to foretell what would befall campesinos in other countries where
structural adjustment programs were just beginning.[25] In 1988, before the PFSA
seized the initiative for regional organizing, the Costa Ricans had already formed
a short-lived three-person committee to seek EEC funds for a gathering of agriculturalists from El Salvador, Nicaragua, and Honduras (Hernández Cascante
1992, 1). Despite the Costa Ricans' concern for regional organizing, the very sophistication of their analyses prevented them from transcending the negative
stereotypes of Costa Ricans held by other Central Americans.[26]

Not all participants in the emerging Central American association rejected
relations with political parties. The Costa Ricans years earlier had broken with
the organized left (Edelman 1991), and UNAG had declared its autonomy from
the FSLN after the Sandinistas' 1990 electoral defeat. The Honduran organizations,
for the most part, did not have "organic ties" with parties, although they constantly cut deals and formed conjunctural alliances with them. In El Salvador, in
contrast, peasant groups on the left, right, and center maintained close links with
parties. These ties were a legacy of the civil war (1980–1991), when each of the five
parties in the guerrilla coalition of the Frente Farabundo Martí de Liberación
Nacional (FMLN) as well as the right-wing and centrist parties sponsored parallel union and peasant organizations. Salvadoran participants in the PFSA and
subsequent regional meetings claimed that they separated union and party loyalties, but they also remained proud members of their respective party groups.[27]
This apparent inconsistency led to charges of "verticalism" from other countries'
representatives, who disliked Leninist-style party discipline and "sectarian" work
styles (Biekart and Jelsma 1994, 10; Hernández Cascante 1992, 3; 1994, 252).

Belize and Guatemala did not participate in the PFSA and were secondary players in the new campesino association. Identified culturally, linguistically, and politically with the English-speaking Caribbean, Belize was little known to PFSA organizers and had few agriculturalist organizations. Moreover, the Belizean government was relatively uninterested in Central American integration because it already belonged to the Caribbean Common Market (CARICOM).[28] Guatemala remained on the sidelines for reasons of its own. The largest Guatemalan organization, the Comité de Unidad Campesina (CUC), maintained ties to the armed left and still operated clandestinely to some degree. The CUC as well as the many smaller and less militant organizations in Guatemala were frequently targeted for brutal repression. Their leaders consequently accorded greater priority to physical survival and the struggle within Guatemala than to establishing high-profile links with counterparts in neighboring countries.[29] They also argued that the emerging association's orientation in favor of "small producers" and cooperativists had limited relevance in Guatemala, where the huge rural proletariat had little or no land and the only agrarian reform had been aborted by the US Central Intelligence Agency and the coup it backed against President Jacobo Arbenz in 1954.

The Organization of ASOCODE

In Tegucigalpa in July 1991, the Primer Conferencia Regional Campesina brought together delegates from throughout the isthmus who agreed to found ASOCODE. The conference approved a position paper to be relayed to the region's agriculture ministers and the tenth Central American Presidents' Summit, which was to meet later that month in San Salvador. This statement—ASOCODE's "productive strategy" (ASOCODE 1991a)—affirmed that small producers were making rational and intensive use of scarce resources but were still "threatened with extinction." It condemned structural adjustment programs, skewed patterns of landownership, the reversal of agrarian reforms, and the "hypocritical protectionism" of the countries providing "food aid" that actually undermined grain producers. Finally, the statement called for several specific changes: offering preferential fiscal, credit, and pricing policies to small producers; allowing participation by peasant organizations in agricultural-sector policymaking bodies and state development banks; giving campesino organizations first-purchase options for public-sector agro-industries undergoing privatization; establishing free trade in grain within the region but with protection from highly subsidized non–Central American producers; and improving the governments' capacity for evaluating and controlling imported technologies, especially biotechnologies.[30]

The presidents' summit produced the Plan de Acción para la Agricultura Centroamericana (PAC), which instructed the agriculture ministers to develop data on the numbers of producers, the production costs, and the output and productivity of each key crop. The PAC included measures to liberalize intraregional trade, especially a reduction in state involvement in commercializing agricultural products and a system of uniform regional "price bands" for basic grains (Presidentes Centroamericanos 1991).[31] To the surprise of many, the final summit declaration resolved "to receive with special interest the proposals of the Asociación Centroamericana de Organizaciones Campesinas para la Cooperación y el Desarrollo and to instruct the appropriate institutions to consider and analyze them in order to find adequate responses to the issues they raise" (ASOCODE 1991b, 23). This gesture was largely rhetorical but represented a degree of recognition that few campesino activists had expected.

In December 1991, campesino organizations throughout Central America sent members to Managua for ASOCODE's founding congress, an event that mixed resolutions, speeches, and association business with "a rich and lively flow of sentiment, denunciation, and synthesis from the singers, poets, and musicians" in the different delegations (ASOCODE 1992).[32] The congress formalized a coordinating commission of two delegates from each national coalition.[33] It also elected as general coordinator Wilson Campos, a charismatic thirty-two-year-old Costa Rican who had played a key role in organizing regional meetings since 1988.[34] Largely at the insistence of the Nicaraguans, the congress decided that if the coordinator was from Costa Rica, then the association's headquarters would have to be in another country. In an effort to balance tensions between Costa Ricans and Nicaraguans, a UNAG functionary was elected vice coordinator, and Nicaragua was chosen as the seat of ASOCODE.

The new association conceived of itself not as a supranational bureaucracy but as a *mesa de encuentro* for national coalitions, where decisions would be made by consensus, as well as a lobby for defending campesino interests in international, regional, and national arenas.[35] The congress specified that these interests included the following:

> (1) Guaranteeing small and medium-sized producers access to land, credit and technical assistance, as well as processing and marketing of their production . . . ; (2) assuring respect for small and medium-sized producers' cultural roots, so that the development of Central American societies will be compatible with their idiosyncrasies and way of life . . . ; (3) achieving full recognition and participation in political and economic decisions at the national, regional, and international levels . . . ; (4) working for a true peace and true respect for the elemental human rights of

small and medium-sized producers . . . ; and (5) promoting conservation of Central America's ecological systems. (ASOCODE 1991b, 25)

The delegates also addressed two resolutions to national governments. They called on Guatemala to free peasant leader Diego Domingo Martín, who was kidnapped by the civil patrol in Ixcumen, Huehuetenango; and they urged the Nicaraguan government to provide titles for all lands "in the hands of campesinos, so that they may obtain credit and become active producers" and "to indemnify or provide new lands for those members of the former Resistencia Nacional [the Contras] whose properties were confiscated" (ASOCODE 1991b, 7–9).

Alternative Messages and Funding the Messengers

How was this challenging agenda to be funded? In 1992 and 1993, three delegations toured Europe. The third and largest group, whose trip was coordinated by the Amsterdam-based Transnational Institute, received a welcome beyond all expectations. Representatives of the governments of Holland, Denmark, Sweden, Norway, Germany, Belgium, and France as well as high-ranking EEC and European Parliament officials met with the ASOCODE envoys, often "for more time than protocol usually requires for this kind of interview" (ASOCODE 1993a). An internal organization report noted that the government representatives "listened with curiosity and at times with surprise at the level of our arguments and our knowledge regarding global economic and agricultural issues and the political, economic, and social problems of our region. In sum, the result is highly favorable to ASOCODE" (ASOCODE 1993a). The tour also reinforced links with European NGOs, foundations, university groups, media, fair-commerce campaigns, and agriculturalists' organizations that, the report declared unselfconsciously, "helped us become aware of our backwardness" (ASOCODE 1993a).[36]

How successful were ASOCODE's European tours and related efforts in securing material support? By the end of 1992, the association inaugurated its headquarters in Managua, a spacious house in an upper-middle-class neighborhood a block from the home of President Violeta Barrios de Chamorro (and around the corner from the UNAG). The office resembled that of any large Central American NGO, with computers and copiers, offices for professional staff, secretaries, a guard, a maid, and a driver with a jeep. By 1993, the organization's annual budget exceeded US$300,000. A monthly subsidy of US$1,000 was paid to each of the seven national coalitions (ASOCODE 1993c, 18). By 1995, this subvention had risen to US$4,000 to $5,000 per month for each coalition (Zavala 1995).[37] The general coordinator's salary in 1993 was $US13,000 a year (not counting the "thirteenth month" year-end bonus), a handsome income for a mid-level professional in Central America (ASOCODE 1993c, 18).

These resources permitted ASOCODE to sponsor frequent seminars with campesino leaders on credit, marketing opportunities, agricultural and agro-forestry technology, administrative and lobbying skills, and other needs. The association also produced a constant flow of proposals and position papers and maintained a regular presence at intergovernmental meetings. In Panama in 1992, after intense ASOCODE lobbying, the Central American Presidents' Summit issued the Compromiso Agropecuario de Panamá (Agricultural Commitment of Panama), a series of guidelines for regional policy. While the Compromiso called for eliminating remaining barriers to free trade, food security also figured as a concern throughout, suggesting that campesino lobbyists had made some impact. The presidents called for protecting small grain producers from "fluctuations and distortions" in international markets; creating a regional fund for improving smallholders' access to technology, credit, and processing facilities; and incorporating "representatives of the public and private agricultural sectors" into policymaking processes and international commercial negotiations (Presidentes Centroamericanos 1992). While it was clear that many of these promises would likely go unfulfilled, the Compromiso nevertheless constituted a significant reference point for future negotiations.

Despite the concessions in the Compromiso, some presidents were far from pleased about having peasant lobbyists attending their regional meetings. Especially since the 1991 confrontation between peasant leaders and government ministers over grain "price band" policies, the more conservative governments had viewed first the PFSA and then ASOCODE with consternation (see earlier discussion on price bands). The government of President Rafael Leonardo Callejas in Honduras took the perceived threat seriously enough to bring right-wing peasant leaders to the Panama summit and then to employ a classic Honduran tactic for dividing popular movements: the creation of a "parallel organization."[38] In early 1993, pro-Callejas campesino groups convoked a meeting to form the Confederación Campesina del Istmo Centroamericano (COCICA), founded "to promote forms of organization that foment harmony among the actors that participate in agricultural development" (COCICA 1993, 3). COCICA leader Nahún Calix put the matter more bluntly, echoing one of the goals of the recently passed Agricultural Modernization Law. Peasants, he declared, "have to get over their fear of associating with foreign capital" (El Heraldo 1993).

Although COCICA attracted a half dozen Guatemalan, Salvadoran, and Costa Rican groups to its founding convention (as well as observers from Nicaragua's UNAG), the organization did not have the human or material resources to compete effectively with ASOCODE. Its links to Callejas, who was widely viewed as aggressively anti-campesino, condemned it to being just one more of the "paper" or "shell" organizations that periodically spring up in Central America, representing themselves as the embodiment of one or another sector of civil society.[39]

ASOCODE rapidly succeeded in gaining regional and international recognition, although at times this pace caused tensions with the participating national coalitions. In December 1993, for example, the association held its second congress in Guatemala and invited President Ramiro de León Carpio to attend. This move was a calculated effort to shield the representatives of the Coordinadora Nacional de Pequeños y Medianos Productores (CONAMPRO), ASOCODE's affiliate in Guatemala, and ASOCODE leaders traveling there, who on earlier occasions had suffered harassment at the airport.[40] CONAMPRO representatives wanted to use de León's presence to raise pressing issues of "massacres . . . , forced [military] recruitment . . . and political persecution."[41] But ASOCODE leaders, concerned about offending the president, exerted pressure to remove all such references from CONAMPRO's statement to the congress. The final version of the CONAMPRO coordinator's speech made only vague allusions to war and repression and to Guatemala's "long and dark night, which has no end in sight" (ASOCODE 1993b, 7).

For ASOCODE, the strategy of lobbying ministers and presidents had several strong points. First, it buffered national organizations against repression. Second, it provided a source of information about impending policy shifts. Third, it demonstrated to international organizations and funders that the peasant movement was not inveterately confrontational and was capable of offering alternative development proposals and willing to negotiate with policymakers. Fourth, the strategy contributed to democratization because peasants and other sectors of civil society gained the right to express their demands and to insist on compliance with government commitments, along with access to the necessary forums. Fifth, it established a presence for popular movements in the new supranational bodies that increasingly direct Central American integration. Sixth, it widened debate over such issues as trade and fiscal policies, vertically integrated production, credit availability, and agrarian reform. Finally, in several countries, this lobbying strategy helped win national organizations' demands for participation in policymaking bodies such as public-sector agrarian banks and bipartite agricultural-sector commissions composed of ministerial and peasant-organization representatives.

Successes in lobbying and negotiations depended significantly on the peasants' growing capacity for appropriating and reshaping official discourse—and not just the presidents' frequent but vague calls for *concertación* (consensus and reconciliation) or for the participation of civil society. The specificity of this approach is suggested in the comments of one Salvadoran activist:

> To speak of the development of El Salvador is to speak of the Lempa River basin: half the country, ten thousand square kilometers, the source of 98 percent of our energy, our main water source. The country's future is bound up with the Lempa basin. . . . We raise this issue to make the traditional demands of the peasant movement: land titling, credit, marketing, technical assistance. But we negotiate around what most interests the country: energy and water. Who lives on the slopes of the Lempa basin? Poor agriculturalists producing basic grains without technology or assistance. They can't change their relation to the land because their rights to it have not been recognized. Even the US agriculture department recognizes that if people don't own their land, it's difficult to change their relation to natural resources. So in negotiations we raise the banner of the Lempa basin. "You're interested in energy? We don't even have energy. We don't have light. You're interested in preventing sedimentation of the dams? You invest millions of dollars in dredging. But if you want to prevent runoff and sedimentation, we have to conserve the soils and only the agriculturalists can do that. . . ." This argument is like a new weapon for negotiation.[42]

But however adroit peasant negotiators had become at appropriating and reshaping official rhetoric, their success in lobbying depended on the willingness of those in power to compromise. By mid-1994, members of ASOCODE's coordinating commission agreed that the region's governments "lacked political will." The promises of the Compromiso Agropecuario de Panamá—and many others—had not been met. Wilson Campos summed up the mood: "We've forced them to recognize us as a legitimate force. But now, after two years, we've been in four summits and over twenty regional forums. We're seeing that they've made a lot of promises that haven't been kept" (Edelman 1994).

Governmental intransigence brought calls from within ASOCODE for a return to traditional pressure tactics: marches or even highway blockades or building occupations. Most agreed, however, that any demonstration should be carried out simultaneously in all seven countries and without abandoning efforts to affect policy through other means. Even before any show of force, the mere threat of action won concessions. As a coordinating commission report from September 1994 indicated, "in November, for the first time, we will have an [entire] day to work with the Central American Agriculture Ministers; but we only obtained this one-day audience because we sent a letter saying that

ASOCODE was considering the possibility of regional pressure and their response was to immediately give us that working day" (ASOCODE 1994, 5).

The possibility of regional pressure had already been determined. On October 10, 1994, organizations in five of the seven countries staged simultaneous marches to protest these governments' unwillingness to modify national structural adjustment policies (no demonstrations occurred in Belize, which was celebrating its national day, or in Nicaragua, where the government banned demonstrations during a visit by US Vice President Albert Gore to the Central American Ecological Summit). The large turnouts—especially in Honduras and Costa Rica, where the presidents received delegations of demonstrators—constituted a significant show of strength and a useful morale builder. But the marches appeared to do little to break the impasse between the governments and the peasant organizations.[43] At the Central American Presidents' Summit in March 1995 in El Salvador, ASOCODE did not receive the customary invitation to address the meeting, despite the event's focus on issues of social welfare (Zavala 1995). Increasingly, the association turned inward, leaving lobbying activities at presidential summits to the Iniciativa Civil para la Integración Centroamericana (ICIC), a coalition of labor, peasant, and small business organizations (ASOCODE 1995a, 13; Lemus 1997). ASOCODE continued to seek common ground with the region's agriculture ministers, with modest successes. But the main focus of its work shifted to strengthening the national coalitions and alliances with non-peasant organizations, identifying whatever opportunities might arise as part of the free-market transition, and fostering campesino technical, entrepreneurial, and administrative capacities (ASOCODE 1997a, 1997b; Cáceres Baca 1997). In Honduras, El Salvador, and Guatemala, organizations linked to ASOCODE staged major land occupations in 1995 and 1996, producing occasional concessions but also new victims of state repression.[44]

Transnational movements to organize peasants in Central America raise significant questions regarding social scientific approaches to transnationalism, collective action, and agrarian change. "Peasants," as Kearney (1996) has rightly suggested, constitute an "ambiguous" and "disruptive" classificatory category. But while this characterization may seem troublesome or precarious to social scientists, it is less so to those Central Americans who assume a "campesino" identity; it is not their "essential" or "univocal" identity but a central part of a spectrum of possible social positions. Nor does a politically inclusive subjective identification as "campesinos" prevent Central American peasants from making analytical distinctions between smallholders, cooperativists, squatters, and the landless. These differences loom large in the everyday work of creating programs, building organizations, and struggling for specific demands. Even though peasant politics now have a profound transnational dimension, they hardly reflect a "decline of class identity" or a displacement of political work from the space of the nation-state (Kearney 1996). On the contrary, material aspirations still occupy a privileged place in a peasant political practice directed simultaneously at particular nation-states and the supranational institutions to which the states now belong (Tarrow 1994, chap. 11).

Despite the evident successes of the transnational peasant movement in Central America, it faces troubling dilemmas. ASOCODE has proved to be more than the sum of its distinct national parts and much more than a project of European NGOs or governments. It has accomplished a great deal in strengthening its constituent organizations and advocating forcefully on behalf of small agriculturalists at a time when discussions about development among Central American elites are largely hostile to (or at best, silent about) peasants and their concerns. Yet it is not surprising that ASOCODE's most significant lobbying successes have been with foreign cooperation agencies rather than with multilateral lenders, presidential summits, or national governments. Many European and Canadian cooperation organizations are favorably disposed to peasant movements to begin with and are receptive to a kind of information and image projection that cannot by itself possibly achieve such major goals as altering the outcome of Central American agrarian struggles or the application of World Bank structural-adjustment programs.

In Central America in the late 1980s and early 1990s, diverse sectors of civil society formed regional networks to defend their interests, often building on transnational ties established during the upheavals of the previous decade. In the case of the peasant organizations that formed ASOCODE, European backing was and still is key, even if threats to a cherished smallholder identity and livelihood goaded them to action at the individual or national level. Without foreign "cooperation," something resembling ASOCODE might have emerged anyway, but with a smaller budget and a lower profile. A mildly critical participant in the Central American labor-union group COCENTRA alluded to ASOCODE's higher profile in suggesting that its leaders should be "taking buses to Guatemala or Honduras the way we do rather than airplanes the way they do."

The flow of European (and other) funds inevitably raises questions about the mix of motives of those leading national and transnational peasant organizations, the long-term possibilities of movements vulnerable to the growing fiscal conservatism of European societies, and the ultimate political and economic impact of internationalization. ASOCODE leaders assert that "no governmental or nongovernmental organization has the right to represent itself as the parent or creator of this process" (ASOCODE 1992, 4).[45] Nevertheless, peasant identity is actively created and represented these days—sometimes consciously, sometimes not—with an awareness of the images, information, and discourses that play best before international audiences. To some extent, the agenda of ASOCODE and its constituent organizations is now driven by donors—a less onerous kind of conditionality than the domination of earlier peasant organizations by political parties but one that nonetheless preoccupies some of its constituents. Much of the attention devoted to gender, Indigenous, and (to a lesser extent) environmental issues appeared at first to derive primarily from European rather than Central American sensibilities (Candanedo and Madrigal 1994, 119).[46]

Being a *dirigente* (leader), moreover, has become a career path, with the security of a salary and possibilities for advancement and foreign travel.[47] As ASOCODE's economic support for the national coalitions has increased, the number of activists on the payroll has grown. Even when these cadres conduct themselves with the utmost integrity (as generally appears to be the case), the perception that they form a privileged group causes frictions.[48] Those outside the top leadership sometimes mutter about *"yuppis campesinos," "el jet set campesino,"* or *"la cúpula de cúpulas."* In traditional Central American peasant politics, receiving a salaried position was often a payoff and a cause for envy. Today, it can still convey an odor of corruption, even when the employer is not a government but a popular organization and the newly fortunate employee is scrupulously honest.

Information flows between ASOCODE and national- and base-level organizations are often less than agile, which is a problem that fuels the perception that regional leaders constitute a distant elite. ASOCODE's concentration on high-level lobbying and organizational consolidation also meant that many ambitious alternative development plans hashed out in regional seminars have yet to be applied on the ground—that is, they have yet "to land" or "come down to earth," as the frequent fliers in the leadership put it. Clearly, it is easier and cheaper to be effective in transnational lobbying and information politics than in the protracted and frustrating work of domestic organizing or the formidable struggle to raise rural living standards.

As a campesino movement, ASOCODE has broken with the local and agrarian protest orientation that historically characterized so many peasant mobilizations in Central America and elsewhere. At the same time, ASOCODE rejects the strategy of "peasant wars," which consumed so many of its supporters in the 1980s. Campesino involvement in lobbying, establishing international networks, building alliances with nonagricultural sector groups, and elaborating detailed and sophisticated development proposals marks a new stage in a social movement that is both very old and very new, as well as a new variety of "globalization from below."

Central America's regional peasant movement does not share the "classless-ness" and the emphasis on "cultural struggles" over "material struggles" said to typify other identity-based "new social movements" that have formed transnational networks, such as those of feminists, environmentalists, and Indigenous peoples (Escobar 1992; Jelin 1990; Melucci 1989; Olofsson 1988). The movement's embrace of "development"—in the names of organizations and in the aspirations of participants for greater well-being—suggests that it was peasants' political and economic marginality that led them to organize and opened the doors to international recognition and alliances (compare Brysk 1996). The case of cross-border peasant organizing in Central America seems to confirm the argument of some theorists in transnational relations that cooperative structures of international governance tend to legitimize transnational activities and to increase their access to national polities (Risse-Kappen 1995, 7). Here, the examples are the Sistema de Integración Centroamericana (SICA), Parlamento Centroamericano (PARLACEN), and the San José Dialogue, a framework for Central American-European cooperation on development and human rights issues. It is less clear, however, that attaining access or building effective coalitions translates into sustained policy impact. The very conditions that made ASOCODE possible—the end or decline of armed struggle, the rise of organizations in civil society, the opening and regional integration of Central American economies, the weakening of states affected by neoliberalism, the availability of foreign "cooperation"—also make it easier for the dominant groups to simply ignore pressure from below.

Yet in just a few years of existence, ASOCODE has surmounted several historical sources of weakness and division in peasant movements. Its rejection of political party ties, genuine ideological pluralism, and commitment to internal and external dialogue and consensus building have permitted the association to coordinate a diverse group of organizations in different national settings and to achieve a remarkable degree of regional and international recognition.

Perhaps the most encouraging aspect of these contradictions is that they are understood, debated, and addressed within ASOCODE with a frankness and sophistication that have few antecedents in peasant movement practice. Campesino organizations are political projects, not profit-generating enterprises, and many of these tensions are probably unavoidable (compare Landsberger and Hewitt 1970). In Central America, at least, even elite business lobbies have relied heavily on foreign "cooperation," usually from the USAID (Rosa 1993; Sojo 1992). The fact that the peasant movement has sought funds abroad could even be interpreted as an indication of growing realism, specialization or professionalization, and maturity. Given Central American peasant movements' long history of factionalism, ASOCODE's success in bringing together such a diverse and fractious collection of groups from seven different countries is nothing short of remarkable.

WHEN NETWORKS DON'T WORK

The Rise and Fall and Rise of Civil Society
Initiatives in Central America

Scholars of collective action rarely examine why many, if not most, social movements fail. This chapter analyzes the roots of competing conservative and progressive visions of "civil society," discusses the inadequacy of Gramsci's concept of "organic intellectuals" for the study of agrarian movements, and examines the demise and subsequent reemergence of transnational peasant organization networks in Central America. The chapter notes the problems of "fictitious," "shell," or "paper organizations" and gatekeeper groups that vet movements seeking to affiliate with transnational networks, as well as the occasionally problematical representation claims of the peasant organizations. It constitutes an experiment in self-criticism and a corrective to the overly optimistic interpretation in chapter 4, which was written in a moment when transnational peasant politics in Central America was ascendant, before processes of organizational decomposition and massive out-migration made the project of regional solidarity ever more challenging. But as the chapter also points out, even as some networks collapsed, others emerged to confront elite-dominated regional integration plans.

"Civil society," "network," and "social movement" are imprecise, frequently contested terms. Many social scientific discussions of collective action are characterized by considerable slippage in the use of these and other, similar concepts. To a large extent, this reflects the emergence of new, hybrid organizational forms, as contemporary social movements network with one another, form coalitions, and seek to establish claims to constitute part of national and global civil society. While this chapter indicates that it may be heuristically helpful to refine distinctions between these categories, it argues that it is probably more useful to integrate insights from the too often separate streams of scholarship that focus, respectively, on civil society, networks, and social movements. In particular, the rise in the 1990s of transnational Central America–wide civil society initiatives (and their decline and reemergence) suggests that (1) contested notions of civil society have a real-world impact on the shape and activities of diverse social movements and nongovernmental organizations; (2) "networks," far from being durable and potent organizational forms (as scholars of the right and left have forcefully maintained) are at times quite fragile and ephemeral and characterized by periodic cycles like those of social movements (Arquilla and Ronfeldt 2001b; Castells 1996; Tarrow 1994); and (3) the new prominence of "networks," whether as political claims or as linked computers or social movements, exacerbates a problem with profound methodological, political, ethical, and representational dimensions that is acknowledged only occasionally in the social movements literature—the appearance of "fictitious" or "shell" organizations and, more recently, "dot causes" or internet-based advocacy organizations with minuscule or indeterminate constituencies (Tilly 1984, 311; Anheier and Themudo 2002, 209–210).

Real-World Impacts of Civil Society and Network Debates

It has become commonplace to refer to the 1980s in Latin America as "the lost decade." With the hindsight of today, it is clear that in many respects, the "lost" maxim was not hyperbolic. Despite occasional and scattered signs of progress, the continent is still reeling from the impact of the debt crisis (the result, in part, of overvalued currencies and the "exhaustion" of statist models of development but also of soaring interest rates in the 1970s, falling commodity prices, and anemic taxation systems); an increasingly volatile global economy; the intractable poverty that continues to affect more than a third of the population and that, in most countries, is little changed in relative terms since 1980 (CEPAL 2002, 64–65); and continuing instability in Argentina, Ecuador, Colombia, Venezuela, and elsewhere. The end of the military regimes and the democratization processes of the early 1980s generated tremendous hopes and opened up political space, but two decades later, Latin Americans express very low levels of satisfaction with how "democracy" works in their countries (Latinobarómetro 2002).

In the small nations of Central America, the 1980s were doubly lost. Affected by economic crises and restructuring (like the rest of the hemisphere), these countries also became a locus of superpower competition and massive social struggles, suffering levels of violence and destruction that beggar the imagination.

The crisis of the 1980s, however, also gave rise to an unprecedented mobilization of diverse sectors of civil society, particularly in the latter part of the decade and in the decade that followed when the civil wars ended or ebbed. There were several sources of this political effervescence. The reduction of civil conflict and the democratization of the political systems opened up "space" for new kinds of actors to express demands from sectors of society that had been on the defensive during the wars but also felt empowered as a result of their participation in a decade or more of arduous struggle. The accords that settled the wars included specific provisions for resettling refugees, incorporating ex-combatants into institutional life, and involving civil society in processes of building peace and strengthening national reconciliation. Throughout the region, new notions of rights had taken hold among highly politicized populations, and politicians across the spectrum articulated a new discourse of *concertación* (consensus and reconciliation). Intellectuals who had been downsized as part of public-sector retrenchment, as well as those who returned from exile or from the mountains, flocked to a growing number of nongovernmental organizations (NGOs). Finally, external actors who had been active in the region throughout the 1980s—notably the United States and the European Community—intensified their support for what were, broadly speaking, two competing civil society projects.

"Civil society" is, of course, a contested notion, with a complex genealogy that is beyond the scope of this chapter. For our purposes, it is worth noting that contrasting theoretical conceptions about how to bound the "civil society" category are often tied to distinct political-economic agendas and views of democratization. Different perspectives generally agree that civil society is the associational realm between the household or family and the state. Beyond that, however, at the risk of oversimplifying too much, it is possible to distinguish two polar positions, separated by opposing views on whether to include markets and firms within civil society. Those who argue for considering markets and corporations as part of the category typically back a conservative agenda (something ironic, given this position's roots in Hegel and Marx) that sees civil society as a domain outside of and morally superior to the state. They posit choice and freedom of association as fundamental characteristics of both the market and civil society, making support for economic liberalization and civil society institutions not only entirely compatible but complementary strategies for checking state power. In contrast, theorists who exclude the market and firms from civil society usually consider it a domain of associational life that attempts to defend autonomous collective institutions from the encroachments of *both* the market and the state. Frequently, they invoke Gramsci, while conveniently ignoring or downplaying his suggestion that achieving working-class hegemony within civil society could be a prelude to seizing state power. In comparison with conservative theorists, they tend to accord much greater analytical importance to how social inequality and power differentials structure or limit political representation (J. Cohen and Arato 1992; J. Cohen 1995; Hearn 2001; Keane 1998, 2001; Macdonald 1997; Nielsen 1995).

This theoretical polarization between differing visions of civil society was reflected in Central America in two political projects promoted by the two key external actors: the United States and the European Community (after 1993, the European Union). Each project—and here, for heuristic purposes, I am again ignoring some complexities—had a contrasting understanding of the underlying causes of the conflicts and a corresponding conception of democratization. In essence, Washington, and particularly the administrations of Ronald Reagan and George H. W. Bush, saw the region's revolutionary movements, wars, and related unrest as rooted fundamentally and almost exclusively in communist subversion and Soviet-Cuban interference. European policymakers—especially (but not only) the Spanish, Scandinavian, and German social democrats—emphasized inequality, poverty, systematic human rights violations, and authoritarian rule as central causes of the upheavals. The US approach was overwhelmingly military until the late 1980s, although it also involved encouraging free elections, legal reforms, privatization of public-sector entities, and rapid economic liberalization. Its civil society component involved strong backing for private-sector lobbies and export promotion organizations, many of which received large subsidies from the US Agency for International Development (Cuenca 1992; Echeverría 1993; Escoto and Marroquín 1992; Rosa 1993; Sojo 1992).

European governments, apprehensive about the possibility of a major Central American war that might eventually compromise their own region's security, actively promoted diplomatic efforts (first Contadora and then Costa Rican President Oscar Arias's initiative that culminated in the 1987 Esquipulas Accords). Since 1984, they sponsored annual European–Central American ministerial-level meetings (called the San José Dialogue) to hammer out "cooperation" or aid agreements. Most of the sudden increase in flows of European cooperation, however, was channeled through donor NGOs rather than bilateral or official European Union agencies. These European NGOs frequently received most of their funding from their respective governments (e.g., Ibis-Denmark or Novib-Holland). They nonetheless placed great emphasis on establishing "horizontal" relations with grassroots "counterparts" that permitted medium- and long-term, rather than project-specific, funding. The European vision of democratization aimed to rein in the excesses of the market and empower historically powerless sectors of the population (the poor, Indigenous and minority groups, women) so that they could participate effectively in political institutions and combat structural inequalities, poverty, and environmental destruction (Biekart 1999; Freres 1998; Fundación Arias 1998; Grabendorff, Krumwiede, and Todt 1984; Hansen 1996; Macdonald 1997; Reuben Soto 1991; Roy 1992; Sanahuja 1996; Schori 1981).

Increasingly, over the course of the 1990s, efforts to theorize civil society—and "global" or "transnational" civil society, in particular—employed the notion of "network" as an analytical category, a metaphor for a social condition, and a description of emerging organizational and institutional forms, communications technologies, and knowledge practices. "Network" has come to have diverse meanings (again, beyond the scope of this chapter), though its genealogy is nowhere near as lengthy as that of the similarly complicated "civil society." As in the civil society literature, with which it overlaps, "network" scholarship is characterized by a pronounced left-right split. Here, though, the division is less about how to bound the object of study than over, alternatively, the emancipatory potential versus the danger that network organization implies. In the former camp, one study of "new social movements" (Riechmann and Fernández Buey 1994) is optimistically titled "Networks That Give Liberty" (*Redes que dan libertad*). Two key works on transnational activism conclude that "dense" networks, with many nodes, are most likely to be effective (Keck and Sikkink 1998, 206; J. Smith 1997, 54–55). Manuel Castells's ambitious examination of this "new social morphology"—which includes case studies of diverse social movements as well as organized crime—suggests that "networks are open structures, able to expand without limits, integrating new nodes as long as they are able to communicate within the network" (Castells 1996, 470). While acknowledging intellectual debts to Castells, John Arquilla and David Ronfeldt of the RAND Corporation argue that "nimble bad guys"—terrorists, criminals, and "militants"—have become more adept than "good guys" at deploying "network" forms and waging "netwar" (Arquilla and Ronfeldt 2001a). Concerned primarily with elaborating new counterinsurgency or "counter-netwar" military doctrine, at times these authors have a troubling tendency to conflate international human rights activists with Al Qaeda or Colombian drug cartels: "They know how to penetrate and disrupt, as well as elude and evade. All feature network forms of organization, doctrine, strategy, and technology attuned to the information age . . . They are proving very hard to beat; some may actually be winning" (Arquilla and Ronfeldt 2001a, v).[1] Across the spectrum, from "Networks That Give Liberty" to "Networks and Netwars," a strong consensus exists about the potency and durability of network forms. As in the broader collective action literature, where the study of unsuccessful social movements is distinctly undertheorized (Edelman 1999, 2001), only a few lone voices—notably Annelise Riles in her ethnographic tour de force *The Network Inside Out*—row against the current and call attention to the possibility that the network may be "a form that supersedes analysis and reality" and that its "'failure' is endemic, indeed, . . . [an] effect of the Network form" (2000, 174, 6).[2] While perhaps not applicable to all networks in all times and places (as Riles seems to claim), this latter perspective deserves consideration when analyzing the rise and decline of certain civil society networks in Central America in the 1990s. I will return to it in the conclusion.

Regional Civil Society in Central America

This chapter examines these issues primarily in relation to the recent history of Central American peasant and small farmer organizations. It looks, in particular, at the meteoric rise and subsequent decline of a regional network of campesino groups, the Association of Central American Peasant Organizations for Cooperation and Development (Asociación Centroamericana de Organizaciones Campesinas para la Cooperación y el Desarrollo, ASOCODE), which briefly enjoyed an extraordinarily high profile in isthmian politics, attending, for example, numerous presidential and ministerial summit meetings and generating a number of related networks that included both non-agrarian and non–Central American organizations. Founded in 1991 as an outgrowth of a European-sponsored food security education program, ASOCODE rapidly took on a life of its own and garnered growing legitimacy with its elite interlocutors and foreign funders, as well as with campesino activists from different countries who increasingly recognized that their counterparts elsewhere confronted similar problems and shared the same concerns. ASOCODE was, nonetheless, beset from the beginning by a variety of tensions that ultimately contributed to its undoing, among them differences of nationality and political orientation, entrenched patriarchal traditions, and leadership styles (Edelman 1998). Dependence on foreign donors also created unexpected vulnerabilities. Finally, the meager gains from transnational activism and the continuing salience of national political struggles eventually led some peasant organizations to question their earlier commitment to globalization-from-below and regional-level struggles.

The charismatic and energetic leadership of Wilson Campos, a young Costa Rican activist, helped to maintain tensions within manageable limits and to cement relations with foreign cooperation institutions during ASOCODE's first five years. Campos moved easily in a range of milieus, from rural farmsteads to presidential summits to UN agencies in New York and foundation offices in Europe. Adept at making those with whom he came in contact feel heard and appreciated, he attracted considerable sympathy in policymaking and donor circles. This role, however, entailed serious costs in greatly reduced attention given to local and national organizations in Costa Rica (in which Campos had previously been a key player) and in growing centralization in a single person of duties relating to ASOCODE's international and internal organizational relations. Other leaders, often distrustful of Costa Ricans to begin with, also resented this concentration of affective attachments and organizational responsibilities.

One way to gain a sense of ASOCODE's rise and fall is by outlining its funding strategy, which clearly responded to a shift in European cooperation strategies in the late 1980s and early 1990s, when multilateral, bilateral, and NGO donors let it be known that they preferred to support projects that had a Central American regional, as opposed to a national or local, focus (Biekart 1999, 204–206). In 1992 and 1993, three ASOCODE delegations toured Europe, meeting with NGO, European Community, and European Parliament officials and representatives of the governments of Holland, Denmark, Norway, Germany, Belgium, and France. By 1993, the organization had an annual budget of over US$300,000, almost entirely from European (and a few Canadian and US) donor groups. A monthly subsidy of US$1,000 per month was paid to each of the seven national coalitions that made up ASOCODE. The general coordinator's salary was US$13,000 per year (handsome compensation for a mid-level professional in Central America, especially when other perquisites were included, such as the "*aguinaldo*" or "thirteenth month" year-end bonus, the use of vehicles, and free housing in Managua). By 1995, the subvention to each national organization had risen to $4,000 or $5,000 per month for each coalition, most of which was spent as salary for the two representatives who each country assigned to part-time work in ASOCODE's coordinating council (Edelman 1998). In 1996, the association's budget rose to US$1.5 million (Biekart 1999, 280).

The sudden abundance of resources created a heady atmosphere. Indeed, in the 1994–1997 period, according to an internal organizational report, "cooperation resources were so abundant that they exceeded the capacity of the headquarters" to administer them (ASOCODE 1999, 24). Perhaps not surprisingly, success in fundraising, together with an intense round of activities, could easily be mistaken for political impact and influence. It also accentuated the top-down character of ASOCODE, lessening its accountability to its national components, and simultaneously created "new needs" that essentially responded to donor offers and priorities (Biekart 1999, 286–293).

In the competition for European funding, claiming to be a "popular organization" that "represented" an historically marginalized sector of the population came to be increasingly important. In ASOCODE's case, the degree of "representativity" could be established by summing the impressive, though not always unexaggerated, membership figures of its constituent organizations. A certain hubris or even grandiosity tended to accompany claims of this sort. By 1997, for example, ASOCODE leaders asserted confidently that within a short time they would have expanded the "Campesino a Campesino" extension program—which had only a modest presence outside of Nicaragua—to all of Central America.[3]

Given the historical antagonism in Central America between "popular organizations" and NGOs, it is striking how much the two forms converged. Analyzing Latin American feminist movements, Sonia Alvarez (1998) calls this a process of "NGO-ization" of popular organizations. ASOCODE, headed by some of the most belligerent anti-NGO activists in the region, resembled nothing so much as a large NGO (a 1999 internal retrospective evaluation indicates candidly that by 1994, the ASOCODE had institutionalized its "function as a cooperation agency"). Headquartered in a spacious house in an upper-middle-class neighborhood of Managua, the association had all of the typical NGO trappings: computers, photocopy machines, faxes, secretaries, maids, a driver, technicians who generated a never-ending stream of project proposals and "strategic plans," and foreign "cooperators," first from Denmark and later Canada. It published a glossy bimonthly newsletter in Spanish and English (the latter, some said, was for the Belizeans, although others conceded that it was primarily for foreign consumption). ASOCODE leaders and technical staff from outside Nicaragua would often dash home (sometimes in ASOCODE vehicles) to Honduras or Costa Rica for the weekend. Many became fluent in the banal and repetitive "NGO speak" ("sustainability," "transparency," "participation," "accountability," and so on), as devastatingly lampooned in Argentine human rights activist Gino Lofredo's 1991 parody, "Get Rich in the 1990s. You still don't have an NGO?"[4]

Part of the sense that ASOCODE was ascendant derived from its very real access to presidential and ministerial summit meetings and from its membership in the Consultative Council of the Central American Integration System (Sistema de Integración Centroamericana, SICA), Central America's main supranational regional governance institution. Several of the national coalitions that participated in ASOCODE used their newfound access to funds to carry out rural development programs and to support struggles for land rights, credit, and technical assistance. At the regional level, however, the principal activity continued to be summit-hopping lobbying, organizational meetings, and training workshops and seminars.

In the early to mid-1990s, ASOCODE also initiated or encouraged the formation of several new networks: the Indigenous and Peasant Community Agroforestry Coordinator (Coordinadora Indígena y Campesina de Agroforestería Comunitaria, CICAFOC); the Central American Indigenous Council (Consejo Indígena Centroamericano, CICA); the Civil Initiative for Central American Integration (Iniciativa Civil para la Integración Centroamericana, ICIC); the Latin American Coordinator of Rural Organizations (Coordinadora Latino-americana de Organizaciones del Campo, CLOC); and the Via Campesina/Peasant Road, which eventually included representatives of farmers' organizations from some fifty countries (Desmarais 2002; Edelman 2003). Following the massive devastation of Hurricane Mitch in October 1998, ASOCODE, together with CICAFOC and a regional network of small coffee producers, set up a new Central American Rural Coordinating Group (Coordinadora Centroamericana del Campo) to join a broader Central America Solidarity Coordinating Group (Coordinación Centroamérica Solidaria) at the Stockholm meeting of European cooperation organizations involved in the reconstruction effort. The proliferation of networks meant a sharp rise in the number of regional meetings, many of which were attended by the same individuals. Some of the more enterprising activists reportedly received full-time salaries simultaneously from more than one network, rather like what Riles (2000, 47) reports in the South Pacific.

Decomposition and Recomposition: "Crisis," "Rupture," and "Transition"

Networks beget networks. The phenomenon is noteworthy because new organizational structures were assumed or claimed to correspond to new political or economic functions or objectives. Ironically, the most intense period of ASOCODE involvement in creating new networks occurred just before its own decomposition. This section describes an organizational decline that some viewed as a demise and that others euphemistically called a "transition." The conclusion that follows suggests why processes of network genesis and decomposition are not coincidental but rather integrally related to each other.

In 1997 and 1998, ASOCODE entered into a period that its own internal evaluation characterizes as "crisis and rupture" (ASOCODE 1999, 25). First, the English and then the Spanish edition of its newsletter ceased publication. Organizational divisions involved more and more energy, and ASOCODE diminished its lobbying at regional and international meetings. Much of the discord manifested itself in a factional split—present from the association's beginnings—between the Panamanian and Salvadoran "verticalists" (with orthodox Leninist proclivities), on the one hand, and the five other countries' representatives, on the other. Additional controversies divided the coordinating council along different lines—for example, whether the association should be a regional campesino lobby or attempt to resolve immediate on-the-ground problems in the member countries. The diversity of the constituent organizations and their social bases (i.e., agricultural workers,

Indigenous groups, independent peasants, cooperative members), which were once seen as a strength, became a further source of polarization as some countries' representatives (Nicaraguans and Costa Ricans, in particular) argued for a narrower orientation toward smallholding producers. Worsening disputes between headquarters and the different national coalitions over control of resources also led some significant organizations to withdraw and others to be expelled from the national coalitions. Sometimes this occurred because national organizations saw the coalitions that represented them at the regional level as too involved in ASOCODE to attend to pressing issues at home.

In 1999, ASOCODE abandoned all efforts at lobbying international, regional, and national institutions. When donor organizations became aware of the turmoil and withdrew their support, the downward spiral accelerated. Some agencies indicated that henceforth they would reverse their previous practice of funding regional initiatives and channel support earmarked for ASOCODE to its constituent national organizations. The coalition that had represented Guatemala in ASOCODE dissolved once it was decimated by the loss of cooperation funds and eclipsed by the rise of other, more dynamic alliances of Guatemalan peasant organizations (in which it had briefly participated). The lavish headquarters in Managua—an example of what one prescient critique termed network "macrocephaly" (Morales Gamboa and Cranshaw 1997, 55)—closed its doors. "Since March 2000," an internal report commented, "we have not had any financial support from any cooperation agency or organization . . . the different activities have been carried out with the support provided by their organizers. Operating expenses until December 2000 . . . were obtained through the sale of equipment from the headquarters" (ASOCODE 2001, 1).

In April 2001, twenty-five delegates (fifteen of them women) from five countries met in Tegucigalpa (representatives from Belize and Guatemala were invited and confirmed their participation but never arrived). Their agenda was to consolidate what some described as a "transition." Instead of a costly headquarters and a regional coordinating committee, ASOCODE decided to divide into issue-specific working groups that would communicate virtually or meet physically on an ad hoc basis. The Honduran member coalition, already host to the global Via Campesina network, agreed to serve as ASOCODE's office as well and to begin the paperwork needed to establish its legal personality in Honduras (and to obtain a Honduran email account). Despite the near demise of the association, the transition commission's report pointed to a wide range of activities over the previous year: regional "encounters" on agrarian problems and the landless in Honduras, El Salvador, and Nicaragua; on rural women in Nicaragua; and on preparing proposals for the civil society Consultative Council of the SICA in El Salvador, as well as participation in forums in Montreal, Madrid, Bangalore, and Nairobi.

Nor did the Tegucigalpa "transition" meeting neglect public relations. The ASOCODE brochure was updated, a press conference scheduled at the end of the event, and plans were made to announce the new organizational structure on the association's web page. The Panamanians, in a move consonant with Riles's (2000, 32, 89) observations about how networks fetishize their own reports, urged the rest of the delegates "to reaffirm the presence of ASOCODE in Central America, taking advantage of all the documents on the letterhead of the different national coalitions [*mesas*], adding the name of ASOCODE [to each, for example] APEMEP-ASOCODE, ADC-ASOCODE, COCOCH-ASOCODE" (ASOCODE 2001, 8).[5]

Some Reasons Why Networks Don't Always Work

It would be tempting to explain the decline of ASOCODE, its lowered profile in Central American regional politics, and the demise of some of its spin-off networks as the result of bitter factional infighting, a macrocephalic organizational structure, battles over money, or an exaggerated dependence on foreign donors. This would not be wrong. But behind the conflicts between "verticalists" and their opponents, the often-opportunistic pursuit of individual or organizational economic security, the currying of favor with European cooperation agencies, and the propagation of donor-driven agendas lie some lessons that speak to the role of nation-states in the global economy and the broader limitations of transnational civil society projects.

Networks are typically represented by social scientists and by their participants as two-dimensional linkages between nodes or focal points of equal weight or significance. This portrayal—whether of "chain," "star and hub," or "all channel" network forms (Arquilla and Ronfeldt 2001b, 8)—often fails to capture how networks are experienced by those who participate in them (Riles 2000). Network activists, like other overworked professionals, feel the tug of disparate demands emanating from the regional, national, and local organizations in which they take part. The network diagrams that show ties between national coalitions (which are very much the same in Central America and in the Pacific) fail to indicate the existence of this third dimension that links national coalitions to their very diverse constituent member groups. Concretely, the same individuals who mobilize delegates for international network conferences may also have to put together a legal team to defend disputed property titles, follow up on late orders for a cooperative's rubber boots, or harvest a field of cabbages. Unlike electrical engineering diagrams, which typically indicate resistance to flows, formal network organigrams imply agile and unobstructed movement of information between nodes or focal points. The network's representation of itself erases political, historical, and personal forces that might, in practice, impede the networking process.

The two-dimensional representation of networks—in part an artifact of commonly used graphics software—effaces not just this third dimension of linkages between a "hub" and its components but also the fourth dimension of how time and periodicity affect civil society initiatives. Social movements everywhere rise and fall, often as part of broader "cycles of protest" (Tarrow 1994; Tilly 1984). US, European, and autochthonous civil society projects of the late 1980s and early 1990s in Central America shared an urgency born out of a decade or more of severe crisis and inconceivable violence. Over the course of the 1990s, these imperatives receded in importance. Donors experienced fatigue, became enamored of new fashions, and shifted their attention to other regions—notably Eastern Europe and southern Africa—where needs seemed more immediate and political hopes appeared to have greater possibilities of realization. In Europe, in particular, the rightward shift in several key countries led to diminished official support for grassroots organizations in the third world. And in several countries in Central America, as democratization advanced, traditional political forms—parties, unions, and lobbies—assumed as their own many of the demands initially articulated through civil society initiatives.

Analysts of transnational politics increasingly question the pundits' facile vision of contemporary globalization as a zero-sum game in which states lose as markets and supranational governance institutions gain. Saskia Sassen, for example, points out that while states everywhere are forfeiting their historical role as regulators of financial markets, they continue to play a major role in extending the interstate consensus in favor of globalization if for no other reason than that national legal systems remain the principal means through which the contracts and property rights so essential in the world economy are enforced (Sassen 2000, 61; Helleiner 1994). Sidney Tarrow, similarly, emphasizes "that states remain dominant in most areas of policy," such as domestic security, border control, and exercising legal dominion with their territories. "Citizens," he says,

> can travel more easily than before and can form networks beyond borders . . . , but they still live in states and, in democratic ones at least, they have the opportunities, the networks, and the well-known repertoires of national politics. . . . Those are incentives to operate on native

ground that the hypothetical attractions of "global civil society" cannot easily match. (Tarrow 2001, 2–3)

The tensions within ASOCODE between the possibilities of regional, transnational organizing and the imperatives of national politics need to be seen in this light, even though for many global networkers (and especially for rural ones) the "attractions" of international travel and a more cosmopolitan lifestyle might be greater than Tarrow indicates. Jorge Hernández Cascante, a longtime campesino organizer in Costa Rica, had been a founder in the early 1980s of the politically centrist National Union of Small and Medium Agricultural Producers (Unión Nacional de Pequeños y Medianos Productores Agropecuarios, UPANACIONAL), still by far the country's largest peasant organization. Later, he had a leading role in the creation of the ASOCODE and the Via Campesina networks and saw UPANACIONAL, his "base organization," marginalized from both. An astute, committed activist who was present as part of a Via Campesina delegation at the "Battle of Seattle," Hernández explained in 2002 why he and his organization had decided to eschew regional politics and concentrate on national-level struggles:

> From UPANACIONAL's point of view, we discerned two serious problems in ASOCODE. One was the social composition of the movement. There were some groups clearly made up of small and medium-size agriculturalists and others which had labor and other sorts of demands. At the same time that movements like UPANACIONAL were interested in the right to make the land produce—because we live from the land—there were others who were concerned about rural wages, the [cost of] the "basic market basket" [i.e., cost of living]. This began to divide the movement. The other question concerned representation. We valued highly representative organizations, not so much purely in terms of numbers of members, which is important, but also in terms of actions in practice, in real struggle. These exist in all of Central America. But we also saw that there were organizations whose support base wasn't very clear. . . . They had a great name, but at the moment when pressure tactics were needed, to block a highway or stage a demonstration, their supporters didn't appear and the leaders still talked about how they had "X" quantity of members. . . . This was notorious, and even the cooperation agencies began to talk about organizations that were like shells. . . . We considered that it wasn't worth being in a process where the concepts of representation were so thin. . . . The organization that has an agenda of very intense internal, national work prefers to leave aside that type of problem and not get involved in that type of dispute. . . . It's

very exhausting. Moreover, the national agenda doesn't wait. The government's policies don't wait, nor the free-trade treaties, nor the pressure that has to be brought on the legislative assembly. If one doesn't do it now, they pass a law or a tax or a new free-trade treaty, and they put us there without any protection for grain producers or [growers of] potatoes or onions. So the organization has concentrated more on this agenda, which is our responsibility as representatives of the small and medium-size Costa Rican agriculturalists, and much to our regret, it has had to leave aside that regional, more Latin American, world level. In that whirlwind of events and seminars, which often were just images to project to the outside, there was a lot of discussion, a lot of politics, but very little advance in plans that might effectively aid the region's producers. (Hernández Cascante 2002)

The conflict was not simply one of global or regional versus national politics. The tension between politics and the agricultural production that was so central to ASOCODE's claimed identity also became a source of contention and disputed legitimacy. Sinforiano Cáceres, a longtime leader of Nicaragua's National Federation of Cooperatives (Federación Nacional de Cooperativas, FENACOOP), served as ASOCODE's general coordinator from 1996 to 1998. Somewhat later, factional disputes led FENACOOP to withdraw from the UNAG. Since the national coalitions—UNAG in this case—were the conduits for participating in ASOCODE and had to vouch for their own member groups that sought participation in the regional association, FENACOOP (and Cáceres) found itself excluded. "A campesino organization," Cáceres remarked,

can't be directed by people who aren't campesinos. . . . In ASOCODE— in confidence, through friendship, and all that—we realized that there were people who weren't agriculturalists, who didn't understand. If I'm not an agriculturalist and to understand the problem of production I have to read a document, that puts me at a disadvantage. Because, in addition to reading it, I have to commit myself, to take it to heart [asumirlo]. But if I'm an agriculturalist, I definitely understand the crisis of maize—that's my production: maize, cassava, citrus. I understand it because I live it; moreover, I've committed my family's economic base and my intellect to it. There's a combination of the personal, the social, the interest group [gremio], and the political. . . . We're not outside, nor [are we] on top. We're on the inside. The critical thing is that [the leader] be a producer. He can be an old-timer or someone who recently got involved, or who inherited the farm—not necessarily just a campesino from the countryside but someone who is a producer. When we talk

about leaders, when we get together among ourselves, we say that we
need an embrace that encourages us and not an embrace that strangles.
(Cáceres Baca 1997)

The depictions of ASOCODE as a "whirlwind of events and seminars" or "an
embrace that strangles" unknowingly echo Annelise Riles's assertion that a key
distinctive characteristic of network activity is "its dual quality as both a means
to an end and an end in itself" (2000, 51). While the Fijian and Pacific women's
organizations that Riles studied might not seem the most obvious point of comparison for analyzing a male-dominated peasant association in Central America, the organizational forms and knowledge practices of each are strikingly
similar and suggestive of patterns that are likely ubiquitous in global civil society. First, there is the constitution of networks that appear, formally, to link
organizations but that also, informally, are based significantly on personal ties
between activists (and between activists and funders) and on processes of exclusion which, despite a pervasive rhetoric of inclusion and consensus, reflect
an unwillingness to accommodate political differences (or a tendency to explain
them as personal in nature), even when these do not exceed the statutory or self-
defined mission of the network. Second, there is an aesthetics that manifests
itself in network "artifacts," such as glossy newsletters for external consumption
and "agendas," directories, "platforms for action," and funding proposals for internal and donor consumption. And, third, there is a proclivity for demonstrat-
ing the effectiveness of the network with reference to its own self-description and
activities. Network practices of representation—submitting proposals, organizing
meetings, collecting data, drafting documents—are, Riles argues, all too familiar to academics, which is perhaps one reason scholars of social movements and
civil society have often been unable to establish analytical distance from their
objects of study. "In its parody of social scientific analysis . . . ," she writes, "the
Network plays on academic sentimentality about finally having found a 'people'
who speak our language, who answer our questions on our own terms. It ap-
peals to our collective fantasy about linking up with our subjects and finding in
the 'data' exactly what we set out to find" (Riles 2000, 174).

Why are processes of network genesis and decomposition so integrally related, as I suggested earlier in this chapter? This becomes clearer if we accept as
a working hypothesis Riles's position that network activity has a "dual quality
as both a means to an end and an end in itself." In the case of ASOCODE, the
formation of new networks was ostensibly intended to broaden common struggles by incorporating new constituencies. The Central American Indigenous
Council, for example, founded at a 1994 ASOCODE meeting in Panama, sought
to involve native peoples alongside non-native peasants in a wide range of

campaigns. It also served, however, as a new institutional vehicle for approaching donors and attracting funds. Unable to shake its image as a creation of European Union cooperation agencies, its impact was minimal (Tilley 2002, 542–550). As ASOCODE entered into decline, the other regional and extra-regional networks it generated took on increasing importance for some of its leaders as sources of employment and outlets for continued activism. This activism, however, remained largely confined to the existing network modes—seminars, workshops, and congresses, each with its corresponding declaration, poster, and funding agency report.

As if to make this dynamic even clearer, in 2001, two new transnational peasant networks emerged in the Central American region. A decade earlier, the most salient elite-led regional free-market project was the SICA, and peasant efforts to "globalize from below" took place within the Central American region and in explicit opposition to the vision of the dominant groups. Now, however, anxieties about the SICA had shifted and political space was reconfigured as a result of Mexican President Vicente Fox's proposed Plan Puebla-Panamá (PPP), a new regional integration project, funded primarily by the Inter-American Development Bank, that sought to link southern Mexico and the Central American isthmus in a single free-trade and development zone. One network—the Mesoamerican Peasant Meeting (Plataforma Encuentro Campesino Mesoamericano, ECM)—arose to oppose the PPP, fueled in part by Guatemala's CONIC (National Indigenous and Peasant Coordination, Coordinadora Nacional Indígena y Campesina) and by the CLOC, another network that had recently moved its headquarters to Guatemala. While Central America (without Mexico) was the key regional reference point for regional cross-border peasant organizing in the 1990s, the PPP expanded the relevant space to Mesoamerica, which is usually understood to include Mexico and most of Central America. In 2002, the president of an almost moribund ASOCODE joined Mexican organizations in convening the meetings and remarked that the new ECM network "was betting on Mesoamerica as a space of convergence" (CCS-Chiapas 2002; Bartra 2002). The group's action plan called for gaining the ECM "public recognition as Regional Coordinator" of the organized peasantry in Mexico and Central America, a status previously claimed, in the latter zone at least, by ASOCODE. Thus the ECM's declarations made no mention of earlier networks in the region that had raised similarly militant opposition to free trade (and that still existed, or claimed to), or of the implications of the redundancies of old and new networks operating in largely the same terrain, made up of many of the same organizations and advancing similar demands (ECM 2002a, 2002b).

The second network to emerge in 2001 had a more ambivalent position regarding PPP and was concerned primarily with influencing the impending free-trade treaty between the Central American countries and the United States and, secondarily, the proposed Free Trade Area of the Americas. The Meso-american Initiative on Trade, Integration, and Sustainable Development (Iniciativa Mesoamericana de Comercio, Integración y Desarrollo Sostenible, commonly known as Iniciativa CID) brought together organizations excluded from ASOCODE and the Via Campesina as well as other peasant organizations (such as Honduras's COCOCH) that were key players in both. It also included a range of research and action-oriented NGOs from Mexico and Central America, suggesting that the geographical scope of network activity was broadening irrespective of political orientation. Ironically, both of the activists quoted above as eschewing transnational networking in favor of national politics, Jorge Hernández and Sinforiano Cáceres, were participants in this new initiative, along with their respective organizations in Costa Rica and Nicaragua (Iniciativa CID 2002). Supported in part by Oxfam International and the AFL-CIO, this group sought to dialogue with the Inter-American Development Bank and to identify possible "opportunities" that might exist for grassroots organizations in the proposed free-trade treaties. This orientation, as well as the funding sources, was suggestive of an emerging fissure in the peasant networks between pragmatic elements who, along with Oxfam, called for making trade fair, and what might be termed "rejectionists" who, like Food First, demanded that agriculture be taken out of the World Trade Organization and who favored strengthening localized rather than global markets for small agriculturalists' output (curiously invoking new interpretations of concepts such as "subsidiarity," which is the EU governing principle—articulated first in the Maastricht Treaty—that decision making should be as close to the community level as possible).

It would probably overstate the case to suggest that networks don't ever work or that they simply propagate endlessly with no measurable impact. The development in Central America of a significant sector of highly sophisticated peasant activists could be viewed as one indicator of impressive success and of the inadequacy of Gramsci's concept of "organic intellectuals," whom he assumed would never emerge from the peasantry (Gramsci 1972, 6). Of the various networks ASOCODE helped to initiate, several are moribund (or virtually so), but others—like those just mentioned that were born in 2001—maintain intense programs of activity. Those that survive seemed to have learned different lessons from the experience of the 1990s. The Via Campesina, headquartered in Honduras, has a lean organizational structure, which suggests that the dangers of network macrocephaly have been taken into account. It has also achieved a high profile in global justice movements, singled out by *Newsweek* following the 2001 Group of Eight (G8) summit in Genoa as one of eight "kinder, gentler globalist" groups behind the anti-G8 protests (Newsweek 2001, 17). Ironically, though, its presence in Honduras is entirely due to the erstwhile strength of ASOCODE, which was once perceived as the most dynamic of the regional units of Via Campesina. The diversity of rural interests that became a source of conflict in ASOCODE and the strong influence of organizations with pronounced verticalist tendencies (such as the Brazilian Landless Rural Workers Movement, Movimento dos Trabalhadores Rurais sem Terra, MST) have, however, contributed to processes of exclusion from the Via Campesina. The CICAFOC network has shown itself to be similarly vital, in large part by keeping overhead low and by prioritizing the on-the-ground needs of its local base organizations.

"On the ground" is an inescapable dimension of successful social movements, though not necessarily of the kind of networks that incorporate social movements or that—like the "dot causes," internet-based advocacy groups with immeasurable constituencies (Anheier and Themudo 2002)—describe themselves unproblematically as social movements. The appearance of "dot causes" and "shell" organizations and networks clearly complicates social scientists' (as well as donors' and policymakers') efforts to evaluate activists' claims. Some suggest that research focus not on organizations, which tends to privilege their claims and obscure less formal processes of political and cultural change, but on the broader "social fields" in which organizations operate (Burdick 1998); this, though, is more easily done with place-based social movements than with transnational networks. The phenomenon of virtual or fictitious organizations also raises thorny questions of accountability, democracy, and representation. Part of the potential power of virtual organizations is that their representational claims are difficult or impossible to evaluate, and they may have an impact that is out of proportion to their real numbers—including, at times, impacts that contravene or obstruct the decisions of democratically elected, genuinely representative institutions. While global civil society groups have rightly sought to hold supranational governance institutions, such as the World Bank, responsible for their actions, the nature of the accountability that ought to be expected of NGOs and social movement organizations and networks is far from clear. As if the emergence of hybrid organizational forms were not enough, responsibilities to elected and appointed leadership bodies, dues-paying members and affiliated organizations, donors and beneficiaries, real and imagined constituencies, and broader publics can become hopelessly confused and a source of considerable contention.

Tellingly, even before the ASOCODE network's decline, the images that peasant activists used to describe its shortcomings were rich in metaphors of flight and distance from the ground (and some of my richest interviews for this project have occurred—or been arranged—at airports and in the planes that shuttle between Central America's capital cities). Some activists in the mid-1990s grumbled about the leadership as a "*jet set campesino*," while others noted the network's seeming inability to "land" or bring its ambitious "action platforms" to the ground (*aterrizar*). In a moment of self-critical, retrospective candor, ASOCODE's first general coordinator recognized that "when a leader originates at the base [and then] becomes bureaucratized and distant from the base, the people say that he's become like a kite (*se papaloteó*), that he goes up and up into the sky, and then suddenly the string breaks and he's lost" (Campos Cerdas 2001).

Part 3

SUBSISTENCE CRISES AND FOOD SOVEREIGNTY

BRINGING THE MORAL ECONOMY BACK IN . . . TO THE STUDY OF TWENTY-FIRST-CENTURY TRANSNATIONAL PEASANT MOVEMENTS

In 2003, the American Anthropological Association held a presidential session at its annual meeting on *Moral Economies, State Spaces, and Categorical Violence: Conversations with James Scott*. This chapter, which was originally presented there, appeared two years later as part of a special issue of *American Anthropologist*.

In this chapter, I would like to revisit one of James Scott's earlier works—*The Moral Economy of the Peasant* (1976)—and argue for its continuing relevance for understanding peasant movements of the late twentieth and twenty-first centuries. There are several reasons for these arguments. First, Scott's entire oeuvre is firmly grounded in the study of agrarian politics, and the other articles in this special section of *American Anthropologist*, apart from K. Sivaramakrishnan's introduction, focus primarily on its implications for a range of non-agrarian social scientific debates. Second, a consideration of certain instances of peasant collective action in relation to Scott's work on "moral economy" and early twentieth-century Southeast Asian peasant rebellions can highlight how agrarian movements, politics, and economies have changed in recent decades. In particular, now that peasant and small farmer movements have a significant transnational dimension, it is worth asking how the content of notions such as "moral economy" and "subsistence crisis"—both elaborated mainly with reference to localized struggles and disasters—shifted in the context of changing forms of peasant economy and politics. And third, revisiting *The Moral Economy of the Peasant* will allow an examination of some of the diverse theoretical

currents that converged in this extraordinary book as well as its impact on subsequent debates in agrarian studies.

Moral Economy

One of the more thorough efforts to trace the origins and shifting boundaries
of this idea is E. P. Thompson's essay on "The Moral Economy Reviewed" (1991),
which appeared twenty years after his famous, pioneering article on the English
crowd and fifteen years after Scott's *Moral Economy of the Peasant*. Thompson
locates the first mentions of "moral economy" in the late eighteenth and early
nineteenth centuries, when Chartists and other critics of capitalism juxtaposed
it to the laissez-faire "political economy" espoused by "'quacks'" (1991, 336–337).[1]
Surveying with his characteristic piquant skepticism the diversity of approaches
spawned by his essay on the English crowd, Thompson reminds us that his own
conception of the moral economy was "in general . . . confined to confrontations
in the market-place over access (or entitlement) to 'necessities'–essential food,"
and particularly over profiteering and the beliefs, usages, forms, and deep emo-
tions that surround "the marketing of food in time of dearth" (1991, 337–338).
The eighteenth-century protesters and rioters Thompson celebrated railed
against grain hoarding and windfall profits, agriculturalists who sold to intermediaries instead of in weekly markets, millers and bakers who short-weighted
or adulterated products, exports that received "bounties," and prices that were
not customary or to their liking.

Scott's use of "moral economy" does not stray far from Thompson's. It places
somewhat less emphasis, however, on consumers' participation in food markets
than on values or mores, specifically producers' expectations about and notions
of a right to "just prices" (including "just" rents and taxes), as well as other sorts
of entitlements, such as access to land, gleaning or fishing rights, rights-of-way
across landowner properties, and redistributive mechanisms and forms of reciprocity that linked peasants with elites and with each other. Scott's approach,
incorporating these other elements, is also more explicitly concerned with developing a "phenomenological theory of exploitation" (Scott 1976, 161, 31).[2] Most
peasants, according to Scott, held deeply rooted beliefs about the right to "subsistence security" (1976, 35). They manifested a generalized aversion to risks that
might threaten this security and an utter dread of those "thresholds" past which
a household could spiral downward to hunger and misery (1976, 101). These subjective elements or *mentalité* in turn become key determinants of where, in any
given conjuncture, peasants ended up on the shadowy continuum between apparent quiescence and open rebellion.[3]

Peasant conceptions of justice, as described by Scott for Southeast Asia in the late nineteenth and early twentieth centuries, are not, in their general outlines, very much different for other times and places (say, late twentieth-century Latin America), which is part of why his book has had such resonance. "Just price" or "price over cost"—*precio sobre costo*, as I have heard dozens of contemporary Central American agriculturalists put it, often with a spark of outrage in their eyes—is at the core of this thinking. Also significant are the expectations, developed over long historical time, of what states and elites may claim and in turn must also provide in times of necessity. Finally, the issues of what values are commensurable, of what can be turned into a commodity, and of what natural or commonly held resources can be appropriated for private use and profit also loom large in the rural poor's understanding of justice. Today, the specific resources targeted for commodification are different from a century ago, but the moral discourse of the affected peasants is remarkably similar. The "right of subsistence," too, remains important, but for peasant movements in recent decades and in diverse world regions (as I shall describe in more detail below), it has broadened to the "right to continue being agriculturalists." This means, in essence, the right to continue living from the land, and it means the protection of a patrimony both of public-sector institutions (which made being an agriculturalist possible and which are now targeted by neoliberal privatizers) and of plant germplasm and cheese cultures that peasants' antagonists now sometimes euphemize and covet as "intellectual property." Moreover, in many countries those public-sector institutions—commodities boards, extension agencies, land reform and irrigation programs, among others—generated upward "historical movement in subsistence expectations" (Haugerud 1995, 10–11). While the "subsistence standard" was probably never static in any society, rising expectations, fueled in many cases by government programs and politicians' rhetoric, have meant that landlord-, market-, or state-based threats to economic opportunity, accumulation, or *improved* welfare are now at least as important as challenges to village autonomy or historical practices of reciprocity.

One of the enduring contributions of Thompson and Scott was to highlight the extent to which "markets" are political constructions and outcomes of social struggle. This may be appreciated by returning for just a moment to a revealing phrase that occurs in Thompson's definition of moral economy: *"confrontations in the market-place."* A marketplace, of course, evokes a concrete location. From our vantage point today, it is sometimes difficult to grasp that even in the mid-nineteenth century, "market" by itself often referred primarily to a specific physical location where particular types of goods were stored and traded (Moreno Fraginals 1985, 11). Only later did it assume the metaphorical and deterritorialized qualities that increasingly adhere to it. The political sleight of hand that accompanied this semantic shift involved making the institutions that actually shaped markets invisible, as well as creating the appearance of a separate and autonomous economic domain disembedded from society. The great achievement of Adam Smith, David Ricardo, Thomas Malthus, and other classical political economists was, as Michael Perelman (2000) demonstrates, to promote the extension to new domains of "free" markets while simultaneously obscuring the brutal dispossession that accompanied their spread and promoting interventionist measures, which thoroughly contradicted laissez-faire doctrine, to force the poor to work. Indeed, as Joseph Stiglitz (2001, ix) remarks in his forward to the new edition of Karl Polanyi's *Great Transformation*, "Truly free markets for labor or goods have never existed." Nonetheless, Scott, in *The Moral Economy of the Peasant*, states that he deliberately accords only summary treatment to the role of market forces as threats to peasants' subsistence security because, unlike the "more politically salient" landlords and state, they were "more or less impersonal processes without any readily identifiable human agency" (1976, 58).[4] It remains largely true today that the invisible hand has no identifiable face, and peasants' "confrontations in the market-place" now occur more and more in a marketplace that no longer has a "place" in it, which naturally affects the character of their political responses. Much of the work of contemporary peasant activists consists of trying to name and put in the spotlight the institutional agency behind the increasingly deterritorialized and invasive market forces that buffet them from all sides.

Institutions, Households, Markets, Influences

The Moral Economy of the Peasant was a major intervention in the emerging field of peasant studies, in theories of collective action, and in debates about the history of the market and human nature and institutions. The Vietnam War, which ended in a crushing US defeat one year before Scott's book appeared, was of course the "defining moment" that contributed to the upsurge of interest in the late 1960s in contemporary peasantries. Also important, if more problematic, were the "Great Proletarian Cultural Revolution" in China, smaller "wars of liberation" in Latin America and in the colonies and recent colonies of Africa and Asia, and the broader question of how the agrarian structures of poor, largely rural countries had shaped—and might influence in the future—processes of underdevelopment and development (Bernstein and Byres 2001, 2; Salemink 2003).

Early in the twenty-first century, it may be hard to recall that only forty years ago this understanding of the peasant as a major historical protagonist was widely shared by scholars, policymakers and revolutionaries.[5] Scott's *Moral Economy* came toward the end of a wave of foundational books in peasant studies, both building on such works and insistently injecting a new cultural and even psychological dimension that they sometimes lacked or downplayed. Eric Wolf's *Peasant Wars of the Twentieth Century* (1969)—itself "an outgrowth of the [Vietnam] teach-in movement" (Roseberry 1995, 161)—analyzed six cases that argued for peasantries' central role in some of the most dramatic upheavals of the decades since the 1910 Mexican Revolution.[6] In *Social Origins of Dictatorship and Democracy* (1966), Barrington Moore compared eight cases (England, France, Germany, Russia, the United States, China, Japan, and India) and linked agrarian relations—and particularly the fate of reactionary landlord classes—to distinct bourgeois democratic, capitalist authoritarian, and revolutionary socialist routes to modernity. The rediscovery and translation into English (and Spanish) of Russian economist A. V. Chayanov's *Theory of Peasant Economy* (1966) enriched understanding of peasant household dynamics, identified specific peasant forms of economic rationality, and sparked heated polemics over whether rural social differentiation produced distinct classes of wealthy and poor peasants or, alternatively, whether such differences resulted from the age and demographic makeup of rural households, with younger units having more dependents and fewer workers and thus less wealth than older units.[7]

Moore's and Wolf's analyses, in somewhat different ways, revolved principally around states and agrarian structures, positing societal explanations for political-economic outcomes. For example, Moore considered "certain agrarian social features"—such as a weak landed aristocracy or the "taming" of peasants through their incorporation into "appropriate" forms of commercial agriculture (or their near-complete displacement, as in England)—to be key in explaining why some societies successfully achieved a bourgeois democratic modernization. Other societies, where commercial agriculture relied on repression of rural labor and alliances formed between landowners and emerging industrial interests, suffered reactionary "revolutions from above" or, where large rural proletariats existed and landowners with a weak market orientation dominated the state, communist revolutions from below (Moore 1966, 414–660). While Moore maintained that reciprocity between peasants and landlords, as well as peasant "moral standards" about justice and risk sharing, contributed to political stability in agrarian societies, he considered culture "an intervening variable" and adamantly rejected the idea that the subjective experience of exploitation might alone trigger rebellion (1966, 468–471, 485, 497).

Wolf, much like Moore, pointed to "traditional arrangements" and the "accustomed institutional context" as features that reduced peasants' risks and, if subverted, produced "psychological, economic, social, and political tensions" that could, given the right conditions, lead to rebellion (1969, xiv–xv). In a related observation in an earlier work, he suggested that peasants are required to divide the wealth they produce between a replacement fund (for biological survival), a ceremonial fund (that reinforces village-level solidary relations), and a fund of rent for landlords, moneylenders, and the state (Wolf 1966). The ceremonial fund, in this conception, consists of resources for reinforcing horizontal relations of reciprocity (one aspect of what Scott later termed "moral economy"). Wolf's central conclusions in *Peasant Wars*, however, dealt only indirectly with the experiential impact of unraveling "traditional arrangements" and was concerned instead with the prominent role of "middle" peasants (and of "free" peasants in peripheral zones) in successful agrarian rebellions and revolutions. Put simply, these social groups, located in comparable ways in systems of class relations, were most vulnerable to market-induced threats and most exposed to ideological influences originating in urban areas (Wolf 1969, 290–295). Wolf did not consider violations of traditional arrangements unimportant in explaining rural unrest, but he emphasized changing property relations and modes of labor mobilization more than peasants' subjective experience of such changes.

Chayanov, in contrast to Moore and Wolf, was less concerned with broader political processes than with elucidating household dynamics, specifically the tendency of peasant families both to engage in "self-exploitation," squeezing available labor as much as possible for tiny increments in production, and to underutilize labor when marginal returns to increased work resulted in subjectively unacceptable levels of "drudgery" (Chayanov 1966, 81–85). Scott's view of the rural household in *The Moral Economy of the Peasant* reflects Chayanov's thinking, particularly in its portrayal of peasant families as seeking stable subsistence rather than higher-risk maximum returns (Scott 1976, 15–19). Employing—a bit uncharacteristically—the language of neoclassical economics (much as Chayanov did), Scott writes that peasant labor is characterized by low opportunity cost (i.e., a near absence of alternative employment possibilities) and "high marginal utility of income for those near the subsistence level" (1976, 14–15). Two claims of Chayanov thus stand out as influences on Scott: the claim that there is a *subjectively* unacceptable level of drudgery past which individuals will cease to work and that the rural poor engage in an unremitting pursuit of subsistence, as opposed to accumulation (although, as noted above, a rising living standard and accumulation have been incorporated into many contemporary peasants' expectations about subsistence).

One objective of *The Moral Economy of the Peasant* is to move beyond Chayanov's restricted focus on family units to the exclusion of other social relations, such as village-based networks of solidarity and mutual support, but to nonetheless examine the implications of his insights into household economics and psychology for larger political transformations. Scott's book thus bridged the scholarship focused on states and agrarian structures, on the one hand, and the scholarship that was concerned primarily with the peasant family, labor allocation, and household budgets, on the other. It did so with greater attention to the role of subjectivity in political contention than was present in the work of others, such as Wolf, whose historical-structural approach also sought, somewhat differently, to connect these different levels of analysis.

The Moral Economy of the Peasant, like Chayanov's *Theory of Peasant Economy*, makes an anti-maximizing argument, and it is here that Scott's intervention in the collective action debates is most apparent. In the Vietnam War era, there was at once a worldwide efflorescence of social movements and the emergence of influential, interrelated paradigms that stressed the self-interested rationality of individual actors and the difficulties, if not the impossibility, of producing collective goods. Paradoxically perhaps, given the thousands who were marching in the streets for civil rights and against the Vietnam War, Mancur Olsen (1965) argued that individuals (presumably in all times and places) were so rational that they would not risk joining collective action because they could benefit from others' activity by pursuing low-risk, self-interested "free rider" strategies at the expense of the group. Like Garrett Hardin's (1968) "tragedy of the commons" model (and the growing body of social scientific work on prisoner's dilemma games, incentive problems, and moral hazards), the "collective action problem" assumed collaboration could only occur if individuals—each epitomizing a universal, calculating *homo economicus*—were induced to join group efforts through rewards or sanctions.[8] The critiques of Scott's book, most famously Samuel Popkin's *The Rational Peasant* (1979), employed this language of individual rationality and "free riders" to argue that for peasants, the "insurance" of village norms of reciprocity and traditional patron–client relations was less reliable, and the potential gains of markets more favorable, than Scott and the other "moral economists" had indicated.[9]

While space constraints preclude giving the critics their due here, it is worth observing that they often engaged in a romanticization of the market rather like the romanticization of village communities—which, they charged, characterized the work of the moral economists. Popkin (1979, 72), for example, asserted that

> while exposure to international and national markets does subject peasants to new and different kinds of uncertainty, larger markets tend to maintain steadier prices and far more certain supplies of food over time. . . . With expansion . . . the actual "insurance value of money," that is, the probability that money saved in a good year will find food

to buy in a bad year, itself increases and peasants have a form of protection which they did not have within smaller market areas.[10]

Popkin's comment is, of course, emblematic of one pole in a larger debate over market society. In *The Moral Economy of the Peasant*, Scott (1976, 5n8) pays "tribute" to the "formative" role that Polanyi's *Great Transformation* (1957) played in his thinking. While this appreciation is given little explicit acknowledgment elsewhere in *The Moral Economy*, Scott's vision of peasant economy as embedded in a framework of intra- and inter-class reciprocal relations echoes Polanyi's rejection of the presumption that economy constitutes an analytically autonomous domain apart from social institutions. Scott maintains that village-level systems of reciprocity produce, over long historical time, widely held moral expectations. Market forces (sometimes in combination with environmental ones) pose challenges to these expectations and may, when thresholds of what is culturally acceptable are crossed, produce rebellion and collective resistance.

Curiously, given the central place that Scott accorded these long-standing expectations and the upheavals that accompany their violation, Popkin charged that the moral economic approach wrongly considers peasant society "stable" (1979, 29). William Booth, a more recent critic, claims that it is "oriented toward the static state" and that "one of the major inadequacies of the moral economic model . . . [is] that it has only thin theoretical resources with which to explain economic change—why economic regimes come into being and pass away" (1994, 658).

These interpretations miss another significant influence on the author of *The Moral Economy of the Peasant*, although one that is again, like that of Polanyi, barely made explicit. In Scott's preface, he acknowledges a debt to the *Annales* "school of historiography" and particularly to Marc Bloch, Emmanuel Le Roy Ladurie, and those researchers working on *mentalités populaires* (Scott 1976, viii). The Annales historians were, of course, too disputatious to constitute a coherent school—"with a Pope, or two, at the top," as Lucien Febvre, one of the journal's first editors, once remarked (Aguirre Rojas 1999, 12). Moreover, in different periods, the approaches that dominated the Annales group varied considerably, from the painstakingly detailed studies of rural life of Bloch and Le Roy Ladurie to the anthropological history of the scholars of mentalités populaires. While the concern with subjectivity of the latter group resonates with Scott's emphasis on the importance of culturally defined consumption standards (and with Chayanov's treatment of "drudgery"), a third Annales tendency—the serial history of *longues durées* pioneered by Ernest Labrousse and made famous by Fernand Braudel—also raised issues that figure as important analytical underpinnings of Scott's *Moral Economy of the Peasant*. This is especially evident, it

seems to me, in Scott's consideration of the factors that mediate between subsistence crises and peasant rebellions.

Subsistence Crises

Subsistence crisis surely has a genealogy that goes back to the neolithic. Crop
diseases, pest infestations, floods, droughts, and frosts have frustrated agriculturalists and contributed to social upheavals for ten millennia. In the contemporary social sciences, subsistence crisis and similar ideas have often raised
the tension between the quantifiable measure and the subjective experience of
shortage that Scott handles so deftly in *The Moral Economy*. Annales-style serial history brought a new emphasis on graphing prices and wages, agricultural
yields, land rents, and costs of living and on identifying seasonal, cyclical, and
long-term trends. While this did not signify a complete break with the earlier
approaches of Bloch and his collaborators, it did tend to displace attention from
land use, agricultural technology, property systems, and the juridical status of
rural labor. Even though proponents of the new serial history claimed to be seeking alternatives to empty economic reductionism, the very nature of their
sources and research procedures sometimes encouraged interpretations that gave
short shrift to the cultural and political mediation of crises, particularly when
they led to collective action.

Ernest Labrousse, for example, one of the pioneers of quantitative serial history (and a leading figure in the Annales group), asked in one of his earliest empirical studies and in his major methodological treatise whether France in 1789
was a "revolution of misery or prosperity." He proceeded to invoke as a proximate
cause of the French Revolution a two-year "subsistence crisis" that led to increased fiscal demands and that dashed rising expectations (among the peasantry, proletariat, and bourgeoisie) generated during a much longer period of
expanding prosperity (Labrousse 1962, 365–366). Similarly, Enrique Florescano
ascribed the 1810 Mexican War of Independence in large part to preceding agricultural crises and famines, despite a recounting of struggles between peasants
and authorities redolent with discourses of moral economy (1969, 4:172–179).[11]

Explanations such as these—and the term "subsistence crisis" itself—raise a
host of questions. First, of course, is the empirical validity and interpretation of
the data series themselves. Le Roy Ladurie (1996, 491 n50), for example, termed
Labrousse's account of the French Revolution "debatable" and "unconvincing,"
and asked why the conclusions of this work have been "piously repeated for almost half a century." Second, narrowly conceived serial history was often notable for what it left out. The role of the Napoleonic Wars in weakening Spain's

hold over its American colonies, to cite another case, received scarcely a mention in Florescano's examination of the years leading up to Mexican independence. Third, the term "subsistence," especially but not only when applied to contemporary agriculturalists, suggests self-provisioning, autarchic "subsistence farmers" or "subsistence peasantries" and tends to obscure the relation with the market that small producers may have, especially in years of high yields and surpluses (or in years of low yields, as consumers of purchased staple foods acquired at high prices).[12] Fourth, and most important, shortening the analytical distance between graphs of price movements and revolutionary upheavals risked simplifying the complexities of popular expectations, social relations, and even "human nature" itself. It was, Thompson commented, a manifestation of

> the schizoid intellectual climate, which permits this quantitative historiography to co-exist (in the same places and sometimes in the same minds) with a social anthropology which derives from Durkheim, Weber, or Malinowski. We know all about the delicate tissue of social norms and reciprocities which regulates the life of Trobriand islanders, and the psychic energies involved in the cargo cults of Melanesia; but at some point this infinitely-complex social creature, Melanesian man, becomes (in our histories) the eighteenth-century English collier who claps his hand spasmodically upon his stomach, and responds to elementary economic stimuli. (Thompson 1971, 78)

If "moral economy" (and English "cultural history") thus emerged as an alternative to "spasmodic" or economic reductionist history, the incorporation of greater complexity inevitably generated analytical tensions.[13] In *The Moral Economy of the Peasant*, Scott develops the concepts of "subsistence minimum" or "level" and "subsistence crisis" as part of an effort to understand the impact of the longue durée on daily life. He illustrates the instability of peasant agriculture over time (a dimension of his work largely overlooked by critics such as Popkin and Booth) and the consistency of elites' claims on it with both hypothetical and actual data series (Scott 1976, 15–16, 29–31, 118–120).[14] At times, he accords considerable weight to the trends themselves, as when he indicates the likelihood that per capita income and rice prices declined in Vietnam in the 1900–1940 period, the last decades of the major peasant uprisings in the northern and north central parts of the country as well as in lower Burma, which was similarly affected by the Great Depression of the 1930s (Scott 1976, 56–57, 120). But when Scott employs such serial reasoning, it is in the service of a more subtle argument about the interplay between the objective indicators and subjective experiences that shape the subsistence crisis. In early twentieth-century Southeast

Asia, according to Scott, subsistence crises arose as a result of fluctuations in natural yields, world-market prices, and "mono-crop" prices (1976, 197), all combined with a subjective experience of each event and elite responses to it that led peasants to view it as a violation of the moral order. "Beyond . . . brute physiological needs," he writes, "there is clearly an historical dimension to subsistence levels in which minimum standards bear some relation to previous experience" (Scott 1976, 17).

How has the nature of subsistence crises changed in the late twentieth and twenty-first centuries, and to what political effect? In most places, peasant involvement with markets has only intensified in the past few decades. For thinking about what a subsistence crisis means today, Scott's emphasis on fluctuation of prices and yields may be a bit too historically specific. The downward secular trend in the prices of many internationally traded agricultural commodities has lasted twenty or more years—that is, almost a generation.[15] There are still occasional booms in particular markets (e.g., soybeans), but the periodicity in agricultural prices, particularly of key staple foods and internationally traded commodities (e.g., cereals, oilseeds, coffee, cotton, sugar, cacao) appears to have greatly diminished or, in some cases, even disappeared (FAO 2000; Aksoy and Beghin 2005). There is little reason to suppose that the downward price trend will reverse itself more than momentarily, given the ever greater linkages between marketplaces, the high-yielding technologies that fill the silos and warehouses and glut the markets, the persistence—despite the World Trade Organization (WTO) and all the neoliberal discourse—of European Union (EU) and US export subsidies and dumping, and the efforts of the major agribusiness corporations to drive down prices at the farm gate.[16]

A frost in the coffee-growing regions of Brazil, for instance, used to be cause for rejoicing in Colombia, Central America, and East Africa, but it is no longer. Indeed, the 1994 frost in Brazil had only minimal impact on international coffee prices (Aksoy and Beghin 2005, 304). In the past decade, Vietnam and Indonesia, traditional tea-drinking countries encouraged to enter coffee production by the World Bank, glutted the market so thoroughly that many Latin American and East African coffee producers have simply given up.[17] In most coffee-producing countries, the dismantling—as a consequence of neoliberal reforms—of single-desk marketing agencies or state commodities boards has meant that supply management mechanisms are difficult or impossible to enforce. The stories for the other commodities are different, but the broad picture is not dissimilar. The subsistence crisis has become a permanent state.

Changing Peasantries

The peasants of today are not the same peasants of the 1960s and 1970s, when "peasant studies" began to occupy an important place in the social sciences in Latin America, Asia, Africa, Europe, and North America. Nor are they entirely the same peasants of *The Moral Economy of the Peasant*. Particularly since the global economic upheaval signaled by the 1970s collapse of the Bretton Woods fixed exchange rate system and controls on capital movements (Helleiner 1994), the rural world has experienced deepening, interconnected crises. In many societies, urbanization has diminished the political clout of rural areas and contributed to the reconfiguration and, at times, the disintegration of peasant household enterprises.[18]

Already in 1976, Mexican anthropologist Arturo Warman wrote of the "devilish dialectic" that tormented the peasants of central Mexico:

> To satisfy the demands of "growth and development" the campesinos have intensified their activity, making it more diverse, complex and arduous to meet a rate of exploitation that is higher, and more ubiquitous and harsh. To be "modern"—to graft fruit trees, to fertilize with chemicals, to harvest products that are too expensive for them to consume—the campesinos have had to become more "traditional." They have to plant the maize that they are going to eat . . . [and] establish reciprocal relations for the direct, non-capitalist exchange of labor and resources. They have had to reproduce themselves and expand the size of their surplus labor force. (Warman 1976, 15)

In Mexico and elsewhere, the situation today is usually, if anything, harsher and the rate of exploitation higher still than when Warman wrote about Morelos. In *The Moral Economy of the Peasant*, Scott (1976, 85) points to "rude shocks . . . linked to the world market" as destroying subsistence security in early twentieth-century Asia, but he is mainly referring to commodities and, secondarily, credit markets. Today, multiple and intensified involvements in markets—for commodities, credit, technology, land, services of all kinds—have brought growing and interconnected vulnerabilities. Peasants' widespread adoption of modern technologies, even when employed in traditional cultivation systems, has deepened dependence on the cash economy and exacerbated the multiple environmental and health catastrophes too often associated with industrial agriculture. The subsistence crises of droughts, floods, insects, crop blights, animal diseases, and plummeting prices still occur, but they are compounded by new risks and more uncertainty and by the punishing impacts of two decades of economic liberalization and institutional restructuring. The cumulative effect of today's "rude shocks" is arguably more violent and brusque than in 1930s Southeast Asia. The secular decline in agricultural prices mentioned above is part of this, but so are privatizations of state development banks, extension agencies, and commodities boards and the ever-growing concentration and vertical integration among the giant corporations that supply inputs and control the lion's share of agricultural trade. The disappearance of subsidies once provided by now debilitated welfare states, even in some less-developed countries, has put small producers ever more at the mercy of local loan sharks, intermediaries, and increasingly capricious and distant invisible forces. The evisceration and reversal of agrarian reforms, which elites abhor as obstacles to the free play of market forces, have contributed to reducing the peasant land base and shattering hope (Zoomers and van der Haar 2000). Nonagricultural employment and entrepreneurial activity have almost everywhere become essential for the rural poor's survival.[19]

Not surprisingly, given this grim panorama, diasporas of country people have scattered throughout the world, affecting rural livelihoods and reshaping peasant imaginaries and politics. Today's campesinos, when they remain on the land, have frequently had to learn not just about fertilizing with chemicals or grafting fruit trees, as Warman suggested, but about the language of bankers and lawyers, market intelligence and computers, business administration and phytosanitary measures, biotechnology and intellectual property, and at least the rudiments of trade policy and macroeconomics. They have had to become sophisticated and worldly.

In recent years, urban and rural culture have converged in so many ways that it is necessary to consider the possibility of a new, contemporary, rural moral economy informed by an urban imaginary and urban consumption expectations. To some extent this convergence, the rising "subsistence standard" referred to above, stems from demographic shifts that create new strains internal to peasant households. Expanding the size of the "surplus labor force" (as Warman put it) of peasants is no longer a simple matter. Even in rural areas, improved access to schooling, growing reliance on off-farm employment, and declining average fertility reduce the numbers of available family laborers and intensify pressures on those who are still farming to provide an ever higher level of consumption for the entire household. This in turn strains extended family ties and limits possibilities of participating in diverse kinds of collective endeavors. At the same time that the expectations of peasants have risen, in many less-developed countries the rural–urban gap (in living standards, in consumption, in life chances) has only widened. This combination of converging expectations and diverging life chances has potentially explosive consequences. As Uruguayan essayist Eduardo Galeano (2000, 25) observes, "Advertising enjoins everyone to consume, while the economy prohibits the vast majority of humanity from doing so. The command that everybody do what so many cannot becomes an invitation to crime." Or, one might add, to collective action.

"There Is No World Market": Moral Economy and Today's Peasant Movements

Polanyi saw the countermovement or resistance that always accompanied the advance of "market society" as largely local or perhaps national in scope (1957, 130–134). Scott, similarly, speaks of the moral criteria of village redistributive norms. In *The Moral Economy of the Peasant*, he emphasizes that "the development of capitalism, the commercialization of agrarian relations, and the growth of a centralizing state represent the historical locus of peasant revolts in the modern era. For, above all, these large historical forces cut through the integument of subsistence customs and traditional social relations to replace them with contracts, the market, and uniform laws" (Scott 1976, 189).

In the past three decades, however, since the breakdown of the Bretton Woods system that ushered in the globalization era (and since the publication of *The Moral Economy of the Peasant*), there has occurred yet another disembedding of the market from society and a "de-moralizing of the theory of trade and consumption," to use Thompson's (1971, 89) description of the late eighteenth-century laissez-faire revolution. Whether the state has weakened under globalization or simply assumed new functions, it is often no longer the principal focus of the countermovement to the market. New supranational governance institutions, such as the WTO, International Monetary Fund and World Bank, have become major targets as well.

Peasant politics in the past two decades reflects this and has taken new, often transnational forms largely unanticipated by the peasant studies scholars of the 1960s and 1970s. Movements in different countries and regions that only a decade ago barely knew of one another's existence now routinely exchange information and delegations and mount joint lobbying, research, and protest actions. The success of the Brazilian Landless Rural Workers Movement (Movimento dos Trabalhadores Rurais sem Terra, or MST) in pressing for agrarian reform has influenced peasant organizations throughout the Americas and as far away as South Africa. Global networks of peasant and small farmer organizations, such as La Via Campesina (LVC) and APM-Mondial (Réseau Mondial Agricultures Paysannes, Alimentation et Mondialisation), link coalitions of national groups that operate within Europe, Latin America, Asia, and Africa. With their own sometimes meager resources and additional backing from European (and a few other) nongovernmental organizations (NGOs) and foundations, they have come to have a high profile in the global justice movement, including the World Social Forums in Porto Alegre and Mumbai and the anti-WTO protests in Seattle, Cancún, and elsewhere (Edelman 2003). Their member organizations have also contributed to toppling national governments, as in Ecuador in 2000 and in Bolivia in 2003.

The history of the formation of transnational peasant and small farmer networks and movements can only be outlined here.[20] The main impetus for cross-border organizing by peasants and small farmers was the 1980s world farm crisis sparked by the rapid liberalization of global agricultural trade. Small agriculturalists' organizations feared—largely correctly, as it turned out—that a more liberal trade regime would lead to lower commodity prices, the consolidation of giant agribusinesses, a homogenization of the global food system, and the erosion of supply management mechanisms and public-sector supports for farmers. Some small agriculturalists, much as Popkin predicted (see above), adapted to the newly globalized economy by entering specialized, export-oriented market niches. Many more, as Scott (1976, 59) had indicated about an earlier period in Asia, found the insecurities of the new economic situation much greater than those they traditionally faced in protected local or national markets.

Transnational networking by small agriculturalists occurred not just as a result of growing market-based threats but from a globalization of moral economic norms. In the late 1980s and early 1990s, in Europe, North America, and Central America, the advance of regional economic integration led small agriculturalists to form cross-border coalitions with counterparts in nearby countries. In India, peasant organizations questioned whether life forms that small farmers had selectively bred over hundreds of years, such as basmati rice or the seeds of the neem tree (which produced an excellent pesticide), could be privately appropriated or patented. Their protests brought worldwide attention to the Trade-Related Intellectual Property Rights (TRIPS) agreement, part of the General Agreement on Tariffs and Trade (GATT), which became the WTO in 2004. European farmers sparred with giant corporations that sought to claim exclusive ownership of age-old cheese cultures or that counterfeited local cheeses. In the early 1990s in Europe, the final round of GATT talks sparked huge demonstrations, some of which were attended by farmers from Asia, Africa, and the Americas, as well as from all over Europe. In 1993, as anti-GATT protests mounted in Europe, representatives of peasant and small farmer organizations from several dozen countries met in Belgium and founded a transnational coalition called La Via Campesina (Edelman 2003, 204–205).[21]

In just a few years, LVC had affiliated around eighty organizations in some fifty countries. Its membership is highly heterogeneous, "ranging from small dairy farmers in Germany to landless peasants in Brazil, from farm surplus-producing farmers in Karnataka (India) to land-poor peasants in Mexico, from farm workers in Nicaragua to rice farmers in South Korea" (Borras 2004, 9). Ideologically, LVC is also diverse, and participating groups frequently disagree over strategy, though all share a broad opposition to neoliberalism (albeit for sometimes different reasons and with different degrees of flexibility or intransigence). Since 1995, when LVC representatives attended the Global Assembly on Food Security in Quebec City, the coalition has had a rising international profile (Desmarais 2002, 103). Over the next decade, LVC and its member organizations have organized and participated in dozens of "parallel summits," NGO forums, and international conferences on food, agriculture, and land questions. While member groups have at times lobbied and pressured national governments around human rights and agrarian reform issues (Edelman 2003, 206–212), LVC still sees its principal political strategy as mass mobilization (Borras 2004, 24). At the same time, however, the coalition and most of its constituent organizations engage in a conscious practice of tactical flexibility and "venue shifting," seeking the local, national, or international locations—institutional and geographical—that will permit them to exercise effective pressure or otherwise attain key objectives.[22]

What are the projects of these transnational peasant and small farmer organizations, and how do they reflect moral economic sensibilities? Here again, for reasons of space, I can only begin to sketch out an answer. The demands and political campaigns of LVC focus on human rights, agrarian reform, environment and sustainable agriculture, biodiversity and genetic resources, state reform, and trade, among other issues. Many of these interrelated efforts are indicative of the continuing salience of moral economies in understanding peasant protest, although just two will be considered here. The first is the call to remove agriculture from the purview of the WTO; the second is the quest for "food sovereignty," a concept to which I will return shortly.

The demand to "take agriculture out of WTO," heard with increasing frequency since the 1999 Seattle protests and the commencement of the WTO Doha Round in early 2000, is based on several premises: (1) that agricultural production is not about just producing commodities but is a means of livelihood and nourishment for peasants and small farmers;[23] (2) that since most of the world's agricultural output is consumed domestically, global trade rules should apply only to that portion that is traded internationally;[24] (3) that "there is no 'world market' of agricultural products" but rather an international trade in surpluses of milk, cereals, and meat dumped primarily by the European Union, the United States, and members of the Cairns Group;[25] and (4) that "the WTO is undemocratic and unaccountable, has increased global inequality and insecurity, promotes unsustainable production and consumption patterns, erodes diversity, and undermines social and environmental priorities" (LVC 2001, 6). For LVC and its supporters, taking agriculture out of the WTO means not just scrapping the Agreement on Agriculture (AoA) but removing or amending relevant clauses in all other WTO accords, including TRIPS, the General Agreement on Trade in Services (GATS), Sanitary and Phytosanitary Measures (SPS), Quantitative Restrictions (QRs), and Subsidies and Countervailing Measures (SCM).

While the AoA allows national governments some leeway in protecting their producers and provides for "special and differential treatment" for less-developed WTO member nations, its overall thrust is toward a rapid phasing out of tariffs and dramatically accelerated trade liberalization. The European Union and the United States, however, have been required to make only minor reductions in their vast subsidy programs, largely because they have been able to argue that direct income supports for farmers that are "decoupled" from production levels or prices have at worst only minimal trade-distorting effects. LVC has maintained, in contrast, that such "green box" subsidies are really hidden export subsidies and that they go, in any case, primarily to large producers who are then unfairly advantaged.[26] Its activists reserve special scorn for the AoA article that prevents member countries from invoking WTO dispute settlement rules intended to provide protection from dumping. While WTO prohibits dumping (albeit with weak sanctions) as one of the most unfair and distorting trade practices, the problem persists as a result of EU and US subsidy policies. In general, however, the peasant organizations have been reluctant to attack developed-country farm subsidies except when they affect international commodity prices, dumping, and market access. This reluctance does not stem from concern that the subsidy question could be a fault line separating farmer organizations in developed countries, especially Europe, from those in poorer countries (even though in Europe, as in the United States, the vast majority of subsidies go to large producers). As Rafael Alegría, Honduran activist and LVC coordinator (1996–2004), explained in an interview:

> As an organization we can't be against subsidies, since that's precisely one thing that permits the European agriculturalists to live, to survive. More important than subsidies, though, are just prices. And the French and other European agriculturalists are very conscious of that. They say, "we'll renounce subsidies but we want good prices, 'just prices,' that we don't have now." And isn't it precisely the multinationals that get most of the subsidies? They take advantage of us and buy cheap, store it, and then sell. We're for reorienting the agro-export model, the industrial

agriculture model, in favor of an agriculture that's more sustainable and based more on the internal market. Because that other [export-oriented] model of Europe or the industrialized countries is exactly what destroys local and national markets. It's what produces social and economic dumping, as we call it. (Alegría 2001)

Alegría's remarks are suggestive of the fundamentally moral bases of contemporary transnational peasant mobilization. "Just prices," in particular, is a demand that parallels the moral economic principles that Scott described for early twentieth-century Southeast Asia. Here, though, it is invoked as a transnational or even universal norm, rather than a local or national one. Some of the actors have changed, and the relevant social field has widened to encompass global markets, but "just" behavior by the more powerful is an aspiration that still forms part of contemporary peasant activists' implicit moral economy. The language employed—more complex than in the early twentieth century—indicates familiarity with esoteric aspects of trade policy. "Dumping," for example, despite its colloquial origin, has come to have a technical definition in global trade accords (see above). As in earlier moral economy discourses, the state is viewed ambivalently, here as a benevolent provider of direct and indirect price supports, but also as an antagonist and promoter of a destructive model of production and commerce. The goal of reorienting agriculture toward the internal market would require a shoring up of the state—earlier one of the peasants' main adversaries—as a bulwark against supranational forces. The multinationals, in Alegría's view, epitomize the market actor whose weight is so great that it unfairly appropriates resources that ought to go to small producers. The rule-governed local market figures as an endangered space, the only one in which peasants have a real chance of making an adequate living. Most significant, though, for LVC, is that an anti-subsidy stance, particularly one that opposes payments for limiting production or for environmental services, would contradict the demand for "food sovereignty."[27]

"Food sovereignty" was first raised as a demand by the LVC in the mid-1990s, notably at the 1996 United Nations Food and Agriculture Organization (FAO) Food Security Conference in Rome. The concept later received greater theoretical elaboration at an international conference in 2001 in Havana that was attended by dozens of APM and LVC member organizations, then in meetings in 2002 and 2003 sponsored by the Tuscan regional government and the International Commission on the Future of Food, and in other new networks of civil society and NGOs such as the International Planning Committee for Food Sovereignty. The FAO's definition of "food security" refers to a situation—at the world, national, or household level—in which all people at all times have physical and economic access to adequate nutritious food. While FAO officials speak of food *security* as an "entitlement," LVC activists maintain that technical balances based on supplies and mouths to feed ought to be replaced with a commitment to food *sovereignty*, a broader concept that considers food a human right rather than primarily a commodity, that prioritizes local production and peasant access to land, and that upholds nations' rights to protect their producers from dumping and to implement supply management policies. "Food security . . . ," according to Peter Rosset of the Institute for Food and Development Policy, which works closely with LVC, "says nothing about where . . . food comes from or how it is produced" (Rosset 2003). "Food sovereignty," on the other hand, "does not negate trade, but rather . . . promotes the formulation of trade policies and practices that serve the rights of peoples to safe, healthy and ecologically sustainable production" (LVC 2001, 2).

Peasant and farm activists have pressed for food sovereignty in international organizations, particularly the FAO, which since 1996 regularly invites them to its conferences. They have also staged a number of events that build on a longer peasant traditions and current social movement practices of theatricality and carnivalesque protests, among them José Bové's famous "dismantling" of a half-built McDonald's restaurant in southern France; Indian peasants' attacks on the Bangalore offices of multinational grain giant Cargill; Brazilian MST supporters' uprooting of genetically modified crops; and the involvement of Basque, French, Brazilian, and Honduran activists in actions in support of Palestinian olive farmers (see chapter 1). In July 2004, for example, an International Food Sovereignty Tribunal convened in Quito, Ecuador, with the participation of Nobel Peace Prize winner Adolfo Esquivel and a panel of distinguished jurists and Indigenous and peasant organization leaders from throughout the Americas. The tribunal, which attracted massive media attention in South America, put the World Bank and the Inter-American Development Bank "on trial" for policies that have led to"the looting of natural resources through deceptive promises, pressure on governments to privatize their enterprises and national patrimony, loan negotiations that involved no consultation with the populations of our countries, and failed plans and projects throughout Latin America" (Váscomes 2004).

In September 2004, a thirty-day People's Caravan for Food Sovereignty, organized by the Pesticide Action Network, kicked off in Malaysia and wound its way through twelve other Asian countries, culminating in Nepal, where Maoist guerrillas briefly captured twenty participants and burned their vehicles (Loone 2004). The caravan held forums, carried out joint protest actions with diverse local and national peasant organizations, visited "ecological farms" and sustainable agriculture projects, and again drew large crowds and garnered substantial media coverage. Among the participants was Percy Schmeiser, a Saskatchewan farmer, who fought the Monsanto Corporation in the Canadian courts after his organic farm was contaminated with genetically engineered canola from neighboring properties. Filipino farmers who claimed to have suffered gastrointestinal ailments, skin allergies, and other symptoms after they planted Monsanto's Bt corn joined Schmeiser in a forum and rally with the banner "David vs. Goliath: Farmers Take on Monsanto."[28] Some two dozen caravan members split off from the main group and toured France, Belgium, and Germany—sponsored by the German-based Food First Information and Action Network and the French global justice organization ATTAC—where they participated in roundtable discussions with agronomists, farmers, and food activists (Wolff 2004).[29] The caravan's final declaration highlights the moral economic aspirations behind this multifaceted transnational demonstration:

> Food Sovereignty is **the inalienable RIGHT** of peoples, communities, and countries to define, decide and implement their own agricultural, labour, fishing, food and land policies which are ecologically, socially, economically and culturally appropriate to their unique circumstances. It includes the true right to food and to produce food, which means that all people have the right to safe, nutritious and culturally appropriate food and to food producing resources and technologies and the ability to sustain themselves, their resources and their societies. The People's Caravan is calling for an International Convention on Food Sovereignty in order to enshrine the principles of food sovereignty in international law and institute food sovereignty as the principal policy framework for addressing food and agriculture. (People's Caravan 2004)

In conversations with peasant and farmer activists in Latin America, North America, and Europe, I have often questioned them about the feasibility of food sovereignty and of taking agriculture out of the WTO. Two of the thorny issues that would have to be resolved are (1) defining how a bushel of wheat can be produced under different rules for export or for domestic consumption and (2) when an agricultural product ceases to be agricultural and becomes an industrial product subject to WTO rules. The activists' responses, however, tend not to focus on such intricacies but rather on two main themes: that conditions were better before the founding of the WTO and that WTO rules are profoundly hypocritical and especially so for agriculturalists in developing countries. Karen Pedersen, a young Saskatchewan beekeeper and Canadian National Farmers Union activist, attended the 2001 FAO "Rome+5" meeting on food security as part of a LVC delegation. "How practical is it to keep agriculture in the WTO?" she asked, recounting discussions at the Rome conference.

At some point we have to stop and look at our rural system the way that it is and say, "You know what? It's not working. . . . It's not distributing food. It's producing more and more food, it's exporting more and more food, but it is not distributing it. We're not gaining on world hunger." If we leave agriculture there in WTO? I mean, all we're gonna have is, we're going to have lost all our small farmers, and when the system collapses, we're not going to have any expertise to rebuild the system. . . . Agriculture is the food industry. And I'm not convinced that you should be shipping, for example, hogs around the world. It's not just that that's the problem. Shipping bacon is also a problem. Is the making of bacon considered industry? Yeah, it is. But does it need to be removed [from WTO] too? Yes, it does. So, to me, it's not enough to just take the raw product out. That's not just the agriculture. Agriculture is—you know, we like to call it agri-industry now or agribusiness—but we used to call it agriculture, and that's what it is. It's just we've changed the terminology. (Pedersen 2002)

Pedersen's comments, like Alegría's, invoke moral norms against the rules and bureaucratic structures that govern global markets: "distribution" as opposed to production, "elimination of hunger" rather than exports, and the identification of "agriculture" with food, sustenance, and local places. Small farmers, she asserts, have expertise that large industrial operators lack, and they are more respectful of the land. Finally, language itself and the definition of "agriculture" must be reclaimed in order to wrest power from agribusiness corporations and supranational governance institutions such as the WTO.

The activists have proffered various proposals for alternative institutional frameworks for managing global agricultural trade. LVC has pointed to article 11 of the 1996 International Covenant on Economic, Social, and Cultural Rights (ICESCR), which establishes the human right to food, and interpreted it as recognizing peasant communities' right to retain access to productive resources (Verhagen 2004, 16). Some LVC organizations are hopeful that the FAO or the UN Conference on Trade and Development (UNCTAD) can assume some regulatory functions in agricultural trade. French farm activist José Bové, a LVC supporter, has called for an International Trade Tribunal modeled on the International Human Rights Court (Bové 2001, 95–96). Underlying these discussions, which involve arcane aspects of the supranational governance bureaucracies, is an older and more fundamental discourse about rights, whether the ICESCR's recognition of a human right to food or the more generalized demand for "just prices" unaffected by the unethical trade practices of the rich and powerful. Here are echoes of earlier peasant demands and struggles, like those described by Scott in *The Moral Economy,* but infused with the sort of specialized expertise that contemporary transnational social movements frequently generate (Keck and Sikkink 1998, 30).

The projects of food sovereignty and removing agriculture from the WTO may or may not be quixotic or utopian. They may even smack of the atavism that elites have almost always considered typical of agrarian movements. But the discourse of "rights" and justice, of a "reliable subsistence," and of a "moral economy" embedded anew in society—albeit global society—are clearly their central pillars.

The organizational and historical continuities and links between local, national, regional, and transnational peasant activism, as well as the political experiences of the transnational activists, which often traverse these varied levels, provide a means through which to grasp the continuing salience of moral economic demands in peasant struggles. The connection between plummeting prices at the farm gate and subsidy and trade policies that encourage dumping, for example, is now widely comprehended among peasants and farmers of the most diverse circumstances in the most varied places. In the lifetime of a single activist, the struggle may have moved from seeking justice from local elites to defending a public-sector development bank against privatization and helping to stall a WTO negotiating round. The old moral economic discourses about just prices, access to land, unfair markets, and the greed of the powerful have echoes in today's struggles against global trade liberalization, the World Bank's market-based agrarian reform programs, and corporate efforts to gain greater control of the food supply and plant germplasm. State and market—the antagonists of old—still threaten peasant livelihood today, along with the new supra-state forms of governance. These supra-national governance institutions are also (as Scott described the state and local markets) "forces [which] cut through the integument of subsistence customs and traditional social relations to replace them with contracts, the market, and uniform laws" (1976, 189).

The rise of transnational peasant activism draws on a deep, historical reservoir of moral economic sensibilities, as well as on old protest repertoires and agrarian discourses. For the activists, however, the pressures of globalized markets and the demands of transnational collective action have required new degrees of political sophistication, new alliances, and moving through strikingly different geographical and institutional spaces. These leaps in the space of politics may occur over the course of a lifetime, but at times they happen in a single week. They reflect both the density of cross-border networking and the increasingly global and complex character of agriculture itself. Asserting moral economic demands in new political spaces has given participants in the transnational peasant and farmer networks an unprecedentedly dynamic sense of themselves as political actors. Empowered with new knowledge, conceptions of solidarity, and tools of struggle, they are passionate about moral economic sensibilities, but in most other respects they are as dissimilar as can be imagined from the unsophisticated rustics that urban elites and academics still often imagine them to be.

FOOD SOVEREIGNTY

Forgotten Genealogies and Future
Regulatory Challenges

> **As is well known, criticizing one's friends is more demanding and therefore more interesting than to expose once again the boring errors of one's adversaries.**
>
> —Albert O. Hirschman, *A Propensity to Self-Subversion*

I wrote this chapter for a 2013 conference at Yale University sponsored by its agrarian studies program and the Initiative for Critical Agrarian Studies based at the International Institute of Social Studies in The Hague. The event brought several hundred scholars, activists, and scholar-activists together to debate "food sovereignty" and the struggles and policies necessary to achieve it. The research from the Yale conference marked a significant advance in specifying what had previously been a shape-shifting concept (Edelman et al. 2016).

Since the mid-1990s, "food sovereignty" has emerged as a powerful mobilizing frame for social movements, a set of legal and quasi-legal norms and practices aimed at transforming food and agriculture systems, and a free-floating signifier filled with varying kinds of content. It is at once a slogan, a paradigm, a mix of practical policies, a movement, and a utopian aspiration. As a banner or frame, it contributed to the formation of broad-based transnational coalitions such as the People's Coalition on Food Sovereignty based mainly in Asia (PCFS 2007), the International Planning Committee for Food Sovereignty involved in pressuring the UN Food and Agriculture Organization (FAO) since 2002, and the Nyéléni Forum, which includes La Via Campesina (LVC) and various other coalitions of peasants, pastoralists, and fisherfolk. It has been the subject of regional presidential summit meetings, as in Managua in 2008 (Cumbre Presidencial 2008). As a set of policy prescriptions, measures intended to enhance food sovereignty run the gamut from relatively conventional types of protectionism to innovative forms of linking small-scale producers and consumers. Food sovereignty has been incorporated in legal norms, sometimes at the level of national constitutions, in a growing number of nation-states including Venezuela, Senegal, Mali, Nicaragua, Ecuador, Nepal, and Bolivia (Beauregard 2009; Beuchelt and Virchow 2012; Gascón 2010, 238–242; Muñoz 2010), and in localities (Field and Bell 2013, 44; Sustainable Cities Collective 2011). Some civil society organizations have sought to institutionalize food sovereignty at the international level through an international convention that would supersede and obviate multilateral free-trade agreements (PCFS and PAN AP 2004; Bové 2005; PCFS 2005; Windfuhr and Jonsén 2005; Claeys 2013a, 4), though this initiative has languished in recent years.[1]

This chapter acknowledges right up front that the idea of food sovereignty has gained extraordinary traction and that it has contributed in numerous ways and in many parts of the world to the realization of a progressive agenda on food and agriculture issues. At the same time, the concept and the way it is typically understood have several evident limitations.[2] The chapter cannot and does not pretend to cover the burgeoning literature on food sovereignty. Its objective instead is merely to broaden the discussion by briefly analyzing several dimensions of food sovereignty that thus far have received insufficient attention and that are arguably important in understanding the history of food sovereignty and in advancing food sovereignty policies. At the outset, it is important to emphasize that the skeptical observations that follow are offered in a spirit of deep sympathy and solidarity with the food sovereignty project, which can only advance further if its proponents sharpen their critical focus and acknowledge how daunting the challenges are.

The Origin Story

All social groups have origin stories and myths. These serve to reaffirm shared identities and values, to mobilize and bound collectivities, to define adversaries, and to connect the present to the past. Like other invented traditions, they are not necessarily about accurate historical reconstruction but instead often serve to legitimize contemporary practices and doctrines (Hobsbawm 1983). Intellectual and social movements—and not just tribes or other imagined or epistemic communities—also typically have origin myths (McLaughlin 1999). Some of them are almost as fanciful as the tale about how the goddess Minerva was born fully grown from the head of Jupiter, wearing her armor and accompanied by her wise owl.

In the case of food sovereignty, the canonical account is repeated more or less the same way in almost every analysis, whether by pro-food sovereignty scholar-activists (Focus on the Global South 2013; Martínez-Torres and Rosset

2010; Windfuhr and Jonsén 2005, 45–52; Wittman, Desmarais, and Wiebe 2010) or by skeptics (Beuchelt and Virchow 2012, 260; Hospes 2014). The following elements recur in most of the now very substantial food sovereignty literature:

(1) Food sovereignty was first discussed by La Via Campesina at its Second International Conference at Tlaxcala, Mexico, in 1996.[3]

(2) LVC and its allies "launched" or went public with a call for food sovereignty at the FAO-sponsored World Food Conference in Rome in 1996.

(3) They juxtaposed food sovereignty with "food security," which was seen as a contrary, deficient, and "mediocre" (Rosset and Martínez-Torres 2013, 6) concept, for reasons that will be elaborated below.

(4) The idea and practice of food sovereignty were refined at various international conclaves of peasant and farmer movements and other civil society organizations, including those in Havana (Foro Mundial 2001), Rome (NGO/CSO Forum 2002), Sélingué, Mali (Nyéléni Forum 2007), and Mexico City (LVC 2012).[4]

A few accounts of the history of food sovereignty provide greater specificity, though not much. Chaia Heller, for example, remarks that "the precise origin of the term is unclear." She notes, however, that "on December 4, 1993, [the French] union paysans joined eight thousand other smallholders from across Europe to travel to Geneva, carrying a banner that for the first time read *Souveraineté alimentaire* (Food sovereignty)" (Heller 2013, 97).

There's an additional wrinkle to the food sovereignty origin story, which concerns academics who have written on the concept and its regional origins. In October 2012, Olivier De Schutter, the UN Special Rapporteur on the Right to Food, delivered a keynote address at an event where an annual Food Sovereignty Prize was awarded by Why Hunger, a New York–based nongovernmental organization (NGO), to several social movement groups. De Schutter began his speech to the audience of New Yorkers by remarking that "the first researcher who actually used the concept of food sovereignty is somebody from New York. He is Marc Edelman in a book called *Peasants against Globalization* in 1999" (De Schutter 2012; Edelman 1999, 102–103).[5] Not long after, Priscilla Claeys, a member of the Special Rapporteur's research team and one of his PhD students, echoed this claim, albeit in less categorical terms, in an article in the journal *Sociology* (Claeys 2012) and, more definitively, in a personal communication with the author (Claeys 2013b).[6]

I was unable to attend Why Hunger's Food Sovereignty Award ceremony. Alerted by a colleague who was present, I viewed the video of De Schutter's keynote, feeling flattered of course but also experiencing a certain disbelief, since I did not recall having "used" the words "food sovereignty" in *Peasants against Globalization* (though I did remember that by the late 1980s, peasant activists in Costa Rica occasionally employed the term).[7] At first, I went back to the index of the book and then to field notes and transcriptions of recorded interviews from the late 1980s and 1990s, where I found scattered references to *"soberanía alimentaria"* (food sovereignty), usually in relation to the dumping of US surplus maize, which undermined domestic producers.

In Central America, and especially in Costa Rica, these scattered mentions of "food sovereignty" occurred (and gradually became more frequent) in a flow of much more commonly used but related terms that peasant movements employed during their apogee in the late 1980s. At least as early as 1988, for example, the term "food autonomy" (*autonomía alimentaria*) was used by more radical Costa Rican peasant groups, such as the Atlantic Region Small Agriculturalists Union (Unión de Pequeños Agricultores de la Región Atlántica, UPAGRA), which was made up mainly of maize producers (La República 1988, 3). UPAGRA was the dominant force in a coalition of peasant movements called the Justice and Development Council (Consejo Justicia y Desarrollo), several leaders of which played key roles in founding LVC.

The politically centrist National Union of Small and Medium Agricultural Producers (Unión Nacional de Pequeños y Medianos Productores Agropecuarios, UPANACIONAL), similarly, demanded "food self-sufficiency [*autosuficiencia alimentaria*] and rejection of the importation of agricultural products at 'dumping' prices . . . [and the] promotion and the establishment of sovereignty in exports, so that these do not concentrate in the hands of transnational companies" (UPANACIONAL 1989, 2).

At least one UPANACIONAL leader attended some early LVC events, although his organization later withdrew from most international work (Desmarais 2007, 182).

The documentary record of a roundtable held in early 1991 again indicates that Costa Rican rural activists employed the term "food sovereignty" in relation to dumping and also to argue for "sovereignty in exports" (*soberanía en las exportaciones*) (Alforja 1991, 1, 7). They understood this as meaning that foreign firms ought not to control Costa Rica's agricultural export trade. Notably, at least two of the activists at the roundtable, including the one who spoke of "soberanía alimentaria," were involved two years later in some of the earliest meetings of LVC. In April 1991, a letter that three other peasant leaders sent to the president of the republic similarly specified "soberanía alimentaria" as an objective "so that [the country] would not have to depend on surpluses from other countries that could vanish and the prices of which are subject to the international market" (Campos, Fernández, and González 1991).[8]

Importantly, Central American governments of varying orientations occasionally used similar kinds of language at least as early as the 1960s (J. Boyer 2010, 322) and very explicitly in the 1980s. In Nicaragua in 1983, for example, the Sandinista government's Ministry of Agricultural Development and Agrarian Reform (Ministerio de Desarrollo Agropecuario y Reforma Agraria, MIDINRA) produced a major "strategic framework" that viewed "food security" as (1) access to an adequate quantity and quality of food by the entire population and (2) national self-sufficiency (*autosuficiencia*) in the supply of food (Biondi-Morra 1990, 64).[9] In 1989, in Costa Rica, the then-minister of agriculture, an individual generally hostile to the peasant organizations, claimed "to back the policy of self-sufficiency [*autoabastecimiento*] in [rice] and other basic grains" (La República 1989, 10A).

Another important source of "food sovereignty" talk was the Food Security Training Program (Programa de Formación en Seguridad Alimentaria, PFSA), funded by the European Community, which held seminars in Panama for peasant activists from throughout Central America in late 1990 and 1991 (see chapter 4). This followed a related food security program that focused on empirical research in the different countries of the region. While the abundant documentary materials these programs produced contain few, if any, mentions of "soberanía alimentaria," the peasants who returned from the seminars sometimes began to use term, although often almost interchangeably with "seguridad alimentaria."[10]

An important new tool for lexicographical research sheds additional light on the origins of food sovereignty and also refutes once and for all De Schutter's notion that I was "the first researcher who actually used the concept." Google—ever respectful of norms governing intellectual property—usually won't let researchers view all of the pages it has scanned for its Google Books database, but it does provide a search tool called the Ngram Viewer that permits them to search for the relative frequency with which particular words or phrases appear in the texts.[11] It is possible, as well, to explore specific sources that employ the search term within delimited periods. Figures 7.1 and 7.2 provide a graphical representation of Ngam data for "food sovereignty" and "soberanía alimentaria," respectively. Both graphs show a steep increase in mentions of the search terms at the end of the 1990s, a reflection of the growing traction at that time of the food sovereignty concept as employed by LVC and its allies. Both graphs, however, also show a significant though smaller upturn in the early to mid-1980s. Scrutiny of this data complicates the origin story of food sovereignty still further.

In 1983, the government of Mexico announced a new National Food Program (Programa Nacional de Alimentación, PRONAL) (Comisión Nacional de Alimentación 1984).[12] The first objective of PRONAL was "to achieve food sover-

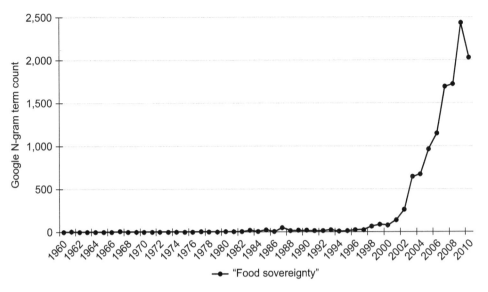

FIGURE 7.1. Relative frequency of "food sovereignty" in Google Books English database, 1960–2010.

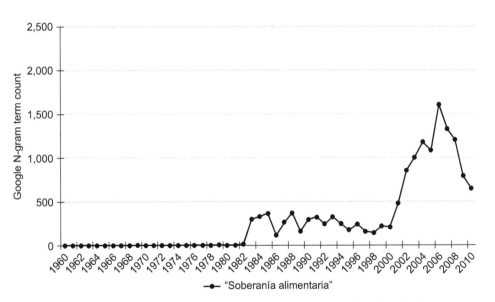

FIGURE 7.2. Relative frequency of "soberanía alimentaria" in Google Books Spanish database, 1960–2010.

eignty," a concept that was understood as "more than self-sufficiency in food; it implies national control over diverse aspects of the food chain, thus reducing dependency on foreign capital and imports of basic foods, inputs and technology. The key factor of this strategy is the adoption of a holistic focus on policies related to the phases of production, transformation, commercialisation, and consumption" (Heath 1985, 115).

While it is beyond the scope of this chapter to discuss PRONAL in any depth, it is clear that the upward blips in the graphs in the mid-1980s are directly related to this Mexican government program and its rhetoric about "soberanía alimentaria."[13] Many researchers writing in English and Spanish—including Gustavo Esteva (Esteva 1984; Austin and Esteva 1987), John Richard Heath (1985), and Steven Sanderson (1986)—used the term in this context. The genealogical complication that this represents for the LVC food sovereignty origin story (and its near-universal acceptance by scholars) is obvious.[14] What is less clear (and probably unknowable) is whether Mexico exported the language of "food sovereignty" to Central America, through mass media or actual contact between peasant movements or other civil society groups, or whether the emergence of the term in Central America is a case of simultaneity of invention.[15]

How Different Is Food Security?

In 1996, LVC advanced food sovereignty as an alternative to the FAO's concept of food security.[16] Some analyses describe food sovereignty versus food security as a "global conflict" characterized by "fundamental antagonisms" (Schanbacher 2010, ix); others describe it as a "counterframe" (Fairbairn 2010, 26–27) or as part of a "conflict between models" (Martínez-Torres and Rosset 2010, 169–170). Raj Patel points out that food sovereignty was "very specifically intended as a foil to the prevailing notions of 'food security'" (2009, 665).[17]

But are these diametrically opposed ideas? Even in the mid-1990s there were about 200 definitions of "food security" in published writings (Clay 2003). One FAO study sensibly advises that "whenever the concept is introduced in the title of a study or its objectives, it is necessary to look closely to establish the explicit or implied definition" (Clay 2003, 25). A number of those 200 or so definitions overlapped substantially with the emerging idea of "food sovereignty."[18] And—as Patel acknowledges—"food sovereignty is . . . over-defined. There are so many versions of the concept, it is hard to know exactly what it means" (2009, 663).

According to Flavio Valente, "the concept of 'food security' was first utilised in Europe after World War I. In its origin it was profoundly linked to the concept of national security and to the capacity of each country to produce its own food so that it would not be vulnerable to possible politically- or militarily-related sieges [*cercos*], embargos or boycotts" (Valente 2002).

Food security was considered part of the human rights agenda as early as the 1943 Hot Springs, Virginia, conference of allied governments, which gave rise to the FAO (Valente 2002; D. J. Shaw 2007, 8–10). Three decades later, the 1974 World Food Summit, held in the context of worsening scarcities, narrowed the definition of food security to the "availability at all times of adequate world food supplies of basic foodstuffs to sustain a steady expansion of food consumption and to offset fluctuations in production and prices" (quoted in Clay 2003, 27). Notably, this definition focuses on countries and on overall consumption rather than on the household or individual level. During this period, the concept of "food security" became increasingly delinked from human rights concerns and centered instead on production and supply in relation to criteria of physical and nutritional necessity (D. J. Shaw 2007; Valente 2002). Over the next two decades, the FAO added additional elements to its definitions, including "access" for all people, food safety and nutritional balance, and cultural preferences (Clay 2003). This new emphasis on consumption and on access by all people, including vulnerable populations, reflected the influential work on "entitlements" of Amartya Sen (1981). Omawale, among others, has argued that Sen's concept of "entitlement" constituted a "bridge between the structural and human rights approach[es] to food in development" (Omawale 1984; see also Schanbacher 2010, 110–111). But entitlement theory also contributed to a shift in food security thinking away from the nation and toward the household or individual as the relevant secure or insecure unit (Fairbairn 2010, 24).

Some of the most frequently cited definitions of food security developed in the 1980s and early 1990s contain elements that figure later in the idea of food sovereignty. Take, for example, Solon Barraclough's definition, developed as part of a study sponsored by the United Nations Research Institute on Social Development:

> Food security can be defined as sustained and assured access by all social groups and individuals to food adequate in quantity and quality to meet nutritional needs. A food system offering food security should have the following characteristics: (a) capacity to produce, store, and import sufficient food to meet basic food needs for all groups; (b) maximum autonomy and self-determination (without implying autarky), reducing vulnerability to international market fluctuations and political pressures; (c) reliability, such that seasonal, cyclical and other variations in access to food are minimal; (d) sustainability such that the ecological system is protected and improved over time; and (e) equity, meaning, as

a minimum, dependable access to adequate food for all social groups. (Barraclough 1991, 1)

Note the concern with "autonomy and self-determination," "sustainability" and the protection of "the ecological system," and "equity." Now compare LVC's "original"—from 1996—statement at the Rome World Food Summit:

> Food security cannot be achieved without taking full account of those who produce food. Any discussion that ignores our contribution will fail to eradicate poverty and hunger. Food is a basic human right. This right can only be realized in a system where food sovereignty is guaranteed. Food sovereignty is the right of each nation to maintain and develop its own capacity to produce its basic foods respecting cultural and productive diversity. We have the right to produce our own food in our own territory. Food sovereignty is a pre-condition to genuine food security. (quoted in NGLS Roundup 1997)

Like the FAO definitions of food security, the relevant unit of sovereignty is the nation, and respect for cultural diversity is a paramount concern. The "right to produce food" is indeed a novel addition, as is the mention of "territory," a term that has historically figured in the demands of Indigenous peoples but that here appears to refer to nation-states.

Perhaps more indicative of the slippage between food security and food sovereignty is the 1996 NGO Forum Statement to the World Food Summit: "Profit for Few or Food for All," subtitled "*Food Sovereignty and Security* to Eliminate the Globalisation of Hunger" (italics added). This extensive declaration highlighted six key elements that are summarized in highly synthetic fashion here: (1) strengthening family farmers, along with local and regional food systems; (2) reversing the concentration of wealth and power through agrarian reform and establishing farmers' rights to genetic resources; (3) reorienting agricultural research, education, and extension toward an agroecological paradigm; (4) strengthening states' capacity for ensuring food security through a suspension of structural adjustment programs, guarantees of economic and political rights, and policies to "improve the access of poor and vulnerable people to food products and to resources for agriculture"; (5) deepening the "participation of peoples' organizations and NGOs at all levels"; and (6) ensuring that international law guarantees the right to food and that food sovereignty takes precedence over macroeconomic policies and trade liberalization (NGO Forum 1996; see also Shaw 2007, 355–356).

By 2002, with the Rome+5 Summit and the formation of the International Planning Committee (IPC) for Food Sovereignty (a massive coalition of civil society organizations, including LVC), an important shift occurred in the prevailing discourse about food sovereignty. In particular, the IPC replaced "nation" with "peoples, communities, and countries" in its definition. As Otto Hospes (2014, 122) points out, this "suggests a pluralistic approach to the question of who is the sovereign."

By 2007, the Declaration of the Nyéléni Forum for Food Sovereignty reduced the scope of sovereignty simply to "peoples": "Food sovereignty is the right of peoples to healthy and culturally appropriate food produced through ecologically sound and sustainable methods, and their right to define their own food and agriculture systems" (Nyéléni Forum 2007, 9).

"Healthy and culturally appropriate food," of course, was already part of earlier FAO definitions of food security. As this and many other examples cited above suggest, in its origins and its contemporary expressions, food sovereignty intersects considerably and sometimes even converges with food security. Both have been protean concepts, frequently imprecise, always contested, and in ongoing processes of semantic and political evolution.

The question of who is the sovereign in "food sovereignty" is of crucial importance, since it is inevitably tied to the administration of food sovereignty. Is it the nation-state, a region, a locality, or "the people"? Is the meaning of food sovereignty the same in a giant country (e.g., Canada) or a tiny one?[19] If the sovereign unit is a region defined as "a local food ecosystem that bases its boundaries on ecological parameters like water flow, rather than on arbitrary state lines" (Field and Bell 2013, 59), then how will the relevant constituency be demarcated? What political institutions will administer "food sovereignty"? How will these differ from existing state institutions? What processes will establish their democratic legitimacy?

Another rarely examined question is the meaning of sovereignty itself and its relevance (or the lack of it) in an increasingly globalized world. Food sovereignty advocates face a paradox because efforts to strengthen food sovereignty at the national level inevitably strengthen the states with which they are frequently in an otherwise adversarial relationship. Moreover, efforts to theorize sovereignty—even by critical scholars (e.g., Agamben 1998) who see institutionalized illegality, violence, and "biopolitical" domination of the citizenry as central to how states work—commonly hark back to conservative, pro-Nazi philosopher Carl Schmitt's hackneyed claim from 1922 that the "sovereign is he who decides on the state of exception" (2005, 1, 5). This deeply authoritarian premise would seem to have little to offer democratically minded proponents of food sovereignty. It does, however, point squarely at an issue about which most food sovereignty advocates have been evasive at best, even those who conceive of the present moment as characterized by a "conflict between models" (Martínez-Torres and Rosset 2010,

169–170). This is the question of the scope of the food sovereign's power and how it will be consolidated, maintained, and enforced.

Long-Distance Trade and Firm Size

The ambiguous nature of the sovereign that characterizes most discussions of food sovereignty is suggestive of another set of problems that require specification if food sovereignty is to make the leap from appealing slogan to on-the-ground policy.[20] The idea of food sovereignty draws on a rich set of ideas and practices related to local food sheds, alternative food networks, and the localization of economies as a defense against globalization. These include reducing "food miles" (the miles that a food item has to travel to reach the final consumer [with the attendant costs in fuel, refrigeration, etc.]); promoting direct marketing and geographical origin indications; local sourcing for restaurants and institutions such as schools, universities, hospitals, nursing homes and prisons; and maintaining greenbelts around urban areas. Food sovereignty advocates differ as to the role of market forces, though most insist that food is not simply a commodity. They also differ as to the role of long-distance and especially international trade in a food sovereign society and have generally been silent on the question of small producers who depend on export production (of coffee, cacao, and so on) for their livelihoods (Burnett and Murphy 2014, 1068–1070). Some food sovereignty proponents explicitly call for tariff protections and "an end to international trade agreements and financial institutions that interfere with the sovereignty and sustainability of food systems" (Field and Bell 2013, 8–9).[21]

Imagine for a moment a flourishing small farm in a food sovereign society (see figure 7.3). It produces a wide variety of high-quality foods for nearby markets using sustainable agroecological practices. It does as much of the postharvest processing, packaging, storage, and transport as possible in order to capture value-added that would otherwise accrue to intermediaries, agroindustries, and retailers. It pays a living wage and benefits to its hired hands and has excellent occupational safety and health standards. Perhaps it has direct links with urban or other consumers through weekly farmers' markets, farm stands, or community-supported agriculture (CSA) groups. It generates significant returns because of its varied production (which minimizes environmental and economic risks and generates year-round sales), its low-input (and thus low-cost) technological mix, its highly productive workforce (which appreciates the decent treatment), its financial backing from CSA subscriptions rather than commercial lenders (which lowers costs and protects against risks of price fluctuations, foreclosure, bad weather, pests, and pathogens), and its savvy marketing strategies

FIGURE 7.3.   "Imagine a small farm . . . ," Noyack, New York, 2009. Photo by the author.

(which also create a risk cushion and fuel further demand). It can, of course, re-invest those profits in the existing farm and in its amortization fund and take some as income or worker bonuses. It may also decide that it wants to expand the scale of its operations by purchasing or renting additional land and hiring more workers (or, if a cooperative, enlisting more associates). It might even de-cide that it wants to sell some of its products in markets on the other side of the country or abroad. How does a "food sovereign" society, one in which "the people define their own food and agriculture system," handle this type of dizzying suc-cess and these kinds of aspirations?

Like proponents of the many efforts to "localize" economies in the face of glo-balization (Halweil 2002; Hines 2000; Nonini 2013), food sovereignty advocates rarely consider what sort of regulatory apparatus would be needed to manage questions of firm and farm size, product and technology mixes, and long-distance and international trade.[22] Food sovereignty implies limits on all of these. Who would enforce those limits? One of the ironies of posing the question in these terms is that many food sovereignty enthusiasts favor abolishing or diminish-ing regulation of local trade and of preferred products (e.g., raw milk and raw milk cheeses). In this respect, their vision sometimes converges with that of the detested neoliberals who tend to view all regulation as onerous for business, large and small. "They [Maine farmers] don't need inspectors to make sure they are following good practices," Tony Field and Beverly Bell declare. "Keeping their neighbors, families, and long-time customers in good health is an even better incentive" (2013, 43).

Both post-Washington Consensus neoliberalism and food sovereignty movements manifest interest in decentralization and local empowerment, albeit with very different rationales. The neoliberal vision backs decentralization as a top-down method of institutional reform that increases "efficiency" and (allegedly) empowers communities vis-à-vis higher orders of governance. Food sovereignty movements, on the other hand, favor decentralization because it might create space for an alternative version of development based on small-scale farming and agroecology. The neoliberal approach assumes a congruence of interests between distinct classes of "stakeholders," with the market resolving questions of trade and firm size. The food sovereignty approach is premised on an ongoing tension between market and society, but it prefers to assume—on the basis of what evidence is unclear—that the market can be kept at bay through direct democracy and "the people" exercising control over "their" food system. Again, the question of what that "control" might look like is rarely specified in sufficient detail for it to become workable policy.

My concern here is with two specific imperatives—limiting firm and farm size and long-distance trade—both of which probably imply relatively draconian state control, though of what kind remains little discussed and unclear. It is worth examining briefly, however, the broader gamut of regulatory possibilities that might arguably be implemented in a food sovereign society. What kinds of control have been tried, and what might be learned from these experiences? State-level anticorporate farming laws in the United States have not been notably successful in stalling the advance of giant agribusinesses (CELDF n.d.). The commodities boards that existed in so many countries before the advent of neoliberalism (and that still survive in some places in hollowed-out form) were designed to provide price supports and to regulate foreign trade in a few internationally traded products. Sometimes they were also in charge of supply management and reserves. Even if resources and political will could be mustered to resurrect and revitalize them, they would not likely be capable of administering the complex product mix of highly diversified food sovereign farms or controlling the successful ones that might want to engage in long-distance trade or even move into potentially profitable monocultures. Ceilings on farm size, which have been a feature of many agrarian reform programs, might begin to check the consolidation of large properties. But such measures have proved notoriously easy to circumvent through titling by different family members or separate corporate

entities.[23] Environmental protection and food safety agencies (and nongovernmental certifying organizations) could conceivably exercise some control over
technology and the use of banned substances or practices, but these would require vastly greater resources in order to be effective and to overcome possible
perverse incentives, such as "cheating" with agrochemicals or suborning inspectors. There is no indication that the "local food policy councils" hailed in some
enthusiasts' analyses would be up to any of these daunting enforcement tasks
(Field and Bell 2013, 70; Halweil 2002, 8; Hassanein 2003, 79–80; Holt-Giménez,
Patel, and Shattuck 2009, 170–171). Some food sovereignty advocates call for
"confederalism": "Nurturing and strengthening citizen-centered food systems
and autonomy calls for forms of political and social organisation that can insti-
tutionalise interdependence without resorting to the market or the central state.
Confederalism involves a network of citizen groups or councils with members
or delegates elected from popular face-to-face democratic assemblies, in villages,
tribes, towns and even neighborhoods of large cities" (Pimbert 2006, xii).

In this view, "confederalism" would, if all goes well, be followed by a linking
of federations and confederations that would produce "a significant counter-
power to the state and transnational corporations" and result in a stage of "dual
power" (Pimbert 2006, xii, 26). This phrase is, of course, redolent of earlier historical experiences that ultimately did not go so well for small farmers.[24]

In an insightful 2008 essay, Boaventura de Sousa Santos pointed to a reciprocal myopia that afflicts both the heterogeneous progressive forces that come
together in the World Social Forums (WSF) and traditional Marxists. On the
one hand, "the conventional left parties and the intellectuals at their service have
stubbornly not paid any attention to the WSF or have minimized its significance."
On the other, "the great majority of the activists of the WSF"—and by extension, one might add, food sovereignty advocates—have shown "contempt . . . for
the rich left theoretical tradition, and . . . militant disregard for its renewal"
(B. de S. Santos 2008, 256–257). In thinking about the limitations of food sovereignty as policy, it is necessary to go beyond Santos's affirmations and recognize
that apart from their respective refusals to acknowledge the other, neither
group has really grappled with the economic lessons that might be learned from
what used to be called "actually existing socialism." This failure results in a
notable shortsightedness when it comes to thinking through the implementation of food sovereignty and particularly the need for strong regulatory oversight of firm size and long-distance trade.

The centrally planned economies were and are (to the extent that they still exist) notoriously unsuccessful in providing their citizens with basic consumer
goods and, in particular, with sufficient fresh and varied foodstuffs. The stress
and wasted time that people endured in a system that used queuing up rather

than purchasing power as the rationing principle for basic goods was arguably an important aspect of the erosion of legitimacy that eventually contributed to those societies' demise (Shanin 1990b, 71; Verdery 1996, 26–29).[25] The Achilles' heel of the command economies was the "plan indicator," a production goal that could be expressed in tons, meters, pairs (e.g., of shoes), or some other measure or combination of measures. In effect, "the center" set targets for enterprises and then negotiated its provision of inputs and the managers' delivery obligations. Frequently, this led to hoarding of materials and labor, considerable waste, and absurd outcomes, such as extra-heavy sheet metal and pipes (an indicator in tons), oversupply of small shoe sizes and undersupply of large sizes (an indicator in pairs), or overly bright light bulbs (an indicator in watts) (Nove 1991; Verdery 1996). These results reflected two fundamental and unresolvable problems: first, the aggregation—for management and planning purposes—of impossibly large numbers of discrete products (e.g., types of light bulbs, sizes and styles of footwear) and second, the failure of the microeconomic signals from end users to be heard or to correspond to the specific products needed or desired.

The conclusion, which some food sovereignty advocates may find lamentable, is that (1) market mechanisms, even if they frequently generate injustice and inequality, can be especially efficient at delivering a wide product mix to consumers, and (2) micromanaging the consumer goods sector—and particularly the agriculture and food sector—has almost always proved counterproductive. This is not to say that supply management and commodities boards and so on are doomed; indeed, these or similar mechanisms will be essential for any meaningful version of food sovereignty. Rather, this conclusion points very specifically to the strong regulatory control that will also be required to localize and domesticate trade and to maintain farm and firm sizes within tolerable bounds. But the onus is on food sovereignty enthusiasts to grapple with the history of the command economies and to come up with creative mechanisms that encourage diversity, that balance and meet the needs of producers and consumers, and that achieve the basic contours of a truly democratic "food sovereign" production and distribution system. The issues of regulating trade and firm size that are implicit in so much of the food sovereignty literature are rarely acknowledged and have sadly received little or no serious attention.

Consumer Taste in a Food Sovereign Society

Kim Burnett and Sophia Murphy (2014) rightly draw attention to the food sovereignty movement's silence on the question of small producers who depend on export crops for their livelihoods and food security. They argue that having such producers shift from (sometimes) lucrative export crops to low-cost staples for domestic consumption risks exacerbating inequalities by reducing producers' incomes. Gerardo Otero, Gabriela Pechlaner, and Efe Can Gürcan (2013, 265) point out that while many developing countries have become dependent on imports of industrially produced cereals and oils, the "dependency" of developed countries is mainly in the sector of high-value "luxury" foods that make only a small contribution to total nutritional intake. A related question concerns consumer tastes and needs (even if the latter are not strictly physiological but socially constructed).

Sidney Mintz (1986) famously analyzed the role of sugar imported from the Caribbean in fueling the workforce that initiated the industrial revolution in England. Together with stimulants—first tea and somewhat later coffee—caffeine and sugar became basic necessities in numerous countries where they were not produced. They powered workers (Jiménez 1995), actual and would-be elites (Roseberry 1996), and military machines (Haft and Suarez 2013). They kept innumerable sleep-deprived academics, policymakers, and activists alert during interminable meetings. A food sovereign society could completely eschew these products, but if prohibition of coffee and tea is not politically popular, then long-distance international trade is essential for providing them (unless, of course, we contemplate anti-economic greenhouse production of these crops in cold climates).

If coffee, tea, and cane sugar have been constructed as necessities, there is also the question of consumer predilections and whims—the construction of tastes for nonnecessities—in a food sovereign society. In Costa Rica in the early 1980s, in the midst of the country's worst economic crisis since the Great Depression of the 1930s, kiwis from Hawaii suddenly started to appear in supermarkets in upscale neighborhoods and frequent radio spots extolled the "exoticness" and "deliciousness" of this novel fruit. The seductive voice in the radio ads became the butt of comedians' jokes and impressions. Archbishop Román Arrieta denounced the squandering of scarce foreign exchange on kiwis and plaintively asked if there was a more delicious fruit in the world than Costa Rican pineapple, which, he reminded people, was cheap, abundant, and locally produced.[26] This implicit plea for a kind of food sovereignty identified one problem but masked another.

Food is not just a source of physiologically necessary nutrients; it is also a major source of pleasure and sociality. Some food sovereignty proponents, such as Slow Food, make this a central part of their political (and culinary) practice, but most others—and especially those most concerned with policy—have given this dimension little systematic attention. Consumers in cold, northern countries have come to enjoy not only pineapples and kiwis but an extraordinary cornucopia of perishable tropical fruits and other products (e.g., chocolate, macadamia nuts). They have come to expect these delicacies all year round. Once they have tasted pineapple (or mangos or açaí or bananas), they are unlikely to take kindly to food sovereignty scolds who insist on their consuming only local products during those long northern winters.[27] The problem is not just how to reverse tastes constructed over long historical time, something that is probably close to impossible, but also how to build political support for "the people" democratically exercising control over "their" food system—that is, for food sovereignty. Limiting access to delectable exotic foods is almost certainly a poor road to consensus. An additional, related paradox is that food sovereignty as a set of diverse practices has advanced by incremental steps, while its advocates typically insist that nothing short of a complete overhaul of food and farming—along with associated changes in values—will be sufficient to reverse the juggernaut of corporate agriculture (Hassanein 2003).

Food sovereignty activists and scholars, almost without exception, attribute the invention of food sovereignty to La Via Campesina and accept the claim that "food sovereignty" and "food security" are diametrically opposed concepts. This chapter has shown instead that the proximate origins of the phrase are in a Mexican government program in the early 1980s and that its adoption by Central American peasant movements occurred in a context where, for some time, "food security," "food sovereignty," and several similar terms overlapped, blended into one another, and were used largely interchangeably. Suggestions that I was the first researcher to mention "food sovereignty" are misplaced, since numerous Mexican and foreign scholars earlier analyzed the Mexican government program. Several (though not all) of the Central American activists who began to speak of food sovereignty in the 1980s eventually went on to participate in the founding of LVC.

Food sovereignty proponents have been remarkably vague about who or what is "the sovereign" in food sovereignty, with different organizations and theorists either disagreeing, ignoring the issue entirely, or shifting over time between pointing to the nation-state, a region, a locality, or "the people." This question matters because it speaks to the crucial point of how a food sovereign society will be administered. Will a food sovereign society permit a successful small farm to expand its operations or to enter international markets? If so, up to what point? Who will draw the line and enforce it? There is an urgent need for devoting more attention to the political institutions needed for food sovereignty, as well as to the issues of how these will intersect with or differ from existing state institutions, and how they will establish and maintain democratic legitimacy.

The nature of sovereignty itself, similarly, is rarely scrutinized in the food sovereignty literature or by food sovereignty movements, most of which find themselves in adversarial relationships with the states in which they operate. The policies that would strengthen food sovereignty at the national level inevitably imply strengthening the states with which the movements are typically in conflict. The experience of the centrally planned economies suggests that the strong state actions required to impose limits on farm and firm size and on long-distance and international trade could easily give rise to unintended consequences that would negatively affect both small agricultural producers and the consumers who sympathize with and depend on them.

The localization of production and consumption that is central to most conceptions of food sovereignty raises a host of further problems that again have received far too little consideration. How much extra-local trade would be tolerated or encouraged? What will become of the millions of smallholders who depend for their livelihoods on export production and whose incomes would plummet if they were required to switch, say, from cacao or African palm production to cassava and maize? Localization also raises fundamental problems for consumers dependent on or even addicted to necessities, such as coffee, which are produced in far-off places. Both needs of this sort and predilections for other exotic products are indicative of the extent to which food has deep cultural roots and meanings, formed over long historical time, that go beyond those typically adduced in the food sovereignty literature. Attempts to reverse these tastes and needs would be extremely difficult and would doubtless raise widespread opposition to any food sovereignty program that sought to do so.

Food sovereignty advocates thus find themselves in an interesting and fertile moment. A proliferation of concepts, experiments, and experiences provides abundant material for reflection and for practical efforts to solidify the paradigm on the ground and, hopefully, to scale it up. At the same time, the almost willful neglect of some key theoretical and policy issues impedes further progress. If we are to imagine not only a successful small farm in a food sovereign society but a successful food sovereign society built on a dynamic small farm sector, we need to devote considerably more attention to some of the challenges and paradoxes that this chapter has outlined.

Part 4

PEASANTS' RIGHTS AND THE UNITED NATIONS

HOW THE UNITED NATIONS RECOGNIZED THE RIGHTS OF PEASANTS AND OTHER PEOPLE WORKING IN RURAL AREAS

The chapter outlines the process that led to the adoption in December 2018 of the UN Declaration on the Rights of Peasants and Other People Working in Rural Areas (UNDROP). It describes my involvement in the negotiations and drafting of this new international instrument. Most anthropological research on global governance has a strong institutionalist and legalistic orientation. This chapter, in contrast, emphasizes the ethnographic encounter. It proposes a new way of thinking about the origin of international norms and an alternative to the "vernacularization" approach dominant in anthropological studies of law. UNDROP is a case of vernacularization-in-reverse, in which the subjects of rights bring their own conceptions to Geneva and New York and author laws that apply to them.

Amid the ebullient atmosphere at the 2001 World Social Forum in Porto Alegre, Brazil, an encounter between an Indonesian peasant leader and a radical Swiss activist from a nongovernmental organization (NGO) launched a prolonged campaign to push international human rights norms beyond established limits. Henry Saragih, of the Indonesian Peasants Union, and Florian Rochat, of the Europe-Third World Center (Centre Europe-Tiers Monde, CETIM), meeting for the first time, hatched a plan to have the United Nations adopt a new international convention or a declaration on the rights of peasants (Saragih 2011; Rochat 2012).[1] Fifteen years later, in a forum at a Geneva university, Saragih hailed "brother Florian" for his solidarity and recalled his own astonishment in 2001 at being able to speak against neoliberalism and for human rights in a UN building.[2] Seventeen years after Saragih first went to Geneva, I huddled in the balcony of the UN

General Assembly in New York with a Bolivian diplomat, the youth vice president of the Canadian National Farmers Union, an activist from the NGO Why Hunger, and an American jurist friend as the Declaration on the Rights of Peasants and Other People Working in Rural Areas became international law (UNDROP 2018).

The UN General Assembly adopted UNDROP on December 17, 2018.[3] This chapter analyzes the rights enshrined in this new legal instrument, the arguments and the forces for and against it, and national-level efforts to implement its provisions before and after it received approval from the Human Rights Council and the General Assembly.[4] The chapter proposes a novel framework for understanding new human rights norms. Rather than viewing this through the lens of "vernacularization," which emphasizes local interpretations and implementation of international norms, I suggest that drafting new global human rights standards more closely resembles "vernacularization-in-reverse."[5] This downside-up process involves rights holders from diverse world regions who arrive at common understandings, build alliances, and collaborate in authoring international norms that apply to them.

The chapter is also a meditation on the limitations of ethnographic approaches for research on the construction of international law and diplomacy more broadly.[6] While the peasant activists I have encountered in Central America and elsewhere—including Geneva—were usually eager to be quoted by name in anything I might write, UN diplomats were mostly cagey (see box 8.1). I had so many conversations that were "off the record," "for background," or "not for attribution." Diplomats liked to check everything "with capital," which meant that often they could not say much of substance. In one 2011 side event, the chair—an NGO activist—laid down "Chatham House rules," which allow attendees to report what was said but not who said it. At key junctures, well-informed actors casually reported fascinating rumors that were difficult to corroborate. The research required patience, too—and frequent caffeinated drinks. Many states' contributions to debates were formulaic and not infrequently hypocritical. Yet, as soporific as these interventions sometimes were, it was essential to remain alert for minor shifts in position, subtle suggestions of openness to something new, and the occasional telling sound bite. UN negotiations often involve parsing meanings of words and bartering terms that states do not like for others that seem more acceptable. The ambiguity of the ethnographic experience contrasted with the immense corpus of UN documentation, which presented a historical record—seemingly written in stone—that reflected numerous unacknowledged quid pro quos and that sanitized and condensed intense conflicts over issues affecting the future of humanity. Working with these sources required reading between the lines. This was only possible because of the dif-

---

Box 8.1. Off the record, not for attribution

"If I were to quote you in something I write, could I refer to you as a German diplomat?"

"No, I don't think so."

"How about a European diplomat?"

"No, that's much too specific."

—Interview for background with a diplomat in the UN's Bar Serpent, 2014

---

fuse, if often vague, "background" derived from observation, informal interviews and conversations, and direct experience.

The UNDROP contains a lengthy preamble and twenty-eight articles and is available in six official UN languages (since its adoption it has been translated into several more languages). It reiterates rights—both civil and political and economic, social, and cultural—enshrined in other international instruments. Significantly, it states that peasants and other people working in rural areas may exercise these rights as individuals but also "in association with others or as a community"—a circumlocution repeated in many UNDROP articles that both advocates and opponents of the declaration correctly interpreted as a step toward the institutionalization of collective rights. It further establishes rights that are arguably "new," such as the rights to seeds and biodiversity, to land and natural resources, and to food sovereignty. Like other international laws, UNDROP calls on states to "respect, protect, and fulfill" the rights it contains and to "consult and cooperate in good faith with peasants and other people working in rural areas . . . who could be affected by decisions before those decisions are made" (UNDROP, art. 2.3). One goal of UNDROP proponents was to produce a single, accessible document that gathered "all" the rights that peasants and other rural people are supposed to enjoy and that could be a tool in on-the-ground struggles.

Indonesian Origins

If the rights of peasants are violated in dozens of countries, why did the campaign for a UN peasants' rights instrument commence in Indonesia? The toppling of the nationalist and anti-imperialist Sukarno government in 1965–1966 and the rise two years later of Suharto's "New Order" involved a bloodbath of astonishing proportions. Some 500,000 to one million people were murdered in a period of two years. Most of them were peasants believed to be militants or sympathizers of the Indonesian Communist Party, many others were simply beneficiaries of the Sukarno-era agrarian reform, and a smaller number were ethnic Chinese, whose prominent role in commerce was used by Suharto partisans to foment resentment (B. Simpson 2008; Melvin 2018). The repression had a strongly agrarian dimension; in many cases, victims' land was seized for large-scale plantations of oil palm, rubber, and other crops.

The *reformasi* era that followed the 1998 fall of Suharto saw extraordinary ferment, political opening, and understandably (given what had transpired under the dictatorship), a florescence of demands phrased in human rights language (Bey 2011; Ikhwan 2011). In 2001, a meeting on agrarian reform in the Jakarta suburb of Cibubur, attended by over a hundred peasant and NGO activists, produced a "Declaration on the Human Rights of Farmers" (Lucas and Warren 2003, 102; Dillon 2011).[7] The Indonesian organizations brought this document to the Asian Region of La Via Campesina (LVC), which decided to turn it into an international instrument. The Indonesian draft, with sixty-seven articles, became the prototype for the first LVC draft UN declaration on peasants' rights. This appeared in a trilingual English, French, and Spanish pamphlet, awkwardly translated from Bahasa, which began to circulate among LVC organizations beyond Asia (LVC 2002a). In 2001, Henry Saragih of the Indonesian Peasants Union first traveled to Geneva to present a statement about peasants' rights in debates on the "right to development" in the UN Human Rights Commission (CETIM, WFDY, and LVC 2001).[8] He was to return every year thereafter to press the cause, each time accompanied by agrarian activists and allies from Indonesia and other countries.

The question of why a peasants' rights declaration originated in Indonesia implicitly asks why it did not emerge or gain strong backing from activists in other countries where peasants' rights were routinely violated. The Brazilian Landless Rural Workers Movement (MST) exercised an outsized influence among Latin American agrarian organizations and the LVC. Despite its involvement in legal training and legal struggles at home, it appears to have been skeptical of the Indonesian campaign, even after its adoption by LVC. The inability of the United Nations to enforce rights covenants and the enormous power of the five permanent members of the Security Council were among the limitations that skeptics raised (Reed 2005; Bové 2005). These concerns reflected a critique of the supposed impartiality of judicial institutions and the effectiveness of legal protections in their own societies, as well as doubts about devoting resources to a prolonged international legal struggle with a remote and uncertain outcome (Houtzager 2005; Glock 2012; Monsalve Suárez 2013). Agrarian movements concerned with seeds and intellectual property reinforced these misgivings, asserting that corporate interests had hijacked the rights discourse, conflated human rights with property rights, and put it at the service of transnational seed companies (Kneen 2009). In its most extreme form, articulated by the NGO GRAIN and its collaborators, this approach condemned the concept of rights as "clearly harmful to communities," "truly diabolical," and "knowingly or unknowingly promot[ing] fictitious and autonomous subjects . . . that locate the essence of personhood in the privatisation and colonisation of nature, resources and knowledge, thus breeding violent competition that culminates in war and destruction."[9]

The 2008 Food Crisis and UNDRIP

In 2008, a global spike in commodity prices triggered hunger riots in dozens of countries and unleashed a worldwide wave of land grabbing, which further threatened peasants' right to food. In 2007, the UN General Assembly adopted the Declaration on the Rights of Indigenous Peoples (UNDRIP), probably the first international instrument where the rights holders participated actively in the more-than-two-decades-long drafting process. The conjunction of these two events breathed new life into the campaign for a UN peasants' rights declaration and allayed the concerns of some skeptics. The impact of the food crisis made it easier to link peasants' rights to the broadly accepted right to food and spurred several UN bodies and agencies to act. UNDRIP served as an inspiration for peasants' rights advocates and as a model of the language acceptable in the UN system and the process necessary to achieve adoption (Edelman and James 2011, 94–95). In late 2008, LVC's Human Rights Commission and Indonesian and European jurists affiliated with human rights NGOs met in Bilbao to rewrite the 2002 draft declaration to make it legally, politically, and stylistically more compatible with existing international law. At least one of the lawyers at the Bilbao meeting, Christophe Golay, had significant "insider" knowledge because he worked in Geneva as a consultant to Swiss sociologist Jean Ziegler, a member of the Advisory Committee of the UN Human Rights Council.[10]

What kinds of rights were contemplated in the 2008 proposed declaration? Many were rights already protected in international law, such as gender equality, freedom from discrimination, and rights to water, food, housing, and freedom of expression and association. Others involved radical new claims, notably rights "to benefit from land reform," "to get a fair price for their production," "to determine the varieties of seeds they want to plant," and "to actively participate in policy design, decision-making, implementation, and monitoring of any project, program or policy affecting their territories." The document also claimed a "right to reject all kinds of land acquisition and conversion for economic purposes" and "intellectual property rights of goods, services, resources and knowledge that are owned, maintained, discovered, developed or produced by the local community" (LVC 2009a). Several of these claims provoked fierce opposition from developed-country states, and in subsequent versions of the text, the language was again modified in the interests of building greater support.

UNDROP in Geneva and New York

In the aftermath of the 2008 food crisis, the proposed Declaration on the Rights of Peasants garnered growing support from rural social movements within and beyond La Via Campesina, as well as from UN member states. The movement of the draft declaration through the UN Human Rights Council (UNHRC) and the General Assembly can be summarized as follows:

(1) In 2008, in response to the global crisis, the UNHRC Advisory Committee—the council's think tank—began a study on "discrimination in the context of the right to food." In 2010, it submitted its preliminary report, which included as an appendix the 2008 version of LVC's peasants' rights declaration (UNHRC Advisory Committee 2010).

(2) In 2011, the Advisory Committee presented its preliminary study "on the advancement of the rights of peasants and other people working in rural areas," which echoed LVC's proposals and argued for a "new legal instrument" (UNHRC Advisory Committee 2011).

(3) In 2012, the Advisory Committee voted unanimously to submit to the council its final study on advancement of the rights of peasants and other people working in rural areas, which contained an appendix with its own declaration on peasants' rights, a text very similar to the LVC draft (UNHRC Advisory Committee 2012).

At that point, according to José Bengoa, a Chilean anthropologist and Advisory Committee member, "The draft Peasants' Rights Declaration is from now on an official UN document. . . . From the moment that this type of instrument becomes part of the public debate about international law, its content and proposals can be considered a reference point with regards to the standards that are discussed and the policies to develop" (Bengoa 2012).

(4) Later in 2012, the council voted to create an open-ended intergovernmental working group to finalize a UN Declaration on the Rights of Peasants

and Other People Working in Rural Areas. The Plurinational State of Bolivia sponsored the resolution and ten additional countries cosponsored it. The United States and most European Union (EU) countries voted "no," while China, India, Indonesia, Russia, and almost all developing-country UNHRC member states voted in favor. Even Chile and Guatemala, then governed by conservative administrations, backed the resolution.

(5) Between 2013 and 2018, the working group met five times. Each one-week session heard presentations from invited panelists and debated the UNDROP text. After the first session, in 2014–2015, the Bolivian Mission received a mandate to redraft the Advisory Committee-LVC text to make it more compatible with existing international law and to address concerns raised by several states. The Bolivian Mission, after bilateral consultations with states and other "stakeholders," also introduced additional modifications to the text after the fourth working group in 2017.

(6) On September 28, 2018, the UNHRC passed a resolution to send the UNDROP to the General Assembly's Third Committee in New York. The Third Committee recommended adoption on November 20, 2018. One month later, on December 17, the General Assembly plenum adopted the declaration by a vote of 121 in favor to eight opposed, with fifty-four abstentions.

A Difficult Negotiation

The road to the adoption of UNDROP was bumpy but also unusually dynamic for a UN negotiating process. Bolivia long had "a visionary agenda" at the United Nations, particularly around issues of Indigenous rights, the right to water, and the climate crisis (Bjork-James 2013, 244). As chair of the working group on the rights of peasants, Bolivia upended UNHRC rules that only permitted civil society representatives to intervene on a topic after states had delivered their statements and that limited participation to representatives of organizations with ECOSOC consultative status (which many NGOs have but social movements typically lack). Particularly in the later negotiating sessions, this meant that debates were punctuated by passionate interventions not just from LVC member organizations and their NGO allies but also from transnational and local movements of artisanal fishers, pastoralists, Indigenous peoples, and rural women.[11] The Bolivian Mission included social movements' representatives on the "expert" discussion panels at the beginning of each negotiating session.[12] As Christophe

Golay pointed out, "Recognizing that rural people are the 'experts' when it comes to the realities of rural life changed the dynamic of the negotiations."[13]

From the beginning, some developed countries, particularly the United States and the European Union, raised budgetary and procedural objections that were thinly veiled efforts to mask opposition to the substance of the Declaration. They asserted that the UNHRC did not have a mandate to negotiate a new declaration and that matters pertaining to food and agriculture properly belonged in the Food and Agriculture Organization. The European Union objected to the Declaration's use of the term "people" and argued that it ought to say "persons," which would indicate that all human rights are held by individuals, not collectivities. The repeated references to a "right to reject" that were part of the 2008 LVC and Advisory Committee drafts aroused considerable indignation, as did the assertion of peasants' "right to determine the price [of their production], individually or collectively," which fueled the impression that the draft was a Trojan horse to establish collective rights, as well as an anti-market manifesto (UNHRC Advisory Committee 2012). Opponents questioned the mention of "Mother Earth" in the text, arguing that there was no accepted language in international law that referred to this concept. Within the European Union, the United Kingdom was the most hostile to UNDROP. An Austrian diplomat, commenting on the pejorative connotations of the word "peasant" in English, told me that "the British colleagues make fun of 'peasant.' They laugh and do impressions from a British TV show where one of the characters yells, 'Out of my way, peasant!' We don't have that problem in other languages."[14]

The issues that excited most opposition in the negotiations involved collective rights, rights to seeds and intellectual property, and rights to territory. Opponents of the Declaration insisted that human rights are only held by individuals and that only Indigenous peoples could be holders of collective rights to land and natural resources, even though many UN member states have long histories of granting various kinds of tenure based on community and of recognizing that many individual rights are exercised collectively (Nuila 2018).[15] The "right to save, use, exchange and sell . . . farm-saved seed," as well as provisions about benefits sharing and the need to have intellectual property and seed certification laws respect the realities of peasant agriculture and traditions, similarly aroused heated opposition from developed countries and—in later years—from large agro-exporting countries such as Brazil and Argentina, whose governments had moved to the right. "Territory" is a concept central to the Declaration on the Rights of Indigenous Peoples and implies an exclusive group right to an area. While earlier versions of UNDROP mention peasants' right to territories, this demand did not survive in the version the General Assembly adopted.

The arguments that states opposed to the Declaration deployed evolved over time. In 2012 and 2013, European countries and the United States frequently raised procedural concerns and eschewed substantive observations on the draft. Around 2014, more of these delegations, while still expressing reservations, reluctantly engaged in discussions of substance (see box 8.2). While they continued to raise doubts about collective or group rights (so-called new rights) and the definition of the rights holders, they appeared to recognize that developing-country member states outnumbered them and resigned themselves to trying to shape the declaration around its edges.

In working group debates and those in the full UNHRC on reauthorizing the group's mandate, it was possible for a while to observe growing support for UNDROP. If in 2012 most EU countries opposed the establishment of the working group, by 2014, when Bolivia proposed extending the group's mandate, the EU bloc split, with most countries abstaining and only the Czech Republic and the United Kingdom opposed.[16] By 2015, when Bolivia sought a three-year extension of the group's mandate, the UNHRC approved the measure by a vote of 31–1, with the United States casting the only negative vote and with all EU

Box 8.2. My country, 'tis of thee . . .

"I saw that guy sitting with the Bolivians," a mid-level US diplomat whispered to his colleague, thinking I was out of earshot, as I walked away after requesting an off-the-record informational interview that I never got.

The United States opposed UNDROP and only engaged (albeit unenthusiastically) in substantive debate during the third working group session in 2016, toward the end of President Barack Obama's administration. It frequently raised budgetary and procedural arguments, maintaining that the UN Human Rights Council did not have a mandate to negotiate a new declaration, that the UNHRC was not the right UN forum for the discussions, and that no new human rights instruments were needed. In 2018, President Donald Trump's administration withdrew the United States from the UNHRC (President Joseph Biden's administration rejoined in 2021).

countries abstaining. Beginning in 2015, however, momentum slackened. With the election of Mauricio Macri in Argentina, the Group of Latin American and Caribbean Countries (GRULAC), which previously was a bastion of UNDROP, began to fragment. The rise of right-wing governments in the Americas and beyond made it increasingly clear that negotiations needed to be concluded as quickly as possible. In 2017, for example, in the fourth working group session, Guatemala, which earlier supported the Declaration, became a vocal opponent, echoing US arguments and posturing as a defender of Indigenous rights. "With respect to collective rights," the Guatemalan delegate declared, "any professor of law will tell you that collective rights belong to the peoples (*los pueblos*) and that each time we try to extend those rights we are diminishing those rights of the indigenous."[17]

If states' interventions in debates were, with few exceptions, predictable and bland, passion and determination infused the oral remarks of peasant and other civil society representatives. As Coline Hubert describes the five negotiating sessions,

> Peasant delegations were formed, with as many as 30 representatives from various regions of the world attending at any one time. . . . In 2017, the LVC and its allied social movements spoke 60 times during the week of negotiations. With an average of 50 interventions per session, the peasants gradually laid out their positions and demands before the diplomats, illustrating them with descriptions of their daily life. . . . Because the LVC works on the principle of decentralization, it was particularly important to avoid the emergence of an elite of peasant leaders that would dominate the discussions of the Declaration. On the contrary, all LVC members had to learn the procedures and get involved. Not only did that keep the process in tune with the reality on the ground, it also paved the way for implementation of the Declaration in the future, for those involved in the negotiations could pass on their experience and knowledge. The delegations were selected in such a way as to be the embodiment of, on the one hand, the diversity of peasants and, on the other, their single-mindedness in working towards the Declaration; also for their daunting negotiating skill, contributed by a seasoned hard-core of particularly committed and well-prepared peasants. (Hubert 2019, 38–39)

LVC lobbyists maintained detailed spreadsheets on the positions, sensitivities, and influence of states that were UNHRC voting members or active participants and cornered delegates on the floor of the council, in their missions' offices, in the halls of the Palais des Nations, or around the coffee bar. Often activists and allies would lunch together in the UN cafeteria or squander their per diems on evening meals in Geneva. Over the course of five years of negotiations, several other transnational rural movements became more active in the debates. These included FIMARC (International Federation of Rural Adult Catholic Movements), WAMIP (World Alliance of Mobile Indigenous People), WFF (World Forum of Fish Harvesters and Fish Workers), WFFP (World Forum of Fisher Peoples), IITC (International Indian Treaty Council), ROPPA (Network of Peasant and Agricultural Producers Organizations of West Africa), and the IUF (International Union of Food, Agricultural, Hotel, Restaurant, Catering, Tobacco, and Allied Workers' Associations).

The rights claimed in the declaration shifted over time, following the first working group's request that the Bolivian Mission present a new draft more in

---

Box 8.3. Vernacularization-in-reverse

"I believe that this Declaration must guarantee the right to health and, within that right, even if it seems strange, the right to not be fumigated, the right to not be sprayed with poison."

—Diego Montón, intervention at the second intergovernmental working group, National Peasant Indigenous Movement (MNCI), LVC, Argentina, November 12, 2014

"Peasants and other people working in rural areas have the right not to use or to be exposed to hazardous substances or toxic chemicals, including agrochemicals or agricultural or industrial pollutants."

—UNDROP, article 14.2

"I learned . . . how to translate 'peasant language' into legal language and the other way around."

—Paula Gioia, Working Community on Peasant Agriculture (AbL), LVC, Germany (quoted in Geneviève Savigny and Paula Gioia, "European Peasants Fighting for Recognition and Human Rights," in Claeys and Edelman 2020).

accord with "accepted language" under international law and that reflected input from non-LVC rural organizations, such as those mentioned above.[18] The non-peasant constituencies backing UNDROP insisted on provisions not contained in earlier drafts, such as the right to social security (which the IUF defended) and the obligation of states to "take appropriate measures to cooperate with a view to addressing transboundary tenure issues affecting peasants and other people working in rural areas that cross international boundaries" (UNDROP 2018, art. 7.2, which nomadic pastoralists championed). The redrafting involved participation from these groups, as well as from a multinational collection of specialists drawn from the UN system, academia, and labor and human rights organizations. Some of the most contentious language was toned down: The "right to reject," for example, became a more anodyne "right not to accept," while the "right not to be fumigated," which had not appeared in the 2008 draft but which farmers from Argentina, France, and elsewhere insisted on in consultative forums, became "the right not to use or to be exposed to hazardous substances or toxic chemicals" (UNDROP 2018, art. 14.2), "right to safety and health at work" (UNDROP 2018, art. 16), and the "right to a safe, clean, and healthy environment" (see box 8.3) (UNDROP 2018, art. 20). Opponents of UNDROP, particularly the United States and the European Union, questioned the

---

Box 8.4. Value chains and buyer power

"Dominican avocados are the best avocados in the world," a Dominican delegate pronounced during the fourth working group on May 17, 2017. It was the first and only time that the Dominican Republic intervened in the negotiations. "And when I bite into a corpulent Dominican avocado, when I inhale its scent, when I allow it to melt on my tongue, I am transported back to Santo Domingo, to my homeland."

I experienced a surreal shock as he spoke, not only because of the unbridled display of Caribbean Latino masculinity and the botanical nationalism, which was over-the-top and borderline inappropriate in the formal discourse of UN debates, but because the accent and attitude were those of my upper Manhattan neighborhood. But the shock subsided when I saw where the paean to avocados was heading.

"And when I miss my homeland," he continued, "and I go to the supermarket here in Geneva to buy a Dominican avocado, which are the best in the world, it costs me four Swiss francs and twenty cents, which is 200 Dominican pesos that I reluctantly pay, because I really want that Dominican avocado. And of those 4.20 francs [US$4.30] that the supermarket receives, do you know how much the Dominican campesino receives? The Dominican campesino receives less than one franc. I always buy Dominican avocados hoping that one of those francs gets to some Dominican campesino. . . . And that is like what every other agriculturalist at the end of a long value chain receives, which is why I feel compelled today to speak in favor of this Declaration."

need for a new declaration since the rights protected were amply covered in other international instruments. Proponents pointed to the advantages of gathering all the provisions that cover a vulnerable population in one easily accessible document and argued that the remit of the UN Human Rights Council was the extension of safeguards to groups that require protection (see box 8.4).

A Different Kind of Field Research

Instead of wearing boots, jeans, and a broad-brimmed hat, as in earlier fieldwork in Central America, in Geneva I donned a suit and tie, shined my shoes, and hung my UN accreditation badge around my neck. Relevant activities in Geneva rarely lasted much more than one week, so I barely had time to get over my jet lag before flying home. I had to recuperate my rusty French for use around Geneva, but I also had to learn a new language—the arcane jargon of the UN human rights system ("special procedures," "interactive dialogue," "procedure 1503," "Like-Minded Group"). I quickly grasped that when diplomats said "We take note," it meant that they were not keen on whatever they were taking note of.

The research did not just involve sitting in UN debates or side events, interviewing participants, and collecting documentation. On weekends, LVC's Swiss organization, Uniterre, would invite visiting "allies" to farms on the outskirts of Geneva, where we shared bread and cheese, hopes and anecdotes, and—in 2011—practiced Asian martial arts with *bo* staffs under the stern direction of an energetic Swiss *paysan*. The Swiss farmers (and nearby French) organized demonstrations in support of UNDROP at every negotiating session, massing across the street from the UN and driving aging tractors and trucks covered with placards around the Palais des Nations. The research also took me to locations as varied as Indonesia, Honduras, and Germany, but space constraints preclude a full discussion here.

Commensality in fieldwork was not limited to the offerings of the coffee bar, the UN cafeteria, and the deli sandwiches that always appeared right before lunchtime side events where rural activists spoke and mingled with diplomats and journalists (and that inexplicably always included multiple prosciutto selections, despite the presence of many Muslim and vegetarian attendees) (see box 8.5). For their off-campus meals, the Indonesian activists favored a Malaysian Chinese restaurant near the train station, where they bantered in Bahasa with the owners. At the conclusions of the different negotiating sessions, UNDROP supporters would gather in bars or restaurants in the center of Geneva. On one occasion, the Bolivian Mission hosted an Aymara celebratory banquet or *apthapi*, with a dozen multicolored quinoa and potato dishes, right outside Salle XX, the UN Human Rights Council's meeting hall. European diplomats politely picked at the unfamiliar fare, while more adventurous NGO activists and visitors from the Global South dug in with gusto.

It must be acknowledged that I was not exactly a neutral observer. During earlier research in Central America in the late 1980s and early 1990s, I became friendly with several peasant leaders who later—in 1993—were among the founders of La Via Campesina, and I had followed and written about the movement for many years. I saw the campaign for UNDROP, which LVC had initiated, with the same eyes that had witnessed violations of the human rights of peasants in Latin America and elsewhere. In the years following the 2008 global food crisis and the upsurge of land grabbing that accompanied it, I was acutely aware of the worsening human rights situation in the countryside and of the need for new international standards. Together with Carwil Bjork-James, I authored a preliminary analysis of the UNDROP campaign for a 2010 Yale Law School conference on "Developing Food Policy" (Edelman and James 2011). The following year, I went to Geneva to follow discussions about UNDROP (an abbreviation that nobody used then) in the Human Rights Council's Advisory Committee.[19] While I began to study UNDROP as a sympathetic observer, I

Box 8.5. A different fieldwork site

The Bar Serpent's massive windows extend upward to the third floor of Building E of Geneva's Palais de Nations. The bar looks out on manicured lawns with sculptures, cedar and pine trees, and the glistening waters of Lake Geneva, with snowcapped Alpine peaks, including the distinctive anvil-shaped Mount Blanc, visible in the distance on clear days. The bar is a place of intrigue. Diplomats huddle at round glass tables and parse the wording of upcoming resolutions. These first and second secretaries and the occasional ambassador are usually smartly attired in European business dress, though some African, Middle Eastern, and South Asian delegates appear resplendent in multicolored robes and saris. Cuban men in impeccable long-sleeve guayaberas, Islamic women in hijabs and niqabs and men in jalabiyas and dishdashas, Indonesian and Malaysian men in songkok or peci caps, and African women in kaftans and boubous round out the sartorial smorgasbord. Young multilingual NGO activists converse in a dozen varieties of English, French, or Spanish and hunch over laptop screens earnestly drafting position papers and oral interventions. Civil society activists circulate through the bar distributing leaflets for roundtables, side events, and interactive dialogues on issues ranging from the empowerment of women in conflict zones, the plight of refugee children, the right to education in Bahrain, freedom of expression in Sri Lanka, or the proposed binding treaty on transnational corporations' human rights obligations. Enormous abstract photographs, in garish tones suggestive of acrylic paint, grace one wall, though the exhibit changes from time to time, often featuring pictures of UN programs, almost always in the poorest regions of the poorest countries. The Bar Serpent is where the action is at the UN, and it is one of the few places in the extraordinarily expensive city of Geneva where one can get a decent cup of coffee for less than three dollars.

became increasingly involved as a participant in its production. In 2012, FIAN International, an important NGO ally of LVC, invited me to participate in an International Public Hearing and Seminar on the Human Rights Situation of Peasant Communities in the Bajo Aguán, Honduras, an area of violent agrarian conflict (Edelman 2012; Edelman and León 2013; Edelman 2017, chap. 4). The Honduras event highlighted severe cases of violations of the rights of peasants in part to build support for UNDROP. The following year, the Office of the High Commissioner for Human Rights (OHCHR) invited me to be a panelist at the first session of the intergovernmental working group mandated with negotiating the text of the declaration.[20] The charge was to present a briefing paper on definitions of "peasant" that could strengthen the draft text's article 1 on the rights holders (see chapter 9). In 2014 and 2015, I joined an informal group that advised the Bolivian ambassador when she had to present a new draft declaration to the UNHRC that was more compatible with "accepted language" in international law (Claeys and Edelman 2020) (see box 8.6). As the lone anthropologist on the team, I was tasked with responsibility for article 1 (definition of the rights holders) and the article on cultural rights (article 26 in the final version of UNDROP).[21]

In earlier work, I expressed skepticism about how foundational thinkers in agrarian studies—or peasant studies, as it was then called—prefaced every analysis with highly specific definitions of "peasant" (Shanin 1990a; Wolf 1966). It was, I suggested, more interesting to examine when, how, and for what purposes political actors invoked and bounded the category (Edelman 1999, 189–193). The imperative of defining the rights holders in a human rights instrument disabused me of this academic pretension (see box 8.7). I proposed a text that drew significantly on LVC's earlier definition that was as inclusive as possible of the different rural sectors (fishers, pastoralists, Indigenous peoples) that were clamoring to be represented, that drew on a substantial corpus of peasant studies literature, and that echoed accepted language on "non-monetized sectors of the economy" from article 14.1 of the Convention on the Elimination of All Forms of Discrimination against Women (CEDAW 1979). The challenge of refining the draft article on cultural rights was different. Starting with the wording that originated with LVC and then the UNHRC Advisory Committee, I sought accepted language from international agreements that might address the supposed contradiction between collective or group rights and the individual rights of persons within the group, an objection that European and other diplomats repeatedly raised and that genuinely concerned me. I finally found in the UNESCO Universal Declaration on Cultural Diversity language that formed the basis for the relevant sentence in UNDROP article 26.1: "No one may invoke cultural rights to infringe upon the human rights guaranteed by international law or to limit their scope" (UNDROP 2018, art. 26.1).[22]

Box 8.6. Accepted language

"Any additions that are not accepted language are difficult to accept."

—Indian delegate's intervention, fifth intergovernmental working group session, April 9, 2018

"Soft Law," Implementation, and Future Perspectives

Given the severity and complexity of the rights violations that rural people face, does it make any difference that the UN adopted the Declaration on the Rights of Peasants and Other People Working in Rural Areas? Declarations, in contrast to conventions, are nonbinding "soft law," and many states are loath to abide even by their own national laws much less international ones that apply to them. In this regard, it is instructive to look at the experience of Declaration on the Rights of Indigenous Peoples (UNDRIP) since its adoption in 2007. Provisions in UNDRIP have been incorporated in national laws and Indigenous movements routinely invoke this "soft" international law as if it were "hard" and binding. That policy-makers and law enforcement bodies do not always grasp this distinction works to the advantage of Indigenous peoples' claims. Even when they understand the difference between "soft" and "hard" law, they may treat nonbinding agreements as hard regulations, since shaming can be an effective mechanism of coercion (Zerilli 2010, 5). "Moreover," as Priscilla Claeys and I argue elsewhere, "in contested agrarian landscapes, distinct legal regimes—customary, local, national and international law—frequently overlap, creating spaces of contention in which 'soft law' may attain increasing legitimacy as an unquestioned standard. In a context of growing involvement of civil society in international law-making, new instruments increasingly derive their visibility, legitimacy and force from the participatory way in which they were elaborated" (Claeys and Edelman 2020, 11).

In addition, in states with "monist" or "constitutional block" legal traditions, international agreements (particularly treaties but also declarations) have force in domestic law, potentially providing a tool for peasants seeking access to justice.[23]

This section on "soft law" briefly considers three efforts to use UNDROP's provisions even before it received UN approval. Its aim is merely to signal, not to analyze in depth, creative uses of an international "soft law" still under construction

Box 8.7. Asserting the dignity of the peasants, defending Article 1 of UNDROP

"Mr. President, this article 1 affects me emotionally in a special way, because I am a son, grandson, and great-grandson of campesinos. I know well how it is to live as a peasant, and I know how this has been with the passage of time. My grandfather said with great pride that he was a campesino. He had some hilly land, a few goats, and olive trees from which he got the oil for the whole year for the family. My father no longer said he was a campesino. He said he was an agriculturalist and cattleman. In his time, being a campesino was held in contempt; it was the worst thing, and that is why he didn't want me to be a campesino, either. But over the years I insisted on being a campesino and working the land and with animals. I am very happy and enjoy this because I am a lover of the land and my profession and because I consider it a point of pride to produce quality food in the quantity necessary to feed society. And of course, it is a very dignified profession, of which I do not have to be ashamed. That is why I believe that the definition in this article 1 perfectly reflects the concept of a peasant. I understand that this definition is essential to value and dignify the work of so many women and men who live and keep the rural world alive, preserving knowledge, cultures, and biodiversity, and creating employment. We are tired of our work being scorned. But still, we continue working and taking care of our lands, with much effort and little profitability, because we love them and because we understand that land is not an inheritance from our parents, but a loan to our children, as an intelligent proverb says. I would like to convey my hope and my emotion, which are like those of millions of peasants who look forward to their rights being recognized with the approval of this declaration. We who are here have the great re-

> sponsibility to reach the necessary agreements so that this historical fact becomes a reality."
>
> —Intervention of José Manuel Benítez Castaño, Coordination of Agriculturalists' and Livestock Producers' Organizations (COAG), Spain, in the fifth intergovernmental working group session, April 12, 2018

to shape national-level human rights practice. The examples include (1) a 2012 International Public Hearing and Seminar on the Human Rights Situation of the Peasant Communities in the Bajo Aguán, Honduras; (2) the *Manual para Juezas y Jueces sobre la protección de los derechos de las campesinas y campesinos*, published in Mexico in 2013, but with an intended audience of judges throughout Latin America; and (3) the varied uses of UNDROP in resolving the armed conflict in Colombia (Edelman 2012; Emanuelli and Gutiérrez Rivas 2013; Castilla Salazar 2016).[24]

The Bajo Aguán region of Honduras was the center of the Honduran agrarian reform in the 1970s and of agrarian counterreform in the 1990s. Since the 2009 military coup that toppled the elected government of President José Manuel Zelaya, the region has been immersed in a brutal conflict between militant peasant movements and large landowners, with both involved in African palm production (Edelman and León 2013). In 2012, several Honduran and international human rights groups held a public hearing in Tocoa, Colón, a small city in the center of the Aguán, that was loosely modeled on the International War Crimes Tribunal that Bertrand Russell organized in the 1960s. For several days, national and international observers received testimonies from victims of human rights violations and debated how to address military, police, and private violence and the prevailing impunity in the region. Discussions included the pros and cons of lobbying with the inter-American and United Nations human rights systems, the European Union and its member states, the US government, the World Bank (which financed the largest plantations), and the International Criminal Court. While peasant organizations in the Aguán reported reductions in violence after the hearing, it is likely this had more to do with the heightened visibility, international attention, and the protection accorded by foreign "accompaniment" rather than with specific lobbying efforts, many of which did not benefit from sustained follow-up.

The *Manual para Juezas y Jueces sobre la protección de los derechos de las campesinas y campesinos*, published in 2013 by Habitat International's Mexico office and the Ibero-American Network of Judges (REDIJ), took the draft peasants' rights declaration as an established standard, citing its articles one after another, even though it was still under consideration in the UN and far from finalized. The *Manual*, amply disseminated throughout the Americas and available online, seeks to heighten awareness among judges about agrarian and peasant issues, to provide new arguments about which cases are "justiciable" or appropriate for review, and to call attention to model cases that could serve as precedents when judges are writing decisions. The model cases include one from Argentina, "Peralta, Viviana vs. Municipalidad de San Jorge," which prohibited pesticide fumigation in a peri-urban zone with the objective of protecting the environment and the population's health. The example is suggestive since, as mentioned above, one Argentine farmer in Geneva demanded the "right not to be fumigated" (vernacular version), which was subsequently incorporated into UNDROP using other language (international "soft law" norm) and which in turn returned to Argentina through the court decision analyzed in the *Manual para Juezas y Jueces* (completing the circle of vernacularization-in-reverse).

The third effort examined here outlines the uses of UNDROP standards to address the rural crisis and armed conflict in Colombia. Beginning in 2014, national and local peasant movements, notably the Cumbre Agraria, demanded that the government uphold standards specified in UNDROP and that the foreign ministry indicate its backing for the declaration in the UN. UNDROP's draft provisions also became part of the peace negotiations—concluded in 2016—between the FARC guerrillas and the Colombian government.[25] Arguing that "for the peasantry to count, it must be counted," DeJusticia, a Colombian human rights organization, initiated a legal action (*tutela*) in 2017 on behalf of 1,770 campesinos and campesinas that sought to have diagnostic, UNDROP-inspired questions added to the national population census with a view to generating evidenced-based policies that would better support peasant communities. The census had already begun by the time the Supreme Court ruled in favor of DeJusticia in 2018, so the necessary questions—developed by a commission that included specialists chosen by the peasant organizations—were not included. They were, however, incorporated into the subsequent agricultural census and national household survey (DeJusticia 2019; Uprimny 2018).

Another, more ambitious proposal that took the draft peasants' rights declaration as an established standard, even before the UN adopted it, was the proposed reform of article 64 of the Colombian constitution, introduced in Congress in 2016 by Senator Alberto Castilla of the Polo Democrático Alternativo (Castilla Salazar 2016). This measure, which drew heavily and explicitly on the draft UNDROP text and other UN documentation, sought to replace language that referred to the *trabajador agrario* (agrarian worker) with *campesino* and *campesina*, while also establishing rights to territory, to seeds, and to free prior and informed consent. In effect, it aimed to close protection gaps in the 1991 constitution, which established important rights for Indigenous and Afro-descendant peoples, and to recognize the peasantry as a social group with a particular identity and practices rather than merely a category of producer. Importantly, this proposed constitutional reform would have provided a framework for the legal resolution of conflicts over land and territory that were both causes and consequences of Colombia's long civil war and that were central to the peace accords. Castilla's attempt at recognizing peasants as "social subjects" did not prosper in the conservative Colombian Senate, which in late 2016 defeated it by a vote of 28–25 (Congreso Visible 2016).

After the UN General Assembly adopted UNDROP, discussions about implementation moved to another level. Because the adoption is so recent, many ideas are under discussion, and many are still preliminary. Some activists who pushed for UNDROP now advocate for the creation of new UN mechanisms, such as a special rapporteur or independent expert on peasants' rights. Others seek to make UNDROP better known among grassroots movements by translating it into additional languages and preparing didactic materials to support on-the-ground struggles. Several point to the need to lobby for national-level laws that incorporate UNDROP language or to engage with regional human rights systems, such as the Inter-American Commission on Human Rights or the European Union. All, however, are cognizant of the difficulties of implementing a peasants' rights agenda in a world where authoritarianism is on the march and where the interests of capital almost everywhere prevail over human needs.

In an interview shortly after the adoption of UNDROP, Natalia Pacheco, a counselor at the Bolivian Mission in Geneva who was deeply involved in the negotiations, asserted that the declaration contributed to decolonizing the international human rights system in three ways:

> First, its objective and spirit address in a holistic way the situation of vulnerability of a historically [defenseless] group. Second, its vision of human rights embraces not only individual civil rights, but also collective rights, both civil and political as well as economic, social and cultural rights. These include human rights to land and seeds, showing the human being's dependence on Mother Earth. Third, the Declaration incorporates unconventional concepts and notions, such as food sovereignty, which reflect a much broader and decolonizing narrative.[26]

Pacheco's observation about decolonization could be extended to the main paradigm that anthropologists have employed to analyze how human rights are created and lived. As I suggest above, the vernacularization understanding of norms creation and diffusion is an overly linear, top-down approach that reproduces a conventional North–South split, with the North as the producer and source of human rights and the South as consumer of standards elaborated in Geneva or New York. This framework gives short shrift to two developments. The first is the participation of rights holders in authoring international norms that apply to them, as occurred in the lead-up to the 2007 UN Declaration on the Rights of Indigenous Peoples and has now taken place with the Declaration on the Rights of Peasants and Other People Working in Rural Areas. The second, as illustrated by the Honduran, Mexican, and Colombian cases outlined above, is the creative appropriation in national contexts of international norms still under construction to convert future "soft law" into defensible rights and justiciable "hard law," even before the soft law is finalized. This closely resembles the vernacularization approach but is different because it occurs as an outgrowth of a parallel process of norms construction from the bottom up. Transnational agrarian movements and their national affiliates have actively participated in the construction and implementation of new international human rights law, while at the same time their national-level campaigns have contributed to the vernacularization of the very norms that they constructed in Geneva.

The history of UNDROP is also a chapter in the wider effort to understand how international law is sometimes constructed from below and to decenter narratives about the origins of human rights that are focused on the Global North.[27] It is not just that grassroots movements, often from marginalized populations, have clawed their way into the UN system and coauthored international law. At the state level, histories of human rights—whether the point of departure is the French Revolution's Declaration of the Rights of Man or the 1948 Universal Declaration of Human Rights—have tended to downplay or obscure non-Western and non-developed-country origins. A growing body of scholarship examines the centrality of countries such as India and Jamaica in the construction of what we today call the UN human rights system (Bhagavan 2012; Jensen 2016, 2015).

Finally, it is essential to situate the UNDROP within the long sweep of an expanding conception of human rights (and of categories of rights holders), which some jurists call their "evolutionary character" (Lauren 2011, chap. 9). The EU delegates who in the UNDROP negotiations repeatedly inveighed against what they saw as "new rights" were in denial about this history. UN recognition of the rights of peasants is simply one more chapter in the long history of struggles of other internationally recognized "vulnerable groups," a category that includes women, children, the elderly, people living in poverty, Indigenous peoples, minorities, migrants, refugees and internally displaced persons, people with disabilities, prisoners, and people living with or affected by HIV/AIDS. International law sees vulnerable groups as lacking human rights protections and as suffering from discrimination or from marginalization of their legal status. It assumes that granting special protection for vulnerable groups or individuals is not contrary but complementary to the principle of nondiscrimination. The inclusion of peasants in the list of vulnerable groups and the recognition of their rights is a long overdue acknowledgment of the discrimination and human rights violations that they routinely suffer. This recognition was the fruit of the peasants' own struggles, persistence, and imagination—a small victory in the early part of an otherwise inauspicious twenty-first century.

DEFINING "PEASANT" AT THE UNITED NATIONS HUMAN RIGHTS COUNCIL

I wrote this chapter at the invitation of the Office of High Commissioner for Human Rights as a contribution to the negotiations in the first session in 2013 of the Intergovernmental Working Group on a United Nations Declaration on the Rights of Peasants and Other People Working in Rural Areas (UNDROP). As I indicate in chapter 8, drafting this text for an audience of diplomats involved a delicate analytical and political balancing act. In the UNDROP negotiations, the very idea of "peasant" evoked skepticism and frontal attacks. This chapter was an effort to have an elite audience normalize a category that much of the world had no trouble at all accepting.

In many (though not all) international human rights instruments, article 1 is used to define the rights holders. Normative definitions of this sort can be controversial (e.g., in debates over who is a "child" in the lead-up to the Convention on the Rights of the Child), as can their absence (as was the case with the Declaration on the Rights of Indigenous Peoples). The question of how to define "peasant" and "peasantry" has a long, complicated, and contentious history. Definitions of human groups arise or are created for different purposes, including social control, legal protections, social scientific analysis, collective action, and colloquial description. Such definitions may or may not overlap and coincide. Sometimes groups that are subject to discrimination appropriate, invert, and celebrate previously pejorative labels. Moreover, cognate terms in different languages are hardly ever completely coterminous (e.g., "peasant," "*campesino*," "*paysan*," "крестьянин [krest'ianin]"). Even though normative definitions appear to fix an object in a timeless way, in practice, definitions always change over time and manifest varying degrees of "strictness."

This chapter is a highly synthetic overview and, for reasons of space, has had to ignore or gloss over many key discussions.[1] It does not pretend to be comprehensive, nor does it purport to resolve the debates. It distinguishes for heuristic purposes four different kinds of definition of "peasant." These are:

(1) Historical definitions, such as those from societies where peasants constituted an estate-like, caste-like, corporate, or subordinated social group characterized by specific restrictions on geographical or social mobility, limited rights, and obligations to provide services and perform particular deference behaviors for superordinate groups;

(2) Social scientific definitions from anthropology and sociology and from the interdisciplinary fields of peasant studies and agrarian studies;

(3) Activist definitions employed by agrarian movements, particularly La Via Campesina and its constituent organizations that self-identify as "peasants" (or "campesinos");

(4) Normative definitions proposed by civil society organizations and by the Advisory Committee of the Human Rights Council.

The first two categories will be examined at greater length than the last two, which will just be the subject of brief comments. It should be noted at the outset that definitions that arise (or arose) in the context of one of these categories sometimes spill over into one or more of the other categories. The legal and institutional codification of "campesino" in Mexico (C. R. Boyer 2003) and in Bolivia (Lagos 1994) in the twentieth century, for example, has in each case dimensions that are at once historical and normative, and these in turn influenced both social scientists and agrarian activists in the respective countries.

Historical Definitions

The word "peasant" appears in English in late medieval and early modern times, when it was used to refer to the rural poor, rural residents, serfs, agricultural laborers, and the "common" or "simple" people. As a verb in that period, "to peasant" meant to subjugate someone as a peasant is subjugated. Earlier Latin and Latinate forms (e.g., French, Castilian, Catalan, Occitan) date as far back as the sixth century and denoted a rural inhabitant, whether or not involved in agriculture. Very early on, both the English "peasant," the French "paysan," and similar terms sometimes connoted "rustic," "ignorant," "stupid," "crass," and "rude," among many other pejorative terms (Oxford English Dictionary 2005).

The word could also imply criminality, as in thirteenth-century Germany where "'peasant' meant 'villain, rustic, devil, robber, brigand and looter" (Le Goff and King 1972, 71).

These derogatory meanings are indicative both of peasants' extreme subordination and of a ubiquitous elite practice of blaming peasants for a variety of economic and social ills. These included (and include) a supposed reluctance to work hard, since their consumption expectations seemed to be easily satisfied; a failure to use land "efficiently" and thus of standing in the way of "progress"; having too many children; and constituting a "dangerous" class not suitable for or capable of full citizenship. These elite imaginings were typically espoused in order to promote policies aimed at pushing peasants off the land and turning them into laborers (Handy 2009).

According to anthropologist George Dalton, "Peasants were legal, political, social, and economic inferiors in medieval Europe. The structured subordination of peasants to non-peasants was expressed in many ways, *de jure* and *de facto*, from restraints on their physical movement to sumptuary restrictions on what kinds of weapons, clothing and adornments they could wear and use, and foods they could legally consume" (Dalton 1972, 391; original italics). As late as the eighteenth century in British-ruled Ireland, Catholic peasants were legally prevented from renting land worth more than thirty shillings a year and from making a profit from land of more than one-third of the rent paid (Ignatiev 1996, 34). In Russia, until 1861, peasants constituted a "social estate," bound to landlords' properties with no right to geographical mobility, and those in serfdom directly to the state were only emancipated in 1867 (Shanin 1972, 19). Analogous forms of bondage existed in Japan and China (Moore 1966). In much of Latin America, de jure and de facto systems of debt peonage and unpaid labor persisted until at least the mid-twentieth century, called *huasipungo* in Ecuador, *colonato* in Bolivia and Central America, *yanaconaje* in Peru, *inquilinaje* in Chile, and *cambão* in Brazil (Barraclough and Domike 1966, 399; Huizer 1973, 9). In some cases, in a particularly grotesque display of patriarchal power reminiscent of the medieval European practice of jus primae noctis, Latin American peasants were required to provide their daughters for the sexual pleasure of the landlords (Huizer 1973, 9).

Social upheavals and economic changes in the twentieth century ended many of the more egregious forms of unfree labor and obligatory service, although these persist in some regions of South Asia and elsewhere (Kapadia 2000). Nonetheless, even the Russian and Chinese revolutions, which sought to upend the old order, reinstated restrictions on the geographic mobility of rural residents, in effect legally tying most peasants to particular production units in the countryside and thus according them second-class citizenship. In both cases, residence restrictions persisted even following decollectivization. Especially if they migrate to other regions without permission, rural residents in these societies have few labor protections and diminished rights to social services, housing, and education (Gang and Stuart 1999; Chan and Zhang 1999).

Other twentieth-century social revolutions created less onerous but nonetheless specific categories for "peasants" that distinguished them from the rest of society. Following the Mexican Revolution, for example, the term "campesino" achieved a new salience and widespread use as a self-ascribed marker of political identity, even among rural people skeptical of aspects of radical agrarian ideology. By the 1930s, "[peasants] were insisting that it was possible to be a campesino *and* Catholic, or a campesino *and* indigenous, or a campesino *and* a resident of such and such a village. . . . They undermined the proposition that campesinos have a unidimensional social essence based solely on their economic interests and replaced it with a hybrid sense of campesino-ness that accommodated multiple and sometimes cross-cutting cultural values" (C. R. Boyer 2003, 44–45).

In Bolivia, similarly, following the revolution of 1952, campesino became an official governance category, with the creation of a Ministry of Peasant Affairs. The term substituted for and came to mask an understanding of the highly diverse and overwhelmingly Indigenous nature of the rural population (Rivera Cusicanqui 1985). Importantly, however, the reassertion of Indigenous identity in the 1990s and after occurred largely alongside and not in opposition to campesino identity (Albó 2008, 40).

Social Scientific Definitions

During the 1960s and 1970s, peasants excited new interest among social scientists. Over the previous half century, peasant wars and revolutions—in Mexico, China, Algeria, and Vietnam, among other places—indicated that peasantries had become important political protagonists (Wolf 1969). Development imperatives in what was then widely termed the "third world" required in-depth understanding of rural populations. East–West geopolitical competition and spreading anticolonial struggles also fueled concern about the peasantry, which was at the time and by almost any definition the majority of humankind.

Anthropologists' early efforts to define peasants emphasized that peasantries emerged in order to provision the first cities and market towns. The category "peasant" was thus only meaningful in relation to a larger society that included non-peasants. Such definitions tended to be ample, often including rural artisans, fisherfolk, pastoralists, and small-scale miners in addition to agriculturalists. Some scholars emphasized generic cultural or "folk" characteristics of peasants (Silverman 1979) while others, notably Eric R. Wolf, sought to delineate social structural "types" based on whether they had secure land rights or, alternatively, were tenants, sharecroppers, or resident laborers on large properties. Peasants tended to be distinguished from farmers; peasants aimed for "subsistence" and produced cash crops primarily for survival and to maintain their social status rather than to invest and expand the scale of their operations, as was allegedly the case with farmers (Wolf 1955). In several widely separated zones of the world, such as in much of Latin America and Indonesia, peasants were found to be living in territorial "corporate communities" that barred membership to outsiders, held exclusive rights to land, and systematically redistributed surplus wealth through obligatory ritual expenditures. Indeed, as David Mosse points out, "Almost every region of the world that experienced colonial rule had some form of 'government through community'" (Mosse 2008, 83). The "closed" communities Wolf analyzed contrasted with others elsewhere in which residence was more open, property and market relations more fluid, and cash crop production more extensive (Wolf 1957, 1986). Wolf further argued that peasants characteristically had to produce a "replacement fund" that provided a caloric minimum and ensured biological reproduction; a "ceremonial fund" to support weddings, community festivals, and other social responsibilities; and a "fund of rent" that consisted of wealth in labor, produce, or money transferred to superordinate sectors, such as landlords, moneylenders, intermediaries, religious specialists, and tax collectors (Wolf 1966).

Teodor Shanin, another leading peasant studies scholar, defined peasantry as having "four essential and inter-linked facets": "the family farm as the basic multi-functional unit of social organisation, land husbandry and usually animal rearing as the main means of livelihood, a specific traditional culture closely linked with the way of life of small rural communities and multi-directional subjection to powerful outsiders" (Shanin 1973, 63–64).

In addition, Shanin recognized the existence of "a number of analytically marginal groups which share with the 'hard core' of the peasantry most but not all of its major characteristics" (Shanin 1973, 64). These included the "agricultural labourer lacking a fully-fledged farm, a rural craftsman holding little or no land, the frontier squatter or the armed peasant who at times escaped centuries of political submission along frontiers or in the mountains," as well as pastoralists and "peasant-workers in modern industrial communities" (Shanin 1971, 16).

Concurring with the overall thrust of Wolf's and Shanin's definitions, Sidney Mintz noted "the fact . . . that peasantries nowhere form a homogeneous mass or agglomerate, but are always and everywhere typified themselves by internal differentiation along many lines" (Mintz 1973, 93). He also pointed to "the need for middle-range definitions of peasantries and of peasant societies: definitions that fall somewhere between real peasant societies 'on the ground,' so to speak, and the widest-ranging level of definitional statement, adequate to describe all of them" (Mintz 1973, 92). "Definitions or typologies of peasantries," he asserted, "will have to deal with different 'mixes' of peasant classes, or of ethnic groups, in different societies" (Mintz 1973, 94). Despite this recognition of the heterogeneity of peasantries, Mintz was reluctant to define "landless, wage-earning agricultural workers" as peasants, since they were inserted in very different kinds of economic relations. He nonetheless qualified this skepticism in acknowledging the "simultaneous participation of large groups of people in activities associated with" both rural wage labor and small-scale agricultural production (Mintz 1973, 95).

The Inter-American Committee for Agricultural Development (ICAD), which carried out land tenure studies in seven Latin American countries in the mid-1960s, classified farms as subfamily, family, multifamily medium, and multifamily large.[2] This typology—based on census data on farm size and on what extension could sustain a household at a culturally acceptable standard of living—remained extremely influential in the social sciences in Latin America and beyond (Hewitt de Alcántara 1984, 123–128; Roseberry 1993, 321–333). Numerous subsequent studies have echoed ICAD's finding that smallholdings used the factor land much more productively and efficiently than large farms (IAASTD 2009; Netting 1993). The ICAD study employed the term "campesino" to refer to indebted laborers who were bound to large estates, but it also used "smallholder" and "farm owner" interchangeably to describe agriculturalists in possession of the smaller categories of farms. This marked a significant conceptual difference with the anthropological and sociological frameworks of Wolf, Mintz, and Shanin, which tended to view "peasant" and "farmer" as contrasting categories, with different economic logics.

In recent decades, a growing number of social scientists have sought to incorporate a gender dimension into understandings of the terms "peasant" and "peasantry." They point out, for example, that the peasant household or family farm, which Shanin viewed as a quintessential element of the peasant economy, is typically characterized by a gender division of labor and gendered internal power relations; in many world regions, women are the primary agriculturalists, and women's participation in small-scale agriculture and nonfarm rural activities appears to be increasing, in part as a result of growing male migration (Appendini and De Luca 2005; Deere 1995; Razavi 2009). These analyses constitute an important corrective to the implicit male bias of many earlier efforts to define "peasant" because they insist on and document both the significant participation of women in rural agricultural households and their frequent invisibility in discussions of "peasantry" and related issues such as agrarian reform.

It is worth acknowledging that several currents of scholarly thought, particularly (but not only) those influenced by traditional cultural anthropology, orthodox Marxism, or postmodernism, rejected the possibility of defining "peasants." Some cultural anthropologists in the 1960s insisted that most rural African cultivators were "tribals" rather than "peasants," although by the 1970s there was a strong social scientific consensus that these groups fit the criteria for peasants outlined by Shanin and others (Fallers 1961; Isaacman 1993, 206; Saul and Woods 1971). Henry Bernstein, arguing from a Marxist perspective, asserted that the terms "peasant" and "peasantry" were only useful in considering "pre-capitalist societies, populated by mostly small-scale family farmers . . . and processes of transition to capitalism." Under capitalism, he suggested, peasants differentiate into classes of "small-scale capitalist farmers, relatively successful petty commodity producers and wage labour" (Bernstein 2010, 3–4). Anthropologist Anthony Leeds lambasted scholars who used the term "peasant," charging that it was "a folk term adopted into social science" and had "no precision whatsoever" (Leeds 1977, 228). He asserted that the concept confused "persons" and "roles" and noted that rural cultivators constantly shifted in and out of a variety of roles, including wage laborer, squatter, job contractor and urban service worker. Other scholars, while not rejecting the peasant language, similarly noted that the rural poor engaged in "occupational multiplicity," a phenomenon that was later widely discussed as "pluriactivity" or the "new rurality" (Comitas 1973; Kay 2008).

Postmodernist theorists such as Michael Kearney also remarked on the diversity of nonagricultural economic activities practiced by the rural poor and saw this as evidence that the peasant concept was obsolete, particularly in an era of intensifying migration and transnational household strategies in Mexico, his main empirical referent (Kearney 1996). He proposed a neologism, "polybian," which was supposed to denote the multifaceted identities and livelihood practices characteristic of the contemporary rural poor. Unfortunately for Kearney, his book went to press right as a major peasant and Indigenous rebellion unfolded in the southern Mexican state of Chiapas, led by an explicitly agrarian movement that claimed the mantle of the early twentieth-century revolutionary Emiliano Zapata. While the Zapatista uprising tended to vitiate Kearney's argument about the obsolescence of the term "peasant," it did point to a significant deficiency in many of the definitions of "peasant" that social scientists had debated since the 1960s. As Shanin noted, peasants "are not only an analytical construct . . . but a social group which exists in the collective consciousness and political deed of its members" (Shanin 1990a, 69). Similarly, "peasant" could be understood not just as a role or a social structural position but also as a form of identity and self-ascription—and not necessarily a primordial or overarching one, since it could coexist in the same person alongside multiple other identities, ranging from Indigenous to "microentrepreneur," migrant, teacher, or electri-

TABLE 9.1. Estimates of the world's agricultural, rural, and economically active in agriculture populations

	IN 1,000s	% WORLD POPULATION
World population	7,130,012	100%
Agricultural population	2,621,360	37%
Rural population	3,445,843	48%
Economically active in agriculture*	1,320,181	19%

Source: Food and Agriculture Organization, FAOstat database, June 21, 2013.
* Economically active population in agriculture includes household heads who sustain larger numbers of nonactive dependents.

cian (Edelman 2008, 251–252). In light of this, some social scientists maintained that what was most revealing about the "peasant" category was to see when and why it was invoked and by whom. This, of course, generally involved grassroots agrarian movements, but it also at times implicated rural elites, including large landowners, who sought to euphemize their position and claimed to be "peasants" for political or other purposes (Edelman 1999, 190–191).

Probably the most significant recent social scientific effort to theorize the notion of peasant and peasantry is Jan Douwe Van der Ploeg's book *The New Peasantries*. Van der Ploeg (2008) locates "peasant farming" on a continuum—rather than as a contrasting category—with "entrepreneurial farming." Key features of "the peasant condition" include minimizing monetary costs, crop diversification to reduce economic and environmental risks, cooperative relations that provide an alternative to monetary relations and market exchange, and a struggle for autonomy, which includes nonmoney forms of obtaining inputs and labor. Importantly, Van der Ploeg sees these elements as central not only to peasants in developing countries but also to the many multifunctional farms in Europe and North America that rely on the same principles to ensure survival in a hostile economic environment. Finally, Van der Ploeg contrasts "the manufactured invisibility" of peasants with their striking "omnipresence"—there are now, he maintains, more peasants than ever before in history, and they still constitute some two-fifths of humanity (see table 9.1) (Van der Ploeg 2008, xiv; Weis 2007, 25).

Activist Definitions

"Peasant," "campesino," "paysan," and similar terms are long-standing identity markers that have served to inspire the collective action of diverse kinds of rural movements. With the rise in the 1990s of transnational agrarian organizations such as La Via Campesina (LVC), "today arguably the world's largest social movement" (Provost 2013), peasants have a heightened global political profile and the "peasant" label has newfound contemporary resonance (Borras, Edelman, and Kay 2008).

In defining "peasant," the imperatives of social movements—and transnational ones, in particular—are different from those of social scientists. Activists typically seek to attract the maximum number of adherents and allies by casting a wide net, while at the same time bounding their movement so as to exclude sectors unsympathetic or opposed to their objectives. In the case of peasants, the transnational agrarian movement LVC includes national organizations that represent quite varied constituencies, from rural workers and small and medium-size cultivators in developing countries to small and medium-size commercial farms in the developed North. The process of grouping these diverse sectors under a single tent has involved highlighting common concerns (e.g., economic vulnerability in globalizing commodities markets, heightened risks resulting from climate change) and deemphasizing possible areas of discord or divergent interests (e.g., developed-country farm subsidies that disadvantage developing-country agriculturalists). Boundary maintenance for the movement has meant limiting affiliation to organizations that share certain minimum principles. Many large farmer organizations are in effect excluded from LVC, not because of the size of their members' holdings per se but rather because of their support for unfettered trade liberalization, industrial chemical-intensive agriculture, and genetically engineered crops.

The umbrella concept central to LVC's definition of "peasant" is "people of the land." This hews closely to the original meaning of terms in Latinate languages, such as "campesino" and "paysan," which literally refer to people from the countryside, whether or not they are agriculturalists. Contemporary agrarian activists insist on the commonalities of "peasants" and "farmers," adducing arguments much like Van der Ploeg's reflections (cited above) on the "peasant condition" of economic vulnerability combined with a quest for autonomy. Today's activists often use the words "peasant" and "farmer" interchangeably—in conversation, in written analyses, and in their movements' names (e.g., the European Farmers Coordination and the Coordination Paysanne Européenne refer to the same organization). As Nettie Wiebe, a LVC activist and past president of the National Farmers Union of Canada, remarked in an interview:

> If you actually look at what "peasant" means, it means "people of the land." Are we Canadian farmers "people of the land"? . . . People of the land—peasantry everywhere, the millions of small subsistence peasants with whom we think we have so little in common—identifies

them, and it identifies us. . . . As long as you keep us in separate categories, and we're the highly industrialized farmers who are sort of quasi-business entrepreneurs and they're the subsistence peasants, then we can't see how closely we and all our issues are linked. (Wiebe 2002)

LVC—a coalition or movement with member organizations in over seventy countries—has been the main force advocating for a new international instrument on peasants' rights. The "people of the land" focus is evident in article 1 of its 2009 proposed draft declaration on peasants' rights:

A peasant is a man or woman of the land, who has a direct and special relationship with the land and nature through the production of food and/or other agricultural products. Peasants work the land themselves, rely[ing] above all on family labour and other small-scale forms of organizing labour. Peasants are traditionally embedded in their local communities and they take care of local landscapes and of agro-ecological systems. The term peasant can apply to any person engaged in agriculture, cattle-raising, pastoralism, handicrafts-related to agriculture or a related occupation in a rural area. This includes Indigenous people working on the land.

The term peasant also applies to landless. According to the UN Food and Agriculture Organization . . . , the following categories of people are considered to be landless and are likely to face difficulties in ensuring their livelihood:

1. Agricultural labour households with little or no land;
2. Non-agricultural households in rural areas, with little or no land, whose members are engaged in various activities such as fishing, making crafts for the local market, or providing services;
3. Other rural households of pastoralists, nomads, peasants practicing shifting cultivation, hunters and gatherers, and people with similar livelihoods. (LVC 2009a)

This definition shares with the social scientific definitions examined above an emphasis on the household or family farm and embeddedness in a community as essential characteristics of the peasant condition. Like the social scientific definitions, it includes diverse rural livelihoods that, strictly speaking, are not agricultural, such as fishing, pastoralism, and artisanal crafts production. It includes some categories, such as hunters and gatherers, which would not be included in most social scientific definitions.

Normative Definitions

In 2010, the Advisory Committee of the Human Rights Council issued its "Preliminary Study of the Human Rights Council Advisory Committee on Discrimination in the Context of the Right to Food," which included as an appendix the LVC draft text quoted above (UNHRC Advisory Committee 2010, 32). Two years later, it released the "Final Study of the Human Rights Council Advisory Committee on the Advancement of the Rights of Peasants and Other People Working in Rural Areas." This document contained the committee's own text, which accepted verbatim the definition in the annex to the Preliminary Study (UNHRC Advisory Committee 2012, 6). According to advisory committee member José Bengoa, the LVC draft text—and by extension its definition of "peasant"—became "an official document of the United Nations" (Bengoa 2012). This hardly means, however, that the draft definition in these UN documents had to be "written in stone." The challenge for the intergovernmental working group is to debate and refine the definition of rights holders so that it is significantly inclusive of the very wide variety of vulnerable rural populations in the world today. At the same time, the working group ought to be attentive to the possibility that once identity categories become fixed in law, there is a risk that they may generate new forms of exclusion if they fail to recognize "invisible" or stigmatized groups or if conditions shift and new vulnerable groups emerge (Claeys 2013). The Advisory Committee of the Human Rights Council's definition, for example, gives little explicit attention to rural migrant workers who are not members of households, such as displaced youths, economic and political refugees, or women who have fled domestic or other violence.

Several conclusions may be extracted from the brief overview presented above:

(1) The terms "peasant" and "peasantry" and their cognates in other languages have long and complicated histories that reflect both peasants' vast presence in most societies—even today—and their political and social subordination in those societies.

(2) The pervasive pejorative uses of these terms are also indicative of the historical and contemporary oppression of peasants in many societies and of the discrimination to which they are subject.

(3) In many parts of the world, peasants are still second-class citizens, with legal and de facto restrictions on their geographical mobility, limited access to social services (e.g., healthcare, education, housing), insufficient access to land, and few labor protections.

(4) In some countries where agrarian revolutions occurred (e.g., Mexico, Bolivia), "peasant" became a legal category intended to confer special group rights, particularly rights to land.

(5) Social scientific definitions of "peasant" generally recognize both that the category is extremely heterogeneous and that individuals and groups in the category typically engage in multiple forms of livelihood, including agriculture, wage labor, pastoralism and livestock production, artisanal production, fishing and hunting, gathering of plant or mineral resources, petty commerce, and a variety of other skilled and unskilled occupations.

(6) "Peasant" may be both a category of social scientific analysis and a self-ascribed identity.

(7) As a social scientific category, "peasant" usually includes landless rural people who either work other people's land or who aspire to obtain land of their own (or both).

(8) In some parts of the world (e.g., Mesoamerica, the Andes, Central Java), peasant communities had (and have) a "closed" corporate structure with hereditary membership and widely recognized territorial rights.

(9) While early social scientific definitions of "peasant" tended to contrast the category to "farmer," more recent analyses (Van der Ploeg 2008) locate peasant farming on a continuum with "entrepreneurial" or industrial farming. Peasants and small farmers share key features, particularly the constant quest to reduce economic and environmental risks by minimizing monetary costs and by diversifying crops and livelihood practices.

(10) Activist definitions of peasantry tend to be capacious, since social movements seek to build coalitions. These definitions, such as that elaborated by LVC, nonetheless generally hew closely to social scientific ones. Many small-scale agriculturalists today use the terms "peasant" and "farmer" interchangeably.

(11) The definition of "peasant" advanced by the Advisory Committee of the Human Rights Council is the same as that proposed earlier by LVC. In its deliberations, the Intergovernmental Working Group could consider broadening this definition to encompass closely related vulnerable groups, particularly rural migrant workers who are not members of households, such as displaced youths, economic and political refugees, or women who have fled domestic or other violence.

(12) Groups that might reasonably be classified as peasants have diminished as a proportion of the overall global population, but in absolute numbers, they are more numerous than ever before in history.

Part 5

ENGAGED RESEARCH

SYNERGIES AND TENSIONS BETWEEN RURAL SOCIAL MOVEMENTS AND PROFESSIONAL RESEARCHERS

> There has been a certain timidity on the part of the professional, perhaps apathy. And on our part, a certain bitterness or resentment because of everything that has happened to us. There are people who have abused us. . . . At times we feel that we're cows. The [researchers] give us a big milking and somebody else gets to drink the milk. You understand?
>
> —Sinforiano Cáceres Baca, Federación Nacional de Cooperativas, Nicaragua (1994)

This chapter was first written for a 2006 conference on Land, Poverty, Social Justice, and Development: Social Movements' Perspectives at the Institute of Social Studies in The Hague. The event was striking for its heated debates in several languages, something perhaps not surprising since it included progressive academics, World Bank representatives, and activists from human rights organizations in Europe and agrarian movements in the Americas, Africa, and Asia. My essay was a provocation not only to positivist-minded social scientists but also to those who view themselves as militant allies and sometimes become uncritical cheerleaders for the movements they study. As a provocation, it may have gone too far in attributing the decline of the United Farm Workers (UFW) union solely to toxic internal dynamics. These issues were surely real, but as Randy Shaw (2008) has shown, broader contextual factors, from California politics to the Mexican peso crisis, also contributed, and many ex-UFW activists went on to play leading roles in other progressive campaigns of the twenty-first century.

Can and should rural social movements and professional or academic researchers work with each other and, if so, under what conditions and in pursuit of what objectives? In what ways are professional or academic researchers and movement researchers similar and in what ways are they different? What types of collaboration and cooperation might be fruitful? When do the relations between social movements and academic or professional researchers become problematical? What are some possible models or ways of specifying or negotiating mutually beneficial relationships? Who gets to "drink the milk," and could the "milking" metaphor be transcended?

This chapter attempts to sketch some approaches to these issues. It starts with an analytical distinction between three categories of people: movement activists, academic researchers in universities and similar institutions, and professional researchers in other kinds of institutions, such as nongovernmental organizations (NGOs). It then argues, however, that the distinction is partly, though not entirely, a heuristic one and that the lines between activist researchers and other researchers are in practice often blurred.[1] To make matters worse, or at least more complicated, another useful heuristic that breaks down under even minimal scrutiny is central to the way the problem here is framed. That is, the distinction between activists and researchers (of all kinds) rests to a large extent on a spurious distinction between "doing" and "thinking." While such distinctions are dubious in practice, they nonetheless retain some limited analytical value because activists and professional researchers (of both academic and other varieties) often occupy different social roles and institutional spaces and emphasize different kinds of social action.

The chapter does not pretend to provide definitive answers but aims instead at stimulating reflection, debate, and mutual understanding. It draws on a reading of materials produced by movement and professional and academic researchers, on many conversations over the years, and on my own experience as a researcher sympathetic to and yet critical of some of the movements that I have studied. I should state at the outset that I do not see the approaches of movement and academic or other professional researchers as incompatible or even necessarily as all that distinct. This does not mean, however, that the relations between them or their knowledge production practices are entirely unproblematic. Indeed, when professional (academic and nonacademic) researchers and activists enter into relations, tensions may always be present, in greater or lesser degrees and sometimes in subterranean forms, unrecognized by one or both parties. This does not necessarily mean, however, that the relation cannot be fruitful for each. It is also important to note at the beginning that (1) the chapter focuses mainly on peasant and farmer movements, particularly transnational ones, even though many of the issues raised are likely relevant as well for other kinds of activist projects and for the researchers in and out of universities who accompany, study, and write about and partner with them, and (2) the discussion of approaches to engaged research, of activists' concerns about researchers, and of the history of professional researchers' acting for and against movements draws heavily on examples from anthropology. In part, this results from my own disciplinary location, but more importantly, it reflects anthropology's role in the social scientific division of labor as the field assigned to "the savage slot" (Trouillot 1991) of less developed countries, the rural and urban poor, and peasant and Indigenous peoples.

Academics and Activists: Blurred Boundaries

Contemporary social movements engage in knowledge production practices much like those of academic and NGO researchers, and the boundaries between activists and researchers are not always as sharp as is sometimes claimed. These blurred boundaries and shared practices can create synergies in activist-researcher relations. There are nonetheless some critical differences that may give rise to tensions. While tensions between social movements and NGOs are notorious and widespread, they generally involve questions of representation and competition over access to resources and decision-making forums (Borras 2004, 2008b; Desmarais 2007, 21–26). Tensions between activists and academics, on the other hand, tend to revolve more narrowly around the research process and the purpose and methods of knowledge production and dissemination.

The complex challenges facing today's social movements have required activists to become researchers. In many cases, researchers in the social movements (and their NGO allies) employ methods, technical language, and publication practices that resemble those of academics. Examples are numerous but include many fine reports on biotechnology, global trade and Canadian agriculture written and published by the National Farmers Union (Canada).[2] Leading figures (or, in some cases, former participants) in the transnational peasant and small farmer organizations have also written rigorous and perceptive "insider" histories of their movements, at times in academic journals (Bové 2001; Bové and Dufour 2001; Desmarais 2002, 2007; Holt-Giménez 2006; Stédile 2007; Borras 2004, 2008b). In other cases, nonfarm intellectuals and farm activists have collaborated closely in producing political and historical analysis (Alegría and Nicholson 2002; Stédile and Fernandes 1999). A few of these nonfarm intellectuals have been integrally involved in formulating strategy, publicizing movement platforms and activities, and carrying out research and training directly geared to movements' needs (Du Plessis 2008; Monsalve Suárez et al. 2008; Rosset 2003).[3] All of these are potential synergies between social movement activists and nonfarm researchers that could be put into practice more systematically.[4]

Some movement activists view academics as coming from an alien world. They draw sharp distinctions between activists and academics (and sometimes between movement organizations and NGOs, even though these lines are frequently more blurred than certain activists like to acknowledge).[5] Yet many leading activists also have considerable academic experience and credentials. They do not always "wear these on their sleeve," since they are participants in and leaders of organizations that represent—or seek to represent—people who typically have much less formal education and sometimes none at all.[6] For a few movement activists involved in farming, the off-farm employment that permits them to survive as agriculturalists includes holding academic positions available only to those who have obtained a postgraduate degree.[7]

The movements have also produced, though their own training programs or those carried out in conjunction with various NGOs, a significant cadre of grassroots intellectuals.[8] Elsewhere, for example, I have written about the development in Central America of a large group of highly sophisticated peasant activists, trained in diverse areas such as trade policy, cooperative administration, and agroecology (see chapter 4; see also Rappaport 2005). These could be viewed as one impressive indicator of movement success, even when peasant movements in the Central American region have suffered major reverses in other aspects of their work (Edelman 2008).[9]

To summarize briefly, then, some important synergies between social movements and academics could involve exchanges of knowledge and contacts, joint strategy discussions, publicizing organizations' platforms and activities and analyzing their histories, and engaging in collaborative research and training.

Sources of Tension

Relationships between academics and social movements are, not surprisingly, sometimes characterized by tensions. Activists expect that academic research will be immediately applicable to their struggles, and academics expect that movement participants will accommodate their needs. Moreover, professional intellectuals, and perhaps especially those who work in academic institutions, are often deeply invested in the search for detail and complexity and for comprehensiveness and "truth," even when they recognize the illusory, relative, and unattainable nature of the latter two objectives. Some of the best work of professional intellectuals, like that of good investigative journalists, involves probing beneath the surface, questioning appearances, and asking uncomfortable questions both of their movement interlocutors and of data that they may have obtained elsewhere (conversely, some of the worst work fails to do precisely this). The uncomfortable questions alone may generate frictions, but more fundamental is the activists' investment in presenting overly coherent "official narratives" about their movements and in making representation claims that may or may not have a solid basis.[10] At times, academic researchers and other professional intellectuals knowingly or unknowingly collude in producing and propagating those narratives and in "airbrushing" (or "photoshopping") out dimensions of activists' biographies and social movement practice that conflict with or complicate the official picture or line. Whether or not this cosmetic approach, which in its more extreme manifestations critics sometimes characterized as "self-censorship," "uncritical adulation," or even "cheerleading," really serves the needs of social movements is an important question, which I will have more to say about shortly.[11]

Academic researchers and social movement activists, even if they have similar knowledge production practices, sometimes seek to produce knowledge for different objectives.[12] Or, even if the objectives of each are similar, they rank the same objectives differently. To be more concrete, a movement researcher and a university-based researcher might each wish to write a book that examines agrarian struggles in country X. Each might genuinely want the results of the research to serve the needs of contemporary and future movements for change. The university-based scholar, however, would likely be at least somewhat more interested in writing the book for an audience of professional intellectuals, addressing arcane academic debates and publishing with a prestigious academic press.[13] The movement-based author of such a book, on the other hand, would be more likely to seek a politically progressive publisher that will guarantee a large print run, wide distribution, and perhaps a low price for the work. The author would also possibly put more energy into a collective discussion of the research findings and into translating any published work into the main language of country X, if it was not first written in that language.

The point is not that academic researchers are selfishly pursuing riches or hoping to inflate their curricula vitae at the expense of, or using knowledge generated by, the social movements. Virtually all university researchers who study or accompany social movements are profoundly sympathetic to the activists' goals (the exceptions are usually those who study right-wing extremist and religious fundamentalist movements).[14] Academics have political projects, too, and those who study or partner with social movements tend to do so because they see in activism the realization of some of their goals and hopes and movement toward a more just world and the kind of society in which they would like to live. Almost all the scholarly books that academics write generate trivial amounts of royalties (though what is "trivial" may appear different in the Global South, and very occasionally, of course, academic books actually become bestsellers).[15] Rather, it is the institutional situation of university-based researchers that powerfully shapes the extent to which different objectives seem important to them. Especially for early-career academics in major universities, the possibilities of continuing to be able to work in their chosen fields depend mightily on the kinds of journals and presses that have published their work (and on the language in which they publish). It is not that they are generally persecuted for publishing in other kinds of outlets or for translating their work into other languages; it is just that these activities typically have to be something "extra," carried out alongside and in addition to the more traditional—I am tempted to say, more soporific and dry—academic work that secures their careers (which, in the United States at least, must almost always be in English). This extra effort, of course, entails risks and has costs in time and career advancement that need to be anticipated by the professionally vulnerable, early-career academic and that, in the interest of real transparency, also ought to be brought to the attention of and acknowledged by one's social movement interlocutors or collaborators. My observations may reflect the particular characteristics of academia in the United States (and particularly the more exalted "Research I" institutions) where "engaged" or "action" research and acting as a public intellectual are less accepted than in Europe or Latin America (Greenwood 2008, 322).[16] But the rules of promotion and tenure in European and Latin American universities do not vary much from their North American counterparts, which is the important thing here in terms of explaining academics' priorities.

The time frames of academic and movement-based researchers are also different. The movement-based researcher typically wants research results to serve immediate political needs. Many social movements function in a permanent crisis-response mode as they attempt to adapt to fast-changing political events. They do not enjoy the luxury of long-term reflection that academics aspire to have (even if this rarely exists in reality). Moreover, the organization of university work, with its summer and sabbatical research leaves, "is incompatible with any form of activism" or at least makes the academic largely unavailable to "external stakeholders" between fieldwork periods (Greenwood 2008, 333–334).[17] Academics, unlike journalists, are socialized in the universities to write slowly. Sometimes, they have also unlearned the ability to write clearly and succinctly.[18] Nor do academics always have access to great audiences or powerful media, as some activists seem to think. It is exceedingly difficult, for example, to place an opinion column in a major daily newspaper in the United States, and very few scholars manage to do it more than occasionally, if at all.[19] Academic journals are notoriously slow in publishing research reports, and I am convinced that very few people actually read most of them.[20] These differences of pace, style, perception, and audience between activists and academics may be another source of tension.

Among social movement activists, the perception sometimes exists that university-based researchers control huge economic resources. This is rarely the case. University jobs, especially in the public universities, tend to be poorly paid in most countries, at least in comparison with those available in other sectors of the economy and individuals with comparable advanced training. The grants that university-based researchers receive are frequently insufficient to cover their costs. Young graduate student researchers commonly live in quite precarious circumstances. Academic and NGO-based researchers can hopefully be an *intellectual* or *political* resource for social movement activists, able to connect them to knowledge, information, and policymakers. Researchers may also be able to facilitate activists' connections to certain funding agencies. But academics themselves are unlikely to be a direct source of money resources or to have significant funds to contribute to the movements.

Another problem that arises from the academic-activist relation is the activist's fear that the academic might be gathering intelligence or functioning as an agent provocateur.[21] This reflects activists' well-founded anxieties about omnipresent imperial or state power, even as it is also suggestive of their sometimes-exaggerated belief in their own political significance. The involvement of supposedly neutral academic researchers in intelligence work dates back to World War I and the first decades of professional social science, when the Mayanist archaeologist Sylvanus Morley reported from Mexico's Yucatán Peninsula to the US Office of Naval Intelligence on Germany's sympathizers in the region and its shipping in the Caribbean (Sullivan 1991; Harris and Sadler 2009). In the interwar years, British anthropologists, in particular, worked among colonized peoples and, while their work tended "to obscure the systematic character of colonial domination" (Asad 1975, 109), their advice to the authorities was rarely sought and, when offered, was almost always ignored (James 1975, 48–49). During World War II, numerous anthropologists lent their skills to the struggle against Nazism and Japanese imperialism and to the administration of local populations, particularly on Pacific islands that had been retaken by the United States (Price 2002; Wolf and Jorgensen 1970). In the postwar era, anthropologists and other social scientists were involved in research and in intelligence and military work that came to be viewed as ethically and morally questionable in a range of Cold War hot spots, including Guatemala, Thailand, Vietnam, and Chile (Berger 1995; Gusterson 2003; Horowitz 1967; Newbold 1957; Price 2002; Wakin 1992; Wolf and Jorgensen 1970).[22] More recently, US social scientists have deployed to Afghanistan, and at least one anthropologist played a key role in authoring the US Army's new counterinsurgency manual (R. J. González 2007; Rohde 2007).[23]

Clearly, then, the activist's fears regarding the researcher's possible covert activities or loyalties are not based solely on febrile imaginings. Nonetheless, three important points deserve consideration. First, it is worth remembering, especially if suspicion falls on a foreign researcher, that most countries' secret services almost always employ nationals of the country in which they are operating, rather than their own nationals, to do most of the actual spying.[24] Second, it is only a tiny minority of outside researchers who are compromised by ties to intelligence agencies, and false accusations of such links have occasionally resulted in tragedy.[25] Third, in various world regions, outside (and frequently foreign) researchers are among those who have produced many of the most compelling exposés of powerful institutions, structural violence, and militarization, as well as the most trenchant critiques of the deficiencies of mainstream punditry, scholarship, and policymaking.[26]

Even if the academic researcher is entirely beyond reproach, activists are also concerned that the data gathered or the reports published might find their way into the wrong hands or strengthen the analytical capabilities of their antagonists. If these concerns arise, they need to be addressed explicitly, and clear agreements need to be reached about how to ensure that no harm results from the researcher's activities. Much academic research—probably most—does not do any direct or indirect harm, and it does not do much direct good either, since, as I noted above, hardly anybody usually reads it.[27] But activists can and ought to do background research on academic researchers if they have doubts about them. Other academics might even be able to help with this, although this practice would, of course, run the risk of creating unfounded paranoia and destroying cooperative relationships (Price 2002, 17).

Some academic researchers expect that the people they accompany or study will or ought to accommodate their needs for time-consuming conversations or other contributions (searching for documents, photocopying, making introductions, chauffeuring them to meetings, and so on).[28] This expectation, perhaps the outcome of the exalted status that some university professors enjoy in their home institutions and societies, understandably irritates movement activists. Like overworked university faculty members, activists have many demands to which they must respond. The benefits of meeting the researcher's needs may be unclear or abstract, minimal or nonexistent, or realizable only far in the future. Not all human relationships, fortunately, require a clear quid pro quo, but ongoing ones do usually require some sort of reciprocity. Attending the academic researcher can become yet another burden and source of stress for the activist. How might each party to this relation see the other more clearly? How might the expectations and perceptions each has of the other be made more explicit? What can each party offer the other?

Some Models of Activist-Academic Relations

It may be useful, in addressing the question of activist-academic relations, to distinguish two types of researchers that enter into relations with rural social movements: first, the researcher who has knowledge or connections sought by the activists, such as an expert understanding of agronomy, trade policy, intellectual property, web design, foundations, or legislative processes and lobbying; and second, the researcher who seeks to study and write about the rural social movements.[29] I have already suggested that the first kind of academic or NGO-affiliated expert may be an important intellectual or political resource for the movements. The second type is potentially more complicated. This is primarily because the category may include researchers who fall in different places along a wide continuum of epistemologies and political commitment, ranging from a positivist stance of "neutrality" and "objectivity" to a "militant" position that conceives of the researcher's role as a publicist or uncritical supporter of the movement under study.[30] In between these two poles are various degrees of engagement or commitment and at least the possibility of a critical interrogation of both activists' and scholars' activities and knowledge-production practices. Also important, of course, is the specific set of issues that the researcher intends to examine. Some situations of extreme political urgency or polarization—massive human rights violations, structural violence, famines or epidemics, for example—may require that researchers "commit" in more sustained, profound ways. This may not be simply a moral or ethical imperative or a decision that is up to researchers. The research subjects with whom they work may very likely push them in this direction.

Nonetheless, there is no single model of activist-academic relationship that will address all of the tensions, possible synergies, or questions. Some models of relationship will accomplish some things better than others. For this reason, both parties to such relationships might do well to think in terms of creativity and variety rather than in terms of a single desirable model or pattern.[31]

"Militant" or "engaged" research constitutes a range of approaches, although there is not, of course, consensus about the practices and ideas that these rubrics might include or about how much they might overlap. At the more militant end of the spectrum, academic or NGO-affiliated researchers place themselves at the service of an organization, take direction from that organization, work as publicists, and report findings that advance the organization's agenda.[32] Admirable as this commitment sometimes might be, the militant model has some shortcomings, whether seen from the position of the movement or from academia.[33] The work of intellectuals closely identified with particular organizations or political tendencies often has less credibility in the larger society and especially among the media, academia, and policymakers than does the work of intellectuals who are sympathetic to the movement but maintain some critical distance and independence. In the role of advocate or publicist, the formally independent voice is likely to be heard more widely and to be taken more seriously than the one seen as "militant" and compromised. Moreover, as Jennifer Bickham Méndez (2008, 144) argues, "Decision makers might assume research presented by academics to be more rigorous and reliable than that put forth by campaigning NGOs, lending a level of legitimacy and credibility to social justice struggles."

An additional problem derives from the frequent gaps between leaders and grassroots activists and the notorious factionalism (and at times, corruption) that pervade social movements (Edelman 2001, 310–311). To which individuals or groups is the "militant" activist committed? What does that commitment imply about the analytical weight accorded to dissenting voices and alternative claims? Even more troubling can be the problem of what to do "when faced with dirty laundry" (Fox 2006, 35)—that is, when the researcher runs across antidemocratic practices or instances of malfeasance. Jonathan Fox argues compellingly for an approach of "first do no harm." Simple whistleblowing to one or another movement sector (or to donor organizations) may, as Fox indicates, constitute unacceptable, impolitic, and counterproductive external intervention. But, as he also suggests, doing nothing or pretending that nothing is wrong may not help the movement and represents another kind of external intervention, albeit one characterized by inaction.

The degeneration of the United Farm Workers (UFW) since its founding by César Chávez in California in the 1960s is a striking case of what can occur when knowledgeable outsiders (and insiders) eschew speaking out or intervention in the face of questionable practices (Cooper 2005; Pawel 2010; Weiser 2004). In its early years, the UFW led dramatic organizing campaigns and consumer boycotts, and the charismatic Chávez, with his principled dedication to nonviolent direct action, was widely considered a Mexican American version of the great US civil rights leader Martin Luther King, Jr. In the late 1970s, faced with growing tensions among his top lieutenants, Chávez implemented self-awareness encounter sessions (called "The Game") in the UFW modeled on the programs of Synanon, a cultlike authoritarian drug rehabilitation organization, and "drifted toward a more autocratic management style" (Ferriss, Sandoval, and Hembree 1998, 212; Pawel 2010). By 2005, less than 2 percent of California's agricultural labor force belonged to any union, and a mere 5,000 workers had UFW contracts—one-tenth of the organization's peak strength.[34] Following the death of Chávez in 1993, the union largely abandoned its original mission of organizing farm laborers, and his heirs poured their efforts "into a web of tax-exempt organizations that exploit his legacy and invoke the harsh lives of farmworkers to raise millions of dollars in public and private money. The money does little to improve the lives of California farmworkers, who still struggle with the most basic health and housing needs and try to get by on seasonal, minimum-wage jobs. . . . [The] tax-exempt organizations . . . do business with one another, enrich friends and family, and focus on projects far from the fields" (Pawel 2006).

As the UFW began to unravel in the late 1970s, few activists stood up to Chávez or resisted his increasingly erratic leadership, and when his family members began to "enrich" themselves and one another, it was investigative journalists, not internal dissenters or militant researchers, who encouraged greater scrutiny (Pawel 2006).[35]

Another role, not incompatible with "militant" research though not necessarily linked to it either, is being an "engaged" public intellectual and witness. The public intellectual or "citizen-scholar" (R. J. González 2004b, 3) speaks out in the print and electronic media, debates the spokespeople of the opposition, exposes hidden wrongdoing, provides expert testimony in courts and legislatures, discusses lobbying and other strategy with activists, teaches students and colleagues, and brings to a larger public the issues raised by grassroots movements.[36] The public intellectual works fundamentally to bring about political and cultural shifts in society. Often these contributions are not especially dramatic, but they are grains of sand that hopefully contribute to eroding the legitimacy of existing power structures, exposing abuses, strengthening the legitimacy of grassroots movements, and informing broader publics about alternative visions, other experiences, and strategies for change.

Most social movements claim to be representatives of particular sectors of the population (women, farmers, Indigenous people, immigrants, and so on), but it is nearly always a small minority of the group that the movement claims to represent that actually participates in it (Borras, Edelman, and Kay 2008, 182–186). Activists are often baffled about why people fail to join them in larger numbers. One of the most significant contributions of academic researchers to social movements may be reporting patterns in the testimony of people in the movement's targeted group who are sympathetic to movement objectives but feel alienated or marginalized by one or another aspect of movement discourse or practice (Burdick 1998; Bevington and Dixon 2005). Movement activists and leaders are often unable to identify problematical organizational patterns that for them have become "naturalized" and that outside researchers easily detect, such as ethnic or regional imbalances and exclusions. Importantly, the "militant" researcher, closely identified with the movement, is unlikely to do these things as well as a more independent researcher to whom people will speak candidly.[37]

Reporting the testimony of the alienated or uninvolved is one important role, but asking challenging questions more generally is another.[38] Both are delicate matters, since they potentially dispute movements' "official stories," activists' self-concepts, and organizations' strategic visions. In the world of transnational activism, for example, national organizations that participated in cross-border alliances at times withdraw in order to struggle at the national level or to work with alternative transnational networks (Borras 2008b).[39] Because sympathetic researchers tend to assume that transnational strategies and organizational forms will always be the most effective, they rarely pose this assumption as a question, even though activists frequently mention as a problem the conflicting demands of activities at the local, national, and transnational level. The balance of what is gained *and* what is lost in moving from a national to a transnational level (or back) is among the critical issues that activists need to consider as a matter of long-term survival and that researchers need to analyze either as part of a more genuine solidary relation with the activists or as a matter of political-intellectual honesty.[40]

This researcher contribution to the movements—posing difficult questions and especially reporting the testimony of the disaffected—may be more possible when the scale of the research is smaller and place-based rather than when it has a wider, multisited focus (it is also easier when organizations are flourishing than when they are in decline). In my own case, I felt that I was more effective in this way when I did extended field research in the countryside in Costa Rica in the 1980s and 1990s, and when I knew many campesinos in and out of the movements, than when I began to study transnational farmer networks and was constantly moving from place to place and had more superficial, shorter-term interactions almost exclusively with movement participants and few or none with nonparticipants.[41] The issue of nonparticipants in targeted constituencies also raises the broader question of what Fox terms "the *directionality* of the researcher's goals—are we drawing from the movement in order to project analysis *outward*, or are we drawing from the external environment in order to project analysis *inward*?" (Fox 2006, 30, original italics).

The last model of activist-academic relations that I will mention involves a formal contract specifying shared objectives and what each party is expected to do and over what period of time. Some Indigenous peoples have long required that outsiders hoping to carry out research among them be vetted by a council of experts. The Kuna in Panama, for example, require written contracts with researchers and demand that all studies carried out in their *comarca* or district be published in Spanish or Kuna and provided to the group's own archives. The statutes governing their territory specify as a crime "the free giving of Kuna-related data and documents to any institution without an equitable and reciprocal enrichment" (CGK and CISAI 2003).

Would this type of contractual relationship work in the rather different context of relations between social movements and researchers who wish to study and write about them? La Via Campesina and some of its constituent organizations have been moving in the direction of establishing such a written protocol for their relations with researchers and academic and NGOs loosely modeled on similar agreements that Indigenous peoples in Canada have found useful. The goals of this more formalized relationship would include ensuring that the research is of use to the movement, helping the movement to understand what the research is about, and—in some cases—shaping or determining the research agenda.[42] While these objectives seem reasonable, particularly from the point of view of the activists, they also entail potential difficulties. The first relates to what I have called the activists' penchant for presenting overly coherent "official narratives" or "stories" about their movements and in making representation claims that may not have a solid basis. To what extent would the written contract limit researchers in the kinds of testimony they could report or in asking delicate questions? The contractual agreement should ideally include a genuine movement commitment to openly entertain uncomfortable questions or findings and to refrain from personalizing any discomfort experienced in the process. Activists need to ask whether the refusal to countenance challenging questions or consider problematical findings really serves the movement's interests. The second difficulty concerns the potential of the written contract to become a kind of gatekeeping or an ideological litmus test. Gatekeeping of this sort would not only preclude facing uncomfortable research findings, but it could also introduce a burdensome formality and bureaucracy into the relation that consumes activists' (and researchers') time and energy.

Despite these caveats, however, it is essential that researchers recognize that their very presence entails costs for the movements, even if there are also clear benefits of collaboration. The activists' desire for a written contract that spells out the parameters of the relationship is thus eminently understandable. So, too, is the possibility that close collaboration can identify shared objectives and powerful synergies.[43] Researchers in private universities in the Global North, for example, are often able to fund activists' international speaking tours and other activities. Contractual agreements could also contemplate the disposition of royalties from books or other research products, even if these are unlikely in most cases to be very substantial.

What can or should movements ask or insist on from the academic researcher who expresses an interest in doing research with and writing about them? Really anything they would insist on in another political or personal relationship, including any or all of the following: transparency about funding sources and objectives and about how, if at all, the movement might benefit from having a researcher in its midst; frank dialogue and exchanges of opinion about issues of mutual concern; prompt, clear, and succinct reporting of research results in a form accessible to movement participants; coauthorship of publications or visual or other media, if both parties so desire; and collaboration in day-to-day movement tasks. As regards the latter, in the 1980s and 1990s, when I was involved in work in Central America, for example, I sometimes rented jeeps to get myself and activist friends to assemblies in remote areas. I participated in some memorable joint forums with Costa Rican academics, NGO researchers, and peasant leaders that sometimes degenerated into heated arguments from which everybody nonetheless learned a great deal. I occasionally translated correspondence and grant proposals and copyedited the text of the English edition of the ASOCODE newsletter.[44] Several times I hosted ASOCODE representatives on their visits to UN agencies, foundations, and church and university groups in New York. These were small forms of solidarity that I would have offered to anyone, but which I felt especially pleased to share with those throughout Central America who had treated me with the utmost graciousness and hospitality and who expected little or nothing in return for helping me to understand their struggles and write about their lives and aspirations.

The epigraph of this chapter quotes a longtime campesino activist-intellectual lamenting that too often researchers "milk" their subjects, who then don't get to drink any of the milk. Activists (and many researchers, too) have been rightly critical of this extractive, exploitative, and unidirectional model of movement-researcher relations. Yet developing more horizontal and collaborative kinds of relations and research practices is not entirely straightforward, either. Movements frame issues and make claims in ways that may not withstand close examination, even by sympathetic observers, and they may resist hearing information that contradicts the stories they tell about themselves (and possibly ostracize the people who bring that information). Researchers' professional priorities may not coincide and may conflict with those of the movements they study. NGO-affiliated intellectuals, while less constrained by the career imperatives that often shape academics' research and dissemination practices, sometimes assume that they may speak in the name of those on whose behalf they claim to work. All parties to this complicated, multifaceted relation are involved in generating new knowledge. This can be a shared practice, though too frequently differences arise over what knowledge to produce, how to produce it, who should produce it, and what to do with it and who owns it once it is produced. Some of these tensions become explicit, while many others remain uncommunicated and sometimes even unconscious.

What can be done to realize the potential synergies between professional researchers and social movements and to ensure on both sides greater clarity about shared (and divergent) objectives and more realistic expectations and understandings of limitations and possibilities? This chapter has analyzed several models of activist-researcher relations and argued that different approaches are suitable for different goals and that no single approach is able to address or resolve all or even most of the tensions in the relationship. Indeed, I have suggested that some tensions are very likely inherent aspects of any process of collaboration between social movements and researchers. What, then, of a process in which the activist-researcher distinction is erased? This "militant," "engaged," or "committed" stance also entails strains and, in its more extreme versions, a narrow vision that may turn out to be of little help—or indeed, harmful—to the movements themselves. Rather than reifying the "militant" or researcher as a single thing or practice, I have argued that "engagement" and "commitment" are best understood as existing along a continuum that has many dimensions. Sometimes, the most enduring contribution of the researcher to the social movement may be in challenging its activists' assumptions with fresh data and an outsider's insights. Not to do this, as suggested above, can involve an abdication of responsibility that flies in the face of genuine engagement.

EIGHT DIMENSIONS OF LAND GRABBING THAT EVERY RESEARCHER SHOULD CONSIDER

I first wrote this chapter in Spanish for the International Conference on "Lands and Territories in the Americas: Land Grabbing, Resistance, and Alternatives," organized by the Land Deal Politics Initiative and held at the Universidad Externado de Colombia in Bogotá in 2016. In translating it, I tried to conserve its original flavor as an oral text. Land grabbing refers to multifaceted phenomena that cannot be adequately understood through a priori generalizations or big data, but which require historically informed, on-the-ground research that takes into account the dimensions outlined below. Research on financialization of land, which I identified as an urgent need, has advanced considerably since the chapter was written (Clapp and Isakson 2018; Fairbairn 2020).

In recent years, in debates on land grabbing, I expressed concerns about how social scientists and agrarian activists address this problem, which plagues Latin America and various other regions of the planet (Edelman 2013; Edelman, Oya, and Borras 2013; Edelman and León 2013; Hall et al. 2015). These interventions were driven, in part, by considerations derived from previous research on land tenure and *latifundismo* that I initiated in the early 1980s, primarily in Costa Rica. Another motive for these analyses and the one that follows here is the sensation that some analysts do not pay sufficient attention to certain key elements (Edelman 1992; Edelman and Seligson 1994). And more specifically, having studied land grabbing before the 2008 financial and food crises, I was left with questions about interpretations, approaches, and methodological assumptions that permeated the growing literature on the subject, especially that produced by nongovernmental organizations (NGOs), international financial institutions, and academics.

In this brief review, I analyze eight of these doubts in a very synthetic way, not so much with the intention of highlighting disagreements, but rather with the idea of enriching debates and emphasizing the need to accept as our common starting point the complexity of the land grabbing phenomenon, even though the very process of investigation and interpretation always presupposes some necessary simplifications.

What, then, are the eight dimensions of land grabbing that every researcher should consider? In summary, they are as follows:

1. The presence of historical antecedents in current history
2. Problems of scale
3. Falling commodity prices in recent years and the impact of commodity prices on "drivers" of land grabbing
4. The role of national actors
5. Reactions "from below" to land grabbing, ranging from expulsion or displacement to incorporation, under adverse conditions, into grabbers' enterprises or projects
6. The increasingly complex dimensions of financialization and its role in the new context of falling commodity prices
7. Land grabbing for nonagricultural purposes
8. The need to make invisible beings visible

The Current Situation Is Just a Sequel to Everything That Happened Before

The economic and food crisis of 2008 was a "perfect storm" whose causes included the following:

- The bursting of the mortgage bubble in the United States, Spain, Ireland, Iceland and other countries;
- A shortage of cereals in international markets triggered by climatic events in Australia, Ukraine and elsewhere;
- The expansion of biofuels, heavily subsidized in the United States, the European Union, and Brazil, among other countries;
- Growing speculation that affected almost all commodities markets, agricultural and nonagricultural, including oil, gold, and other minerals.

All this gave rise to an unprecedented increase in prices of basic foods and, in many countries, led to riots and looting of supermarkets and warehouses. As is well known, the land grabbers intensified their efforts, often claiming the existence of a neo-Malthusian crisis and pointing to the supposed urgency of producing more food for the hungry masses by whatever means necessary.

The unforeseen and dramatic nature of this financial and food crisis often led researchers to view it as a sui generis and exceptional event, treating the rise of land grabbing as a conjunctural problem and losing sight of the long trajectories of the actors on the ground and the corporations behind it, as well as previous processes of expulsion and land concentration. They attributed several serious problems to post-2008 land grabbing, such as the expulsion of peasant communities from their lands and the expansion of biofuels at the cost of basic grain production. These versions were to some extent accurate, but they tended to see the pre-2008 past as a time when the tragedies the crisis generated were smaller or even absent.

Obviously, I am exaggerating a bit. Nonetheless, Carlos Oya (2013), in a study of 176 academic papers containing assertions about the impact of post-2008 land grabbing in sub-Saharan Africa, found that none of them included baseline data before 2008. This made it impossible to rigorously test authors' claims that the negative effects were results of recent land grabbing and not of other long-standing processes. According to Oya, there was not "a single study . . . presenting an evaluation of impact with a rigorous baseline and a before and after comparison" (2013, 1541).

Apart from the absence of comparative analyses of the situations before and after the 2008 crisis, there are other reasons to insist on a more historical view. Here I will summarize some arguments developed in more detail in a paper on Honduras written together with Andrés León (Edelman and León 2013). The rural areas where the "new" post-2008 land grabbing is occurring are seldom really empty, despite the fact that grabbers and governments often maintain that they are vacant national lands, "deserts," or abandoned places. Even supposed *terra nullius* or "land belonging to nobody" is typically produced by earlier processes of conflict, dispossession, and displacement. Preexisting social formations in these spaces are always characterized by local particularities, such as "formal and customary land tenure, historical configurations of class relations, family networks, gender and settlement patterns, environmental features, actual or potential infrastructure, state policies, international treaties and agreements, as well as forms of insertion in markets, among many other elements" (Edelman and León 2013, 1697–1698). Both the social groups rooted in these territories and the states that intend to govern them have their historical repertoires of political contention, which can also influence the viability (or failure) of a given attempt to seize land. History, then, is part of the present and strongly influences the present, hence the need to take it more into account.

Questions of Scale

Several issues of scale arose in land grabbing studies in the years following the 2008 crisis. During that period, NGO scholar-activists emphasized quantifying the number of hectares grabbed and sometimes neglected other factors, including the quality of the data. NGOs, with a view to influencing public opinion and attracting donations, sometimes competed to make increasingly dramatic allegations about massive areas monopolized by investors that were almost always foreign. In this "hectare fetishism," promoted in part by the Land Matrix and GRAIN databases on large-scale land deals, important elements got lost (Edelman 2013).

First, the largest land grabs were not necessarily associated with more violent and conflictive processes of dispossession and displacement, something that was clear in the Honduran case, which was analyzed with Andrés León (Edelman and León 2013) and also in George Christoffel Schoneveld's 2014 study of land grabbing in Africa. Schoneveld warns that the largest land concessions are almost always intended for logging, a use whose impact on the surrounding communities tends to be much lower than with agricultural and mining projects. The inclusion of these large concessions in the Land Matrix and GRAIN databases tends to skew global trends, increasing sharply the total number of hectares grabbed. In addition, the scale of some projects featured in the first land grabbing reports was so exaggerated that it was unlikely they would work out, and investigators rarely paid attention (and still pay little attention) to diseconomies of scale that could affect farms of several hundred thousand hectares. The collapse of several of these megaprojects is notorious, in some cases because of financing problems and in others because of excessive ambition on the part of the investors or resistance either from affected communities or state apparatuses.

Second, in several parts of the world, such as India and East Africa, large-scale land deals often occur after a series of purchases of and expulsions from very small plots. Typically these are run by brokers or sometimes by the state, with both working in the interests of the end buyers (Kandel 2015; Levien 2013; Mollett 2016). This "ant work" is not always very visible or fast, so researchers have to be on the ground to detect and understand it, even though such processes have generated large population movements and significant resistance movements (Sampat 2015).

Third, we need to think more about scale—not only the extensions of land grabbed but also other factors. The most significant is the capital associated with a particular land grabbing project (Edelman, Oya, and Borras 2013, 1527; Edelman 2013, 488). This affects several other elements, including the durability or fragility of the project, the political and financial alliances behind it, and the displacements it causes. As investors target agricultural land, as well as forests, water, minerals, areas of urban and industrial potential, carbon sinks, and so on, researchers could think more systematically about the different scales they apply to these types of cases (e.g., the cubic meters of water instead of hectares, or the value of carbon credits that are appropriated).

Collapsing Commodity Prices

The debate on land grabbing began at a time when cereal, oil, and other commodity prices were rising sharply. But after prices of most agricultural and non-agricultural commodities peaked in 2012 and 2013, they experienced a fall as dramatic as the 2008 rise.

The sudden and unforeseen nature of the financial and food crises of 2008 led researchers to focus, perhaps a bit simplistically, on "drivers" of land grabbing. If prices of agricultural products were high, they incentivize land grabbers. The implicit corollary—that low prices would discourage them—did not take into account the variety of motives behind land grabbing.

The NGO GRAIN, which in 2008 was the first organization to raise alarm about the new wave of land grabbing (GRAIN 2008), issued a report in which it argued that despite the fall in commodity prices, the number of land transactions continues to grow, but that growth has slowed since 2012. Several of the largest "projects" have collapsed, resulting in a decline in the total number of hectares. The problem, however, will not go away (GRAIN 2016).

Part of the problem, at least in Latin America, lies in the overdependence of many countries on energy and mineral rents and the counterintuitive effect that price declines had on these societies. As commodity prices and government revenues from oil, mineral, and other sources have fallen, two worrying trends emerged. On the one hand, governments and companies allied with them are intensifying the search for new sources of foreign exchange derived from extractive activities, trying to compensate for low prices with increases in volume. On the other hand, following the same extractive logic, they are emphasizing high-value-added flex crops frequently associated with land grabbing, such as African palm, soybeans, and sugarcane (Alonso-Fradejas et al. 2016; Hidalgo Pallares and Hurtado Pérez 2016; McKay 2017). Both tendencies mean that pressure on the lands of peasant, Indigenous, and Afro-descendant communities remains strong even after the end of the commodity boom. Moreover, the despair of governments and investors about finding new revenue streams reinforced the importance of the land resource as an object of financial speculation.

National Actors

In a 2013 paper written with Carlos Oya and Jun Borras (Edelman, Oya, and Borras 2013), we proposed a periodization of activist and academic literature on land grabbing. Starting in 2008 and going until about 2012, researchers and activists were trying to understand an unusual phenomenon and to document and denounce it. Starting in 2012, a significant number of in-depth and small-scale case studies emerged that shed new light on the variety of processes and actors involved in land grabbing. If the emphasis at the beginning was on foreign investors and the "grabbing" of land, over time researchers realized the significant role played by national actors. It turned out that they could be just as nefarious as foreigners and that they very often collaborated with them, forming joint ventures, facilitating contacts in state apparatuses, providing services, serving as "national" facades for outsiders, and using their knowledge and cultural capital to accelerate appropriation of land, water, forests, and other resources.

The complexity of relationships between domestic and foreign actors is such that a recent report insists on the impossibility of specifying with certainty the "nationality" of most large land transactions. It also notes the difficulty of distinguishing between various types of private and public actors, given the new importance of public-private partnerships (Borras et al. 2016). Another recent analysis of Africa indicates that domestic projects are often "less visible" than foreign ones, since governments and the media do not monitor them closely (Schoneveld 2014).

The fact that nationals are involved in land grabbing together with foreigners should not be surprising, as this has been the case throughout Latin America and in many other regions for at least 150 years (Edelman 1992). However, there are two reasons why "foreignization" still deserves attention. The first has to do with new corporate forms such as sovereign wealth funds, public-private partnerships, and other entities that seize "opportunities" in a globalized economy (Anseeuw, Cotula, and Taylor 2012). National actors are a reality, but this does not mean that the preoccupation with foreign investors in the first studies on land grabbing is wrong, only that it would have to be understood in terms that are more complex and less black-and-white (Keene et al. 2015).

The second reason is perhaps less obvious but more interesting and has to do with the discursive construction of land grabbers by the groups that are resisting them. In many contexts, calling landowners "foreigners" is a way of discrediting them and fomenting nationalist and local resistance. And this can happen even if investors are citizens of the same country as those who are resisting them, such as if they belong to a minority group or are a naturalized immigrant, if they have an unusual surname, or if they associate with foreigners. The largest and most notorious land grabber in Honduras, for example, Miguel Facussé, who died in 2015, was of Arab descent but came from a family that had been in the country for more than a century (N. L. González 1993, 191). Peasant movements nevertheless considered him a "Turk" (*turco*) and a foreigner and appealed to nationalist sentiments to mobilize the population against him (Edelman and León 2013).[1]

Reactions "from Below"

The previous section mentioned the proliferation of case studies, which began to appear around 2012 and forced us to recognize the extremely diverse processes of land grabbing taking place in different areas of the world. One aspect that became clear then was the variety of reactions of subaltern groups that land grabbing affected. If researchers and NGOs initially assumed that large land transactions always involved mass displacement of peasants and Indigenous people and that they always resisted what was happening, over time and with the accumulation of more data, it became obvious that the impacts on the affected communities were more varied and interesting than what the first wave of reports had suggested.

In an analysis written by a team coordinated by Ruth Hall (Hall et al. 2015), we emphasized the need to question some a priori assumptions common in contemporary agrarian studies. These include the ideas that land grabbing always generates resistance and that certain crops, such as African palm, are always promoted by large landowners and that small farmers therefore oppose them, as well as the notion that small peasants cannot exist alongside large agro-industrial farms. We also noted that the reactions of subaltern groups registered empirically have ranged from expulsion and resistance to incorporation under adverse conditions in investors' projects, whether as contract farmers, laborers, or owners who rent plots to a company. Between these two extremes of expulsion with resistance and adverse incorporation were other possibilities, among them expulsion without resistance, struggles for better indemnification by the displaced, and "competitive exclusion" when the farmers do not manage to compete with big companies. In addition to struggles for better terms of incorporation in companies, as contract producers or as workers, we acknowledged that some communities (or sectors of them) actively seek insertion in new capitalist enterprises and mobilize against those who are resisting large land transactions (Hall et al. 2015). Similarly, we pointed to cases in which small producers and cooperatives are enthusiastic about cultivating African palm, a crop that researchers and activists tend to associate with large landowners and land grabbing but which is a source of income and employment for many peasants (Castellanos-Navarrete and Jansen 2015; Edelman and León 2013). For large enterprises, incorporating peasants into supply chains devolves production and market risks downward and solves the question of how to attract and discipline labor. It also extends territorial control without having to enter into exhausting and possibly unsuccessful conflicts over land. These situations are "difficult political dilemmas" (Hall et al. 2015). Labor justice demands are not always compatible with agrarian justice demands, and these in turn could be incompatible with demands for biodiversity and environmental justice.

Different bottom-up reactions to land grabbing reflect an accumulation of the historical elements mentioned in the first section of this chapter: traditions and repertoires of contention, preexisting forms of land tenure, and collective and individual aspirations and identities. And here it could be stressed that some of these elements (e.g., gender and especially generation) have received very little attention from land grabbing researchers and should be more present in future research.

Financialization of Land

Researchers are using the concept of financialization more frequently to refer to the influence of financial capital on land markets and agribusiness in general and also to point to the growing importance of profits derived not from agricultural production but from financial mechanisms. Even after pioneering studies on the subject (Clapp 2014; Fairbairn 2014; Knuth 2015; Sippel, Larder, and Lawrence 2017), we have done little more than scratch the surface. Databases, for example, that document actors and quantify the extent of land grabbing, such as the Land Matrix, generally focus on companies and pay little attention to their funding sources (Borras et al. 2016, 13).

Researchers have emphasized the importance of partnerships between land grabbers and international banking and multilateral institutions such as the World Bank. They have also pointed out how land is a hedge in the portfolios of large pension funds and other institutional and individual investors. Diversification also occurs at the geographic level as large investors seek opportunities in different hemispheres and regions to minimize chances of negative climate events (Sippel, Larder, and Lawrence 2017).

Land prices do not fluctuate in the same way as bond and stock prices, so investment advisers often tell clients to keep some of their net worth in the form of farm property. Recently, there have been studies of specific actors such as the US pension fund TIAA-CREF, which has problematic investments in Brazil (Rede Social et al. 2015), the United States, and elsewhere, and of European corporations that encourage land grabbing outside the European Union (Borras et al. 2016). The latter report warns:

> When looking at the investment chains of land deals, there are different types of actors: business managers of the agricultural project; parent companies who . . . own the business managing the project . . . ; investors/shareholders who invest money in a company in return for shares; lenders who make loans to a project or a company . . . ; governments who offer land to the business managing the project and allow a company to be registered and operate in their country or region; brokers who play a role in helping to secure business deals and communicating between or supporting different actors involved; contractors who carry out certain jobs on the ground on behalf of the project; and buyers who buy the produce grown or processed by the project. . . . These actors are not always based in one single country, which makes attributing accountability to one state inadequate. (Borras et al. 2016, 19)

For a researcher or even a sophisticated multidisciplinary research team, it is difficult to uncover complex networks of financial and commercial relationships, especially because companies are often nested shells or fictitious entities, domiciled in tax havens where there is little transparency. Flows of loans and profits are intentionally hidden the same way. Commonly, the activities and legal entities of the companies involved cover several jurisdictions, further complicating the task of deciphering their structures (Cotula and Berger 2015, 11). It is important to see this complexity as part of a broader process—the ascendancy since the 1980s of a capitalism characterized by minimal regulation and a strong bias toward the financial and real estate sectors to the detriment of productive sectors. In the mid-1970s in the United States, for example, the regulations governing large public pension funds were changed, leading them to diversify their investments beyond the state bonds that had formed their economic foundation up to then and to inject large sums into nontraditional sectors: first equities, then commercial real estate, and eventually much riskier and obscure instruments. As risks increased, funds had to diversify more and seek new hedges against market downturns.

Researchers have hardly touched on the fiscal dynamics behind the new wave of land grabbing. Land grabbers often invest in lands abroad to hide resources from their country's tax authorities while also benefiting from juicy tax concessions from host governments (Geisler 2015, 244). In the 1980s, the United States and many other countries began significant reductions in taxes on capital gains and, to a lesser extent, on corporate earnings. These changes benefited financial and real estate sectors at the expense of other sectors of society and other fractions of capital. In other words, the new fiscal structures tend to inflate real estate prices and deflate the "real economy" of industrial and agricultural production and service provision, which was subjected to asset-stripping at the hands of leveraged-buyout and private equity investors (Alexander 2017).

The new tax frameworks lend themselves to the proliferation of new forms of investment, such as REITs (real estate investment trusts), a kind of fund invented in the United States that now exists in at least thirty countries. REITs invest in a portfolio of properties, charge high entrance fees, and pay no taxes. By law, they must distribute 90 percent of their income to the members every year, and these are the ones who are liable for capital gains taxes. In the last fifteen years, REITs first experienced a rapid expansion and then, more recently, the popping of a speculative bubble. However, since about 2000, they have been a major driver of the rise in land and real estate prices. REITs, like other institutional investors, have always been more interested in lands as an asset in a diversified portfolio than in their productive potential. This tends to foment price inflation and a short-term mentality among investors.

Economist Michael Hudson offers some remarks about financialization that should also prompt reflection. According to Hudson, approximately 70 percent of bank loans in the United States, Britain, and Australia are for urban and rural real estate, and 80 percent of capital gains in the United States are derived from increases in land prices (Hudson 2012, 146, 215; Gunnoe 2014, 480). He suggests that we are witnessing the birth of a new stage of capitalism, based on an unprecedented integration of financial capital and land ownership, which he calls "neo-rentier society" (Hudson 2012, 407). Despite what Sarah Elisabeth Knuth (2015) indicates in an excellent analysis of financialization, short-termism and a neo-rentier mentality are not necessarily opposing orientations. Neo-rentier investors can easily enter and exit a series of projects according to the possibilities they offer for generating revenue, while managing both short- and long-term investments.

Part of the logic of neo-rentier society and increasing investor interest in land may be seen if we examine a series of data from the United States during the period from 1991 to 2015. Figure 11.1 shows the difference between an agricultural property price index compiled by one of the leading real estate trade associations

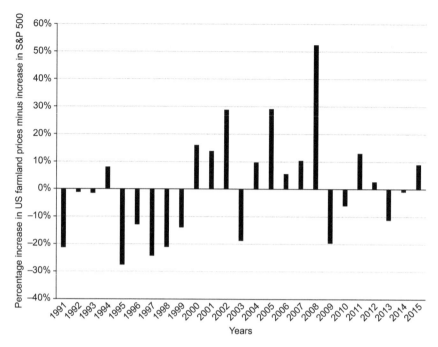

FIGURE 11.1. Annual growth in US farmland prices minus annual growth of S&P 500 index.

Sources: Farmland prices are from the National Council of Real Estate Investment Fiduciaries (NCREIF), July 12, 2016, http://www.ncreif.org/; S&P 500 data are from NYU Stern School of Business, "Historic Returns on Stocks, Bonds, and Bills: 1928–2022," updated January 2023, http://pages.stern.nyu.edu /~adamodar/New_Home_Page/datafile/histretSP.html.

Note: The NCREIF Farmland Index is a quarterly data series that measures prices for a large number of individual agricultural properties acquired in the private market for investment purposes only. All properties in the NCREIF Farmland Index have been acquired, at least in part, by tax-exempt institutional investors, most of them pension funds.

and one of the most important stock market indexes, the Standard and Poor's 500 (S&P 500). The positive percentages in the chart denote the relative advantage each year of having invested in land instead of stocks. Negative values indicate the relative advantage of having invested in stocks rather than land. One interesting aspect revealed by these data is that the incentives to invest in land as a hedge start to become very strong not after the financial crisis of 2008 (which is the starting point for almost all analyses of land grabbing) but after the end of the dot-com boom in 2000. Land Matrix's land deal data are from 2000 onward, too (Land Matrix 2016). Indeed, during the 1990s, apart from 1994, there was no advantage in investing in land rather than equities. After 2000, in contrast, the trend becomes positive in most years, with spectacular gains in some years and losses in negative years lower than they would have been during the 1990s.

Nonagricultural Land Grabbing

I have already mentioned types of land grabbing for nonagricultural purposes. These include logging, mining, energy (oil, hydroelectric projects, and wind farms), water, speculation, urbanization, industrial parks and other infrastructure (roads, airports, military bases), value chain consolidation, protection of ecological zones, ecotourism, and carbon sinks or other sources of payments for environmental services.

Researchers who work on land grabbing have been somewhat agro-centric. It is not that we have neglected other forms of land grabbing. On the contrary, we have excellent studies of many of them (Fairhead, Leach, and Scoones 2012; Franco, Mehta, and Veldwisch 2013; Ros-Tonen et al. 2015; Carter et al. 2017). Where we could go deeper is, first, in the investigation of the interrelations between different forms and, second, in the weight that each has in our vision of the global situation. From the investor's point of view, different forms of land transactions are sometimes seen as complementary and sometimes as alternative strategies. We need to go deeper into factors that influence these different strategies. In the United States in recent decades, for example, investments in timber exploitation have grown much faster than agricultural investment (Gunnoe 2014). In Africa, the largest land concessions are also for logging (Schoneveld 2014). In China and India, the most acute land conflicts often deal with urbanization projects and industrial parks (O'Brien and Li 2006; Levien 2013; Sampat 2015). The agro-centrism of researchers sometimes causes us to lose sight of these other processes, which we need to take more into account.

Invisible Peoples

Researchers must make invisible peoples visible. Policymakers, politicians, the business media, and multilateral organizations discursively construct the spaces where land grabbing occurs as "empty," "underutilized," insufficiently privatized, or populated by people who don't count. The legal doctrine of *terra nullius*—land that belongs to nobody—has a long history in western jurisprudence and is often applied to land that would-be grabbers have in their sights (Milun 2011). Studies of large-scale land deals have long noted that grabbers target zones where there are public or state lands, commons, nonprivate reserves, or overlapping and ambiguous property titles (Edelman 2013; Dell'Angelo et al. 2017). Frequently, Indigenous peoples, swidden agriculturalists, mobile nomads, and transhumant pastoralists inhabit particular parts of their territories only during certain seasons of the year (Gilbert 2014). They may incorporate large expanses into their subsistence and livelihood practices, and some of these expanses are "occupied" only occasionally and intermittently for purposes of hunting or low-impact shifting cultivation, grazing, or extraction of one or a few resources. Not all these territories are legally protected, and in any case, legal protections are sometimes vulnerable to self-interested politicians acting in cahoots with agribusiness interests, as has occurred often in Brazil (Watts 2017; Zimerman 2010). Importantly, as Sarah Mollet has argued for Latin America, elites' practices of racialization frequently depict Indigenous, Afro-descendant, and other rural peoples as "wild," "atavistic," and requiring "civilization." Elites engage in a discursive "inferiorization of nomadic land uses" and assert the identification of sedentary and—more recently—industrial agriculture with "civilization" and "development" (Scott 2011; Mollett 2016, 416).

Invoking "yield gaps" (and also food security and climate change) is another way to justify the expansion of industrial agriculture and corporate farms into territories occupied by mobile peoples and peasant farmers and to disparage the practices of these groups. If resource-poor farmers achieve lower yields than producers of the same crops in the best-endowed, resource-rich regions, then the solution must be to provide advanced technology that will help to close the gap. The yield gap is a key trope and policy plank for multilateral organizations and foundations, notably the World Bank and the Gates Foundation, that seek to develop "uncultivated" lands and to enact technological fixes, especially in Africa, where the yield gap is greatest (Deininger and Voegele 2010; Gillis 2011). These advocates of a "second green revolution for Africa" typically overestimate the yield gap (Ponisio et al. 2014) and put greater stock in genetically modified seeds and "precision" and "climate smart" agriculture than they do in efforts to guarantee smallholders access to adequate resources. The latter would mean facilitating or guaranteeing access to land through agrarian reform and titling programs as well as emphasizing irrigation, credit, storage, processing, transport, markets, and inputs and extension services oriented toward a genuinely resilient agroecology rather than vulnerable and chemical-intensive genetic monocultures (IAASTD 2009). As studies of market-led land reform have shown, titling programs, while potentially securing smallholders' properties and facilitating their access to credit, are sometimes a double-edged sword rather than a panacea (M. Davis 2006, 80; Lahiff, Borras, and Kay 2007). Usually, it is betteroff smallholders that can navigate and pay the costs required by the cumbersome bureaucracies that survey, register, and title farms. Even for them, foreclosure looms when crops fail or more powerful interests target their holdings.

Perhaps the most invisible of those who need to be made visible are those who lived there before and are still present. In Zimbabwe, ancestor spirits associated with particular territories were an inspiration for land and liberation struggles against the white racist "Rhodesian" regime (Lan 1999). Native peoples in many parts of the world inhabit territories that are rich in resources and dotted with sacred sites central to their cultural and physical reproduction. Clashes between mining and petroleum interests and Indigenous peoples are hardly new, but with the extractivist frenzy of recent years, they appear to be intensifying (Colby and Dennett 1996; S. H. Davis 1977; Conde and Le Billon 2017). Sacred sites are a core element of peoples' identities and a generative force for resistance. Their desecration or destruction can also fuel anomie, demoralization, displacement, and defeat.

A letter published in *Science* (Liao et al. 2016) criticized land grabbing studies and pointed out three other important elements: (1) Global land transactions databases underestimate the total number of transactions, especially in countries such as Ethiopia, Peru, and Cambodia. (2) It is difficult to estimate the extent to which land transacted is in production, since not all land is used for agriculture. (3) Findings in the academic literature rely on samples that are not statistically representative of the range of geographic conditions, socioeconomic differences, and contractual arrangements that influence the outcome of attempts to grab land.

This review leaves us with questions and challenges, some of which we already listed. Probably the most important conclusion is that we must accept the complexity of the processes studied as the starting point for all research on land grabbing. Black-and-white simplifications can be counterproductive because they seldom help in understanding what is really happening or in developing strategies for struggle. In some cases, they even succeed in delegitimizing and discrediting movements for social justice (Edelman 2013, 488). Researchers need to take more into account the presence of history in the spaces where land grabbing occurs, the complicated scale issues we outlined, the complexity of land grabbing drivers and the ways in which they have changed in recent years, the underreported role of national actors, the variety of reactions of subaltern groups apart from frontal resistance, and the obscure financial relationships behind large land transactions. We need to restrain our agro-centrism and integrate the study of agricultural holdings with other varieties of land grabbing. The invisible people on the land, past and present, need to be made visible and to be recognized as justifications and inspiration for mobilizations against land grabbing. Finally, as we briefly noted above, the aspects of gender and especially of generation have been neglected and deserve more analysis, not so much because of a desire to foreground different principles of identity but rather because they are dynamics that in many cases manifestly affect the outcomes of struggles for land.

Conclusion

THE LONG MARCH

Historical processes don't stop when a book ends, and analytical certainties are inapt when uncertainty is among the most striking features of human existence (Lechner 1998). In the introduction, I observed that peasants' *absolute* numbers are now greater than at any time in history, even if their *relative* weight in the global population has fallen. This will remain true for a while, but around the time this book appears, rural population growth in less developed regions will turn negative, and those absolute numbers will gradually decline (UN Population Division 2019, 18). As this happens, and as the climate crisis worsens, the unequal "conflict between models" (mentioned in chapter 7)—the conflict between high-input industrial monocropping and the high-output diversified peasant farm—will intensify.

The "conflict between models" frame captures a fundamental contradiction in agricultural policymaking, but with its large-versus-small emphasis, it neglects the important concept of "differential optima" that A. V. Chayanov (1991) advanced one hundred years ago and that Soviet and Western modernizers conspired to consign to oblivion. Chayanov argued for a model that later emerged (independently of any direct influence) in several Central American countries and beyond: farms connected in overlapping scales with machinery, irrigation, postharvest processing, purchasing, marketing, credit, and insurance cooperatives covering large areas and cultivation and field care—usually at smaller scales—geared to the "biological processes" of particular crops. "There would," Chayanov asserted, "be one optimum for the produce of meadow cultivation, another for tillage; . . . one optimum for grain crops, one for intertilled

crops, [and] another for seed production" (1991, 46). One might add that the optimum for grain crops would be larger in temperate zones, where seasonal cold
reduces pests and pathogens to low levels, than in the tropics, where these constitute a year-round threat, manageable only with copious applications of pesticides derived from fossil fuels.

The industrial agriculture's carbon dependence is crucial. It now employs big
data, digitalization, and "surveillance" to boost "efficiency" but relies unsustain-
ably on fossil fuels for fertilization, pest control, traction, packaging, and long-
distance transport (Dietz and Drechsel 2021; Stone 2022b). The peasant food
web—connected mainly to local and regional markets, drawing on fodder-
fertilizer synergies between crop and animal production, seeking resilience
through diversity—persists in the twenty-first century despite all the powerful
policymakers, economists, and philanthropists committed to its destruction. The
outcome of the conflict between models is unclear, but the transnational movements fighting to sustain and extend peasant and small farmer lifeways and production are a key force trying to head off a planetary catastrophe.

What are some of the provisional lessons learned about those movements?

In 2002, in Saskatchewan, Roy Atkinson, a founder of the National Farmers
Union (NFU), asked me a rhetorical question: "What do you notice about the
towns around here that are alive and the ones that are dying?" I have since
thought many times about his answer: "The towns that are alive all have a credit
union and a cooperative grain elevator."

That is lesson one: *Rural zones are sources of wealth, but rural people struggle
to appropriate the wealth that they produce or that is in their territories.* The credit
union or the cooperative are but a few of the tools that people use to circulate
wealth in their communities and to appropriate more of the value-added along
what otherwise might be very lengthy and exploitative commodity chains. In
Costa Rica in the 1980s, peasants in Santa Bárbara de Santa Cruz installed a
small Japanese rice mill to do the same thing, capturing the high protein *semo-
lina* that could be used for feed concentrates rather than giving it as a free "by-
product" to giant industrial rice processors seventy kilometers to the north,
which would sell it and make extra profits. This is the struggle for development—
and it transcends the agrarian economy to include all sources of value in rural
zones, including people's blood plasma (Edelman 2021). The fight against dispossession is another dimension of this ongoing conflict (chapter 11). The productive economy is inseparable from productive autonomy and alternative
approaches to life, which are sometimes rooted in local-level democratic, utopian, and communal traditions (Moguel, Botey, and Hernández 1992; Van der
Ploeg 2008; Escobar 2018; Rosset and Barbosa 2021). Admirers of Karl Polanyi's
The Great Transformation will recognize this as the perpetual pushback against

the liberal fantasy of the "self-regulating market" and its attendant "demolition of society" and "defiling" of landscapes (2001, 74).

It wasn't just Roy Atkinson of Canada's NFU or the small rice producers of Santa Bárbara who led me to think about the active underdevelopment of rural zones. *Agrarian movements are knowledge producers* (Holt-Giménez 2006). To refer to their theorists and researchers as "organic intellectuals"—a term Gramsci believed could not apply to peasants—does not do justice to their expertise, which sometimes differs not at all from that of credentialed "experts" (Claeys and Edelman 2020). Few activities rely more on constant empirical investigation than farming. The knowledge production of agrarian organizations concerns agriculture but goes beyond it. During this research, I encountered rural activists as erudite as anybody in any Global North ivory tower. I met peasants and farmers who were experts on plant genetics and agrarian and human rights law and who had sophisticated understandings of macroeconomics. Some, from South Africa and India, for example, spoke more languages (and spoke them well) than most accomplished developed-country academics. In Central America, I encountered peasant organizations that created their own "think tanks" and founded nongovernmental organizations, an inversion of the more common phenomenon of identified "thinkers," "experts," or funders creating "astroturf" grassroots organizations.

Formally constituted organizations are the most visible, but not necessarily the most significant or meaningful, dimension of social movement activity. Scholars have long been divided between those who see organizations as essential for mobilization (Della Porta and Diani 1999) and those who emphasize that organizations frequently fuel demobilization (Piven and Cloward 1979). Politics, though, occurs inside, outside, and alongside organizations and networks. Sometimes it is opaque to the organizations themselves and certainly to social scientists. This complicates organizing and research, especially for those who want to push beyond movement offices and the claims of spokespeople and leaders. The full dynamics of movements will be hard to grasp, however, without paying attention to the unorganized, the unconvinced, the expelled or organizationally marginalized, and the dropouts, as well as competing movements in the same spaces.

"Protest cycles" and "movement waves" aren't the only periodicity or evolution that social movements experience. Scholars have devoted much attention to how outsider campaigns become institutionalized, co-opted, or demobilized and given relatively little consideration to how they claim new political spaces (Gaventa 2006). Movements—especially transnational ones that incorporate diverse ideologies, nationalities, classes, and cultural idioms—experience profound internal transformations over time. When I initiated this project in Cen-

tral America, most peasant organizations were male-dominated or entirely male. A few had dynamic women leaders, but this was partly tokenism aimed at assuaging European funders' concerns. In some countries, women broke away from male-dominated campesino movements and started their own organizations. The broader social field in which these activists moved was (and remains) deeply patriarchal.

Women's involvement in La Via Campesina (LVC) and its constituent organizations exemplifies how movements change from within. As I describe in chapters 1 and 3, the 1992 call for founding LVC came from the Paulo Freire Foundation in the Netherlands (PFS) and Nicaragua's National Union of Agriculturalists and Livestock Producers (UNAG), where the PFS's director had worked as a cooperator. In 1992, a small meeting of peasant and farmer organizations in Managua issued a declaration that lambasted the liberalization of global agricultural trade under the General Agreement on Tariffs and Trade (predecessor to the World Trade Organization) but that failed to mention any gender-related issues (LVC 1996, 67–69). According to Nettie Wiebe, then the women's president of the NFU of Canada and a longtime LVC activist, the declaration "was the work of the all-male leadership" (Wiebe 2013, 2). At LVC's 1993 launch, in Mons, Belgium, about 20 percent of those present were women, and the same was true at its 1996 conference in Tlaxcala, Mexico. There, when delegates elected an International Coordinating Committee (ICC) composed entirely of men, women delegates rebelled and forced "a tense discussion" that led to reconvening the regional caucuses and to the election of Wiebe—who by then was president of the NFU—as North American representative to the ICC. In succeeding years, LVC and its member movements mobilized to empower women militants, increase their representation at all levels, institutionalize gender equity in decision making, and campaign against violence against women (Desmarais 2003a; Wiebe 2013). *Movements also have their internal "protest waves."*

Since the 1980s in Latin America, as movements pursued autonomy from political parties and sought to occupy newly democratized spaces, agrarian activists spoke more of moving *de la protesta a la propuesta*—from protests to proposals. To be taken seriously and achieve their objectives, movements had to propose viable alternatives rather than only protesting injustices. Much of the knowledge that movements produce involves innovations in policy and agronomy and upending previously unquestioned assumptions. These novel approaches occasionally overflow the bounds of the movements that developed them and become part of larger debates and campaigns (Martínez-Alier et al. 2014). The rise of critical agrarian studies opposed to the hegemonic neoliberal common sense reflects and feeds the questioning that originates in the movements. As David Barkin (2018, 23) observes, "protest" in this conception refers not only to mobilizations and movements but also to the rejection of inherited dogmas and the disappointments associated with them. While Barkin had in mind leftist orthodoxies, I would extend the skepticism of inherited dogmas to include certain canonical academic thinkers and the "grand theory" associated with them, which so many times during this project failed to shed analytical light on messy and surprising empirical realities.

Outcomes are not always immediately apparent and may not relate to movements' explicit goals. Evaluating movement outcomes involves "the micro-, meso-, and macrolevels of political and social life" (Almeida 2019, 122). It must be considered in short-, medium- and long-term perspectives. What Albert Hirschman (1983) termed activists' "social energy" (see chapters 2 and 3) is an incalculable force; movement leaders whose organizations decline, such as the United Farm Workers (UFW) or ASOCODE (chapters 4, 5, and 10), reemerge heading other campaigns. Rebecca Solnit, calling for "a complex calculus of change, instead of the simple arithmetic of short-term cause and effect," captures better than any positivist academic how the long-term outcomes of movements are unpredictable and how this figures in participants' inspiration:

> For many groups, movements and uprisings, there are spinoffs, daughters, domino effects, chain reactions, new models and examples and templates and toolboxes that emerge from the experiments, and every round of activism is an experiment whose results can be applied to other situations. To be hopeful, we need not only to embrace uncertainty but to be willing to know that the consequences may be immeasurable, may still be unfolding. . . . To know history is to be able to see beyond the present, to remember the past gives you capacity to look forward as well, it's to see that everything changes and the most dramatic changes are often the most unforeseen. . . . What you've done may do more than you can imagine for generations to come. You plant a seed and a tree grows . . . ; will there be fruit, shade, habitat for birds, more seeds, a forest, wood to build a cradle or a house? You don't know. A tree can live much longer than you. So will an idea, and sometimes the changes that result from accepting that new idea about what is true, right, just remake the world. (Solnit 2017)

It is my hope that in the pages of this book, the reader has come to know better the seeds that agrarian activists planted and that they may inspire new spinoffs, domino effects, and chain reactions.

Notes

INTRODUCTION

1. Also see Mosse and Nagappan 2021 and Borras 2008b.

2. Edelman and Borras (2016) also discuss the early twentieth-century Green International in Central and Eastern Europe and the Red (Communist) Peasant International.

3. For a critique of Hobsbawm's classification of peasant movements as "primitive" and "archaic," see Edelman 2017, 15–17.

4. The phrases "part-lifetime proletarian" and "semi-proletarian" come from Wallerstein (1974) and refer to those who, over the course of their lives or a single year, depend on waged work and other economic activities, especially agriculture.

5. Not all peasant studies scholars fully embraced critical agrarian studies (CAS). Some, grouped around the *Journal of Agrarian Change*, continued with a narrower emphasis on materialist political economy and the classic agrarian question of traditional Marxism (Bernstein and Byres 2001). For an encyclopedic compendium on CAS, see Akram-Lodhi et al. 2021.

6. Brazil's Movimento dos Trabalhadores Rurais sem Terra (MST), or the Landless Rural Workers Movement, also developed a large program of university-level legal education for its militants (Houtzager 2005). Not all these agroecology institutions prospered. The Latin American University Institute of Agroecology "Paulo Freire" (IALA) in Barinas, Venezuela, for example, became mired in conflict over accusations of corruption (Edelman and Borras 2016, 92).

2. PEASANT-FARMER MOVEMENTS, THIRD WORLD PEOPLES, AND THE SEATTLE PROTESTS AGAINST THE WORLD TRADE ORGANIZATION, 1999

1. Martínez's expanded but less well known version of the essay in *Monthly Review* makes the same argument, but it contains copious information about "people of color" from the United States and elsewhere who *did* participate in the Seattle protests (Martínez 2000b).

2. Jim Glassman, similarly, refers to "the limited presence on the streets of Seattle of any voices from the 'Global South'" (2002, 513). Elsewhere, Tarrow says that although the Battle of Seattle "had relatively little international participation, its capacity to block the Ministerial and its triggering of a police riot gave it remarkable resonance around the world" (Tarrow 2005, 171). I would argue instead that the global "resonance" of N30 derived significantly from the participation of activists from abroad, even if they did not constitute a major proportion of the protesters.

3. Most rural activists today deliberately use the terms *farmer* and *peasant* interchangeably to highlight the common problems of small agriculturalists in developed and less developed countries (and also because equivalent categories in other languages, such as *campesino* or *paysan*, are often more inclusive of the types of individuals and production units that in English are described as both "farmers" and "peasants"). Here I follow the activists' practice of using both terms largely interchangeably, for reasons I have elaborated in detail elsewhere (see chapters 1 and 9).

4. For example, in 2001 meetings in Mexico City in preparation for that year's World Social Forum in Porto Alegre, Brazil, the draft call for new mobilizations was signed by hundreds of organizations from the Americas, Europe, and Asia, declaring, "We form part of a movement that has been growing since Seattle" (Ação da Cidadania conta a Fome a pela Vida 2001, 1). See also Seoane and Taddei 2001a.

5. The 1990 GATT ministerial session in Brussels, for example, was supposed to complete the Uruguay Round negotiations, but protests by small farmer, consumer, and environmentalist groups helped stall the talks, in part because massive street protests made some developing-country GATT delegates feel sufficiently empowered to raise objections to provisions in the draft agreement. Among the estimated 30,000 farmers who joined the 1990 protests were 100 from North America, 200 from Japan, and others from Korea, Africa, and Latin America (Brecher 1993; Kidder and McGinn 1995; Ritchie 1996). These protests—"far bigger than Seattle [1999], but less violent" (Ritchie 2001, 4)—followed other anti-GATT farmers' demonstrations in the United States and Canada. Anti-GATT and anti-WTO protests that did not have international participation were also frequent. In 1998 in Taiwan, for instance, thousands of farmers, protesting the impending opening of markets to US pork and poultry, "threw pig shit at US government offices in their country" (Desmarais 2007, 115).

6. Barlow and Clarke (1998) detail the arguments and campaign strategy that helped to sink the MAI. Seoane and Taddei (2001a), Smith (2002), and Pianta and Marchetti (2007) provide excellent overviews of the diverse transnational movements that emerged in the 1990s.

7. It should be recalled that organized labor participation in N30 was not limited to the United States and Canada. Union representatives from France, Brazil, South Korea, and South Africa, among others, also came to Seattle (Seoane and Taddei 2001a, 113).

8. This section attempts to address in synthetic form a historical deficiency in much anthropological literature on contemporary globalization. In a 2002 review of several books on globalization by prominent anthropologists, Graeber pointed out that "it is difficult to find anthropological essays that so much as mention the WTO, an organization that also does not appear in the index of any of the books here under review—or, for that matter, some recent volumes that actually have pictures of the Seattle protests on their cover!" (Graeber 2002, 1226).

9. Since the 1970s, US livestock producers have used natural and synthetic hormones to increase animals' growth. In 1989, the European Community, predecessor to the European Union (EU), banned imports of beef from cattle treated with growth-inducing hormones. The United States attempted to challenge the ban under GATT but was stymied when European representatives prevented the seating of an expert panel to examine US claims. In 1996, the United States and Canada complained about the EU ban to the WTO's dispute settlement body, whose new rules made it impossible to impede the case, as had occurred earlier under GATT. The WTO ruled against the EU in 1997 (a decision that was upheld on appeal the following year) and permitted the United States and Canada to institute retaliatory tariffs on a range of European luxury goods. In a related matter, in 1994, the US Food and Drug Administration approved the use of Monsanto's genetically engineered bovine growth hormone (recombinant bovine somatotropin or rBST), which is used mainly to boost milk production. European studies, however, indicated that rBST caused mastitis, lameness, and reproductive and other problems in cows. Europe prohibited the use of rBST (as did Canada in 1999). However, the EU eventually relaxed limits on imports of dairy products from cows treated with rSBT.

10. There are numerous accounts of these events (see Bové and Dufour 2001; Heller 2002; Alland and Alland 2001). While Bové is often represented simply as a local sheep farmer, he is actually the son of university professors, spent four years of his childhood

in Berkeley, had a long history of radical activism before he became a farmer, and has a near-native command of English. In many ways, he epitomizes the kinds of transnational peasant activist that, following Tarrow (2005) and others, I have elsewhere termed "rooted cosmopolitans" (see chapter 3).

11. CLOC is the Coordinadora Latinoamericana de Organizaciones del Campo (Latin American Coordinator of Rural Organizations). Founded in 1994 in Lima in the aftermath of the 1992 continental Indigenous campaign against the Columbian quincentenary celebrations, CLOC works closely with LVC. The main business at the Seattle CLOC meeting was the imminent move of the organization's office from Nicaragua to Mexico (Hernández Cascante 2002).

12. Peter Waterman (2001, xix) asks "why there was no significant feminist or women's movement present in Seattle [when] energetic, competent, courageous and outrageous women (young and old) were there in large numbers." The underreporting of the international presence at N30, to which he himself alludes, may have made the international women's activities less visible. US and other women's actions at N30 may have been similarly underreported, though that would have to be the subject of further historical research.

13. UPANACIONAL is the Unión Nacional de Pequeños y Medianos Productores Agropecuarios (National Union of Small and Medium Agricultural Producers). Founded in 1981, it participated in a short-lived effort to found a Central America–wide peasant association (Edelman 2008) and in the formation of the LVC. Because of tensions with another, smaller but internationally well connected (though now defunct) Costa Rican peasant organization, UPANACIONAL was later marginalized and virtually excluded from LVC (Hernández Cascante 2002; Desmarais 2007, 182).

14. IATP is the Institute on Agriculture and Trade Policy, based in Minneapolis.

15. ATTAC, created in 1998 with the backing of the newspaper *Le Monde Diplomatique*, has an unwieldy name: Association pour la Taxation des Transactions Financières pour l'Aide aux Citoyens (Association for the Taxation of Financial Transactions to Aid the Citizenry). It is a French-based global justice network, with branches in various European and Latin American countries, that favors implementation of the Tobin tax on international currency and other financial transactions. On the Tobin tax, see Patomäki 2001.

16. GABRIELA (General Assembly Binding Women for Reforms, Integrity, Equality, Leadership, and Action) is a Philippine women's coalition, founded in 1984, with branches in major US cities. AMIHAN (whose name refers to monsoon winds) is the National Federation of Peasant Women in the Philippines, founded in 1986. KMP (Kilusang Magbubukid ng Pilipinas) is the Peasant Movement in the Philippines, founded in 1985. BAYAN (Bagong Alyansang Makabayan) is the New Patriotic Alliance, founded in 1985.

17. SnB (Sentenaryo ng Bayan) means the People's Centennial of the Philippine Revolution of 1896.

18. It is important to note that not all Filipino organizations present in Seattle participated in the IPA activities. Shortly after the Seattle events, a coalition that included the International South Group Network, AKBAYAN, and numerous other groups issued an analysis that obliquely criticized the IPA: "It is unfortunate for some Filipino groups to claim that the 'battle in Seattle' was a mountain that grew out of a molehill, belittling all other groups' efforts while taking credit for everything" (Mora, Soto, and Bello 1999).

19. Key events included protests against the World Economic Forum in Davos, Switzerland; the tenth summit of the United Nations Conference on Trade and Development; the World March of Women; the IMF and World Bank meetings in Washington, DC; the OECD meeting in Bologna; huge demonstrations in Millau in support of the French

Confédération Paysanne; the G7 summit in Okinawa; the IMF and World Bank meetings in Prague; and the organized labor parallel summit to the Mercosur meeting in Florianópolis, Brazil. The upsurge in Latin America was especially noteworthy, with the Zapatista caravan throughout Mexico, the participation of the Ecuadorian Indigenous movement in toppling the corrupt government of Jamil Mahaud, the "water war" in Cochabamba, Bolivia, and the massive protests against the economic crisis in Argentina (Seoane and Taddei 2001a).

20. Shortly before the Qatar meeting, LVC coordinator Rafael Alegría mentioned to the author that the organization was thinking of chartering a ship to bring protesters to Qatar or at least to anchor offshore. This never transpired (Alegría 2001). In 2005, the WTO again chose to meet on a peninsula, this time in Hong Kong. On that occasion, hundreds of Korean farmers donned orange life vests and dove into the harbor, hoping to swim to the cordoned-off meeting center.

21. "People of color" may be convenient shorthand, but it is also a problematical concept, particularly when employed as a category that includes groups with a wide variety of skin hues. Are blond, blue-eyed Hispanics (of which there are many and who in some places and situations may experience some but not all the oppression that their darker co-ethnics face) "people of color"? If not, what makes them different from olive-skinned, brown-eyed ones or Hispanics of Chinese descent? If historic oppression is the organizing principle for the category, it surely needs to be the subject of deeper analysis and more than skin deep. The "Global South" (which used to be the "Third World" and which includes numerous countries in the northern hemisphere) is similarly problematical. A real "archaeology" of these keywords remains to be carried out, just as the question of developing more appropriate descriptors has hardly ever been raised.

22. Glassman's (2002, 515) assertion that the "actual achievements in Seattle or its immediate aftermath were minimal" fails to acknowledge sufficiently this fundamental point.

23. The Group of Seven industrialized countries or G7 was founded in 1973. Between 1997 and 2014 Russia participated and it was called the Group of Eight or G8.

3. ROOTED, RURAL, AND SUBALTERN COSMOPOLITANS IN TRANSNATIONAL PEASANT AND FARMER MOVEMENTS

1. Nicole Doerr points to the central importance in European-wide civil society gatherings of "activists with multiple political backgrounds or transnational life histories." She argues that the most democratic civil society spaces were those in which "a 'culture of listening' predominated" and which eschewed a lingua franca model and treated "linguistic pluralism as a precious resource" (Doerr 2007, 226–227). Archibugi (2008) mentions the voluntary interpreters group known as Babels that was created to facilitate the World Social Forum and describes the complex debates around interpretation and translation issues in the European Parliament. Boéri (2012) provides a more detailed history of the Babels. The Barcelona-based Collective for the Self-Management of Interpretation Technologies (COATI 2017) also collaborates with La Via Campesina.

2. In more recent years, TAMs have increasingly relied on highly skilled, multilingual staff members to facilitate meetings and other international work.

3. For detailed discussions of LVC, see chapter 1 of this book; see also Edelman and Borras 2016, Desmarais 2007, and Martínez-Torres and Rosset 2010.

4. Other figures not considered here—professional intellectuals, nongovernmental organization (NGO) functionaries, foreign cooperators, politicians—have also contributed to the development and impact of TAMs (see chapter 10). Like many TAMs activists, they are also arguably "rooted" or "subaltern cosmopolitans."

5. The IFAP, a large, seemingly consolidated organization, suddenly collapsed in 2010 because of a severe deficit resulting—ironically—from the refusal of Agriterra, PFS's successor organization, to provide promised funding when IFAP was experiencing internal governance problems (Edelman and Borras 2016, 65–67).

6. One participant in the Mons meeting says that Verhagen did this "almost single-handedly" until 1996. Personal communication from Jun Borras, November 3, 2009.

7. Jonathan Pattenden (2005) argues that despite KRRS's radical antiglobalization rhetoric, its base consists of middle-class and wealthy farmers, led by dominant-caste men, and is personalistic and centralized. In contrast to social movements theorists who emphasize the horizontal and antihierarchical character of intra- and inter-movement communication, Pattenden indicates that KRRS employed two separate sets of messages, one for grassroots followers and another for international allies.

8. GRAIN is an international NGO headquartered in Spain that promotes biodiversity and local control of crop genetic resources. The split in KRRS that sparked this polemic between Shiva and Nanjundaswamy was only resolved in early 2008 (The Hindu 2008).

9. Tikait is a leader of the Bharatiya Kisan Union in Uttar Pradesh. In April 2008, over 10,000 police and paramilitary personnel surrounded Tikait's village, seeking to arrest him for derogatory, "caste-ist" remarks he allegedly directed at Uttar Pradesh Chief Minister Mayawati Kumari, leader of a Dalit political party, who has faced frequent allegations of corruption. Tikait, accompanied by 4,000 supporters, surrendered and acknowledged that "calling Maya names was a mistake" (Mittal and Banerjee 2008).

10. Another account says "Professor Najundaswamy was an assiduous Francophile, who studied at the Sorbonne and went to France to lead the [1999] Intercontinental Caravan for the destruction of GMOs [genetically modified organisms]" (Mittal and Banerjee 2008).

11. The first organizations to establish links with TAMs nonetheless sometimes become gatekeepers, preventing the entrance into international networks of other organizations in their countries or regions. KRRS, an "early linker" to LVC, for a long time blocked other Indian movements from joining LVC (Borras, Edelman, and Kay 2008, 192–193; Pattenden 2005, 1978–182; Edelman and Borras 2016, 47).

12. See Nicholson 2007 and LVC 2000b.

13. Wiebe's family's farm is reportedly 3,225 acres (Wolfwood 2009), medium-size by western North America standards.

14. "I have strong memories of America," Bové remarked in a 2000 interview, commenting on his Berkeley years. "I really like the United States. The language is still in my ears, and it really helps to be able to explain things to the Americans in English" (Bremner 2000).

15. From 1964 to 1969, Chonchol directed the agrarian reform under Christian Democratic President Eduardo Frei, and from 1970 to 1972, he served as agriculture minister in Salvador Allende's Popular Unity government. Vuskovic worked for years at ECLA (UN Economic Commission for Latin America) and was economy minister in Allende's government. Marini, dos Santos, and Bambirra were key exponents of dependency theory.

16. See Gioia 2016; for Moreno's biographical essay, see Claeys and Edelman 2020.

17. These authors point out that classical sociology is "surprisingly negative" about how leaders contribute to a movement's success. These perspectives emphasize the circulation of elites (Pareto 1935), the tendency to oligarchy of elites (Michels 1959), and institutionalizing charismatic leadership (Weber 1958).

18. John Burdick (1998) has an excellent elaboration of this problem and some innovative alternative approaches. Also see chapter 10 in this book.

19. See Bebbington 2005, 938, as well as the introduction and chapter 10 of this book, for discussions of representation politics.

20. Relatedly, the gap between leaders and the social bases of their organizations may result from emphasizing transnational activities over domestic, national, or local politics (see chapter 5 of this book; Edelman 1999, chap. 5; Pattenden 2005).

21. This also occurs in national- and local-level peasant organizations (Edelman 1999, chap. 5).

22. Early twentieth-century peasant studies by US and Mexican anthropologists devoted considerable attention to delimiting boundaries of such taxa as "primitives," "Indians," "folk," and "peasants" and to arguing for making the latter objects of research in a discipline that until then had focused almost exclusively on nonstate tribal peoples (Hewitt de Alcántara 1984, 19–41).

23. These changes are sometimes called the "new rurality" (Kay 2008).

4. TRANSNATIONAL PEASANT POLITICS IN CENTRAL AMERICA

1. This is not a novel argument. Anthony Leeds made much the same point two decades ago in a too-often overlooked essay entitled "Mythos and Pathos: Some Unpleasantries on Peasantries" (1977).

2. Region and regional are used here to refer to Central America as a whole. Other peasant organizations covering all of Central America include sector-specific groups such as the Unión de Pequeños Productores de Café de Centroamérica, México y el Caribe (UPROCAFE), founded in 1989, and the Confederación de Cooperativas del Caribe y Centroamérica (CCC-CA, founded in 1980, which has an agricultural co-op section. Banana workers' unions have participated since 1993 in the Coordinadora de Sindicatos Bananeros de Centroamérica y Colombia.

3. Regional integration accelerated following the Central American Presidents' Summit in Antigua, Guatemala, in June 1990. In December 1991, the Tegucigalpa Protocol created the Sistema de Integración Centroamericana (SICA), which incorporated the periodic regional meetings of presidents and ministers and the regional Central American Parliament (PARLACEN) founded as part of the 1987 Esquipulas Peace Accords. In contrast to the Central American Common Market (CACM) of the 1960s, which relied on high extra-regional tariffs to stimulate industry geared toward regional markets, current integration efforts are antiprotectionist and emphasize nontraditional agricultural exports and maquilas or garment-assembly plants as the engine of growth. The creation of SICA and of regional business lobbies (such as FEDEPRICAP, or the Federation of Private Entities of Central America and Panama) are among the examples that peasant leaders cite in explaining why they felt the need to organize at the regional level. In the Managua Declaration II of September 1997, the Central American countries and the Dominican Republic stated their intention of moving toward a European-style political union.

4. In 1989, negotiations for a new coffee agreement stalled, and world prices plummeted 40 percent in one month to the lowest levels in more than twenty years (Pelupessy 1993, 39–40). Prices registered a modest rise in 1994, tumbled precipitously in 1995, and began a more sustained recovery in 1997.

5. Steven Feierman's masterful *Peasant Intellectuals* (1990) concerned a kind of African leader whose exoticism seems to confirm old social scientific and popular stereotypes of rural peoples. The "peasant intellectuals" discussed in this chapter, in contrast, are probably closer to what Antonio Gramsci (1967) envisioned as "organic intellectuals," although most of them adamantly reject "organic ties" to political parties.

6. "I've taken any number of courses," Amanda Villatoro remarked matter-of-factly. Born in 1961, she finished the ninth grade in eastern El Salvador and went on to become a prominent leader of the Unión Comunal Salvadoreña (UCS). She elaborated, "Statis-

tics, microeconomics, macroeconomics, political theory . . . I have a long curriculum vitae. The UCS helped train me, with very high-level professors, and although I never went to the university nor even finished high school, I believe the knowledge I've acquired is equivalent to the fourth year of [a university] economics [major]. These are the tools we need to interpret the numbers the governments and the business groups present to us" (Villatoro 1994). Jorge Amador, a leader of the Central Nacional de Trabajadores del Campo (CNTC) and the Concejo Coordinador de Organizaciones Campesinas de Honduras (COCOCH), completed a year and a half of high school. But he also received extensive specialized education later: "I've participated in many training programs in Honduras, programs of the CNTC, such as a three-and-one-half-month program called 'technician in agrarian development,' as well as other subjects: sociology, a bit of philosophy, planning, agrarian law. I've also been trained abroad in Panama for three months. I've been in a great number of training programs and traveled to training events in Mexico, Nicaragua, Colombia, and England. . . . I've always taken the initiative to read a little, as much as possible, and I have a little library in my house" (Amador 1994).

7. Another example from El Salvador suggests something about the personal trajectories of these peasant intellectuals, as well as how field research frequently challenged the preconceptions about "campesinos" that I held as an urban writer. In July 1994, I went to an unmarked building in a grimy working-class neighborhood of San Salvador to interview René Hernández, a leader of the Sociedad de Cooperativas Cafetaleras de la Reforma Agraria (SOCRA). Born in 1957, Hernández had managed to complete the fifth grade in his hometown of Candelaria de Santa Ana. A beneficiary of the first stage of El Salvador's agrarian reform, he belongs to a cooperative founded in 1980 that owned 25 manzanas (17.5 hectares) of coffee. In the early 1980s, he attended courses on cooperative administration at the Centro de Capacitación Cooperativista (CENCAP), a government agency. By the late 1980s, he was a leader of FESACORASAL (Federation of Agrarian Reform Cooperatives of the Western Region) and CONFRAS (Confederation of Federations of Cooperatives of the Salvadoran Agrarian Reform), two above-ground cooperative organizations that were nonetheless influenced by one faction of the FMLN (Farabundo Martí National Liberation Front), an armed opposition group (Goitia 1994, 181). As a representative of Salvadoran cooperativism, he traveled to Germany, France, Israel, Mexico, Puerto Rico, and the rest of Central America. Since 1990, he has been on the board of directors of the state agricultural development bank and is a member of its credit commission, a post he received as part of a deal between peasant organizations and the minister of agriculture. Hernández commented, "This has been like a university degree for me." During our conversation, Hernández, at times jumping up to scribble on a whiteboard with a marker, gave me a complex lecture about rediscount policies and interest-rate "spreads," value-added taxes, banks' loan portfolios, and government privatization policies. On the way out, he nodded toward a room down the hall with some computer equipment and asked, "*¿Querés ver el volado?*" ("Do you want to see the thing-amajig?"). Peasants with computers were no longer a novelty to me, but to be polite, I responded "*Va' pues*" ("Okay"). He nudged the mouse, and a screen full of columns of constantly changing numbers appeared. The "Best Investments" modem next to the 486-66 IBM-compatible had a cable running to a huge parabolic antenna on the roof. Hernández had hooked into the New York coffee market and was looking at up-to-the-minute price shifts and futures options. Grabbing the mouse, he started to open up windows with graphs of seven-, thirty- and ninety-day price trends. "You see," he remarked with a sly smile, "now they can't lie to us about the price anymore" (R. Hernández 1994).

8. This goal has sometimes conflicted, however, with organizations' need to mobilize politically, because to a certain extent the peasant-as-rustic remains a critical symbol for garnering sympathy from policymakers and the public (Edelman 1991).

9. In 1994, for example, regional cooperative, community, labor, NGO, small enterprise, and agriculturalist networks formed a lobbying group called the Iniciativa Civil para la Integración Centroamericana (ICIC). Outside the region, ASOCODE has links to the international network called "La Via Campesina." It first met in Mons, Belgium, in 1993, with fifty-five organizations participating from thirty-six countries in the Americas, Europe, Asia, and Africa (Paulo Freire Stichting 1993; LVC 1996).

10. Interviews with Wilson Campos, ASOCODE (Campos Cerdas 1994a, 1994b).

11. Interviews with Carlos Hernández, CCJYD (Hernández Porras 1994); José Adán Rivera, ATC (Rivera 1994); and Sinforiano Cáceres, National Federation of Cooperatives/FENACOOP (Cáceres Baca 1994).

12. Virtually all UNAG leaders belonged to the FSLN, and some held high positions. Nevertheless, as UNAG functionary Amílcar Navarro recalled in an interview that "at that time [circa 1981], to own means of production was to be bourgeois. It was thought that the peasant movement had the same interests as the workers movement, as salaried agricultural workers, but that's not so. . . . The Frente Sandinista supported the workers movement much more than the peasant movement. The Frente had intellectuals, students, workers—and very few campesinos. They didn't understand the campesino who wanted to make his land produce, to sell his products at a good price, to have technical assistance. . . . The workers struggled to work less, five hours instead of ten. But we're employers, and we're paying these guys, so I can't support them when they say they want to work less" (Navarro 1994).

13. Expanding the Campesino a Campesino program to the rest of Central America became a central focus of ASOCODE's work after 1996 (ASOCODE 1997a, 10-11).

14. Relations between the European Community and Central America have been institutionalized in the "San José Dialogue," ministerial-level meetings held each year since 1984 (Sanahuja 1994).

15. CADESCA was originally intended to be a short-term undertaking. In 1994, it ceased to exist as an intergovernmental entity and was replaced by the private Foundation for the Economic and Social Development of Central America (FUNDESCA), which was funded primarily by the European Economic Community, European governments, and Scandinavian NGOs participating in the Copenhagen Initiative for Central America (CIFCA). FUNDESCA took over CADESCA's Panama offices and carried on its existing projects.

16. Subsequent to our 1994 interview, in 1996, Stein was named chancellor (foreign minister) of Guatemala in the government of President Alvaro Arzú.

17. The PL-480 "Food for Peace" program, established in 1954, was intended to win goodwill abroad and to reduce agricultural surpluses in the United States. It provides soft credits to finance grain purchases. Importing countries not only benefit from balance-of-payments savings but also resell the US products at market prices to domestic agro-industries, thus generating local currency that becomes part of government budgets. PL-480 agreements, however, specify which agencies and programs may receive this budgetary support, in effect establishing a new kind of external conditionality like that of the World Bank or the International Monetary Fund (Garst and Barry 1990, 6-15). The EEC and European governments, in contrast, did not share the US insistence on influencing macroeconomic policies. Most US assistance went through bilateral agencies, primarily the US Agency for International Development (USAID), which often attached political conditions to grants or used them to complement military strategies of "low-intensity conflict" (Cuenca 1992; Saldomando 1992; Sojo 1992). This approach contrasted with the European and Canadian practice of channeling most assistance (usually called "cooperation") through private organizations that supported small-scale grassroots efforts at development.

18. The PFSA, in conjunction with CADESCA's French counterpart IRAM (the Research Institute on Applied Development Methods), also carried out a number of short-term field studies on credit, pricing, and profitability issues. The results were reported to local (and not just national) agriculturalists' organizations. This aspect of the PFSA appears to have had relatively little impact, at least partly for reasons that I observed in July 1991, when I accompanied two French IRAM professionals on a one-week tour in northern Costa Rica. One IRAM expert, a middle-aged male credit specialist, did not speak Spanish. The other, a young woman, spoke Spanish fluently. She tried with fervor to convince groups of cooperative members and other campesinos that the era of subsidized production credit had ended and that from now on, they would have to increase productivity dramatically and work with high-interest loans. This bad news, combined with the culture clash involved in having a young European woman address large audiences made up almost exclusively of men, made it difficult for IRAM to get its message across at the grassroots level. PFSA leaders, acting together with the Salvadoran representatives to ASOCODE, later managed to sack the young Frenchwoman, even though some program participants considered her more knowledgeable about the region and the peasant organizations (and less dogmatic) than the young Frenchman who succeeded her.

19. Salvador Arias received a licenciatura in economics from the Jesuit-run Universidad Centroamericana in San Salvador in 1974. From 1975 to 1976, he served in the government, "at a time when efforts were being made to carry out an agrarian reform. I was vice minister, the minister was a military officer," he recalled in a 1995 interview. "In the process of discussion, of defining the character of the agrarian reform, we confronted each other and *el baboso* [the jerk] lost the battle. My position won, he resigned, and I was left [as minister] in charge of the process. But I only lasted four or five months. We pushed [for the reform], but the government backtracked." From 1977 to 1979, Arias studied at the London School of Economics. He returned to Central America in 1979 and 1980, when he served briefly as an adviser to the Sandinista government. He then spent nine years in Mexico and earned a doctorate in economics from the University of Paris VIII with a thesis on biotechnology (Arias Peñate 1990). In 1989, he moved to Panama to direct the PFSA (Arias Peñate 1995).

20. The PFSA's initial contacts tended to be with left-leaning organizations. But as national-level unity proceeded, centrist and occasionally conservative organizations also attended regional meetings. For example, one of the two Honduran representatives elected to ASOCODE's first coordinating commission was Víctor Calix, of the conservative Consejo Nacional Campesino (ASOCODE 1991b, 31; Calix 1994). The centrist Costa Rican union UPANACIONAL (National Union of Small and Medium Agricultural Producers) was also involved in ASOCODE from the beginning.

21. *El corte de chaleco* ("vest cut") is a Nicaraguan expression originally referring to a method of executing prisoners and traitors said to have been used by Sandino's forces during the war (1927–1932) against the US occupation of Nicaragua—after the Marines displayed the heads of captured Sandinistas (Black 1988, 44). As used here, the phrase suggests that free-market policies crippled peasant producers.

22. According to Carlos Hernández (Hernández Porras 1994), "Many of the documents were too technical. Having read a bit, I might be able to understand them, but for other compañeros, it was as if they were given a document in Chinese." Many other PFSA participants echoed these comments. I acquired a sizable box of PFSA documents in 1991 from an articulate activist in northern Costa Rica, a voracious reader who had come close to graduating from high school. While packing his belongings before moving, he threw up his hands and exclaimed, "If these things interest you, take them! I'll probably never read them." But for PFSA Director Salvador Arias, "this was a conscious thing on our

part. At times there is an oversimplification of the training given to campesino leaders. It is almost reduced to ABCs. We didn't agree with that. We said, we'll give them complicated topics and we'll explain them, so that they raise their level. . . . Some resisted, but in the end, it was positive because the campesino leadership began to have a new capacity, a new vocabulary, a new use of social and economic categories. They pressured us to write things in a certain language. But we said, 'No, we're not going to do that. I can explain globalization in the simplest way, and you will understand me. But if you can't handle the terminology used by the politicians with whom you're negotiating, even if you know about globalization, you're not going to understand them because they aren't going to use your categories. You have to use their words. When you're negotiating, you can't ask ministers to negotiate at your level. You have to raise the level.' Now it's easy to find campesino leaders in Central America who can speak about macroeconomics, about economic adjustment" (Arias Peñate 1995).

23. The Honduran campesino movement, despite its large size and deep historical roots, was severely divided. In 1991 and 1992, negotiations over the "agricultural modernization law" exacerbated splits between opponents and supporters of the government of Rafael Leonardo Callejas. In an effort to secure peasant backing for the measure, Callejas provided conservative peasant leaders and their organizations' base groups with considerable state resources, including public-sector jobs, vehicles, and promises of land titling and technical assistance. As a result, several large Honduran organizations split, with one part remaining in the anti-Callejas coalition COCOCH and the other joining the pro-Callejas National Peasant Union (UNC). In 1994, the two sectors began to discuss reuniting, in part because groups that had supported the agricultural modernization law now sought to amend provisions that had negatively affected their constituencies (Reyes Caballero 1994; Alegría 1997; Calix 1994). In Panama, key organizations were especially weak after 1989. The Confederación Nacional de Asentamientos Campesinos (CONAC) was linked closely to populist military leader Omar Torrijos and then to the regime of his successor, Manuel Antonio Noriega, who was overthrown in the US invasion. Following the intervention, CONAC became a target of considerable repression (Bermúdez 1994; Leis 1994, 104–105).

24. This coordinating body, which had incorporated several additional organizations, was renamed the Mesa Nacional Campesina (MNC) two years later. The CCJYD dissolved in 1995 as a result of factional disputes and allegations of financial impropriety.

25. Justicia y Desarrollo leader Carlos Hernández recalled, "The Honduran case was very sharp and definitive. The campesino organizations didn't expect [the structural adjustment program]. When we told them about the impact of adjustment in Costa Rica and what neoliberalism was going to mean in [the rest of] Central America, they thought it impossible that this could affect the Honduran agrarian reform. . . . This was a very clear position of the peasant leaders we saw in the [PFSA] seminars. They said the agrarian reform was a conquest of the people, that there were laws, that it would never happen, that we were crazy" (Hernández Porras 1994). Between 1962 and 1990, the Honduran state distributed over 376,000 hectares of land to some 66,000 rural families (Sierra Mejía and Ramírez Mejía 1994, 59). In March 1990, the government announced plans for a structural adjustment program. Two years later, the Agricultural Modernization Law took effect, permitting private titling and sales of agrarian reform lands (Honduras Poder Legislativo 1992). In 1992 alone (the first year of the law), official data suggest that some 17 percent of reform beneficiaries abandoned or sold their land (Thorpe et al. 1995, 113). Many more subsequently sold their holdings to large investors (Posas 1996, 141–147).

26. As citizens of the region's only demilitarized and democratic social-welfare state, Costa Ricans have long enjoyed levels of literacy, health, and well-being far above those of other Central Americans. Often, they consider themselves more "advanced" than their

"less cultured" and "more violent" neighbors. In turn, other Central Americans often view Costa Ricans as snobbish, pro-gringo, and pacifistic to the point of cowardice. Even though Costa Rican campesino leaders did their best to overcome these prejudices, the fact that many had some higher education and considerable familiarity with urban culture complicated relations with representatives from other countries. An economist who participated in early PFSA seminars said, "The Costa Ricans were tremendously articulate [and] able to speak about the issues. They often ended up speaking most at these meetings. They were never able to get beyond the others' severe anti–Costa Rican attitudes. Their articulateness served them poorly in this dynamic; it was associated with being effeminate. They didn't talk like peasants" (anonymous 1994). A Panamanian social scientist had similar recollections of the PFSA but noted that the Costa Ricans' greater experience with democratic decision making helped the emerging regional peasant association. "That antipathy toward Ticos is always mixed with a bit of envy. 'Costa Rica is a petty-bourgeois, boring country where nothing ever happens and Ticos are all *maricones* [a perjorative for gay males].' They're envious because they know that Costa Rica has a social system and a certain social peace that doesn't exist in the other countries. . . . That capacity for compromise that is part of Costa Rican political culture, one of its positive aspects, has contributed to the process of ASOCODE, to the practice of hard argument followed by consensus" (anonymous 1994). The sophistication of Costa Rican leaders had earlier impressed PSA specialists. In their first meeting in 1988, "the national technicians who worked with the PSA in Costa Rica were surprised by the peasants' arguments. It was not common to hear campesino proposals; it was odder to find that those proposals constituted a broad alternative to what the government's economic team was then negotiating with the World Bank and the [International Monetary Fund]" (Hernández Cascante 1992, 1–2).

27. The 1994–1995 divisions in the FMLN appear to have had little effect on ASOCODE's Salvadoran affiliate, the Alianza Democrática Campesina (ADC). Activists from both the ERP (the Revolutionary People's Army, which quit the FMLN) and the FPL (Popular Forces of Liberation, which remained in the FMLN) continue to participate in the ADC.

28. Ethnic divisions were also more pronounced in Belize than elsewhere. Much commercial agriculture was controlled by Mennonites, who were often not well liked by the English-speaking (and frequently urban) Afro-Belizeans and the Hispanicized Kekchi Maya. These two groups also felt pressured by Guatemalan and Salvadoran refugees who flooded Belize in the 1980s and competed for land and government services. ASOCODE finally attracted Belizean participants after it sent emissaries to identify leaders and cooperative organizations (Ávila 1994). The Belizean representatives came exclusively from the Hispanic and Hispanicized Maya population. They nonetheless were often less comfortable speaking Spanish than English and at first found it difficult to understand the technical and political discussions of the other Central Americans (Tzib 1994); see also Candanedo and Madrigal 1994, 36, 104, and Hernández Cascante 1995.

29. Interviews with Guatemalan campesino leaders, Panama City, June 1994, and New York City, December 1994. All Guatemalans interviewed for this project before the 1996 signing of the peace accords requested anonymity. In a meeting of ASOCODE's coordinating commission that I observed in June 1994, one of the Guatemalan representatives became irate because his name appeared in a draft of the association's newsletter. He insisted that if published, it could have caused him serious problems at home.

30. This mention of biotechnology is one of several factors that suggest that Salvador Arias played a significant role in drafting ASOCODE's 1991 "productive strategy." Arias wrote his doctoral dissertation on the potential dangers of biotechnologies for Central America (Arias Peñate 1990). In more than fifty in-depth interviews with Central

American campesino activists in 1994–1995 and 1997, the subject of biotechnology rarely came up, suggesting that the topic was not a major peasant concern.

31. The "bands" set price ceilings and floors for key basic grains and common tariffs on extra-regional imports well below the levels already established in the GATT negotiations (Ministros de Agricultura de Guatemala, El Salvador, Honduras y Nicaragua 1993; Segovia 1993; Solórzano 1994). Campesino leaders who had attended PFSA seminars participated in the regional meetings of agriculture ministers that led up to the free-trade agreement on basic grains. These discussions in 1991 were so heated that the ministers and World Bank representatives "asked for the head" of the PFSA director, Salvador Arias. He recalled that "the campesinos by now had been studying this for two or three years, and they started a confrontation with the ministers and wiped them out. The campesinos took apart all their arguments. [The ministers] were unable to respond" (Arias Peñate 1995). Under pressure from the angered ministers, CADESCA's director had to urge the campesino leaders to be more diplomatic in future negotiations (Stein 1994). Even though several Central American foreign ministers began to push for Arias's removal from the PFSA, the representatives from Mexico, Colombia, Venezuela, and Panama on CADESCA's board, as well as the influence of the EEC, thwarted their efforts.

32. Individuals and groups at the congress are listed in ASOCODE 1991b. Also present were observers from the CCC-CA, small agriculturalists organizations in Mexico and Cuba, and the Federación Internacional de Productores Agropecuarios (FIPA), an umbrella group with member organizations in fifty-five countries, headquartered in France. Other attendees were representatives of the diplomatic corps, development agencies, the Catholic Church, the Nicaraguan and Honduran governments, and CADESCA functionaries.

33. The participating national coalitions were APEMEP (Panama), CNA (Costa Rica), UNAG (Nicaragua), ADC (El Salvador), COCOCH (Honduras), and BFAC and CCC-B (Belize). The Belizean organizations created a formal coalition (the Belize Association of Producers' Organizations, or BAPO) to participate in ASOCODE only in 1996, years after this step had been taken in the other countries. A range of Guatemalan organizations (including the CUC) attended the congress but asked for observer status because they had not yet founded a national coalition to participate in ASOCODE. CONAMPRO, the coalition that came to represent Guatemala in ASOCODE, was founded shortly after the congress. According to interviews that I conducted with two anonymous CONAMPRO leaders in Panama City in June 1994, its influence was hurt, however, by factional disputes and the withdrawal of its largest constituent organizations: the CUC (the Committee of Peasant Unity) and the CONIC (a group identified with National Indigenous and Peasant Coordination). The CUC and CONIC withdrew as a result of disagreements over NGO support for CONAMPRO and the high priority that ASOCODE gave to agricultural issues rather than to political and human rights concerns (Candanedo and Madrigal 1994, 41). According to Carlos Hernández, CADESCA leaders apparently opposed the participation of the CUC because its identification with the armed left would cause problems with the Guatemalan government (Hernández Porras 1994). The CUC and CONIC went on to found the Coordinadora Nacional de Organizaciones Campesinas (CNOC), which initially competed with CONAMPRO. By 1997, however, CONAMPRO, the CUC, and CONIC were all participating in the CNOC. Even CONAMPRO supporters acknowledged that the CNOC, because of its broader membership, might replace CONAMPRO as the Guatemalan affiliate of ASOCODE (Lemus 1997).

34. Wilson Campos came from a rural community near the central Costa Rican city of Heredia. In a 1990 interview, he recalled that his father had "chosen" him as the one child out of eight who would attend a university. He completed two years at the Universidad de Costa Rica, dropped out to take a position with the health ministry in a remote

northern zone, and in the early 1980s led the formation of the Unión Campesina de Guatuso (UCADEGUA), a member of the Justicia y Desarrollo coalition (Campos Cerdas 1990). In 1996, Sinforiano Cáceres, a Nicaraguan UNAG leader, succeeded Campos as ASOCODE's general coordinator.

35. ASOCODE's statutes specified that the coordinating commission's decisions must be consensual rather than by majority vote (1991b, 30). Members described this practice with pride and wondered at their capacity for dialogue, but this sentiment was mixed with frustration over the heated and sometimes inconclusive nature of the discussions.

36. Interviews with a COCOCH member (Fuentes 1994a, 1994b) also informed me on this topic. Campaigns for fair commerce seek to supply niche markets (like the one for organic or gourmet coffee) or to purchase the output of small producers, cooperatives, and democratically controlled peasant organizations at premium or "just" prices. One of the more notable successes is the Netherlands' Max Havelaar Foundation, which imports coffee from small producers' groups in over a dozen countries. Havelaar coffee is served in eleven out of twelve Dutch provincial government buildings, in 40 percent of municipal offices, and in the National Parliament. It is also available in most Dutch, Belgian, and Swiss supermarkets as well as elsewhere in Europe (Havelaar 1992).

37. ASOCODE's statutes provide for the possibility of the associated coalitions paying dues to ASOCODE (1991b, 26), and its 1993 congress approved in principle a dues payment from each national group (Candanedo and Madrigal 1994, 162). Nonetheless, resources have flowed exclusively in the other direction, from ASOCODE to the national groups.

38. The creation of a "parallel organization" typically involves staged elections for a new board of directors. Government agencies or the courts then award the organization's "legal identity" (along with offices, bank accounts, and other resources) to a favored faction, whether or not it represents the membership (Arita 1994; Lombraña 1989; Menjívar, Li Kam, and Portuguez 1985; Posas 1985; Thorpe et al. 1995, 131–143). According to Salvador Arias, Callejas may have been especially irritated with ASOCODE because he facilitated its first appearance at a summit (in San Salvador in mid-1991) as a result of concessions to ASOCODE's Honduran affiliate COCOCH (Arias Peñate 1995). Well-informed sources indicate that Callejas's effort to form a "parallel" to ASOCODE also involved the government of Alfredo Cristiani in El Salvador.

39. COCICA's moribund status was evident in interviews that I carried out one day apart in 1994 with pro-Callejas peasant leaders Víctor Calix and Marcial Reyes Caballero (Calix 1994; Reyes Caballero 1994). Each one of these leaders told me that the other was COCICA's current president. Clearly, this situation exemplified what Charles Tilly once aptly termed "fictitious organizations" (1984, 311).

40. Similar harassment also occurred in Honduras and El Salvador. ASOCODE leaders wanted to be able to tell threatening Guatemalan police or immigration officials not only that they had met personally with the president but that he had stated his approval of their organization. Similarly, connections with ASOCODE (and ASOCODE's ties to European governments) constituted an important form of protection for national groups in the countries where repression of the peasant movement was ongoing.

41. Interview with anonymous CONAMPRO leaders, Panama City, June 1994.

42. Interview with anonymous ADC leader, San Salvador, July 18, 1994.

43. In Honduras, however, the peasant march forced the creation of a new bipartite commission representing peasant organizations and the public sector to monitor central bank credits provided to the state development bank.

44. On October 23, 1995, Honduran troops killed three campesinos in the Yoro Department and wounded two others when firing into a crowd of seventy demonstrators who refused to leave land claimed by the Ministerio de Recursos Naturales. In December 1995,

Honduran police fired on peasant demonstrators outside the Central American Presidents' Summit, killing one protester. In western El Salvador in October 1995, the ADC and its allies occupied seventeen properties. This initiative led to the formation of a mixed government-peasant-organization commission to investigate farms that exceeded the constitutional ceiling of 245 hectares. The group consisted of representatives of the state agrarian-reform agency and human rights office, the FMLN, the UN Observer Mission, and the ADC. On February 20, 1996, Guatemalan police violently evicted several hundred campesinos from a CONAMPRO-linked organization who were occupying land in San Lucas Tolimán, Sololá.

45. Another internal ASOCODE document offered a franker assessment, describing the group's reliance on foreign "cooperation" as one of its "original sins." The document characterized such funding as "one of the temptations that we will have to face on a daily basis in order to guarantee that ASOCODE has full autonomy and is really at the service of the small and medium-sized agriculturalists of the isthmus" (Hernández Cascante 1992, 6). In one external evaluation of the organization, a number of ASOCODE participants mentioned dependence on foreign funds as a significant preoccupation (Candanedo and Madrigal 1994).

46. Increasingly, however, these concerns are being shared and debated. One internal ASOCODE report on a European tour stated, "The ecological issue . . . is one of the problems of most concern to European civil society. Some groups tend to push us toward changes in our cultivation practices that are too drastic. We told them that we were not prepared for this and proposed a more moderate approach toward chemical-free agriculture . . . , introducing new practices little by little to achieve a gradual change" (ASOCODE 1993a, 4). Similarly, much of the initial impetus for expanding women's participation came from foreign donor NGOs. But once such efforts began, they quickly developed a dynamic of their own, with campesina leaders demanding and attaining greater representation in the organization (ASOCODE 1995b). Nonetheless, as a recent external evaluation noted, "Work with women is still unfortunately conceived of as a problem of the women themselves" (Morales Gamboa and Cranshaw 1997, 27).

47. ASOCODE sought to guarantee rotation of cadres in top posts, barring the coordinator and coordinating commission members from serving more than two terms in office. But the scarcity of skilled organizers in the national and transnational networks of which ASOCODE is a part—the lobbying group ICIC, the CICAFOC (Indigenous and Peasant Community Agroforestry Coordinator), Via Campesina, and so on—suggests that leaders can continue careers well after service to any one organization (compare Keck and Sikkink 1998; Lichbach 1994, 408–409).

48. ASOCODE's second congress in December 1993 resolved to place the two coordinating commission representatives from each country on the ASOCODE payroll because they were devoting most of their time to the regional organization. Some national coalitions later objected that this matter should have been discussed first at the national level, given that these individuals also worked for national- and base-level organizations. Some objected as well to a "lack of transparency" in approving the draft budget, which had not been distributed sufficiently in advance to permit detailed study and discussion (Candanedo and Madrigal 1994, 108).

5. WHEN NETWORKS DON'T WORK

1. Arquilla and Ronfeldt played a key role in codifying the US military's strategy against the Taliban regime in Afghanistan and Al Qaeda (Pisani 2002).

2. John and Jean Comaroff (1999, 33) also call attention to how "Euro-modernist forms" of civil society "may be emptied of substance . . . turned into a hollow fetish . . .

[or] a dangerous burlesque." At the same time, they acknowledge, as Riles rarely does, that civil society nonetheless serves as a vessel for utopian visions and for opening up democratic spaces.

3. On the Campesino a Campesino program, see Bunch 1982; Enlace Sur-Sur 1998; Holt-Giménez 1996; and Núñez Soto, Cardenal, and Morales 1998.

4. For a less jocular approach to the same problem, see Stirrat 1996.

5. APEMEP (Asociación de Pequeños y Medianos Productores de Panamá), ADC (Alianza Democrática Campesina) of El Salvador, COCOCH (Concejo Coordinador de Organizaciones Campesinas de Honduras).

6. BRINGING THE MORAL ECONOMY BACK IN . . . TO THE STUDY OF TWENTY-FIRST-CENTURY TRANSNATIONAL PEASANT MOVEMENTS

1. Samuel Popkin's *Rational Peasant* (1979) echoes this distinction, though without acknowledging its eighteenth-century origins or the pejorative meanings—noted by Thompson—that early critics attached to "political economy."

2. Thompson comes close to this in his discussion of the "ideal existence" of the "paternalist model" of locally administered commerce, though he displays less interest specifically in the subjectivity of the poor than in how encroaching market forces eroded existing regulatory institutions and generated popular resentment (1971, 83–88).

3. I use the phrase *"apparent* quiescence" because even though Scott's *Moral Economy* focused on the consuming question of the peasant studies field—the causes of rebellion—it foreshadowed in many ways his later writing on the "micro-" or "infrapolitics" of resistance (Scott 1985, 1990).

4. In *Weapons of the Weak*, Scott maintains, similarly, that "the personalization of the causes of distress" is a significant dimension of how peasants understand and experience "the large abstractions" such as "capitalism, imperialism, or the green revolution" (1985, 347–348).

5. Buijtenhuijs (2000) argues that the diminished salience of peasantries in the late twentieth century resulted not only from urbanization and related societal shifts but from growing peasant involvement in unattractive "predatory wars" and from changing social scientific fashions that led researchers to categorize in other terms what they would formerly have seen as "peasant wars."

6. That several of the revolutionary movements (e.g., Russia, Algeria, and Cuba) that Wolf classified as "peasant wars" were arguably not entirely or even largely made up of peasants is indicative of the extent to which peasant-centric thinking dominated social scientific discussions at this time. While demobilized soldiers from rural areas sometimes backed revolutionary parties and certainly contributed to ending czarism in Russia (Wolf 1969, 87–89), the insurrections of February and October 1917 were primarily urban in origin. Similarly, Algeria's National Liberation Front waged a mainly urban guerrilla struggle, backed by town dwellers, disaffected veterans, workers, and the nationalist intelligentsia. In Cuba, Fidel Castro's 26th of July Movement guerrillas eventually gained support from some "middle" or "tactically mobile" peasants, but, as Wolf himself suggested, without "outside leadership," they would likely have achieved little (1969, 291–294).

7. On the "consumption" of Chayanov's work by scholars concerned with Russia, Asia, and Latin America, see Bernstein and Byres (2001, 13–15); Hewitt de Alcántara (1984); Roseberry (1993, 333–342); and Shanin (1972). In anthropology, possibly the most innovative use of Chayanov's work was in *Stone Age Economics*, where Marshall Sahlins (1972) maintained that "customary consumption requirements" explained observed levels of production intensification in "primitive" and peasant households.

8. Rational-actor approaches have generated considerable skepticism. See, among many examples, Ostrom 1990 on common property resource management and Tilly 2001 on contentious politics.

9. Other moral economists that Popkin targeted included Eric Wolf, whose analysis of the "closed corporate community" (Wolf 1957, 1986) highlighted "leveling" and redistributive tendencies that market-oriented theorists considered overblown, and Joel Migdal (1974, 69), who similarly viewed peasants' redistributive "prestige economy" as a key survival mechanism.

10. Contrast Popkin's assertion to Scott's position (1976, 59) that "the insecurities of the world market were, on balance, greater than those of the traditional local markets."

11. Echoing Labrousse, Florescano declared, "The revolution of [Mexican] independence, like the French Revolution, explodes in the middle of a storm of high prices. Thus culminated the attack of successive agricultural crises on the weak structures of colonial society" (1969, 4:179).

12. Scott is clearly aware of this dynamic (1976, 14), although in *The Moral Economy*, he usually analyzes peasants' commitment to minimal but reliable returns as part of a trade-off between subsistence production and riskier cash cropping (1976, 20–21). In much of the book, he appears mainly concerned with producers who have only a limited, indirect, and intermittent commercial orientation, as when he refers to peasants' "sale of a portion of the crops (often in the form of a crop loan that is repaid in kind)" (1976, 114).

13. In an earlier work, referring to the period of the early industrial revolution in England, Thompson (1963, 203) declared that "some of the most bitter conflicts of these years turned on issues which are not encompassed by cost of living series."

14. A "subsistence level" assumes, Scott writes, "a pattern of food preferences and is itself therefore culturally determined" (1976, 17n10). Benjamin Orlove, in an important article that elaborates the political implications of this point for early twentieth-century Chile, takes Thompson to task for giving scant attention to such preferences (1997, 236). While Thompson does note the "feelings of status" that attached to the consumption of white bread, his discussion emphasizes the interest that bakers and millers had in producing it instead of making coarser whole grain or non-wheat loaves ("the bread of the poor"), the prices of which were regulated. Bread made for the poor was shunned by more affluent customers who suspected it was adulterated (Thompson 1971, 80–81).

15. While the causes of declining prices (and levels of volatility) vary somewhat for different commodities, the downward co-movement of so many commodity prices, particularly since the mid-1990s, is historically unprecedented.

16. Dumping, which still occurs, even though it is prohibited under WTO rules, refers to the practice of selling products abroad at below their cost of production, typically in an effort to gain market share or undermine local competitors.

17. Also important in the case of coffee after 1989 is the suspension, as a result of disagreements among member countries, of the mandatory export quotas in the International Coffee Agreement.

18. Little-noticed and undertheorized aspects of this trend, however, include "repeasantization" (Edelman 1999, 205–207) and the dispersion of an increasing proportion of the remaining rural population into a growing number of ever smaller, remote communities. Arturo Warman (2001, 41), who described the latter phenomenon for Mexico, remarked somewhat romantically that "this represents a form of resistance to urbanization, a way of reproducing life without changing it, so that it continues to be as before, as it always was, even though it can never be the same."

19. Some social scientists, particularly but not only in Europe, celebrate this phenomenon as the "new" or "postindustrial rurality." If rural areas once provided labor, food, and raw materials for the rise of industry, under the "new rurality," the countryside ex-

periences growth in the service and manufacturing sectors, which no longer require the same degree of spatial concentration as they did in a Fordist economy, and farm families rely more on "pluriactivity" than on agriculture (Eikeland 1999; Llambí 2000; Marsden 1995). The limited applicability of this paradigm to most societies in the Global South, especially those where the urban-based industries of the postindustrial North have now settled, should be obvious.

20. For more detailed treatments, see Borras 2004; Desmarais 2002, 2003b; and Edelman 1998, 2002, 2003.

21. *Via Campesina* may be roughly translated as "Peasant Road"; even non-Spanish speakers, however, refer to the organization by its Spanish name. Its activists deliberately use the terms "farmer" and "peasant" interchangeably to highlight the common problems of small agriculturalists in developed and less-developed countries. I follow this practice here for reasons that I have elaborated in detail elsewhere (see chapter 1).

22. Alison Van Rooy (2004, 20) points out that all social movements engage in "venue shifting" but that this tends to intensify when they participate in transnational networks. Borras (2004, 4–5) describes LVC organizations as "polycentric"—with centers of power located at international, regional, national, and local levels. The networks that link them are, he says, both "actors" and "arenas of actions," since they engage in mobilizations and other pressure tactics while simultaneously serving as a forum for debates and exchanges of experiences among participating groups and individuals (Borras 2004, 4–5).

23. Similarly, LVC's agrarian reform campaign, which seeks to present an alternative to the World Bank's market-based agrarian reform model, states that it rejects "the ideology that only considers land as merchandise" (Borras 2004, 11). The argument is reminiscent of Polanyi's concept of "fictitious commodities": "What we call land is an element of nature inextricably interwoven with man's institutions. To isolate it and form a market out of it was perhaps the weirdest of all undertakings of our ancestors" (Polanyi 1957, 178, 72–73).

24. LVC and its supporters frequently suggest that only 10 percent of world agricultural output is traded internationally (CPE 2004; LVC 2001, 6; A. Simpson 2004). The FAO reports, however, that "around one-third of world [agricultural] output is traded internationally." The proportion of total output traded internationally varies greatly by commodity, from 94 percent of coffee (in 1996) to 20 percent of wheat and 5 percent of rice (FAO 2000).

25. The Cairns Group consists of 17 countries (including Argentina, Australia, Brazil, Canada, Chile, Indonesia, Malaysia, New Zealand, and South Africa) with modern agricultural export sectors and minimal farm subsidies. In international trade talks, it has pushed for the reduction and elimination of export and other agricultural subsidies.

26. WTO categorizes most kinds of agricultural subsidies in "amber," "green," and "blue boxes." The "amber box" (like the caution signaled by the amber color of a traffic light) includes subsidies that are considered trade distorting and must be reduced over time, such as support prices or subsidies directly related to production output. Permitted "green box" subsidies are mainly programs of direct income support not tied to particular products, as well as payments to farmers for environmental conservation. The "blue box" contains amber box–type subsidies that require agriculturalists to limit production. Green and blue box subsidies are not subject to overall national limits. Approximately two-thirds of US subsidies are now in the green box and one-third in the amber box, while EU programs are approximately one-half in the amber box and one-quarter each in the green and blue boxes.

27. Peter Rosset provides a succinct statement of what is probably the majority position within LVC: "Subsidies per se are not the enemy. Their merit depends on how much the subsidies cost, who gets them, and what they pay for. So subsidies paid only to large

corporate producers in the North, leading to dumping and the destruction of rural livelihoods in the Third World, are bad. But subsidies paid to family farmers to keep them on the land and support vibrant rural economies, and subsidies that assist with soil conservation, the transition to sustainable farming practices, and direct marketing to local consumers, are good. The real enemy of farmers is low prices" (2003, 3).

28. The Monsanto Corporation's genetically engineered Bt corn (brand name Yieldgard) produces insecticidal proteins from the soil bacterium (*Bacillus thuringiensis*, or Bt) that resist corn borer infestations. Activists have assailed Monsanto and other biotech seed companies for contributing to the genetic contamination of landraces and other crop varieties, reducing populations of pollinating insects, threatening human and animal health, and requiring agriculturalists to purchase licenses that oblige them not to save seeds for future planting cycles.

29. ATTAC, which campaigns for the Tobin tax on international currency movements and related justice and development issues, has chapters in many countries. Its unwieldy full name is *Association pour la Taxation des Transactions Financières pour l'Aide aux Citoyens* (Association for the Taxation of Financial Transactions to Aid the Citizenry). The European leg of the caravan was only one of several Asian peasant organization caravans to Europe (see chapter 1).

7. FOOD SOVEREIGNTY

1. In contrast, an Intergovernmental Working Group of the UN Human Rights Council, mandated with drafting a Declaration on the Rights of Peasants and Other People Working in Rural Areas, held its first meeting in July 2013 (see chapter 8). The first draft under discussion contained several provisions related to food sovereignty. See Edelman and James 2011; Golay and Biglino 2013. A Convention on Food Sovereignty was one demand of the NGO Forum and allied social movements at the 2001 Rome+5 World Food Conference (D. J. Shaw 2007, 359).

2. As Jennifer Clapp warns, "a broad conceptualization may work well in the early stages of a movement, but it is likely that the concept will need to be more precisely articulated, which may in turn cause it to lose some of its supporters" (2012, 176).

3. The proceedings from this meeting states that "food sovereignty, simply defined, is ensuring that land, water, seeds and natural resources are controlled by small and medium-sized producers. It is directly linked to democracy and justice" (LVC 1996, 21).

4. For a more complete listing of relevant meetings and framing documents, see Windfuhr and Jonsén 2005, 47–52. This process of refinement produced increasingly precise definitions but also "increasing levels of inconsistency" (Patel 2009, 666). Key ideas include protection for food producers, especially small-scale ones; regulation of agricultural production and trade; an end to dumping of developed-country surpluses in developing countries; sustainable, agroecological production practices; and democratic control by "the people," "local producers," or those who "produce, distribute, and consume food"; management of resources, seeds, and territories by small-scale food producers; and gender and other kinds of social equality. Occasionally, food sovereignty enthusiasts (Patel 2009, 666–667) acknowledge that such capacious framings contain internal or even "fatal" contradictions, elisions, and substantial doses of wishful thinking.

5. The relevant section in the book was based on an article of mine that was first published in the now-defunct journal *Peasant Studies* (not to be confused with the *Journal of Peasant Studies*); see Edelman 1991, 229. I also mentioned food sovereignty in another article (Edelman 1998, 59) that was published a year before the book that De Schutter mentioned.

6. In another work, Claeys locates the origins of food sovereignty in Central America in the mid-1980s (2013a, 3).

7. A few years later this was true in Honduras (and perhaps elsewhere in the region) as well. See Amador 1994.

8. These leaders were from leftist and centrist organizations; none of them became involved in LVC.

9. According to Rose Spalding (1994, 73), "In the absence of any competing, long-term national development plan, this MIDINRA document served as the main expression of the regime's economic vision."

10. As late as 2008, the declaration of the Latin American Presidential Summit on Food Sovereignty and Security also used the terms largely interchangeably (Cumbre Presidencial 2008).

11. On the Ngram, see Egnal 2013 and Rosenberg 2013.

12. Two years earlier, the phrase "food sovereignty" appears in discussions of Canada's food aid program, with one speaker asserting that "the first test of any emerging nation's real sovereignty is food sovereignty" (Canadian Institute of International Affairs 1981, 12:107). The term, however, failed to gain traction at the time.

13. Journalist Alan Riding charged accurately that PRONAL "emerged as a SAM without money" (Riding 1986, 286). SAM—the Sistema Alimentario Mexicano—was the previous government's food program (dismantled in 1983) that tried simultaneously to provide support prices to farmers and subsidies to consumers, thus worsening an already critical fiscal deficit.

14. María Elena Martínez-Torres and Peter Rosset are right that "food sovereignty is a concept coined by actively appropriating and inventing language" (2010, 161). What they and other LVC activists fail to realize, however, is that the language appears to have been appropriated, even if indirectly, from PRONAL and then Mexican President Miguel de la Madrid—surely not the most inspiring political-intellectual ancestor for these Mexico-based scholar-activists.

15. On contacts in this period between Mexican and Central American peasant activists, see Boyer 2010 and Holt-Giménez 2006. It may be significant that the 1996 LVC conference that adopted a food sovereignty program was held in Mexico, where local movements would have been aware—at the very least—of the government's rhetoric about "food sovereignty" under de la Madrid.

16. The conventional view is typified by an editorial in the *Nyéléni Newsletter*:

> Food sovereignty is different from food security in both approach and politics. Food security does not distinguish where food comes from, or the conditions under which it is produced and distributed. National food security targets are often met by sourcing food produced under environmentally destructive and exploitative conditions, and supported by subsidies and policies that destroy local food producers but benefit agribusiness corporations. Food sovereignty emphasizes ecologically appropriate production, distribution and consumption, social-economic justice and local food systems as ways to tackle hunger and poverty and guarantee sustainable food security for all peoples. It advocates trade and investment that serve the collective aspirations of society. It promotes community control of productive resources; agrarian reform and tenure security for small-scale producers; agro-ecology; biodiversity; local knowledge; the rights of peasants, women, indigenous peoples and workers; social protection and climate justice (Focus on the Global South 2013).

17. Madeleine Fairbairn rightly suggests that food sovereignty is both a reaction to and an intellectual offspring of the earlier concepts of the "right to food" and "food security'" (2010, 15).

18. Fairbairn's idea that food security is a relatively new concept, dating to the 1970s, clearly requires rethinking (2010, 22–23; 2012, 221).

19. Writing on Canada, Annette Aurélie Desmarais and Hannah Wittman (2014) stress "unity in diversity" as a key principle of food sovereignty. They also point to the Canadian Wheat Board (CWB), which among other things was the country's major exporter, as an institution of "food sovereignty." But they also acknowledge that importing countries would be unlikely to view the CWB that way. Indeed, part of the CWB's early success was that its single-desk buyer system eliminated competition among farmers, "allowing them to achieve greater economic clout in the global grain trade" (Magnan 2011, 116).

20. Of course, some food activists, as Fairbairn (2012) indicates, view food sovereignty as largely a question of consumer choices and express little interest in its policy implications.

21. In 1996, LVC simply demanded the *renegotiation* of "international trade agreements like GATT/WTO, Maastricht, [and] NAFTA" (LVC 1996, 23). Later, of course, it called for getting the "WTO out of agriculture" (Rosset 2006). Food sovereignty advocates' views are evolving. Some "see a gradual acceptance of trade under certain circumstances . . . , with the shift away from focusing primarily on local markets to integrating consideration for fairer trade" (Burnett and Murphy 2014, 1068).

22. Marcia Ishii-Eiteman (2009) and Kim Burnett and Sophia Murphy (2014) are among the very few exceptions to this generalization. C. Clare Hinrichs (2003), Giles Mohan and Kristian Stokke (2000), and Don Robotham (2005) provide unusually thoughtful and grounded discussions of the complexities of constructing "the local."

23. In peri-urban areas in the United States, conservation and similar easements intended to preserve greenbelts and farmland have sometimes had the effect of creating ownership ceilings, even though this is not their intention.

24. See Lenin 1964 and Stalin's unsurprisingly meretricious essay "Dizzy with Success" (Stalin 1955, originally published in 1930).

25. Of course, many (if not most) people didn't just line up but also worked their connections and resorted to the illegal market economy to obtain otherwise scarce necessities. Cubans sardonically refer to this as *sociolismo*, a play on *socialismo* and *socio*, which means "partner" but which they commonly employ to mean "buddy" or "friend."

26. He was apparently unconcerned that pineapple was produced in pesticide-intensive monocultures.

27. The ubiquitous plastic bags of mushy, tasteless McIntosh and Red "Delicious" apples that were the main source of vitamin C during my childhood in 1950s and 1960s New York are but one dismal example of the alternative to long-distance trade. At least there were sometimes oranges from far-off Florida and California. The glories of summer included abundant local peaches, plums, and berries.

8. HOW THE UNITED NATIONS RECOGNIZED THE RIGHTS OF PEASANTS AND OTHER PEOPLE WORKING IN RURAL AREAS

1. See also Henry Saragih, "A Declaration That Is Truly the Voice of the Movement," and Melik Özden and Florian Rochat, "An Extraordinary Tool in the Hands of Peasants," both interviews in Claeys and Edelman 2020.

2. Remarks by Saragih at the forum "En lutte pour la reconnaissance de nos droits ou comment un movement paysan international pousse le Conseil des Droits de l'Homme à agir," Haute école du paysage, d'ingénierie et d'architecture, Geneva, May 17, 2016.

3. See Alabrese et al. 2022; Claeys 2015, 2018; Claeys and Edelman 2020; Edelman and James 2011; Edelman 2014; Golay 2015, 2019; Hubert 2019; Jovanović 2015; Raghu 2018; Salomon 2018; and Vandenbogaerde 2015.

4. The Human Rights Council has forty-seven states as voting members. They are elected by the General Assembly for staggered three-year terms, with seats apportioned as follows: African states (thirteen), Asian-Pacific states (thirteen), Latin American and Caribbean states (eight), Western European and other states (seven), and Eastern European states (six). States that are not voting members frequently participate in its proceedings.

5. On vernacularization, see Levitt and Merry 2009; see also Merry 2006.

6. See Müller 2013.

7. Harbrinderjit Singh Dillon was the presidential special envoy for Poverty Alleviation in Jakarta.

8. The UN Human Rights Commission was the predecessor of the UN Human Rights Council, created in 2006.

9. Remarks by GRAIN, C. R. Bijoy, and F. Mazhar (GRAIN 2007, 3, 5, 14).

10. Golay, "Trust and Complementarity, Ingredients for Success," in Claeys and Edelman 2020.

11. Some of these groups had already elaborated their own declarations (LIFE Network 2010).

12. On the contentious question of "expertise," see Claeys and Edelman 2020.

13. Golay, "Trust and Complementarity, Ingredients for Success," in Claeys and Edelman 2020.

14. Anonymous interview, June 20, 2014.

15. This issue is also discussed by Saúl Vicente Vásquez, "Collective Rights in Theory and Practice," in Claeys and Edelman 2020.

16. One important element was Switzerland's 2013 decision to back UNDROP. While not an EU member, Switzerland not only had influence with some EU countries, but also supported seminars in Geneva that aimed to educate diplomats about UNDROP. The Swiss change of heart was likely an outcome of a campaign by LVC's Swiss affiliate UNITERRE. See Golay, "Trust and Complementarity, Ingredients for Success," in Claeys and Edelman 2020.

17. Remarks during the fourth session of the open-ended intergovernmental working group on a United Nations declaration on the rights of peasants and other people working in rural areas, May 15, 2017.

18. Some scholars (Dunford 2017) with no firsthand exposure to the debates or drafting process assert that this process involved an "erasure of peasant voices" and the "marginalization of grassroots and Southern voices," claims that are entirely unfounded.

19. The Advisory Committee is a "think tank" composed of eighteen specialists from different regions and professional backgrounds that provides the UNHRC with research-based advice.

20. The invitation came from OHCHR, but only after the Bolivian Mission contacted me, apparently at the recommendation of FIAN and CETIM.

21. English was the language of drafting and of the text (which was only available in other UN languages after 2015). Participants in the drafting group all had an impressive command of English, but as one of only two native English speakers in the collective, I did a lot of proofreading.

22. Compare UNESCO 2001, art. 4.

23. On "monism" and "constitutional block," see OHCHR 2018, 125–127; Uprimny 2011, 1592.

24. In English, the 2013 Mexican publication is the "Manual for Women and Men Judges on the Protection of the Rights of Women and Men Peasants."

25. Well-informed sources that requested anonymity reported this as early as 2014. FARC stands for Fuerzas Armadas Revolucionarias de Colombia (Revolutionary Armed Forces of Colombia).

26. María Natalia Pacheco Rodríguez, "Building Hope Together in the International Human Rights System," in Claeys and Edelman 2020.

27. For relevant analyses, see Claeys 2018; Rajagopal 2005.

9. DEFINING "PEASANT" AT THE UNITED NATIONS HUMAN RIGHTS COUNCIL

1. Many of these other discussions are ably summarized in Bernstein and Byres 2001; Bryceson, Kay, and Mooij 2000; Mintz 1973; and Owen 2005.

2. ICAD was created by the Food and Agriculture Organization, the Economic Commission for Latin America, the Organization of American States, the Inter-American Institute for Agricultural Sciences, and the Inter-American Development Bank (Barraclough and Domike 1966).

10. SYNERGIES AND TENSIONS BETWEEN RURAL SOCIAL MOVEMENTS AND PROFESSIONAL RESEARCHERS

Epigraph: "Ha habido cierta timidez de parte del profesional, tal vez cierta apatía. Y cierto resquemor de parte nuestra por todo que nos ha pasado. Hay gente que nos ha abusado . . . Nos sentimos como vacas a veces. Y nos pegan una gran ordeñada y otro se bebe la leche. ¿Entendés?"

1. Moreover, as Irene Carlota Silber (2007, 168) suggests, it is important to examine the "move to theorize a created temporal and spatial community of engagement and suffering as activism."

2. Many of these reports are available at the National Farmers Union website (https://www.nfu.ca).

3. Importantly, however, most of these individuals are associated with NGOs and not academic institutions. The implications of this distinction will be examined more below.

4. Jonathan Fox (2006, 28–29) points to the US environmental justice movement as exemplifying the potential of "partnerships between engaged researchers and grassroots organizations. In the US debate numbers and quantitative analysis were the key battleground for revealing the racial and class imbalance in exposure to toxic hazards. Alternative numbers empowered alternative ideas, turning them into mainstream common sense." See also Hale 2008, 21.

5. On the blurred boundaries between social movements and NGOs, see Alvarez 1998; Bickham Méndez 2008; Edelman 2008.

6. João Pedro Stédile, leader of the Brazilian Landless Rural Workers Movement (Movimento dos Trabalhadores Rurais sem Terra, MST), for instance, reports that "probably the best period of [his] life" was when he was able to study in Mexico for two years in the 1970s. He reported meeting major figures in the Brazilian and Latin American left who were living in exile there, such as Francisco Julião, who had led the Ligas Camponesas (Peasant Leagues) in the early 1960s, and outstanding intellectuals such as Rui Mauro Marini, Vânia Bambirra, Teotônio dos Santos, and Jacques Chonchol (Stédile 2002, 78–79).

7. This is the case, for example, with at least one major figure in the National Farmers Union of Canada.

8. Less commonly, as in Central America in the 1980s and 1990s, peasant organizations have provided the major impetus for creating NGOs to serve movement objectives.

9. This process also points to the inadequacy of Antonio Gramsci's frequently cited concept of "organic intellectuals." As a good Marxist, Gramsci assumed that such intellectuals would come from the working class and, if they did emerge from the peasantry, would never remain loyal to peasant interests (Gramsci 1972, 6). Despite Gramsci's

doubts about peasants' political reliability, in some countries, notably Bolivia, his language of "organic intellectuals" has been widely adopted by militant activists of rural origin (Zamorano Villarreal 2009).

10. On the latter point, see Borras, Edelman and Kay 2008, 182–189, and Edelman 2008, 231. Shannon Speed (2008, 215) suggests that "the multiple tensions and contradictions that exist between anthropologists and those we work with" need to be viewed as "productive tensions that we might strive to benefit from analytically rather than seek to avoid."

11. About self-censorship, Kay Warren (2006, 221) asks, "Does it mean that whole domains of social life have been, in effect, off the table for richer ethnographic analysis?" Douglas Bevington and Chris Dixon (2005, 191) argue that "uncritical adulation" does not provide a movement "with any useful information and does not aid the movement in identifying and addressing problems which may hinder its effectiveness." The cheerleading concept is often invoked in off-the-record conversations among researchers who study social movements and rarely appears in print. Scholars not identified with (or even hostile to) the movements are those most likely to employ the term in publications (e.g., Wickham-Crowley 1991, 4).

12. Samuel Martínez (2008, 191) compares the researcher-activist relation to the rural Haitian *konbit* or communal reciprocal work party: "Activist anthropology puts people to work alongside each other, each side maintaining a distinct project, the anthropologist hoping to harvest academic publications even as he helps activists cultivate political or organizational gains. As in peasant agriculture, the goal of activist anthropology is not generating maximum output but generating sustainable and equitably shared gain."

13. Academics also, of course, are expected to publish not just books but articles in specialized journals. In certain countries (such as the United States) and in some academic disciplines, professional advancement is strongly correlated with publishing in "disciplinary" journals, particularly those affiliated with the main professional associations. More innovative work on social movements, especially that which challenges positivist paradigms or manifests even mild political engagement, tends to be relegated to smaller, less prestigious but frequently more stimulating publications or to those journals that nobody reads but which exist mainly to credential scholars in "second tier" institutions and to make profits for academic publishers.

14. For an excellent synopsis of the relevant literature and issues involved in the latter sort of study, see Blee 2007. Some researchers, while not sympathetic to the goals of rightist movements, nonetheless strive to identify "the human dimension" of even pathologically violent participants (Cívico 2006).

15. In the offices of some very distinguished scholars, I have actually seen royalty checks framed on the wall as ornaments, the amounts so laughably tiny as to make them not worth cashing.

16. The Research I category of universities, developed by the Carnegie Foundation (which discontinued use of the term in the late 1990s), refers to US doctoral-level institutions that place a heavy emphasis on research and obtain large amounts of federal grants. Criteria for promotion and tenure in Research II and other institutions may include a greater emphasis on teaching and service and less on research and publication. It is possible that researchers in these less prestigious institutions, and particularly in fields that in the Research I universities avidly defend their disciplinary boundaries, may actually have greater leeway in pursuing unconventional career paths, integrating activism into their scholarly work, and publishing with other than the supposedly most important journals and presses.

17. Warren (2006, 221) points out that most [academic anthropologists] "are part-time observers." Many nonetheless position themselves in heroic and self-aggrandizing ways

in their written accounts as a way of establishing narrative authority and fail "to acknowledge scholarly networks and lines of transnational solidarity that provide the basis upon which innovative findings and activism are constructed."

18. Conversely, many have been trained to employ deliberately obscure yet high-prestige, jargon-laced prose styles accessible only to a small, initiated group of similarly specialized colleagues. It is not always a simple matter to unlearn these rhetorics of (academic) power in the interests of communicating about or supporting a broader political project.

19. But see R. J. González 2004a and Besteman and Gusterson 2005 for forceful interventions by academics in, respectively, major media and public policy debates.

20. Credentialing, rather than knowledge diffusion, is often the main function of most academic journals. This is rarely evident to nonacademics, however, and is rarely acknowledged by academics. Opinions differ as to whether activists actually read social movement theory produced by professional scholars (as opposed to case study histories of movements). Stevphen Shukaitis and David Graeber (2007) point to intense engagement with certain varieties of "high" theory by (mostly European) anarchist and autonomist activists. Douglas Bevington and Chris Dixon (2005, 189), writing mainly about US political science and sociology's social movement studies, ask: "What does it say if the social movement theory being produced now is not seen as helpful by those persons who are directly involved in the very processes that this theory is supposed to illuminate?"

21. David Price points out that the situation is actually more complex, since scholars may be witting or unwitting participants in research that is directly funded or sought by intelligence agencies or in independent research that is later used by such agencies. "The following four scenarios are possible: Witting-Direct, Witting-Indirect, Unwitting-Direct, Unwitting-Indirect" (Price 2002, 17). He concludes that "most of anthropology's interactions with intelligence agencies have probably been unwitting and indirect, with anthropological work being harvested by intelligence agencies as it enters the public realm through conferences and publications" (2002, 21). Many social scientists have been reluctant to examine scholars' past links to intelligence agencies, arguing that to do so will result in reduced possibilities for field research. Price argues forcefully for scrutinizing such ties, since "we all risk reduced field opportunities as these largely unexamined historical interactions become documented" (2002, 17).

22. Richard N. Adams's survey research with political prisoners in Guatemala, following the 1954 coup directed by the US Central Intelligence Agency, was published in 1957 under the pseudonym "Stokes Newbold," a composite of his own middle name and that of Manning Nash, who collaborated in the research. In a 1998 reminiscence, Adams noted that since his survey did not provide much evidence that the rural population had been influenced by communist proselytizing, as the US State Department had alleged, the US Embassy rapidly forgot about it. Ironically, some left-leaning social scientists subsequently found Adams's survey of considerable value in examining the social class origins and attitudes of Guatemalan rural activists of the 1950s (Grandin 2004, 226n54; Wasserstrom 1975, 464). Adams also indicated that he used a pseudonym at the insistence of his employer, the Pan American Sanitary Bureau, and that "I never hid the fact that I was the author, but it was some years before it became widely known" (Adams 1998, 20n9). Adams had developed a pronounced concern about research ethics (Adams 1967) and a strongly critical stance regarding US policy in Guatemala and the Guatemalan military's abysmal human rights record, as did June Nash, who also participated in the survey. Wolf and Jorgensen (1970, 32) cite a US counterinsurgency specialist in Thailand, who was interviewed by a *New York Times* reporter: "The old formula for successful counterinsurgency used to [be] 10 troops for every guerrilla. . . . Now the formula is ten anthropologists for each guerrilla" (Braestrup 1967).

23. The manual, known as *FM 3–24*, includes a chapter by "Montgomery McFate," a pseudonym for Mitzy Carlough, who received a PhD in anthropology from Yale.

24. The writings of Philip Agee, who worked for the US Central Intelligence Agency (CIA) in Latin America for many years before abandoning the CIA and authoring an exposé, provide abundant evidence of this practice. Agee remarked, however, that it was harder to recruit agents in countries with a higher standard of living and a developed welfare state than in less developed countries. "Uruguayan communists simply are not as destitute and harassed as their colleagues in poorer countries and thus are less susceptible to recruitment on mercenary terms" (Agee 1975, 339).

25. Price (2002, 17) mentions the case of Raymond Kennedy, a US scholar who had worked in the Office of Strategic Services during World War II and then joined the State Department. An opponent of Dutch colonialism in Indonesia, he resigned from the State Department in protest against US policies. Four years later, he was executed in Java by anticolonial fighters who mistakenly believed he was a CIA agent. Similar suspicions fall on non-researchers as well, undoubtedly in larger numbers and with tragic results, especially during revolutionary armed movements. See, for example, Bourgois 2001 for a description of internecine violence among the Salvadoran guerrillas in the 1980s.

26. Examples are many. See, for example, Besteman and Gusterson 2005; Gill 2004; R. J. González 2004a; Lutz 2007; McCaffrey 2002; and Vine 2007. However, the ethical and legal dimensions of foreign activists involving themselves in the politics of other nations are rarely considered in the literature on engaged research. Some, such as Jeffrey Juris (2008) and Nancy Scheper-Hughes (1995), apparently consider such involvement a matter of internationalist or ethical commitment and completely unproblematic. Shannon Speed (2008) is among the few who acknowledge the problem and note its impact on her research.

27. João Vargas notes "that scholars, especially those in the beginning of their career, benefit from their involvement with grassroots organizations in ways glaringly disproportionate to what we can offer them" (2008, 164–165, 178).

28. Dani Wadada Nabudere (2008, 79), writing on Uganda, remarks on the "deep mistrust on the part of people who had developed 'research fatigue' from constant harassment by hordes of researchers since colonialism had first knocked on their doors. They had seen researchers come and go while their own conditions had steadily worsened. This suggested to them, with some justification, that the researchers were part of their problem."

29. Jonathan Fox (2006, 30) remarks that "one kind of contribution that scholars can offer to social actors is to wade through, decipher, and boil down the mind-bending quantities of arcane and hard-to-access information that is produced by mainstream institutions."

30. Given the hegemony of positivist approaches in some disciplines, it may be important to recall that the very origins of modern social science were thoroughly activist, and its practitioners were often deeply involved in what might today be called social movements and in attempting to modify policy (Calhoun 2008; Greenwood 2008).

31. Three colleagues who commented on an earlier version of this chapter pointed out that activist-researcher synergies are most likely to occur when both parties develop strong feelings of trust in each other as a result of daily interactions around small matters. Activists naturally observe outside researchers at least as much as the other way around, and they make decisions about the extent of their collaboration on the basis of how they evaluate the researcher's integrity, sincerity, and decency, among other things.

32. Efforts to theorize these ideas and practices are discussed in Scheper-Hughes 1995; see also Harrison 1991, Hale 2008, and the mostly anarchist-influenced essays in Shukaitis, Graeber, and Biddle 2007. Jeffrey Juris (2008, 20, 319) calls for researchers to practice "proactive solidarity" and remarks that "militant ethnography . . . refers to ethnographic

research that is not only politically engaged but also collaborative, thus breaking down the divide between research and object." This formulation, apart from its emphasis on ethnography to the exclusion of other research practices, obscures the extent to which collaboration between researchers and subjects may be of varied forms and intensity. In other words, it elides discussion of a collaborative engagement that might not be militant in the sense of subordinating the researcher to a larger political project, but still might serve the objectives shared by the researcher and the movement.

33. At times, the "militant" stance, presented as an unproblematic matter of preexisting ethical-political principles, verges on a troubling naivete, as when one prominent US anthropologist—newly arrived in South Africa—identified herself in a squatter camp as "a member of the ANC [African National Congress]" (Scheper-Hughes 1995, 414). At least one critic has charged, in relation to this case, that the "militant" position rests on "an amalgamation of sociobiological and religious ideas" and substitutes an outsider's politics for research itself (Trencher 1998, 122).

34. In part, this resulted from anti-labor policies in the state capital and from growers' increasing reliance on undocumented Mexican workers, many of whom came from Indigenous communities and spoke little Spanish. The UFW lacks organizers who speak Indigenous languages. One Indigenous worker-activist quoted in a press report declared: "We hear a lot about the achievements of Cesar Chavez. But we can't see any of them. Where are they? Truth is, the UFW has no strength here, not among our people. We remember how, when the Mixtecs first began to organize, Cesar called us 'communists.' That's okay, he's gone. We need our own organizations now that speak to our heart, our own union" (Cooper 2005).

35. Family members of UFW leader Dolores Huerta are also prominent in the same organizations. One of the first journalistic exposés of the UFW affiliates wryly remarked that "some would call this nepotism" (Weiser 2004).

36. For examples of mass media interventions of this sort, see R. J. González 2004a.

37. One strand of activist research may simply involve generating critical knowledge— that is, "an effort to understand how things could be different and why existing frameworks of knowledge do not recognize all the actual possibilities" (Calhoun 2008, xxiv–xxv).

38. In a brilliant essay on "Research as an Experiment in Equality," Alessandro Portelli (1991, 44) suggests that the research interaction itself is both laden with political content and an opportunity for political work: "There is no need to stoop to propaganda in order to use the *fact* itself of the interview as an opportunity to stimulate others, as well as ourselves, to a higher degree of self-scrutiny and self-awareness; to help them grow more aware of the relevance and meaning of their culture and knowledge; and to raise the question of the senselessness and injustice of the inequality between them and us."

39. In 2008, for example, several Mexican organizations that had participated in the transnational LVC network wrote an open letter explaining their decision not to attend the organization's Fifth International Conference in Mozambique. They charged that the North American regional coordinating group of LVC engaged in "verticalist and antidemocratic" practices and spread "disinformation" and was more interested in "international activities" than in supporting local and regional initiatives (AMUCSS et al. 2008).

40. In an analysis of the impact of transnational consumer boycotts, "stateless regulation" and NGO monitoring of corporations, Gay Seidman writes, "In an era when most national governments seem weaker than footloose multinational corporations, the international human rights movement and past examples of transnational consumer-based pressure on corporations seem to offer promising new directions for transnational campaigns. . . . I interrogate this promise, hoping not to undermine efforts by

transnational activists to find new approaches to organizing workers, but to provoke discussion: in the effort to create new support for workers' struggles, why do so many activists neglect or bypass local institutions designed to protect citizens, and what might be gained or lost as a result?" (Seidman 2007, 15–16).

41. I do not mean to suggest that I have found it easy to raise challenging questions of activists. On the contrary, at times it can be decidedly uncomfortable for both the researcher and the activist (Edelman 1999, 33–36).

42. Annette Desmarais, personal communication, September 15, 2008.

43. See Juris 2008 and Shukaitis, Graeber, and Biddle 2007 for compelling examples from the perspectives of militant, anarchist-oriented researchers.

44. ASOCODE was the Asociación Centroamericana de Organizaciones Campesinas para la Cooperación y el Desarrollo (Association of Central American Peasant Organizations for Cooperation and Development). Its rise and demise are outlined in Edelman 2008 and in chapter 5 of this book.

11. EIGHT DIMENSIONS OF LAND GRABBING THAT EVERY RESEARCHER SHOULD CONSIDER

1. Throughout Latin America, Arab immigrants and their descendants are frequently called *turcos* or "Turks." This misnomer dates to the nineteenth century and the first wave of immigration from the Levant (Palestine, Lebanon, and Syria), when new arrivals often had Ottoman travel documents.

References

Ação da Cidadania conta a Fome a pela Vida. 2001. "Llamado de Porto Alegre para las próximas movilizaciones." Pamphlet.

Ackerman, Bruce. 1994. "Rooted Cosmopolitanism." *Ethics* 104 (3): 516–535.

Acuña Ortega, Víctor Hugo. 1993. "Clases subalternas y movimientos sociales en Centroamérica (1870–1930)." In *Historia General de Centroamérica, Tomo IV Las repúblicas agroexportadoras (1870–1945)*, edited by Víctor Hugo Acuña Ortega, 255–323. Madrid: Sociedad Estatal Quinto Centenario & Facultad Latinoamericana de Ciencias Sociales.

ACWW. 2002. "Associated Country Women of the World." Associated Country Women of the World. http://www.acww.org.uk/.

Adams, Richard N. 1967. "Ethics and the Social Anthropologist in Latin America." *American Behavioral Scientist* 10 (10): 16–21.

——. 1998. "Ricocheting through a Half Century of Revolution: Kalman Silvert Award Address." *LASA Forum* 29 (3): 14–20.

Agamben, Giorgio. 1998. *Homo Sacer: Sovereign Power and Bare Life*. Stanford, CA: Stanford University Press.

Agee, Philip. 1975. *Inside the Company: CIA Diary*. New York: Stonehill.

Aguirre Rojas, Carlos Antonio. 1999. *La escuela de los Annales: Ayer, hoy, mañana*. Madrid: Montesinos.

Akram-Lodhi, A. Haroon, Kristina Dietz, Bettina Engels, and Ben M. McKay, eds. 2021. *Handbook of Critical Agrarian Studies*. Cheltenham: Edward Elgar.

Akram-Lodhi, A. Haroon, and Cristóbal Kay. 2010. "Surveying the Agrarian Question (Part 1): Unearthing Foundations, Exploring Diversity." *Journal of Peasant Studies* 37 (1): 177–202. https://doi.org/10.1080/03066150903498838.

Aksoy, M. Ataman, and John C. Beghin, eds. 2005. *Global Agricultural Trade and Developing Countries*. Washington, DC: World Bank.

Alabrese, Mariagrazia, Adriana Bessa, Margherita Brunori, and Pier Filippo Giuggioli, eds. 2022. *The United Nations' Declaration on Peasants' Rights*. Abingdon, Oxon: Routledge.

Albó, Xavier. 2008. *Movimientos y poder indígena en Bolivia, Ecuador y Perú*. Cuadernos de Investigación 71. La Paz: Centro de Investigación y Promoción del Campesinado-CIPCA.

Alegría, Rafael. 1997. Interview with the author. Tegucigalpa, Honduras, August 7.

——. 2001. Interview with the author. Tegucigalpa, Honduras, August 2.

Alegría, Rafael, and Paul Nicholson. 2002. "Nous espérons que ce livre aidera à faire connaître les luttes paysannes et à construire des ponts avec d'autres mouvements sociaux." In *Vía Campesina: Une alternative paysanne à la mondialisation néolibérale.*, edited by Marcel Mazoyer, Florian Rochat, Rafael Alegría, Paul Nicholson, and Jean Ziegler. Geneva: Centre Europe-Tiers Monde.

Alexander, Brian. 2017. *Glass House: The 1% Economy and the Shattering of the All-American Town*. New York: St. Martin's Press.

Alforja, ed. 1991. *El campesino ve el ajuste estructural así. Reflexiones de Jorge Hernández (UPANACIONAL), Carlos Hernández (Consejo Justicia y Desarrollo), y*

Oscar Monge (UNAC). San José, Costa Rica: Centro de Estudios y Publicaciones Alforja.

Alger, Chadwick F. 1988. "Perceiving, Analysing, and Coping with the Local-Global Nexus." *International Social Science Journal* 40 (3): 321–40.

Alland, Alexander, Jr., and Sonia Alland. 2001. *Crisis and Commitment: The Life History of a French Social Movement*. 2nd ed. Amsterdam: Harwood.

Almeida, Paul. 2019. *Social Movements: The Structure of Collective Mobilization*. Oakland: University of California Press.

Alonso-Fradejas, Alberto, Juan Liu, Tania Salerno, and Yunan Xu. 2016. "Inquiring into the Political Economy of Oil Palm as a Global Flex Crop." *Journal of Peasant Studies* 43 (1): 141–165. https://doi.org/10.1080/03066150.2015.1052801.

Alvarez, Sonia E. 1998. "Latin American Feminisms 'Go Global': Trends of the 1990s and Challenges for the New Millennium." In *Cultures of Politics/Politics of Cultures: Re-Visioning Latin American Social Movements*, edited by Sonia E. Alvarez, Evelina Dagnino, and Arturo Escobar, 296–324. Boulder, CO: Westview.

Amador, Jorge. 1994. Interview with the author. Tegucigalpa, Honduras, July 29.

Aminzade, Ronald R., Jack A. Goldstone, and Elizabeth J. Perry. 2001. "Leadership Dynamics and Dynamics of Contention." In *Silence and Voice in the Study of Contentious Politics*, by Ronald R. Aminzade, Jack A. Goldstone, Doug McAdam, Elizabeth J. Perry, William H. Sewell, Jr., Sidney Tarrow, and Charles Tilly, 126–154. Cambridge: Cambridge University Press.

AMUCSS, ANEC, CNPA, and FDC. 2008. "¿Por qué no podremos asistir a la 5a Conferencia Internacional de La Vía Campesina?" Asociación Mexicana de Uniones de Crédito del Sector Social, Asociación Nacional de Empresas Comercializadoras de Productores del Campo, Coordinadora Nacional Plan de Ayala, Frente Democrático Campesino de Chihuahua.

Anderson, Perry. 2002. "Internationalism: A Breviary." *New Left Review* 14 (April): 5–25.

Anheier, Helmut, and Nuno Themudo. 2002. "Organisational Forms of Global Civil Society: Implications of Going Global." In *Global Civil Society 2002*, edited by Marlies Glasius, Helmut Anheier, and Mary Kaldor, 191–216. Oxford: Oxford University Press.

Anseeuw, Ward, Lorenzo Cotula, and Mike Taylor. 2012. "Expectations and Implications of the Rush for Land: Understanding the Opportunities and Risks at Stake in Africa." In *Handbook of Land and Water Grabs in Africa: Foreign Direct Investment and Food and Water Security*, edited by Tony Allan, Martin Keulertz, Suvi Sojamo, and Jeroen Warner, 421–435. London: Routledge.

APM-Afrique. 2001. Université Paysanne Africaine. March 16.

APM-Mondial. 2001. "Asie" Zooide. http://www.zooide.com/apm/htm/racti.html (site discontinued).

——. 2002. "Encuentro Mundial Campesino: Declaración de Yaoundé," May 11. http://infotek.alliance21.org/d/f/1158/1158_SPA.msword.

Appadurai, Arjun. 1990. "Disjuncture and Difference in the Global Cultural Economy." *Public Culture* 2 (2): 1–24.

Appendini, Kirsten, and Marcelo De Luca. 2005. "Cambios agrarios, estrategias de sobrevivencia y género en zonas rurales del centro de México: notas metodológicas." *Estudios Sociológicos* 23 (69): 913–930.

Appiah, Kwame Anthony. 2005. *The Ethics of Identity*. Princeton, NJ: Princeton University Press.

Archibugi, Daniele. 2008. *The Global Commonwealth of Citizens: Toward Cosmopolitan Democracy*. Princeton, NJ: Princeton University Press.

Arias Peñate, Salvador. 1989. *Seguridad o inseguridad alimentaria: Un reto para la región centroamericana, Perspectivas para el año 2000.* San Salvador: UCA Editores.

——. 1990. *Biotecnología: amenazas y perspectivas para el desarrollo de América Central.* San José, Costa Rica: DEI.

——. 1995. Interview with the author. Santa Tecla, El Salvador, August 11.

Arias Peñate, Salvador, Juan Jované, and Luis Ng. 1993. *Centro América: obstáculos y perspectivas del desarrollo: un marco cuantitativo MOCECA. Modelo de coherencia económica del istmo centroamericano.* San José, Costa Rica: DEI.

Arita, Carlos. 1994. "El movimiento campesino: Situación actual." *Boletín Informativo de Honduras* 68 (July): 1–14.

Arquilla, John, and David Ronfeldt. 2001a. "Preface." In *Networks and Netwars: The Future of Terror, Crime, and Militancy,* edited by John Arquilla and David Ronfeldt, v–vi. Santa Monica, CA: RAND.

——. 2001b. "The Advent of Netwar (Revisited)." In *Networks and Netwars: The Future of Terror, Crime, and Militancy,* edited by John Arquilla and David Ronfeldt, 1–25. Santa Monica, CA: RAND.

Arrighi, Giovanni. 2010. *The Long Twentieth Century: Money, Power, and the Origins of Our Times.* London: Verso.

Asad, Talal. 1975. "Two European Images of Non-European Rule." In *Anthropology & the Colonial Encounter,* edited by Talal Asad, 103–118. London: Ithaca Press.

ASOCODE. 1991a. "Estrategia productiva de los pequeños y medianos productores del istmo centroamericano. Agosto 1991." Managua: ASOCODE. Photocopy.

——. 1991b. "Memoria [Primer Congreso ASOCODE]. 4, 5 y 6 de diciembre de 1991." Photocopy. Managua: ASOCODE.

——. 1992. "Informe congreso constitutivo." Managua: ASOCODE. Photocopy.

——. 1993a. "Informe general: Gira a Europa." Managua: ASOCODE.

——. 1993b. "Memoria II Congreso General de ASOCODE." Guatemala: ASOCODE.

——. 1993c. "Plan trabajo operativo 1993." Managua: ASOCODE. Photocopy.

——. 1994. "Documento base de trabajo para el taller de seguimiento a la I Conferencia Regional Campesina sobre Cooperación Solidaria." Managua: ASOCODE. Photocopy.

——. 1995a. "Valoración del trabajo de incidencia de ASOCODE, octubre 1995." Managua: ASOCODE.

——. 1995b. "Síntesis de conclusiones: Encuentro 'Mujer y movimiento campesino.'" San Salvador: ASOCODE.

——. 1997a. "Trabajando una plataforma común contra la pobreza. III Consejo Regional Campesino, II Conferencia la Cooperación y el Campesinado, 7 al 10 de abril de 1997."

——. 1997b. "Propuesta de ASOCODE al Consejo Agropecuario Centroamericano: III Consejo Regional Campesino, San José, abril 1997." Managua: ASOCODE.

——. 1999. "Documento para la discusión sobre el 'Proceso de reorganización y reorientación de ASOCODE.'" Managua: ASOCODE.

——. 2001. "Memoria: Encuentro regional de dirigentes campesinos centroamericanos." Tegucigalpa, April 4–5.

Assunta, Mary. 1996. "A Champion of the Farmers, a Foe of the MNCs." *Third World Resurgence,* 67 (March): 35–36.

Austin, James E., and Gustavo Esteva. 1987. "Final Reflections." In *Food Policy in Mexico: The Search for Self-Sufficiency,* edited by James E. Austin and Gustavo Esteva, 353–373. Ithaca, NY: Cornell University Press.

Ávila, Julián. 1994. Interview with the author. Panama City, June 23.

Ayres, Jeffrey McKelvey. 1998. *Defying Conventional Wisdom: Political Movements and Popular Contention against North American Free Trade.* Toronto: University of Toronto Press.

Bachriadi, Dianto. 2010. "Between Discourse and Action: Agrarian Reform and Rural Social Movements in Indonesia Post-1965." PhD diss., University of Flinders, Adelaide, Australia.

Ballantine, Sue. 1986. "International Farm Crisis Summit." *Union Farmer* 37 (6): 10.

Barkin, David. 2018. *De la protesta a la propuesta: 50 años imaginando y construyendo el futuro.* México, DF: Siglo Veintiuno.

Barlow, Maude, and Tony Clarke. 1998. *MAI: The Multilateral Agreement on Investment and the Threat to American Freedom.* New York: Stoddart.

Barraclough, Solon Lovett. 1991. *An End to Hunger? The Social Origins of Food Strategies.* London: Zed Books, UNRISD, South Centre.

Barraclough, Solon L., and Arthur L. Domike. 1966. "Agrarian Structure in Seven Latin American Countries." *Land Economics* 42 (4): 391–424.

Bartra, Armando. 2002. "Sobre la realización del Encuentro Campesino Mesoamericano." *La Jornada*, May 2. https://www.jornada.com.mx/2002/05/02/correo.php.

BAYAN. 1999. "Peoples' Assembly and March-Rally Say NO to WTO," November 28–30. http://list.jca.apc.org/public/asia-apec/1999-November.txt.

Beauregard, Sadie. 2009. "Food Policy for People: Incorporating Food Sovereignty Principles into State Governance. Case Studies of Venezuela, Mali, Ecuador, and Bolivia." Urban and Environmental Policy Department, Occidental College, April.

Bebbington, Anthony. 2005. "Donor–NGO Relations and Representations of Livelihood in Nongovernmental Aid Chains." *World Development* 33 (6): 937–950. https://doi.org/10.1016/j.worlddev.2004.09.017.

Bell, Beverly. 2002. "Social Movements and Regional Integration in the Americas." Center for Economic Justice.

Bellinghausen, Hermann. 2003. "Rompe el silencio la comandancia del EZLN y toma San Cristóbal." *La Jornada*, January 2. http://www.jornada.unam.mx/2003/ene03/030102/003n1pol.php?origen=index.html.

Benford, Robert D. 1997. "An Insider's Critique of the Social Movement Framing Perspective." *Sociological Inquiry* 67 (4): 409–430. https://doi.org/10.1111/j.1475-682X.1997.tb00445.x.

Bengoa, José. 2012. "Declaración Internacional de los Derechos Campesinos." *Le Monde Diplomatique—edición chilena*, March. http://www.lemondediplomatique.cl/Declaracion-Internacional-de-los.html.

Berger, Mark T. 1995. *Under Northern Eyes: Latin American Studies and U.S. Hegemony in the Americas, 1898–1990.* Bloomington: Indiana University Press.

Berlet, Chip, and Matthew Nemiroff Lyons. 2000. *Right-Wing Populism in America: Too Close for Comfort.* New York: Guilford.

Bermúdez, Julio. 1994. Interview with the author. Panama City, June 27.

Bernstein, Henry. 2010. *Class Dynamics of Agrarian Change.* Halifax, Nova Scotia: Fernwood.

Bernstein, Henry, and Terence J. Byres. 2001. "From Peasant Studies to Agrarian Change." *Journal of Agrarian Change* 1 (1): 1–56.

Berthomé, Jacques, and Marie-Rose Mercoiret. 1993. *La Rencontre de M'Balmayo, Cameroun, 26 au 30 Avril 1993.* Cameroun: APM-Afrique.

Besteman, Catherine Lowe, and Hugh Gusterson, eds. 2005. *Why America's Top Pundits Are Wrong: Anthropologists Talk Back.* Berkeley: University of California Press.

Beuchelt, Tina D., and Detlef Virchow. 2012. "Food Sovereignty or the Human Right to Adequate Food: Which Concept Serves Better as International Development Policy for Global Hunger and Poverty Reduction?" *Agriculture and Human Values* 29 (2): 259–273.

Bevington, Douglas, and Chris Dixon. 2005. "Movement-Relevant Theory: Rethinking Social Movement Scholarship and Activism." *Social Movement Studies* 4 (3): 185–208.

Bey, Idham. 2011. Interview with the author. Jakarta, October 27.

Bhagavan, Manu. 2012. *The Peacemakers: India and the Quest for One World*. Noida, India: HarperCollins.

Bickham Méndez, Jennifer. 2008. "Globalizing Scholar Activism: Opportunities and Dilemmas through a Feminist Lens." In *Engaging Contradictions: Theory, Politics, and Methods of Activist Scholarship*, edited by Charles R. Hale, 136–163. Berkeley: University of California Press.

Biekart, Kees. 1996. "Strengthening Intermediary Roles in Civil Society: Experiences from Central America." In *NGOs, Civil Society, and the State: Building Democracy in Transitional Societies*, edited by Andrew Clayton, 141–56. Oxford: INTRAC.

——. 1999. *The Politics of Civil Society Building: European Private Aid Agencies and Democratic Transitions in Central America*. Amsterdam: Transnational Institute.

Biekart, Kees, and Martin Jelsma, eds. 1994. "Introduction." In *Peasants beyond Protest in Central America: Challenges for ASOCODE, Strategies towards Europe*, 7–23. Amsterdam: Transnational Institute.

Biondi-Morra, Brizio N. 1990. *Revolución y política alimentaria: un análisis crítico de Nicaragua*. México, DF: Siglo Veintiuno.

Bjork-James, Carwil. 2013. "Claiming Space, Redefining Politics: Urban Protest and Grassroots Power in Bolivia." PhD diss., City University of New York.

Black, George. 1988. *The Good Neighbor: How the United States Wrote the History of Central America and the Caribbean*. New York: Pantheon.

Blee, Kathleen M. 2007. "Ethnographies of the Far Right." *Journal of Contemporary Ethnography* 36 (2): 119–128.

Blokland, Kees. 1995. "Peasant Alliances and 'Concertation' with Society." *Bulletin of Latin American Research* 14 (2): 159–170. https://doi.org/10.1111/j.1470-9856.1995.tb00004.x.

——. 1998. Interview with the author. Arnhem, the Netherlands, April 24.

Boehm, Terry. 2002. Interview with the author. Saskatoon, Canada, November 21.

Boéri, Julie. 2012. "Translation/Interpreting Politics and Praxis: The Impact of Political Principles on Babels' Interpreting Practice." *The Translator* 18 (2): 269–290.

Booth, William James. 1994. "On the Idea of the Moral Economy." *American Political Science Review* 88 (3): 653–667.

Borras, Saturnino M., Jr. 2004. *La Vía Campesina: An Evolving Transnational Social Movement*. Amsterdam: Transnational Institute.

——. 2008a. "Re-Examining the 'Agrarian Movement-NGO' Solidarity Relations Discourse." *Dialectical Anthropology* 32 (3): 203–209.

——. 2008b. "La Vía Campesina and Its Global Campaign for Agrarian Reform." *Journal of Agrarian Change* 8 (2–3): 258–289. https://doi.org/10.1111/j.1471-0366.2008.00170.x.

Borras, Saturnino M., Marc Edelman, and Cristóbal Kay. 2008. "Transnational Agrarian Movements: Origins and Politics, Campaigns and Impact." *Journal of Agrarian Change* 8 (2–3): 169–204. https://doi.org/10.1111/j.1471-0366.2008.00167.x

Borras, Saturnino M., Jr., Philip Seufert, Stephan Backes, Daniel Fyfe, Roman Herre, Laura Michele, and Elyse Mills. 2016. *Land Grabbing and Human Rights: The Involvement of European Corporate and Financial Entities in Land Grabbing Outside the European Union*. Brussels: European Parliament.

Bourdieu, Pierre. 1986. "The Forms of Capital." In *Handbook of Theory and Research for the Sociology of Education*, edited by John G. Richardson, 241–58. New York: Greenwood.

Bourgois, Philippe. 1989. *Ethnicity at Work: Divided Labor on a Central American Banana Plantation*. Baltimore: Johns Hopkins University Press.

——. 2001. "The Power of Violence in War and Peace: Post-Cold War Lessons from El Salvador." *Ethnography* 2 (1): 5–34.

Bové, José. 2001. "A Farmers' International?" *New Left Review* 12:89–101.

——. 2005. "La réalité locale dépend aussi du contexte global." In *ONU: droits pour tous ou loi du plus fort? Regards militants sur les Nations Unies*, edited by Julie Duchatel and Florian Rochat, 366–368. Geneva: CETIM.

Bové, José, and François Dufour. 2000. *Le monde n'est pas une marchandise: des paysans contre la malbouffe*. Paris: Éditions la Découverte.

——. 2001. *The World Is Not for Sale: Farmers against Junk Food*. London: Verso.

Boyer, Christopher R. 2003. *Becoming Campesinos: Politics, Identity, and Agrarian Struggle in Postrevolutionary Michoacán, 1920–1935*. Stanford, CA: Stanford University Press.

Boyer, Jefferson. 2007. "Review of Eric Holt-Giménez, Campesino a Campesino: Voices from Latin America's Farmer to Farmer Movement for Sustainable Agriculture." *Human Ecology* 35 (6): 779–781. https://doi.org/10.1007/s10745-007-9112-y.

——. 2010. "Food Security, Food Sovereignty, and Local Challenges for Transnational Agrarian Movements: The Honduras Case." *Journal of Peasant Studies* 37 (2): 319–351. https://doi.org/10.1080/03066150003594997.

Braestrup, Peter. 1967. "Researchers Aid Thai Rebel Fight; U.S. Defense Unit Develops Antiguerrilla Devices." *New York Times*, March 20. https://www.nytimes.com/1967/03/20/archives/researchers-aid-thai-rebel-fight-us-defense-unit-develops.html.

Braudel, Fernand. 1972. *The Mediterranean and the Mediterranean World in the Age of Philip II*. New York: Harper & Row.

Brecher, Jeremy. 1993. "The Hierarchs' New World Order—and Ours." In *Global Visions: Beyond the New World Order*, edited by Jeremy Brecher, John Brown Childs, and Jill Cutler, 3–16. Boston: South End Press.

Bremner, Charles. 2000. "The New Asterix: Attacking McDonald's Made French Farmer José Bové a Folk Hero. Now He Is Taking on Other Multinationals." *Times of London*, October 25.

Bringel, Breno M., and Flávia B. Vieira. 2015. "Movimientos internacionalistas y prácticas de cooperación Sur-Sur: brigadas y experiencias formativas del Movimiento de los Sin Tierra de Brasil y La Vía Campesina." *Revista Española de Desarrollo y Cooperación* 36: 65–79.

Bryceson, Deborah, Cristóbal Kay, and Jos Mooij, eds. 2000. *Disappearing Peasantries? Land and Labour in Africa, Asia and Latin America*. London: Intermediate Technology Publications.

Brysk, Alison. 1996. "Turning Weakness into Strength: The Internationalization of Indian Rights." *Latin American Perspectives* 23 (2): 38–57.

Buijtenhuijs, Robert. 2000. "Peasant Wars in Africa: Gone with the Wind?" In *Disappearing Peasantries? Rural Labour in Africa, Asia and Latin America*, edited by Deborah Bryceson, Cristóbal Kay, and Jos Mooij, 112–121. London: Intermediate Technology Publications.

Bunch, Roland. 1982. *Two Ears of Corn: A Guide to People-Centered Agricultural Improvement*. Oklahoma City: World Neighbors.

Burawoy, Michael. 2000. "Introduction: Reaching for the Global." In *Global Ethnography: Forces, Connections, and Imaginations in a Postmodern World*, edited by Michael Burawoy, 1–40. Berkeley: University of California Press.

Burdick, John. 1998. *Blessed Anastácia: Women, Race, and Popular Christianity in Brazil*. New York: Routledge.

Burnett, Kim, and Sophia Murphy. 2014. "What Place for International Trade in Food Sovereignty?" *Journal of Peasant Studies* 41 (6): 1065–1084. https://doi.org/10.1080/03066150.2013.876995.

Bush, Evelyn, and Pete Simi. 2001. "European Farmers and Their Protests." In *Contentious Europeans. Protest and Politics in an Emerging Polity*, edited by Doug Imig and Sidney Tarrow, 97–121. Lanham, MD: Rowman & Littlefield.

Bustelo, Eduardo S., Andrea Cornia, Richard Jolly, and Frances Stewart. 1987. "Hacia un enfoque más amplio en la política de ajuste: ajuste con crecimiento y una dimensión humana." In *Políticas de ajuste y grupos más vulnerables en América Latina: hacia un enfoque alternativa*, 126–156. Bogotá: Fondo de las Naciones Unidas para la Infancia.

Byrnes, Michael. 2001. "Eco-Terrorists May Have Planted FMD Plague-Farmers." *Reuters*, May 15.

Cáceres Baca, Sinforiano. 1994. Interview with the author. Managua, Nicaragua, July 4.

——. 1997. Interview with the author. Managua, Nicaragua, July 31.

CADESCA. 1990. *Los efectos de la política macroeconómica en la agricultura y la seguridad alimentaria*. Panama: CADESCA.

Cadji, Anne-Laure. 2000. "Brazil's Landless Find Their Voice." *NACLA Report on the Americas* 33 (5): 30–35.

Calderón, Vilma, and Clemente San Sebastián. 1991. *Caracterización de los productores de granos básicos en El Salvador*. Panama: CADESCA.

Calhoun, Craig. 1993. "'New Social Movements' of the Early Nineteenth Century." *Social Science History* 17 (3): 385–427.

——. 2002. "The Class Consciousness of Frequent Travelers: Toward a Critique of Actually Existing Cosmopolitanism." *South Atlantic Quarterly* 101 (4): 869–897.

——. 2008. "Forward." In *Engaging Contradictions: Theory, Politics, and Methods of Activist Scholarship*, edited by Charles R. Hale, xii–xxvi. Berkeley: University of California Press.

Calix, Víctor. 1994. Interview with the author. Tegucigalpa, Honduras, July 28.

Campos Cerdas, Wilson. 1990. Interview with the author. San José, Costa Rica, August 1.

——. 1994a. Interview with the author. San José, Costa Rica, July 29.

——. 1994b. Interview with the author. Panama City, June 23.

——. 2001. Interview with the author. San José, Costa Rica, July 27.

Campos R., Carlos, Rogelio Fernández L., and Tobías González. 1991. "Carta al Presidente de la República Licenciado Rafael Angel Calderón Fournier, 22 de abril de 1991." Unpublished manuscript.

Canadian Institute of International Affairs. 1981. *International Canada*. Vol. 12. Ottawa: Canadian Institute of International Affairs and Parliamentary Centre for Foreign Affairs and Foreign Trade.

Candanedo, Diana, and Víctor Julio Madrigal. 1994. "Informe final. Evaluación externa de ASOCODE. Período julio 91–diciembre 93." Managua: ASOCODE.

Carter, Sarah. 2016. *Imperial Plots: Women, Land, and the Spadework of British Colonialism on the Canadian Prairies*. Winnipeg: University of Manitoba Press.

Carter, Sarah, Ameur M. Manceur, Ralf Seppelt, Kathleen Hermans-Neumann, Martin Herold, and Lou Verchot. 2017. "Large Scale Land Acquisitions and REDD+: A

Synthesis of Conflicts and Opportunities." *Environmental Research Letters* 12 (3): 035010. https://doi.org/10.1088/1748-9326/aa6056.

Castellanos-Navarrete, Antonio, and Kees Jansen. 2015. "Oil Palm Expansion without Enclosure: Smallholders and Environmental Narratives." *Journal of Peasant Studies* 42 (3–4): 791–816. https://doi.org/10.1080/03066150.2015.1016920.

Castells, Manuel. 1996. *The Rise of the Network Society.* Vol. 1. Oxford: Blackwell.

Castilla Salazar, Alberto. 2016. "Proyecto de Acto Legislativo N° 12 de 2016 Senado. Por medio del cual se reconoce al campesinado como sujeto de derechos, se reconoce el derecho a la tierra y a la territorialidad campesina y se adoptan disposiciones sobre la consulta popular." Congreso de la República de Colombia. http://leyes .senado.gov.co/proyectos/images/documentos/Textos%20Radicados /proyectos%20de%20ley/2021%20-%202022/PL%20164-21%20Campesinidad.pdf

CCOD. 1990. *Cooperación externa y desarrollo en Centroamérica. Documentos de la II Consulta Internacional de Cooperación Externa para Centroamérica.* San José, Costa Rica: CECADE.

CCS-Chiapas. 2002. "Con la participación de la CNPA, UNORCA, CIOAC y CLOC en Tapachula." Coordinación de Comunicación Social, Estado de Chiapas, May 5.

CEDAW. 1979. "Convention on the Elimination of All Forms of Discrimination against Women." UN Division for the Advancement of Women. http://www.un.org/women watch/daw/cedaw/cedaw.htm.

CELDF. n.d. "Anti-Corporate Farming Laws in the Heartland." Community Environmental Legal Defense Fund.

CEPAL. 2002. *Anuario estadístico de América Latina y el Caribe 2001.* Santiago, Chile: CEPAL.

CETIM, WFDY, and LVC. 2001. "The Opening of the Agricultural Markets and Their Consequences for the Peasants of the South." *CETIM,* November 11. https://www .cetim.ch/the-opening-of-the-agricultural-markets-and-their-consequences-for -the-peasants-of-the-south/.

CGK and CISAI. 2003. "Acuerdo Bilateral Entre el Congreso General de la Cultura Kuna y el Centro Interdipartimentale di Studi Sull'america Indígena dell'Università degli Studi di Siena." Congreso General Kuna and Centro Interdipartimentale di Studi Sull'America Indígena, Università di Siena. http://onmaked.nativeweb.org /acuerdo_bilateral.htm.

Chan, Kam Wing, and Li Zhang. 1999. "The Hukou System and Rural-Urban Migration in China: Processes and Changes." *China Quarterly* 160:818–855.

Chang, Ha-Joon. 2009. "Rethinking Public Policy in Agriculture: Lessons from History, Distant and Recent." *Journal of Peasant Studies* 36 (3): 477–515.

Chayanov, A.V. 1966. *The Theory of Peasant Economy.* Edited by Daniel Thorner, Basile H. Kerblay, and R. E. F. Smith. Homewood, IL: American Economic Association.

——. 1991. *The Theory of Peasant Co-Operatives.* Columbus: Ohio State University Press.

Cívico, Aldo. 2006. "Portrait of a Paramilitary: Putting a Human Face on the Colombian Conflict." In *Engaged Observer: Anthropology, Advocacy, and Activism,* edited by Victoria Sanford and Asale Angel-Ajani, 131–146. New Brunswick, NJ: Rutgers University Press.

Claeys, Priscilla. 2012. "The Creation of New Rights by the Food Sovereignty Movement: The Challenge of Institutionalizing Subversion." *Sociology* 46 (5): 844–60.

——. 2013a. "From Food Sovereignty to Peasants' Rights: An Overview of Vía Campesina's Struggle for New Human Rights." In *La Vía Campesina's Open Book: Celebrating 20 Years of Struggle and Hope,* 1–10. Jakarta: Via Campesina.

——. 2013b. Email to the author, February 1.

——. 2015. "Food Sovereignty and the Recognition of New Rights for Peasants at the UN: A Critical Overview of La Vía Campesina's Rights Claims over the Last 20 Years." *Globalizations* 12 (4): 452–465. https://doi.org/10.1080/14747731.2014 .957929.

——. 2018. "The Rise of New Rights for Peasants: From Reliance on NGO Intermediaries to Direct Representation." *Transnational Legal Theory* 9 (3–4): 386–399. https:// doi.org/10.1080/20414005.2018.1563444.

Claeys, Priscilla, and Marc Edelman. 2020. "The United Nations Declaration on the Rights of Peasants and Other People Working in Rural Areas." *Journal of Peasant Studies* 47 (1): 1–68. https://doi.org/10.1080/03066150.2019.1672665.

Clapp, Jennifer. 2012. *Food*. Cambridge: Polity.

——. 2014. "Financialization, Distance and Global Food Politics." *Journal of Peasant Studies* 41 (5): 797–814. https://doi.org/10.1080/03066150.2013.875536.

Clapp, Jennifer, and S. Ryan Isakson. 2018. *Speculative Harvests: Financialization, Food, and Agriculture*. Black Point, Nova Scotia: Fernwood.

Clark, Ann Marie. 1995. "Non-Governmental Organizations and Their Influence on International Society." *Journal of International Affairs* 48 (2): 507–525.

Clay, Edward. 2003. "Food Security: Concepts and Measurement." In *Trade Reforms and Food Security: Conceptualizing the Linkages*, edited by FAO, 25–34. Rome: FAO.

CLOC. 1997. "First Latin American Assembly of Rural Women." São Paulo: CLOC.

——. 2001. "III Congreso Coordinadora Latinoamericana de Organizaciones del Campo." https://movimientos.org/es/cloc/show_text.php3%3Fkey%3D716.

CNTC. 1992. *El ábaco hindú: una propuesta para la enseñanza-aprendizaje de matemáticas con adultos*. Tegucigalpa: CNTC.

COATI. 2017. "Simultaneous Interpreting Using Radio Frequencies." Colectivo Para La Autogestión de Las Tecnologías de La Interpretación. 2017. https://coati.pimienta .org/articles/index.es.html.

COCICA. 1993. "Acta de Constitución de la Confederación Campesina del Istmo Centroamericano." Tegucigalpa: COCICA. Photocopy.

Cockburn, Alexander, and Jeffrey St. Clair. 2000. *5 Days That Shook the World*. London: Verso.

Cohen, Jean. 1995. "Interpreting the Notion of Civil Society." In *Toward a Global Civil Society*, edited by Michael Walzer, 35–40. Providence, RI: Berghahn.

Cohen, Jean, and Andrew Arato. 1992. *Civil Society and Political Theory*. Cambridge, MA: MIT Press.

Cohen, Mitchell. 1992. "Rooted Cosmopolitanism." *Dissent* 39 (4): 478–483.

Colby, Gerard, and Charlotte Dennett. 1996. *Thy Will Be Done: The Conquest of the Amazon. Nelson Rockefeller and Evangelism in the Age of Oil*. New York: HarperCollins.

Comaroff, John L., and Jean Comaroff, eds. 1999. "Introduction." In *Civil Society and the Political Imagination in Africa: Critical Perspectives*, 1–33. Chicago: University of Chicago Press.

Comisión Centroamericana. 1991. "Posición ante el programa de ajuste estructural, las relaciones con las ONGs locales y la cooperación internacional solidaria." Panama: Comisión Centroamericana de Pequeños y Medianos Productores. Photocopy.

Comisión Nacional de Alimentación. 1984. *PRONAL—Programa Nacional de Alimentación*. México, DF: Comisión Nacional de Alimentación.

Comitas, Lambros. 1973. "Occupational Multiplicity in Rural Jamaica." In *Work and Family Life: West Indian Perspectives*, edited by Lambros Comitas and David Lowenthal, 157–173. Garden City, NY: Anchor Press.

Conde, Marta, and Philippe Le Billon. 2017. "Why Do Some Communities Resist Mining Projects While Others Do Not?" *The Extractive Industries and Society* 4(3): 681–697. https://doi.org/10.1016/j.exis.2017.04.009.

Congreso Visible. 2016. "'Plenaria del Senado niega reconocimiento del campesinado colombiano, al hundir reforma constitucional que buscaba reconocer sus derechos': Senador Alberto Castilla." Universidad de los Andes, December 14.

Consejo Nacional. 1991. "La urgencia del desarrollo exige concertar. Posicion de las organizaciones de los pequeños y medianos productores del istmo centroamericano ante la cumbre presidencial agropecuaria de Centroamérica y Panamá." San José, Costa Rica: Consejo Nacional de Pequeños y Medianos Productores Justicia y Desarrollo. Photocopy.

Cooper, Marc. 2005. "Sour Grapes: California's Farm Workers' Endless Struggle 40 Years Later." *LA Weekly*, August 11.

Cotula, Lorenzo, and Thierry Berger. 2015. *Land Deals and Investment Treaties: Visualising the Interface*. London: International Institute for Environment and Development.

CPE. 2004. "At the WTO, Rischler and Lamy Betrayed the European Farmers and Those from the Southern Countries, to the Only Advantage of the Transnational." Coordination Paysanne Européenne, press release, distributed by Alexandra Strickner to agri-trade@yahoogroups.com, August 3.

Cuenca, Breny. 1992. *El poder intangible: la AID y el estado salvadoreño en los años ochenta*. Managua: CRIES.

Cumbre Presidencial. 2008. "Cumbre Presidencial, Soberanía y Seguridad AlimentarIa: Alimentos para la Vida, Managua, Nicaragua, 7 de mayo de 2008," May 7.

Custers, Peter. 2004. "Farmers Lose a Leading Champion of Their Rights." *Nadir.org*, February 3. https://www.nadir.org/nadir/initiativ/agp/new/swamy.htm.

Dalton, George. 1972. "Peasantries in Anthropology and History." *Current Anthropology* 13 (3–4): 385–407, 411–415.

Davis, Mike. 2006. *Planet of Slums*. New York: Verso.

Davis, Shelton H. 1977. *Victims of the Miracle: Development and the Indians of Brazil*. Cambridge: Cambridge University Press.

De Armond, Paul. 2001. "Netwar in the Emerald City: WTO Protest Strategy and Tactics." In *Networks and Netwars: The Future of Terror, Crime, and Militancy*, edited by John Arquilla and David Ronfeldt, 201–234. Santa Monica, CA: RAND.

De Schutter, Olivier. 2012. "Food Sovereignty Prize Address." Food Sovereignty Prize, October 10. https://www.youtube.com/watch?v=qeht1Q-TwsI.

Deere, Carmen Diana. 1995. "What Difference Does Gender Make? Rethinking Peasant Studies." *Feminist Economics* 1 (1): 53–72.

Deininger, Klaus, and Juergen Voegele. 2010. "Rising Global Interest in Farmland: Can It Yield Sustainable and Equitable Benefits?" World Bank. https://reliefweb.int /attachments/8abd2cbf-6aad-3b01-83b7-d1b659ababf4/88BA6FBA8CDE34E649 257798000CAB2B-wb-sep2010.pdf.

DeJusticia. 2019. "¿En qué va la sentencia que pide medidas para contar al campesinado?" DeJusticia. June 2. https://www.dejusticia.org/asi-va-la-sentencia-que-pide-contar -al-campesinado/.

Dell'Angelo, Jampel, Paolo D'Odorico, Maria Cristina Rulli, and Philippe Marchand. 2017. "The Tragedy of the Grabbed Commons: Coercion and Dispossession in the Global Land Rush." *World Development* 92:1–12. https://doi.org/10.1016/j.worlddev .2016.11.005.

Della Porta, Donatella, and Mario Diani. 1999. *Social Movements: An Introduction*. Oxford: Blackwell.

Desai, Meghnad, and Yahia Said. 2001. "The New Anti-Capitalist Movement: Money and Global Civil Society." In *Global Civil Society 2001*, edited by Helmut Anheier and Marlies Glasius, 51–78. London: Oxford University Press.

Desmarais, Annette Aurélie. 2002. "The Vía Campesina: Consolidating an International Peasant and Farm Movement." *Journal of Peasant Studies* 29 (2): 91–124.

——. 2003a. "The Vía Campesina: Peasant Women at the Frontiers of Food Sovereignty." *Canadian Woman Studies/Les Cahier de La Femme* 23 (1): 140–45.

——. 2003b. "The Vía Campesina: Peasants Resisting Globalization." PhD thesis, University of Calgary, Alberta, Canada.

——. 2007. *La Vía Campesina: Globalization and the Power of Peasants*. Halifax, Nova Scotia: Fernwood.

Desmarais, Annette Aurélie, and Hannah Wittman. 2014. "Farmers, Foodies and First Nations: Getting to Food Sovereignty in Canada." *Journal of Peasant Studies* 41 (6): 1153–1173. https://doi.org/10.1080/03066150.2013.876623.

Dévé, Frédéric. 1989. "Los productores de granos básicos en el istmo centroamericano: Ensayo de síntesis, logros y perspectivas." In *Programa de Seguridad Alimentaria CADESCA/CEE*. Guatemala: CADESCA/CEE. Mimeographed.

Dhanagare, D. N. 2016. "Declining Credibility of the Neoliberal State and Agrarian Crisis in India: Some Observations." In *Critical Perspectives on Agrarian Transition: India in the Global Debate*, edited by Bibhuti Bhusan Mohanty, 138–163. Basingstoke: Routledge.

Diamond, Sara. 1995. *Roads to Dominion: Right-Wing Movements and Political Power in the United States*. New York: Guilford.

Dietz, Kristina, and Franza Drechsel. 2021. "Digital Agriculture." In *Handbook of Critical Agrarian Studies*, edited by Haroon Akram-Lodhi, Kristina Dietz, Bettina Engels, and Ben M. McKay, 569–581. Cheltenham: Edward Elgar.

Dillon, Harbrinderjit Singh. 2011. Interview with the author. Jakarta, October 28.

Doerr, Nicole. 2007. "Multilingualism and Transnational Public Spaces in Civil Society." In *Global Civil Society 2007/8: Communicative Power and Democracy*, edited by Martin Albrow, Helmut K. Anheier, Marlies Glasius, Monroe E. Price, and Mary Kaldor, 226–227. Los Angeles: SAGE.

Dorner, Peter. 1992. *Latin American Land Reforms in Theory and Practice: A Retrospective Analysis*. Madison: University of Wisconsin Press.

Drage, Dorothy. 1961. *Pennies for Friendship: The Autobiography of an Active Octogenarian, a Pioneer of ACWW*. London: Gwenlyn Evans Caernarvon.

Du Plessis, Andre. 2008. *New Global Contract: Values in Conflict: How Trade and Finance Rules Curtail Our Rights*. Minneapolis: Institute for Agriculture and Trade Policy.

Dunford, Robin. 2017. "Peasant Activism and the Rise of Food Sovereignty: Decolonising and Democratising Norm Diffusion?" *European Journal of International Relations* 23 (1): 145–167. https://doi.org/10.1177/1354066115614382.

Echeverría, Carlos Manuel. 1993. "La integración centroamericana y las relaciones extrarregionales fundamentales: La visión de FEDEPRICAP." *Presencia* 5 (19): 100–105.

Eckstein, Susan, ed. 1989. *Power and Popular Protest: Latin American Social Movements*. Berkeley: University of California Press.

ECM. 2002a. "Declaración Campesina de Nicaragua II Encuentro Campesino Mesoamericano," July 15. http://movimientos.org/cloc/show_text.hp3?key=1041 Managua.

——. 2002b. "Plan de Acción II Encuentro Campesino Mesoamericano," July 15. http://movimientos.org/cloc/show_text.hp3?key=1040 Managua.

Edelman, Marc. 1991. "Shifting Legitimacies and Economic Change: The State and Contemporary Costa Rican Peasant Movements." *Peasant Studies* 18 (4): 221–249.

——. 1992. *The Logic of the Latifundio: The Large Estates of Northwestern Costa Rica since the Late Nineteenth Century.* Stanford, CA: Stanford University Press.

——. 1994. "Three Campesino Activists." *NACLA Report on the Americas* 28 (November–December): 30–33.

——. 1998. "Transnational Peasant Politics in Central America." *Latin American Research Review* 33 (3): 49–86.

——. 1999. *Peasants against Globalization: Rural Social Movements in Costa Rica.* Stanford, CA: Stanford University Press.

——. 2001. "Social Movements: Changing Paradigms and Forms of Politics." *Annual Review of Anthropology* 30 (1): 285–317. https://doi.org/10.1146/annurev.anthro.30.1.285.

——. 2002. "Toward an Anthropology of Some New Internationalisms: Small Farmers in Global Resistance Movements." *Focaal—European Journal of Anthropology* 40: 103–22.

——. 2003. "Transnational Peasant and Farmer Movements and Networks." In *Global Civil Society 2003*, edited by Mary Kaldor, Helmut Anheier, and Marlies Glasius, 185–220. London: Oxford University Press.

——. 2008. "Transnational Organizing in Agrarian Central America: Histories, Challenges, Prospects." *Journal of Agrarian Change* 8 (2–3): 229–257.

——. 2012. "International Public Hearing on Human Rights in the Bajo Aguán, Honduras." *Right to Food Journal* 7 (1): 9.

——. 2013. "Messy Hectares: Questions about the Epistemology of Land Grabbing Data." *Journal of Peasant Studies* 40 (3): 485–501. http://dx.doi.org/10.1080/03066150.2013.801340.

——. 2014. "Linking the Rights of Peasants to the Right to Food in the United Nations." *Law, Culture and the Humanities* 10 (2): 196–211. https://doi.org/10.1177/174387 2112456669.

——. 2016. *Estudios agrarios críticos: tierras, semillas, soberanía alimentaria y los derechos de las y los campesinos.* Quito: Editorial del IAEN.

——. 2017. *Activistas empedernidos e intelectuales comprometidos: ensayos sobre movimientos sociales, derechos humanos y estudios latinoamericanos.* Quito: Editorial del IAEN.

——. 2021. "Hollowed out Heartland, USA: How Capital Sacrificed Communities and Paved the Way for Authoritarian Populism." *Journal of Rural Studies* 82 (February): 505–517. https://doi.org/10.1016/j.jrurstud.2019.10.045.

Edelman, Marc, and Saturnino M. Borras, Jr. 2016. *Political Dynamics of Transnational Agrarian Movements.* Halifax, Nova Scotia: Fernwood.

Edelman, Marc, and Carwil James. 2011. "Peasants' Rights and the UN System: Quixotic Struggle? Or Emancipatory Idea Whose Time Has Come?" *Journal of Peasant Studies* 38 (1): 81–108. https://doi.org/10.1080/03066150.2010.538583.

Edelman, Marc, and Andrés León. 2013. "Cycles of Land Grabbing in Central America: An Argument for History and a Case Study in the Bajo Aguán, Honduras." *Third World Quarterly* 34 (9): 1697–1722. https://doi.org/10.1080/01436597.2013.843848.

Edelman, Marc, Carlos Oya, and Saturnino M. Borras. 2013. "Global Land Grabs: Historical Processes, Theoretical and Methodological Implications and Current Trajectories." *Third World Quarterly* 34 (9): 1517–1531. https://doi.org/10.1080/01436 597.2013.850190.

Edelman, Marc, James C. Scott, Amita Baviskar, Saturnino M. Borras, Jr., Deniz Kandiyoti, Eric Holt-Giménez, Tony Weis, and Wendy Wolford, eds. 2016. *Critical Perspectives on Food Sovereignty. Global Agrarian Transformations, Volume 2.* London: Routledge.

Edelman, Marc, and Mitchell A. Seligson. 1994. "Land Inequality: A Comparison of Census Data and Property Records in Twentieth-Century Southern Costa Rica." *Hispanic American Historical Review* 74 (3): 445–91.

Egnal, Marc. 2013. "Evolution of the Novel in the United States: The Statistical Evidence." *Social Science History* 37 (2): 231–254.

EHNE. 2002. "Paul Nicholson, historia de un activista agrario. 25 años comprometido con EHNE." Euskal Herriko Nekazarien Elkartasuna. *EHNE.org*, April 5. https://web.archive.org/web/20050213072505/http://www.ehne.org/prensa_ficha_g.asp?kodea=4.

Eikeland, Sveinung. 1999. "New Rural Pluriactivity? Household Strategies and Rural Renewal in Norway." *Sociologia Ruralis* 39 (3): 359–376.

El Heraldo. 1993. "Presidente del CNC: Campesinos deben romper el temor de asociarse con capitales extranjeros." *El Heraldo*, February 18.

Elshtain, Jean B. 1995. "Exporting Feminism." *Journal of International Affairs* 48 (2): 541–558.

Emanuelli, Maria Silvia, and Rodrigo Gutiérrez Rivas, eds. 2013. *Manual para Juezas y Jueces sobre la protección de los derechos de las campesinas y campesinos.* Mexico City: Habitat International Oficina para América Latina. https://sjlatinoamerica.files.wordpress.com/2014/01/emanuelli-marc3ada-silvia-y-gutic3a9rrez-rodrigo-coords-2013-manual-para-juezas-y-jueves-sobre-proteccic3b3n-de-los-derechos-de-las-campesinas-y-campesinos.pdf.

Engels, Frederick. 1926. *The Peasant War in Germany.* New York: International Publishers.

Enlace Sur-Sur. 1998. "¿Qué es Campesino a Campesino?" Enlace Sur-Sur. 1998.

Escobar, Arturo. 1992. "Culture, Practice and Politics." *Critique of Anthropology* 12 (4): 395–432.

——. 2018. *Otro posible es posible: Caminando hacia las transiciones desde Abya Yala/Afro/Latino-América.* Bogotá: Ediciones Desde Abajo.

Escobar, Arturo, and Sonia E Alvarez. 1992. *The Making of Social Movements in Latin America: Identity, Strategy, and Democracy.* Boulder, CO: Westview.

Escoto, Jorge, and Manfredo Marroquín. 1992. *La AID en Guatemala: Poder y sector empresarial.* Managua: CRIES/AVANCSO.

Esteva, Gustavo. 1984. *Por una nueva política alimentaria.* Mexico, D. F.: Sociedad Mexicana de Planificación.

ETC Group. 2022. "Small-Scale Farmers and Peasants Still Feed the World." Québec: ETC Group. https://www.etcgroup.org/files/files/31-01-2022_small-scale_farmers_and_peasants_still_feed_the_world.pdf.

Fairbairn, Madeleine. 2010. "Framing Resistance: International Food Regimes and the Roots of Food Sovereignty." In *Food Sovereignty: Reconnecting Food, Nature & Community,* edited by Hannah Wittman, Annette Aurélie Desmarais, and Nettie Wiebe, 15–32. Halifax, Nova Scotia: Fernwood.

——. 2012. "Framing Transformation: The Counter-Hegemonic Potential of Food Sovereignty in the US Context." *Agriculture and Human Values* 29 (2): 217–230. https://doi.org/10.1007/s10460-011-9334-x.

——. 2014. "'Like Gold with Yield': Evolving Intersections between Farmland and Finance." *Journal of Peasant Studies* 41 (5): 777–795. https://doi.org/10.1080/03066150.2013.873977.

——. 2020. *Fields of Gold: Financing the Global Land Rush.* Ithaca, NY: Cornell University Press.

Fairhead, James, Melissa Leach, and Ian Scoones. 2012. "Green Grabbing: A New Appropriation of Nature?" *Journal of Peasant Studies* 39 (2): 237–261. https://doi.org/10.1080/03066150.2012.671770.

Falk, Richard. 1987. "The Global Promise of Social Movements: Explorations at the Edge of Time." *Alternatives: Global, Local, Political* 12 (2): 173–196.

Fallas, Helio. 1993. *Centroamérica: pobreza y desarrollo rural ante la liberalización económica.* San José, Costa Rica: IICA.

Fallers, Lloyd A. 1961. "Are African Cultivators to Be Called 'Peasants'?" *Current Anthropology* 2 (2): 108–110.

FAO. 2000. "Trends in World and Agricultural Trade." In *Multilateral Trade Negotiations on Agriculture: A Resource Manual.* Rome: FAO.

——. 2018. "Scaling Up Agroecology Initiative: Transforming Food and Agricultural Systems in Support of the SDGs." Rome: FAO. http://www.fao.org/3/I9049EN/i9049 en.pdf.

Feierman, Steven. 1990. *Peasant Intellectuals: Anthropology and History in Tanzania.* Madison: University of Wisconsin Press.

Fernandes, Bernardo Mançano. 2000. *A formação do MST no Brasil.* Petrópolis: Editora Vozes.

Ferriss, Susan, Ricardo Sandoval, and Diana Hembree. 1998. *The Fight in the Fields: Cesar Chavez and the Farmworkers Movement.* San Diego, CA: Harcourt Brace.

FIAN. 2000. "Land Is Much More than a Commodity." Food First Information and Action Network.

Field, Tony, and Beverly Bell. 2013. *Harvesting Justice: Transforming Food, Land, and Agricultural Systems in the Americas.* New York: US Food Sovereignty Alliance.

Florescano, Enrique. 1969. *Precios del maíz y crisis agrícolas en México (1708–1810): ensayo sobre el movimiento de los precios y sus consecuencias económicas y sociales.* México, DF: El Colegio de México.

Focus on the Global South. 2013. "Editorial: Food Sovereignty Now!" *Nyéléni Newsletter,* March.

FONDAD. 1993. *Campesinos y ajustes estructurales. Informe Encuentro Campesino: Pequeños y Medianos Productores de Panamá.* Panama: FONDAD.

Foro Mundial. 2001. "El Foro Mundial sobre Soberania Alimentaria propone alternativas a las políticas alimentarias que generan hambre y malnutrición," September 3.

Fox, Jonathan. 2006. "Lessons from Action–Research Partnerships. LASA/Oxfam America 2004 Martin Diskin Memorial Lecture." *Development in Practice* 16 (1): 27–38.

Franco, Jennifer, Lyla Mehta, and Gert Jan Veldwisch. 2013. "The Global Politics of Water Grabbing." *Third World Quarterly* 34 (9): 1651–1675. https://doi.org/10.1080 /01436597.2013.843852.

Freres, Christian L. 1998. *La cooperación de las sociedades civiles de la Unión Europea con América Latina.* Madrid: AIETI.

Friedmann, Harriet. 1992. "Distance and Durability: Shaky Foundations of the World Food Economy." *Third World Quarterly* 13 (2): 371–383.

Fuentes, Inés. 1994a. Interview with the author. Panama City, June 24.

——. 1994b. Interview with the author. Tegucigalpa, July 28.

Fundación Arias. 1998. "Elementos para el debate sobre la cooperación y las ONG en Centroamérica." Fundación Arias para la Paz y el Progreso Humano.

GABRIELA (National Alliance of Women's Organizations). 1999. Women's statement against AoA/WTO. Email distributed November 29 by gab@info.com.ph.

Galeano, Eduardo H. 2000. *Upside Down: A Primer for the Looking-Glass World.* New York: Metropolitan Books.

Gang, Ira N., and Robert C. Stuart. 1999. "Mobility Where Mobility Is Illegal: Internal Migration and City Growth in the Soviet Union." *Journal of Population Economics* 12:117–134.

García Canclini, Néstor. 1990. *Culturas híbridas: estrategias para entrar y salir de la modernidad*. Mexico: Grijalbo.

Garst, Rachel, and Tom Barry. 1990. *Feeding the Crisis: US Food Aid and Farm Policy in Central America*. Lincoln: University of Nebraska Press.

Gascón, Jordi. 2010. "¿Del paradigma de la industrialización al de la soberanía alimentaria? Una comparación entre los gobiernos nacionalistas latinoamericanos del siglo XX y los pos-neoliberales a partir de sus políticas agrarias." In *Cambio de rumbo en las políticas agrarias latinoamericanas? Estado, movimientos sociales campesinos y soberanía alimentaria*, edited by Jordi Gascón and Xavier Montagut, 215–259. Barcelona: Icaria.

Gautier, François. 1999. "Le drame du coton transgénique en Inde." *Jaia-Bharati.org*. October 29.

Gaventa, John. 2006. "Finding the Spaces for Change: A Power Analysis." *IDS Bulletin* 37 (6): 23–33.

Geertz, Clifford. 2000. *Available Light: Anthropological Reflections on Philosophical Topics*. Princeton, NJ: Princeton University Press.

Geisler, Charles. 2015. "Trophy Lands: Why Elites Acquire Land and Why It Matters." *Canadian Journal of Development Studies* 36 (2): 241–257. https://doi.org/10.1080 /02255189.2015.1041881.

George, Susan. 2000. "Fixing or Nixing the WTO." In *Globalize This! The Battle against the World Trade Organization and Corporate Rule*, edited by Kevin Danaher and Roger Burbach, 53–58. Monroe, ME: Common Courage Press.

Gidwani, Vinay, and K. Sivaramakrishnan. 2003. "Circular Migration and Rural Cosmopolitanism in India." *Contributions to Indian Sociology* 37 (1–2): 339–367. https://doi.org/10.1177/006996670303700114.

Gilbert, Jérémie. 2014. *Nomadic Peoples and Human Rights*. Abingdon, Oxon: Routledge.

Gill, Lesley. 2004. *The School of the Americas: Military Training and Political Violence in the Americas*. Durham, NC: Duke University Press.

Gill, Lesley, Leigh Binford, and Steve Striffler. 2020. "Introduction." In *Fifty Years of Peasant Wars in Latin America*, edited by Leigh Binford, Lesley Gill, and Steve Striffler, 1–24. New York: Berghahn.

Gillis, Justin. 2011. "Can the Yield Gap Be Closed—Sustainably?" *New York Times*, June 7. https://green.blogs.nytimes.com/2011/06/07/can-the-yield-gap-be-closed -sustainably/.

Gioia, Paula. 2016. "A Real System Change Has to Come from Below, Says Paula Gioia, the European Youth ICC Member of La Vía Campesina." La Vía Campesina, February 9. https://web.archive.org/web/20170313203110/https://viacampesina.org /en/index.php/main-issues-mainmenu-27/youth-mainmenu-66/1970-closing -speech-at-the-iss-conference-by-paula-gioia-the-european-youth-icc-member -of-la-via-campesina.

———. 2019. "Coming Out! Gender Diversity in the Food System." *Right to Food and Nutrition Watch* 11:34–41.

Glassman, Jim. 2002. "From Seattle (and Ubon) to Bangkok: The Scales of Resistance to Corporate Globalization." *Environment and Planning D* 19 (5): 513–533.

Gleave, Alfred P. 1991. *United We Stand: Prairie Farmers 1901–1975*. Toronto: Lugus.

Glock, Clarinha. 2012. "Thematic Social Forum Awash with Criticism for Green Economy." *Ipsnews.Net*. January 30. https://www.globalissues.org/news/2012/01/30/12571.

Goitia, Alfonso. 1994. "Acceso a la tierra en Centroamérica." In *Alternativas campesinas: modernización en el agro y movimiento campesino en Centroamérica*, edited by Klaus-Dieter Tangermann and Ivana Ríos Valdés, 159–188. Managua: CRIES.

Golay, Christophe. 2015. "Negotiation of a United Nations Declaration on the Rights of Peasants and Other People Working in Rural Areas." Geneva Academy of International Humanitarian Law and Human Rights. https://www.geneva-academy.ch /joomlatools-files/docman-files/InBrief5_rightsofpeasants.pdf

———. 2019. "The Implementation of the United Nations Declaration on the Rights of Peasants and Other People Working in Rural Areas." Geneva: Geneva Academy of International Humanitarian Law and Human Rights. https://www.geneva -academy.ch/joomlatools-files/docman-files/The%20implementation%20of%20 the%20UN%20Declaration%20on%20the%20rights%20of%20peasants%20 and%20other%20people%20w.pdf.

Golay, Christophe, and Irene Biglino. 2013. "Human Rights Responses to Land Grabbing: A Right to Food Perspective." *Third World Quarterly* 34 (9): 1630–1650. https://doi.org/10.1080/01436597.2013.843853.

González, Nancie L. 1993. *Dollar, Dove, and Eagle: One Hundred Years of Palestinian Migration to Honduras.* Ann Arbor: University of Michigan Press.

González, Roberto J., ed. 2004a. *Anthropologists in the Public Sphere: Speaking out on War, Peace, and American Power.* Austin: University of Texas Press.

———. 2004b. "Introduction." In *Anthropologists in the Public Sphere: Speaking out on War, Peace, and American Power,* edited by Roberto J. González, 1–20. Austin: University of Texas Press.

———. 2007. "Towards Mercenary Anthropology? The New US Army Counterinsurgency Manual FM 3–24 and the Military Anthropology Complex." *Anthropology Today* 23 (3): 14–19.

González, Vinicio. 1978. "La insurrección salvadoreña de 1932 y la gran huelga hondureña de 1954." *Revista Mexicana de Sociología* 60 (2): 563–606.

Gorneg, Paol. 2001. "Un syndicat agricole 'à la Soviétique': voyage au coeur de la FNSEA." *Le Monde Diplomatique,* January. http://www.monde-diplomatique.fr /2001/01/GORNEG/14741.

Gould, Jeffrey L. 1998. *To Die in This Way: Nicaraguan Indians and the Myth of Mestizaje, 1880–1965.* Durham, NC: Duke University Press.

Grabendorff, Wolf, Heinrich-W. Krumwiede, and Jörg Todt, eds. 1984. "The Internationalization of the Central American Crisis." In *Political Change in Central America: Internal and External Dimensions,* 155–171. Boulder, CO: Westview.

Graeber, David. 2002. "The Anthropology of Globalization (with Notes on Neomedievalism, and the End of the Chinese Model of the Nation-State)." *American Anthropologist* 104 (4): 1222–1227.

GRAIN. 2007. "What's Wrong with Rights?" *Seedling,* October 2007.

———. 2008. "Seized: The 2008 Landgrab for Food and Financial Security," October 24. https://grain.org/article/entries/93-seized-the-2008-landgrab-for-food-and -financial-security.

———. 2016. "The Global Farmland Grab in 2016: How Big, How Bad?" June 14. https://grain .org/article/entries/5492-the-global-farmland-grab-in-2016-how-big-how-bad

Gramsci, Antonio. 1967. *La formación de los intelectuales.* México, DF: Grijalbo.

———. 1972. *Selections from the Prison Notebooks.* New York: International Publishers.

Grandin, Greg. 2004. *The Last Colonial Massacre: Latin America in the Cold War.* Chicago: University of Chicago Press.

Greenwood, Davydd J. 2008. "Theoretical Research, Applied Research, and Action Research: The Deinstitutionalization of Activist Research." In *Engaging Contradictions: Theory, Politics, and Methods of Activist Scholarship,* edited by Charles R. Hale, 319–340. Berkeley: University of California Press.

Greider, William. 2000. "The Last Farm Crisis." *The Nation,* November 20.

Guha, Ranajit. 1999. *Elementary Aspects of Peasant Insurgency in Colonial India.* Durham, NC: Duke University Press.

Gunnoe, Andrew. 2014. "The Political Economy of Institutional Landownership: Neorentier Society and the Financialization of Land: The Political Economy of Institutional Landownership." *Rural Sociology* 79 (4): 478–504. https://doi.org/10.1111/ruso.12045.

Gupta, Akhil. 1998. *Postcolonial Developments: Agriculture in the Making of Modern India.* Durham, NC: Duke University Press.

Gusterson, Hugh. 2003. "Anthropology and the Military—1968, 2003, and Beyond?" *Anthropology Today* 19 (3): 14–19.

Hadden, Jennifer, and Sidney Tarrow. 2007. "The Global Justice Movement in the United States since Seattle." In *The Global Justice Movement: Cross-National and Transnational Perspectives*, edited by Donatella della Porta, 210–231. Boulder, CO: Paradigm.

Haft, Michael, and Harrison Suarez. 2013. "The Marine's Secret Weapon: Coffee." *New York Times*, August 16. http://atwar.blogs.nytimes.com/2013/08/16/the-marines-secret-weapon-coffee/?_r=0.

Hale, Charles R., ed. 2008. *Engaging Contradictions: Theory, Politics, and Methods of Activist Scholarship.* Berkeley: University of California Press.

Hall, Ruth, Marc Edelman, Saturnino M. Borras, Ian Scoones, Ben White, and Wendy Wolford. 2015. "Resistance, Acquiescence or Incorporation? An Introduction to Land Grabbing and Political Reactions 'from Below.'" *Journal of Peasant Studies* 42 (3–4): 467–488. https://doi.org/10.1080/03066150.2015.1036746.

Halweil, Brian. 2002. *Home Grown: The Case for Local Food in a Global Market.* Washington, DC: Worldwatch Institute.

Handy, Jim. 2009. "'Almost Idiotic Wretchedness': A Long History of Blaming Peasants." *Journal of Peasant Studies* 36 (2): 325–344.

Hannerz, Ulf. 2007. "Cosmopolitanism." In *A Companion to the Anthropology of Politics*, edited by David Nugent and Joan Vincent, 69–85. Malden, MA: Wiley-Blackwell.

Hansen, Finn. 1996. *Relaciones Europa-Centroamérica: Ayuda externa y comercio desfavorable.* Managua: CRIES.

Hardin, Garrett. 1968. "The Tragedy of the Commons." *Science* 162 (3859): 1243–48.

Harris, Charles H., and Louis R Sadler. 2009. *The Archaeologist Was a Spy: Sylvanus G. Morley and the Office of Naval Intelligence.* Albuquerque: University of New Mexico Press.

Harrison, Faye Venetia, ed. 1991. *Decolonizing Anthropology: Moving Further toward an Anthropology of Liberation.* Arlington, VA: Association of Black Anthropologists, American Anthropological Association.

Harvey, David. 2009. *Cosmopolitanism and the Geographies of Freedom.* New York: Columbia University Press.

Hassanein, Neva. 2003. "Practicing Food Democracy: A Pragmatic Politics of Transformation." *Journal of Rural Studies* 19 (1): 77–86. https://doi.org/10.1016/S0743-0167(02)00041-4.

Haugerud, Angelique. 1995. *The Culture of Politics in Modern Kenya.* Cambridge: Cambridge University Press.

Hawken, Paul. 2000. "Skeleton Woman Visits Seattle." In *Globalize This! The Battle against the World Trade Organization and Corporate Rule*, edited by Kevin Danaher and Roger Burbach, 14–34. Monroe, ME: Common Courage Press.

Hearn, Jonathan. 2001. "Taking Liberties: Contesting Visions of the Civil Society Project." *Critique of Anthropology* 21 (4): 339–60. https://doi.org/10.1177/0308275X0102100401.

Heath, John Richard. 1985. "El Programa Nacional de Alimentación y la crisis de alimentos." *Revista Mexicana de Sociología* 47 (3): 115–135.

Helleiner, Eric. 1994. "From Bretton Woods to Global Finance: A World Turned Upside Down." In *Political Economy and the Changing Global Order*, edited by Richard Stubbs and Geoffrey R. D. Underhill, 163–175. New York: St. Martin's Press.

Heller, Chaia. 2002. "From Scientific Risk to Paysan Savoir-Faire: Peasant Expertise in the French and Global Debate over GM Crops." *Science as Culture* 11 (1): 5–37. https://doi.org/10.1080/09505430120115707.

——. 2013. *Food Solidarity: French Farmers and the Fight against Industrial Agriculture and Genetically Modified Crops*. Durham, NC: Duke University Press.

Hellman, Judith Adler. 1995. "The Riddle of New Social Movements: Who They Are and What They Do." In *Capital, Power, and Inequality in Latin America*, edited by Sandor Halebsky and Richard Harris, 165–83. Boulder, CO: Westview.

Herman, Patrick, and Christian Boisgontier. 2001. *Confédération paysanne: Changeons de politique agricole*. Paris: Arthème Farard.

Hernández, René. 1994. Interview with the author. San Salvador, July 14.

Hernández Cascante, Jorge. 1992. "Para la evaluación del Congreso Constitutivo de ASOCODE. 6 de enero de 1992." Photocopy.

——. 1994. "ASOCODE: los retos y perspectivas del movimiento campesino centroamericano." In *Alternativas campesinas: modernización en el agro y movimiento campesino en Centroamérica*, edited by Klaus-Dieter Tangermann and Ivana Ríos Valdés, 243–266. Managua: CRIES.

——. 1995. "ASOCODE: Nuestra herramienta de coordinación y desarrollo campesino centroamericano. (Nuestro machete para el desarrollo sostenible centroamericano)." Unpublished manuscript.

——. 2002. Interview with the author. Tibás, Costa Rica, July 27.

Hernández Navarro, Luis. 1992. "Las convulsiones sociales." In *Autonomía y nuevos sujetos sociales en el desarrollo rural*, edited by Julio Moguel, Carlota Botey, and Luis Hernández, 235–60. Mexico: Siglo Veintiuno.

——. 2000. "The Revolt of the Globalized." In *Globalize This! The Battle against the World Trade Organization and Corporate Rule*, edited by Kevin Danaher and Roger Burbach, 41–43. Monroe, ME: Common Courage Press.

Hernández Porras, Carlos. 1994. Interview with the author. San José, Costa Rica, June 16.

Herren, Hans R., Benedikt Haerlin, and IAASTD+10 Advisory Group, eds. 2020. *Transformation of Our Food Systems: The Making of a Paradigm Shift. Reflections since IAASTD—10 Years On*. Zürich: Zukunftsstiftung Landwirtschaft & Biovision. https://www.globalagriculture.org/fileadmin/files/weltagrarbericht/IAASTD-Buch/PDFBuch/BuchWebTransformationFoodSystems.pdf.

Hetland, Gabriel, and Jeff Goodwin. 2014. "The Strange Disappearance of Capitalism from Social Movement Studies." In *Marxism and Social Movements*, edited by Colin Barker, Laurence Cox, John Krinsky, and Alf Gunvald Nilsen, 83–102. Chicago: Haymarket.

Hewitt de Alcántara, Cynthia. 1984. *Anthropological Perspectives on Rural Mexico*. London: Routledge & Kegan Paul.

Hidalgo Pallares, José, and Felipe Hurtado Pérez. 2016. "Ecuador." In *El socialismo del siglo XXI tras el boom de los commodities*, edited by José Hidalgo Pallares and Felipe Hurtado Pérez, 131–184. Quito: Konrad Adenaueer Stiftung.

Hindu, The. 2008. "KRRS Factions Unite for Greater Good." *The Hindu*, February 17.

Hines, Colin. 2000. *Localization: A Global Manifesto*. London: Earthscan.

Hinrichs, C. Clare. 2003. "The Practice and Politics of Food System Localization." *Journal of Rural Studies* 19 (1): 33–45. https://doi.org/10.1016/S0743-0167(02)00040-2.

Hirschman, Albert O. 1983. "The Principle of Conservation and Mutation of Social Energy." *Grassroots Development* 7 (2): 3–9.

——. 1995. *A Propensity to Self-Subversion*. Cambridge, MA: Harvard University Press.

Hobsbawm, Eric J. 1983. "Introduction: Inventing Traditions." In *The Invention of Tradition*, edited by Eric J. Hobsbawm and Terence O. Ranger, 1–14. Cambridge: Cambridge University Press.

——. 1994. *The Age of Extremes: The Short Twentieth Century, 1914–1991*. London: Michael Joseph.

Holt-Giménez, Eric. 1996. "The Campesino a Campesino Movement: Farmer-Led, Sustainable Agriculture in Central America and Mexico." In *Food First Development Report No. 10*. Oakland, CA: Institute for Food and Development Policy.

——. 2006. *Campesino a Campesino: Voices from Latin America's Farmer to Farmer Movement for Sustainable Agriculture*. Oakland, CA: Food First.

Holt-Giménez, Eric, Raj Patel, and Annie Shattuck. 2009. *Food Rebellions! Crisis and the Hunger for Justice*. Oakland, CA: Food First.

Honduras Poder Legislativo. 1992. "Decreto número 31–92, Ley para la modernización y el desarrollo del sector agrícola." Tegucigalpa: mimeo.

Horowitz, Irving Louis, ed. 1967. *The Rise and Fall of Project Camelot: Studies in the Relationship between Social Science and Practical Politics*. Cambridge, MA: MIT Press.

Hospes, Otto. 2014. "Food Sovereignty: The Debate, the Deadlock, and a Suggested Detour." *Agriculture and Human Values* 31 (1): 119–130. https://doi.org/10.1007/s10460-013-9449-3.

Houtzager, Peter P. 2005. "The Movement of the Landless (MST), Juridical Field, and Legal Change in Brazil." In *Law and Globalization from Below: Towards a Cosmopolitan Legality*, edited by Boaventura de Sousa Santos and César Rodríguez-Garavito, 218–40. Cambridge: Cambridge University Press.

Hubert, Coline. 2019. *The United Nations Declaration on the Rights of Peasants: A Tool in the Struggle for Our Common Future*. Geneva: CETIM.

Hudson, Michael. 2012. *The Bubble and Beyond: Fictitious Capital, Debt Deflation and the Global Crisis*. Dresden: Islet-Verl.

Huizer, Gerrit. 1973. *Peasant Rebellion in Latin America: The Origins, Forms of Expression, and Potential of Latin American Peasant Unrest*. Hammondsworth: Penguin.

Humphrey, Caroline. 2004. "Cosmopolitanism and Kosmopolitizm in the Political Life of Soviet Citizens." *Focaal* 2004 (44): 138–152. https://doi.org/10.3167/092012904782311245.

Hussain, Athar, and Keith Tribe. 1981. *Marxism and the Agrarian Question*. Atlantic Highlands, N.J: Humanities Press.

IAASTD. 2009. *Agriculture at a Crossroads: Global Report*. Washington, DC: International Assessment of Agricultural Knowledge, Science and Technology for Development & Island Press.

ICA and IFAP. 1967. *Cooperation in the European Market Economies*. Bombay: International Cooperative Alliance and International Federation of Agricultural Producers.

IFAP. 1952. "FAO Position on International Commodity Problems." *IFAP News*, January.

——. 1957. *The First Ten Years of the International Federation of Agricultural Producers*. Paris: IFAP.

Ignatiev, Noel. 1996. *How the Irish Became White*. New York: Routledge.

Ikhwan, Mohammed. 2011. Interview with the author. Geneva, March 13.

Indigenous Peoples' Caucus. 2000. "Indigenous Peoples' Seattle Declaration." In *Globalize This! The Battle against the World Trade Organization and Corporate Rule*, edited by Kevin Danaher and Roger Burbach, 85–91. Monroe, ME: Common Courage Press.

Iniciativa CID. 2002. "Campaña Regional en Torno al Tratado de Libre Comercio entre los Estados Unidos y Centro América." Managua: Iniciativa Mesoamericana de Comercio, Integración y Desarrollo.

International South Group Network. 2000. "ISGN Forum in Bangkok." Email from Rcpd@info.com.ph, December 28. http://list.jca.apc.org/public/asia-apec/1999 -December.txt.

IPA. 1999. "Statement of the Seattle International People's Assembly Condemning the State of Siege in Seattle." Email from Bayan@iname.com, December 10. http://list .jca.apc.org/public/asia-apec/1999-December.txt.

IRC. 1992. "Cross-Border Links: Where the Action Is." *Interhemispheric Resource Center.*

Isaacman, Allen F. 1993. "Peasants and Rural Social Protest in Africa." In *Confronting Historical Paradigms: Peasants, Labor, and the Capitalist World System in Africa and Latin America*, edited by Frederick Cooper, Allen F. Isaacman, Florencia E. Mallon, William Roseberry, and Steve J. Stern, 205–317. Madison: University of Wisconsin Press.

Ishii-Eiteman, Marcia. 2009. "Food Sovereignty and the International Assessment of Agricultural Knowledge, Science and Technology for Development." *Journal of Peasant Studies* 36 (3): 689–700.

James, Wendy. 1975. "The Anthropologist as Reluctant Imperialist." In *Anthropology & the Colonial Encounter*, edited by Talal Asad, 41–69. London: Ithaca Press.

Jelin, Elizabeth, ed. 1990. "Citizenship and Identity: Final Reflections." In *Women and Social Change in Latin America*, edited by Elizabeth Jelin, 184–207. London: Zed Books.

Jensen, Steven L. B. 2015. "The Jamaican Broker: UN Diplomacy and the Transformation of International Human Rights, 1962–1968." In *Europe and the Americas: Transatlantic Approaches to Human Rights*, edited by Erik André Andersen and Eva Maria Lassen, 91–129. Leiden, The Netherlands: Brill.

——. 2016. *The Making of International Human Rights: The 1960s, Decolonization, and the Reconstruction of Global Values.* New York: Cambridge University Press.

Jiménez, Michael J. 1995. "'From Plantation to Cup': Coffee and Capitalism in the United States, 1830–1939." In *Coffee, Society, and Power in Latin America*, edited by William Roseberry, Lowell Gudmundson, and Mario Samper Kutschbach, 38–64. Baltimore: Johns Hopkins University Press.

Jovanović, Miodrag. 2015. "Constructing Legal Personality of Collective Entities—The Case of 'Peasants.'" Belgrade: Faculty of Law, University of Belgrade. https://papers .ssrn.com/sol3/papers.cfm?abstract_id=2599926.

Juris, Jeffrey S. 2008. *Networking Futures: The Movements against Corporate Globalization.* Durham, NC: Duke University Press.

Kandel, Matt. 2015. "Politics from Below? Small-, Mid- and Large-Scale Land Dispossession in Teso, Uganda, and the Relevance of Scale." *Journal of Peasant Studies* 42 (3–4): 635–652. https://doi.org/10.1080/03066150.2015.1016918.

Kapadia, Karin. 2000. "Responsibility without Rights: Women Workers in Bonded Labour in Rural Industry in South India." In *Disappearing Peasantries? Rural Labour in Africa, Asia and Latin America*, edited by Jos E. Mooij, Deborah Fahy Bryceson, and Cristóbal Kay, 247–261. London: Intermediate Technology Publications.

Kay, Cristóbal. 2008. "Reflections on Latin American Rural Studies in the Neoliberal Globalization Period: A New Rurality?" *Development and Change* 39 (6): 915–943.

Keane, John. 1998. *Civil Society: Old Images, New Visions*. Stanford, CA: Stanford University Press.

——. 2001. "Global Civil Society?" In *Global Civil Society 2001*, edited by Marlies Glasius, Helmut Anheier, and Mary Kaldor, 23–47. Oxford: Oxford University Press.

Kearney, Michael. 1995. "The Local and the Global: The Anthropology of Globalization and Transnationalism." *Annual Review of Anthropology* 24:547–65.

——. 1996. *Reconceptualizing the Peasantry: Anthropology in Global Perspective*. Boulder, CO: Westview Press.

Keck, Margaret E. 1995. "Parks, People and Power: The Shifting Terrain of Environmentalism." *NACLA Report on the Americas* 28 (5): 36–43.

Keck, Margaret E., and Kathryn Sikkink. 1998. *Activists beyond Borders: Advocacy Networks in International Politics*. Ithaca, NY: Cornell University Press.

Keene, Sara, Marygold Walsh-Dilley, Wendy Wolford, and Charles Geisler. 2015. "A View from the Top: Examining Elites in Large-Scale Land Deals." *Canadian Journal of Development Studies* 36 (2): 131–146. https://doi.org/10.1080/02255189.2015.1044503.

Khadse, Ashlesha, and Peter M. Rosset. 2019. "Zero Budget Natural Farming in India—from Inception to Institutionalization." *Agroecology and Sustainable Food Systems* 43 (7–8): 848–871. https://doi.org/10.1080/21683565.2019.1608349.

Kidder, Thalia, and Mary McGinn. 1995. "In the Wake of NAFTA: Transnational Workers Networks." *Social Policy* 25 (4): 14–21.

Klandermans, Bert, Marga de Weerd, José Manuel Sabucedo, and María Costa. 1999. "Injustice and Adversarial Frames in a Supranational Political Context: Farmers." In *Social Movements in a Globalising World*, edited by Hanspeter Kriesi, Donatella della Porta, and Dieter Rucht, 134–147. Basingstoke: Palgrave Macmillan.

Kneen, Brewster. 2002. *Invisible Giant: Cargill and Its Transnational Strategies*. 2nd ed. London: Pluto Press.

——. 2009. *The Tyranny of Rights*. Ottawa: Ram's Horn.

Knuth, Sarah Elisabeth. 2015. "Global Finance and the Land Grab: Mapping Twenty-First Century Strategies." *Canadian Journal of Development Studies* 36 (2): 163–178. https://doi.org/10.1080/02255189.2015.1046373.

Kruijt, Dirk. 1992. "Monopolios de filantropía: El caso de las llamadas "Organizaciones no Gubernamentales" en América Latina." *Polémica* 16:41–47.

La República. 1988. "Las medidas de presión se mantienen en firme—Gobierno pide calma a los agricultores." *La República*, July 28.

——. 1989. "El país no debe importar ni exportar arroz, dice Figueres." *La República*, May 24.

Labrousse, Ernest. 1962. *Fluctuaciones económicas e historia social*. Madrid: Tecnos.

Lagos, María. 1994. *Autonomy and Power: The Dynamics of Class and Culture in Rural Bolivia*. Philadelphia: University of Pennsylvania Press.

Lahiff, Edward, Saturnino M. Borras, and Cristóbal Kay. 2007. "Market-Led Agrarian Reform: Policies, Performance and Prospects." *Third World Quarterly* 28 (8): 1417–1436.

Lan, David. 1999. *Guns and Rain: Guerrillas and Spirit Mediums in Zimbabwe*. London: Currey.

Land Matrix. 2016. "About—LAND MATRIX." Land Matrix.

Landsberger, Henry A, and Cynthia N. Hewitt. 1970. "Ten Sources of Weakness and Cleavage in Latin American Peasant Movements." In *Agrarian Problems and Peasant Movements in Latin America*, edited by Rodolfo Stavenhagen, 559–83. Garden City, NY: Anchor-Doubleday.

Laraña, Enrique, Hank Johnston, and Joseph R. Gusfield, eds. 1994. *New Social Movements: From Ideology to Identity*. Philadelphia: Temple University Press.

Latinobarómetro. 2002. "Latinobarómetro: Opinión Pública Latinoamericana." 2002. http://www.latinobarometro.org/English/iniconst-i.htm.

Lauren, Paul Gordon. 2011. *The Evolution of International Human Rights: Visions Seen.* Philadelphia: University of Pennsylvania Press.

Laxer, Gordon. 1995. "Social Solidarity, Democracy, and Global Capitalism." *Canadian Review of Sociology and Anthropology* 32:288–313.

Laycock, David H. 1990. *Populism and Democratic Thought in the Canadian Prairies, 1910 to 1945.* Toronto: University of Toronto Press.

Le Goff, Jacques, and Edmund King. 1972. "The Town as an Agent of Civilisation, C. 1200-c. 1500." In *The Fontana Economic History of Europe: The Middle Ages,* edited by Carlo M. Cipolla, 71–106. London: Collins/Fontana.

Le Roy Ladurie, Emmanuel. 1996. *The Ancien Régime: A History of France, 1610–1774.* London: Blackwell.

Lechner, Norbert. 1998. "Nuestros Miedos." *Perfiles Latinoamericanos* 13:179–198.

Leeds, Anthony. 1977. "Mythos and Pathos: Some Unpleasantries on Peasantries." In *Peasant Livelihood: Studies in Economic Anthropology and Cultural Ecology,* edited by Rhoda Halperin and James Dow, 227–256. New York: St. Martin's Press.

Leis, Raúl. 1994. "Panamá: movimientos campesinos, transitismo y democracia." In *Alternativas campesinas: modernización en el agro y movimiento campesino en Centroamérica,* edited by Klaus-Dieter Tangermann and Ivana Ríos Valdés, 95–116. Managua: CRIES.

Lemus, Miguel Angel. 1997. Interview with the author. Guatemala City, August 11.

Lenin, V. I. 1964. "The Dual Power." In *Collected Works.* Vol. 24, 38–41. Moscow: Progress Publishers.

León, Osvaldo, Sally Burch, and Eduardo Tamayo. 2001. *Movimientos sociales en la red.* Quito: ALAI.

Lerche, Jens. 2021. "The Farm Laws Struggle 2020–2021: Class-Caste Alliances and Bypassed Agrarian Transition in Neoliberal India." *Journal of Peasant Studies* 48 (7): 1380–1396. https://doi.org/10.1080/03066150.2021.1986013.

Levien, Michael. 2013. "Regimes of Dispossession: From Steel Towns to Special Economic Zones." *Development and Change* 44 (2): 381–407. https://doi.org/10.1111/dech.12012.

Levitt, Peggy, and Sally Merry. 2009. "Vernacularization on the Ground: Local Uses of Global Women's Rights in Peru, China, India and the United States." *Global Networks* 9 (4): 441–461.

Li, Mengyu, Nanfei Jia, Manfred Lenzen, Arunima Malik, Liyuan Wei, Yutong Jin, and David Raubenheimer. 2022. "Global Food-Miles Account for Nearly 20% of Total Food-Systems Emissions." *Nature Food* 3 (6): 445–453. https://doi.org/10.1038/s43016-022-00531-w.

Liao, Chuan, Suhyun Jung, Daniel G. Brown, and Arun Agrawal. 2016. "Insufficient Research on Land Grabbing." *Science* 353 (6295): 131. https://doi.org/10.1126/science.aaf6565.

Lichbach, Mark I. 1994. "What Makes Rational Peasants Revolutionary? Dilemma, Paradox, and Irony in Peasant Collective Action." *World Politics* 46 (3): 383–419.

LIFE Network. 2010. "Declaration on Livestock Keepers' Rights."

Lima, Aparecida do Carmo, Janaina Stronzake, Judite Stronzake, and Rosangela Celia Faustino. 2015. "Contribuições da Vía Campesina em processos educativos agroecológicos na América Latina." *Trabalho Necessário* 13 (22): 80–102.

Llambí, Luis. 2000. "Global–Local Links in Latin America's New Ruralities." In *Disappearing Peasantries? Rural Labour in Africa, Asia and Latin America,* edited by

Deborah Bryceson, Cristóbal Kay, and Jos Mooij, 176–212. London: Intermediate Technology Publications.

Lofredo, Gino. 1991. "Hágase Rico En Los 90. ¿Usted Todavía No Tiene Su ONG?" *Chasqui* 39:15–18.

Lombraña, Martiniano. 1989. *Historia de las organizaciones campesinas de Honduras.* Ceiba: mimeo.

London Times. 1946a. "Conference of World Farmers: Supporting the F.A.O.," May 20.

——. 1946b. "Marketing of Food," May 30.

Loone, Susan. 2004. "People's Caravan Participants Captured by Nepali Maoists and Burn Two of Their Vehicle." People's Caravan 2004 for Food Sovereignty, distributed by Pesticide Action Network to agri-trade@yahoogroups.com.

Lucas, Anton, and Carol Warren. 2003. "The State, the People, and Their Mediators: The Struggle over Agrarian Law Reform in Post-New Order Indonesia." *Indonesia* 76 (October): 87–126.

Ludden, David E. 2008. *An Agrarian History of South Asia.* Cambridge: Cambridge University Press.

Luneau, Gilles. 2001. "Preface." In *The World Is Not for Sale: Farmers against Junk Food,* by José Bové and François Dufour, ix–xii. London: Verso.

Lutz, Catherine. 2007. "Militarization." In *A Companion to the Anthropology of Politics,* edited by David Nugent and Joan Vincent, 318–331. Malden, MA: Blackwell.

LVC. 1995. "Neo-Liberal Food Policies: The Road to Hunger." Press release. *FAO Symposium.*

——. 1996. *La Vía Campesina: Proceedings from the II International Conference of the Vía Campesina, Tlaxcala, Mexico, April 18–21, 1996.* Brussels: NCOS Publications.

——. 1998. "Dakar Declaration of Vía Campesina," November.

——. 1999a. "Mobilization Actions and Incidences Carried Out at Seattle 28th November to 3rd December."

——. 1999b. "Women Farmers in Seattle Say No to WTO." https://viacampesina.org/en/women-farmers-in-seattle-say-no-to-wto/.

——.1999c. "Vía Campesina Sets Out Important Positions at World Bank Events." *Vía Campesina Newsletter,* August.

——. 2000a. "Acciones desarrolladas en el primer año de la campaña." 2000.

——. 2000b. "Via Campesina Position Paper: International Relations and Strategic Alliances." In *III International Conference in Bangalore.* Jakarta: La Via Campesina.

——. 2001. "Priority to Peoples' Food Sovereignty." https://www.citizen.org/wp-content/uploads/wtooutoffood.pdf.

——. 2002a. *Peasant rights-Droits paysans-Derechos campesinos.* Jakarta: Via Campesina.

——. 2002b. "Vía Campesina Demands Respect for the Principle of Food Sovereignty and Right of Palestinian Farmers to Produce and to Remain on Their Land." Email from Viacam-info-palestina@yahoogroups.com, April 5.

——. 2009a. "Declaration of Rights of Peasants—Women and Men." https://viacampesina.org/en/wp-content/uploads/sites/2/2011/03/Declaration-of-rights-of-peasants-2009.pdf.

——. 2009b. *Small Scale Sustainable Farmers Are Cooling Down the Earth.* La Via Campesina Position Paper. Jakarta: Via Campesina. https://viacampesina.org/en/small-scale-sustainable-farmers-are-cooling-down-the-earth/.

——. 2012. "International Internal Seminar on Public Policy for Food Sovereignty (Preliminary Report)." Via Campesina.

——. 2021. "La Vía Campesina Agroecology Training Schools and Processes." La Vía Campesina. https://viacampesina.org/en/schools/.

LVC, ANUC, and FENSUAGRO. 2001. "Statement of the International Seminar on Agrarian Reform for Peace in Colombia." Presented at the International Seminar on Agrarian Reform for Peace in Colombia, Bogotá, June 27.

MAB. 2001. "O valor dos nossos símbolos." São Paulo: Movimento dos Atingidos por Barragens.

Macdonald, Laura. 1994. "Globalising Civil Society: Interpreting International NGOs in Central America." *Millennium-Journal of International Studies* 23 (2): 267–285.

———. 1997. *Supporting Civil Society: The Political Role of Non-Governmental Organizations in Central America*. New York: St. Martin's Press.

Magnan, André. 2011. "The Limits of Farmer-Control: Food Sovereignty and Conflicts over the Canadian Wheat Board." In *Food Sovereignty in Canada: Creating Just and Sustainable Food Systems*, edited by Hannah Wittman, Annette Aurélie Desmarais, and Nettie Wiebe, 114–133. Halifax, Nova Scotia: Fernwood.

Malseed, Kevin. 2008. "Where There Is No Movement: Local Resistance and the Potential for Solidarity." *Journal of Agrarian Change* 8 (2–3): 489–514.

Marcus, George E. 1995. "Ethnography in/of the World System: The Emergence of Multi-Sited Ethnography." *Annual Review of Anthropology* 24: 95–117.

Marsden, Terry. 1995. "Beyond Agriculture? Regulating the New Rural Spaces." *Journal of Rural Studies* 11 (3): 285–296.

Martínez, Alberto. 1990. *Costa Rica: política y regulación de precios en granos básicos*. Panama: CADESCA.

Martínez, Elizabeth. 2000a. "The WTO: Where Was the Color in Seattle?" *Colorlines* 3 (1): 11–12.

———. 2000b. "Where Was the Color in Seattle? Looking for Reasons Why the Great Battle Was So White." *Monthly Review* 52 (3): 141–149.

Martínez, Samuel. 2008. "Making Violence Visible: An Activist Anthropological Approach to Women's Rights Investigation." In *Engaging Contradictions: Theory, Politics, and Methods of Activist Scholarship*, edited by Charles R. Hale, 183–207. Berkeley: University of California Press.

Martínez-Alier, Joan, Isabelle Anguelovski, Patrick Bond, Daniela Del Bene, Federico Demaria, Julien-François Gerber, Lucie Greyl, et al. 2014. "Between Activism and Science: Grassroots Concepts for Sustainability Coined by Environmental Justice Organizations." *Journal of Political Ecology* 21 (1): 19–60. https://doi.org/10.2458/v21i1.21124.

Martínez-Torres, María Elena, and Peter M. Rosset. 2010. "La Vía Campesina: The Birth and Evolution of a Transnational Social Movement." *Journal of Peasant Studies* 37 (1): 149–175. https://doi.org/10.1080/03066150903498804.

Matejka, Michael G. 1979. *The Christian Rural Mission in the 1980's: A Call to Liberation and Development of Peoples*. New York: Agricultural Missions.

McCaffrey, Katherine T. 2002. *Military Power and Popular Protest: The U.S. Navy in Vieques, Puerto Rico*. New Brunswick, NJ: Rutgers University Press.

McCune, Nils, Juan Reardon, and Peter Rosset. 2014. "Agroecological Formación in Rural Social Movements." *Radical Teacher* 98:31–37. https://doi.org/10.5195/rt.2014.71.

McKay, Ben M. 2017. "Agrarian Extractivism in Bolivia." *World Development* 97:199–211. https://doi.org/10.1016/j.worlddev.2017.04.007.

McLaughlin, Neil. 1999. "Origin Myths in the Social Sciences: Fromm, the Frankfurt School and the Emergence of Critical Theory." *Canadian Journal of Sociology* 24 (1): 109–139.

McMath, Robert C., Jr. 1995. "Populism in Two Countries: Agrarian Protest in the Great Plains and Prairie Provinces." *Agricultural History* 69 (4): 516–546.

McMichael, Philip. 1998. "Global Food Politics." *Monthly Review* 50 (3): 97–111.

Meier, Mariann. 1958. *ACWW 1929–1959*. London: Associated Country Women of the World.

Melucci, Alberto. 1989. *Nomads of the Present: Social Movements and Individual Needs in Contemporary Society*. London: Hutchinson Radius.

Melvin, Jess. 2018. *The Army and the Indonesian Genocide: Mechanics of Mass Murder*. New York: Routledge.

Menjívar, Rafael, Sui Moy Li Kam, and Virginia Portuguez. 1985. "El movimiento campesino en Honduras." In *Movimientos populares en Centroamérica*, edited by Daniel Camacho and Rafael Menjívar, 373–408. San José, Costa Rica: EDUCA.

Merry, Sally Engle. 2006. *Human Rights and Gender Violence: Translating International Law into Local Justice*. Chicago: University of Chicago Press.

Merton, Robert K. 1949. *Social Theory and Social Structure*. New York: Free Press.

Michels, Robert. 1959. *Political Parties: A Sociological Study of the Oligarchical Tendencies of Modern Democracy*. New York: Dover.

Migdal, Joel S. 1974. *Peasants, Politics, and Revolution: Pressures toward Political and Social Change in the Third World*. Princeton, NJ: Princeton University Press.

Mignolo, Walter. 2002. "The Many Faces of Cosmo-Polis: Border Thinking and Critical Cosmopolitanism." In *Cosmopolitanism*, edited by Carol A. Breckenridge, Sheldon Pollock, Homi K. Bhabha, and Dipesh Chakrabarty, 157–187. Durham, NC: Duke University Press.

Milun, Kathryn. 2011. *The Political Uncommons: The Cross-Cultural Logic of the Global Commons*. Farnham, Surrey: Ashgate.

Ministros de Agricultura de Guatemala, El Salvador, Honduras y Nicaragua. 1993. "Resolución sobre el sistema de bandas de precios de importación." *Cuadernos de Investigación* [Centro de Investigaciones Tecnológicas y Científicas, Dirección de Investigaciones Económicas y Sociales, El Salvador] 4 (17): 30–40.

Mintz, Sidney W. 1973. "A Note on the Definition of Peasantries." *Journal of Peasant Studies* 1 (1): 91–106.

———. 1986. *Sweetness and Power: The Place of Sugar in Modern History*. New York: Penguin.

Mittal, Anuradha. 1999. "Action Alert: Last Week Seattle . . . This Week Oakland." Email from Foodfirst.org, December 9.

Mittal, Swati, and Sanhati Banerjee. 2008. "Tikait Arrested, Admits His 'Mistake,' Gets Out on Bail." *Economic Times*, April 3. https://economictimes.indiatimes.com /news/politics-and-nation/tikait-arrested-admits-his-mistake-gets-out-on-bail /articleshow/2921511.cms?from=mdr.

Mngxitama, Andile. 2002. "The World Bank Must Still Apologise," July 9.

Moguel, Julio, Carlota Botey, and Luis Hernández. 1992. "Introducción." In *Autonomía y nuevos sujetos sociales en el desarrollo rural*, edited by Julio Moguel, Carlota Botey, and Luis Hernández, 9–11. Mexico: Siglo Veintiuno.

Mohan, Giles, and Kristian Stokke. 2000. "Participatory Development and Empowerment: The Dangers of Localism." *Third World Quarterly* 21 (2): 247–268. https:// doi.org/10.1080/01436590050004346.

Mollett, Sharlene. 2016. "The Power to Plunder: Rethinking Land Grabbing in Latin America." *Antipode* 48 (2): 412–432. https://doi.org/10.1111/anti.12190.

Monsalve Suárez, Sofía. 2013. "The Human Rights Framework in Contemporary Agrarian Struggles." *Journal of Peasant Studies* 40 (1): 239–290. https://doi.org/10.1080 /03066150.2011.652950.

Monsalve Suárez, Sofía, Ulrike Bickel, Frank Garbers, and Lucia Goldfarb. 2008. "Agrofuels in Brazil—Summary." FIAN International, May 26. http://fian.org/en/news /article/agrofuels-in-brazil-summary-616.

Mooney, Patrick H., and Theo J. Majka. 1995. *Farmers' and Farm Workers' Movements: Social Protest in American Agriculture*. New York: Twayne.

Moore, Barrington. 1966. *Social Origins of Dictatorship and Democracy: Lord and Peasant in the Making of the Modern World*. Boston: Beacon.

Mora, Eduardo, Sonia Soto, and Walden Bello. 1999. "The WTO Debacle in Seattle: A Unity Statement of Philippine Social Movements, Labor Groups, People's Organizations, and NGOs." December 10. https://list.jca.apc.org/public/asia-apec /1999-December/001372.html.

Morales Gamboa, Abelardo, and Martha Isabel Cranshaw. 1997. *Regionalismo emergente: redes de la sociedad civil e integración en Centroamérica*. San José, Costa Rica: FLACSO & Ibis-Dinamarca.

Moreno Fraginals, Manuel. 1985. "Plantations in the Caribbean: Cuba, Puerto Rico, and the Dominican Republic in the Late Nineteenth Century." In *Between Slavery and Free Labor: The Spanish-Speaking Caribbean in the Nineteenth Century*, edited by Manuel Moreno Fraginals, Frank Moya Pons, and Stanley L. Engerman, 3–21. Baltimore: Johns Hopkins University Press.

Morgan, Dan. 1980. *Merchants of Grain*. New York: Penguin.

Morris, Aldon D, and Carol McClurg Mueller, eds. 1992. *Frontiers in Social Movement Theory*. New Haven, CT: Yale University Press.

Mosse, David. 2008. "Collective Action, Common Property, and Social Capital in South India: An Anthropological Commentary." In *The Contested Commons: Conversations between Economists and Anthropologists*, edited by Pranab K. Bardhan and Isha Ray, 83–106. Malden, MA: Blackwell.

Mosse, David, and Sundara Babu Nagappan. 2021. "NGOs as Social Movements: Policy Narratives, Networks and the Performance of Dalit Rights in South India." *Development and Change* 52 (1): 134–167. https://doi.org/10.1111/dech .12614.

Müller, Birgit, ed. 2013. *The Gloss of Harmony: The Politics of Policy Making in Multilateral Organisations*. London: Pluto.

Muñoz, Juan Pablo. 2010. "Constituyente, gobierno de transición y soberanía alimentaria en Ecuador." In *¿Cambio de rumbo en las políticas agrarias latinoamericanas? Estado, movimientos sociales campesinos y soberanía alimentaria*, edited by Jordi Gascón and Xavier Montagut, 151–168. Barcelona: Icaria.

Münster, Daniel. 2016. "Agro-Ecological Double Movements? Zero Budget Natural Farming and Alternative Agricultures after the Neoliberal Crisis in Kerala." In *Critical Perspectives on Agrarian Transition: India in the Global Debate*, edited by Bibhuti Bhusan Mohanty, 222–244. Basingstoke: Routledge.

Muzzopappa, Eva, and Ana Margarita Ramos. 2017. "Una etnografía itinerante sobre el terrorismo en Argentina: paradas, trayectorias y disputas." *Antípoda* 29 (September): 123–142. https://doi.org/10.7440/antipoda29.2017.06.

Nabudere, Dani Wadada. 2008. "Research, Activism, and Knowledge Production." In *Engaging Contradictions: Theory, Politics, and Methods of Activist Scholarship*, edited by Charles R. Hale, 62–87. Berkeley: University of California Press.

Navarro, Amílcar. 1994. Interview with the author. Managua, Nicaragua, July 1.

NCC. 2002. "Agricultural Missions 'Education for Rural Justice Tour' Is Underway." National Council of Churches News Service, October 1. http://www.ncccusa.org /news/02news84.html.

Nelson, Diane M. 1996. "Maya Hackers and the Cyberspatialized Nation-State: Modernity, Ethnostalgia, and a Lizard Queen in Guatemala." *Cultural Anthropology* 11 (3): 287–308.

Nelson, Paul. 2004. "New Agendas and New Patterns of International NGO Political Action." In *Creating a Better World: Interpreting Global Civil Society*, edited by Rupert Taylor, 116–132. Bloomfield, CT: Kumarian.

Netting, Robert McC. 1993. *Smallholders, Householders: Farm Families and The Ecology of Intensive, Sustainable Agriculture*. Stanford, CA: Stanford University Press.

Newbold, Stokes. 1957. "Receptivity to Communist Fomented Agitation in Rural Guatemala." *Economic Development and Cultural Change* 5 (4): 338–361.

Newsweek. 2001. "New Face of Protest: A Who's Who." *Newsweek*, July 30.

NFU. 1985a. "1985: A Year of Struggle, Heartache, Victory and Solidarity." *Union Farmer* 36 (7): 6–7.

——. 1985b. "NFU Becomes a Member of NAFA." *Union Farmer* 36 (7): 2.

——. 1985c. "NFU Presents Brief to Wheat Board Minister." *Union Farmer* 36 (3): 5.

——. 1988. "Defending Canada's Rural Communities." *Union Farmer* 39 (8): 6–7.

——. 2001. "The National Farmers Union: Fighting for the Family Farm for over 30 Years."

NGLS Roundup. 1997. "The World Food Summit." United Nations Nongovernmental Liaison Service, January.

NGO Forum. 1996. "Profit for Few or Food for All: Food Sovereignty and Security to Eliminate the Globalisation of Hunger," November.

NGO/CSO Forum. 2002. "Food Sovereignty: A Right for All. Political Statement of the NGO/CSO Forum for Food Sovereignty," June. https://viacampesina.org/en/declaration-ngo-forum-fao-summit-rome5/.

Nicholson, Paul. 2007. "Editorial: Biodiversidad en España." *Biodiversidad, Sustento y Culturas* 54 (October): 1–3.

Nielsen, Kai. 1995. "Reconceptualizing Civil Society for Now: Some Somewhat Gramscian Turnings." In *Toward a Global Civil Society*, edited by Michael Walzer, 41–67. Providence, RI: Berghahn.

NLC and LPM. 2002. "Arrested Landless People's Movement Members Released— National Land Committee and Landless People's Movement." *Focus on the Global South*, August 24.

Nonini, Donald M. 2013. "The Local-Food Movement and the Anthropology of Global Systems." *American Ethnologist* 40 (2): 267–275. https://doi.org/10.1111/amet.12019.

Nove, Alec. 1991. *The Economics of Feasible Socialism Revisited*. 2nd ed. London: HarperCollins.

Novoa, Andre. 2015. "Mobile Ethnography: Emergence, Techniques and Its Importance to Geography." *Human Geographies* 9 (1): 97–107. https://doi.org/10.5719/hgeo.2015.91.7.

Nuila, Andrea. 2018. "Collective Rights in the UN Declaration on the Rights of Peasants and Other People Working in Rural Areas." Heidelberg: FIAN International. https://www.fian.org/fileadmin/media/publications_2018/Reports_and_guidelines/droits_collectifs_UK_web.pdf.

Núñez Soto, Orlando, Gloria Cardenal, and Juan Morales. 1998. *Desarrollo agroecológico y asociatividad campesina*. Managua: CIPRES.

Nussbaum, Martha C. 1994. "Patriotism and Cosmopolitanism." *Boston Review*, October 1. http://bostonreview.net/martha-nussbaum-patriotism-and-cosmopolitanism.

Nyéléni Forum. 2007. "Nyéléni 2007: Forum for Food Sovereignty," Sélingué, Mali, February 23–27. https://nyeleni.org/DOWNLOADS/Nyelni_EN.pdf.

O'Brien, Kevin J., and Lianjiang Li. 2006. *Rightful Resistance in Rural China*. Cambridge: Cambridge University Press.

O'Brien, Robert, Anne Marie Goetz, Jan Aart Scholte, and Marc Williams. 2000. *Contesting Global Governance: Multilateral Economic Institutions and Global Social Movements*. Cambridge: Cambridge University Press.

OHCHR. 2018. "Human Rights and Constitution Making." Geneva: Office of the United Nations High Commissioner for Human Rights. https://www.ohchr.org/Documents /Publications/ConstitutionMaking_EN.pdf.

Olofsson, Gunnar. 1988. "After the Working-Class Movement? An Essay on What's 'New' and What's 'Social' in the New Social Movements." *Acta Sociológica* 31 (1): 15–34.

Olsen, Mancur. 1965. *The Logic of Collective Action: Public Goods and the Theory of Groups.* Cambridge, MA: Harvard University Press.

Omawale. 1984. "Note on the Concept of Entitlement: Bridge between the Structural and Human Rights Approach to Food in Development." In *Food as a Human Right*, edited by Asbjørn Eide, Wenche Barth Eide, Susantha Goonatilake, Joan Gussow, and Omawale, 260–264. Tokyo: United Nations University.

Orlove, Benjamin S. 1997. "Meat and Strength: The Moral Economy of a Chilean Food Riot." *Cultural Anthropology* 12 (2): 234–268.

Ortega, Emiliano. 1992. "Evolution of the Rural Dimension in Latin America and the Caribbean." *CEPAL Review* 47:115–136.

Orwell, George. 1952. *Homage to Catalonia.* New York: Harcourt, Brace.

Ostrom, Elinor. 1990. *Governing the Commons: The Evolution of Institutions for Collective Action.* Cambridge: Cambridge University Press.

Otero, Gerardo, Gabriela Pechlaner, and Efe Can Gürcan. 2013. "The Political Economy of 'Food Security' and Trade: Uneven and Combined Dependency." *Rural Sociology* 78 (3): 263–289. https://doi.org/10.1111/ruso.12011.

Owen, John R. 2005. "In Defence of the 'Peasant.'" *Journal of Contemporary Asia* 35 (3): 368–385.

Oxford English Dictionary. 2005. "Peasant, n. and Adj." In *Oxford English Dictionary.*

Oya, Carlos. 2013. "The Land Rush and Classic Agrarian Questions of Capital and Labour: A Systematic Scoping Review of the Socioeconomic Impact of Land Grabs in Africa." *Third World Quarterly* 34 (9): 1532–1557. https://doi.org/10.1080 /01436597.2013.843855.

Paget-Clarke, Nic. 2008. "Interview with Ibrahima Coulibaly of Mali's CNOP." *In Motion Magazine*, October 22. http://inmotionmagazine.com/global/i_coulibaly_int .html#Anchor-From-49575.

Pahwa, Nitish. 2020. "What's Driving the Biggest Protest in World History?" *Slate Magazine*, December 9. https://slate.com/news-and-politics/2020/12/india-farmer -protests-modi.html.

Palerm, Ángel. 1980. *Antropología y marxismo.* México, DF: Nueva Imagen.

Palley, Marian L. 1991. "Women's Rights as Human Rights: An International Perspective." *Annals of the American Academy of Political and Social Science* 515 (May): 163–178.

Pareto, Vilfredo. 1935. *The Mind and Society.* New York: Harcourt, Brace.

Pasos, Rubén. 1994. Interview with author. Managua, Nicaragua, July 6.

Patel, Raj. 2009. "What Does Food Sovereignty Look Like?" *Journal of Peasant Studies* 36 (3): 663–673.

Patnaik, Utsa. 2011. "The Agrarian Question in the Neoliberal Era." In *The Agrarian Question in the Neoliberal Era: Primitive Accumulation and the Peasantry*, edited by Utsa Patnaik, Sam Moyo, and Issa G. Shivji, 7–60. Oxford: Pambazuka.

Patomäki, Heikki. 2001. *Democratising Globalisation: The Leverage of the Tobin Tax.* London: Zed Books.

Pattenden, Jonathan. 2005. "Trickle-Down Solidarity, Globalisation and Dynamics of Social Transformation in a South Indian Village." *Economic and Political Weekly* 40 (19): 1975–1985.

Paulo Freire Stichting. 1993. "La Via Campesina." Unpublished manuscript.

Pawel, Miriam. 2006. "Farmworkers Reap Little as Union Strays from its Roots." *Los Angeles Times.* January 8. https://www.latimes.com/local/la-me-ufw8jan08-story.html.

——. 2010. *The Union of Their Dreams: Power, Hope, and Struggle in Cesar Chavez's Farm Worker Movement.* New York: Bloomsbury.

PCFS. 2005. "Draft—The People's Convention on Food Sovereignty," February. https://studylib.net/doc/9031792/people-s-convention-on-food-sovereignty.

——. 2007. "People's Coalition on Food Sovereignty (PCFS)." People's Coalition on Food Sovereignty.

PCFS and PAN AP. 2004. "People's Convention on Food Sovereignty." In *Primer on People's Food Sovereignty,* 35–45. Penang: People's Coalition on Food Sovereignty and Pesticide Action Network Asia and Pacific.

Pedersen, Karen. 2002. Interview with the author. Saskatoon, Canada, November 20.

Pelupessy, Wim. 1993. *El mercado mundial del café.* San José, Costa Rica: DEI.

People's Caravan. 2004. "Statement of the People's Caravan for Food Sovereignty 2004: Assert Our Rights to Land and Food!" People's Caravan 2004 for Food Sovereignty, distributed by Pesticide Action Network Asia and the Pacific to agri-trade@yahoogroups.com.

Perelman, Michael. 2000. *The Invention of Capitalism: Classical Political Economy and the Secret History of Primitive Accumulation.* Durham, NC: Duke University Press.

Petras, James. 1998. "The New Revolutionary Peasantry." *Z Magazine* 11:29–34.

PFS. 1993. "La Vía Campesina." Doetinchem, Netherlands: Paulo Freire Stichting.

Pianta, Mario, and Mario Marchetti. 2007. "The Global Justice Movements: The Transnational Dimension." In *The Global Justice Movement: Cross-National and Transnational Perspectives,* edited by Donatella della Porta, 29–51. Boulder, CO: Paradigm.

Pimbert, Michel P. 2006. *Transforming Knowledge and Ways of Knowing for Food Sovereignty.* London: International Institute for Environment and Development. http://pubs.iied.org/pdfs/14535IIED.pdf.

Pino, Hugo Noé, and Andrew Thorpe, eds. 1992. *Honduras: el ajuste estructural y la reforma agraria.* Tegucigalpa: Centro de Documentación de Honduras.

Pisani, Francis. 2002. "'Best Story, Not the Biggest Bomb': How to Fight the Terror Networks." *Le Monde Diplomatique,* June. http://mondediplo.com/2002/06/02networks.

Piven, Frances Fox, and Richard A. Cloward. 1979. *Poor People's Movements: Why They Succeed, How They Fail.* New York: Vintage.

Polanyi, Karl. 1957. *The Great Transformation: The Political and Economic Origins of Our Time.* Boston: Beacon.

——. 2001. *The Great Transformation: The Political and Economic Origins of Our Time.* 2nd ed. Boston: Beacon.

Ponisio, Lauren C., Leithen K. M'Gonigle, Kevi C. Mace, Jenny Palomino, Perry de Valpine, and Claire Kremen. 2014. "Diversification Practices Reduce Organic to Conventional Yield Gap." *Proceedings of the Royal Society B: Biological Sciences* 282 (1799): 20141396. https://doi.org/10.1098/rspb.2014.1396.

Popkin, Samuel L. 1979. *The Rational Peasant: The Political Economy of Rural Society in Vietnam.* Berkeley: University of California Press.

Portelli, Alessandro. 1991. *The Death of Luigi Trastulli and Other Stories: Form and Meaning in Oral History.* Albany: SUNY Press.

Posas, Mario. 1985. "El movimiento campesino hondureño: Un panorama general." In *Historia política de los campesinos latinoamericanos,* Vol. 2, edited by Pablo González Casanova, 28–76. Mexico, D.F.: Siglo Veintiuno.

——. 1996. "El sector reformado y la politica agraria del Estado." In *El agro hondureño y su futuro,* edited by Eduardo Baumeister, 131–166. Tegucigalpa: Guaymuras.

Presidentes Centroamericanos. 1991. "Plan de Acción para la Agricultura Centroamericana PAC, 15 y 16 de julio, San Salvador." El Salvador. Photocopy.

——. 1992. "El Compromiso Agropecuario de Panamá." El Salvador. Photocopy.

Price, David H. 2002. "Interlopers and Invited Guests: On Anthropology's Witting and Unwitting Links to Intelligence Agencies." *Anthropology Today* 18 (6): 16–21.

PROSI. 1996. "Cinquantenaire de la FIPA: Déclaration des agriculteurs du monde." *PROSI Magazine (331)*, August.

Provost, Claire. 2013. "La Via Campesina Celebrates 20 Years of Standing Up for Food Sovereignty." *The Guardian*, June 17. http://www.guardian.co.uk/global-develop ment/poverty-matters/2013/jun/17/la-via-campesina-food-sovereignty.

Qualman, Darrin, and Nettie Wiebe. 2002. *The Structural Adjustment of Canadian Agriculture*. Ottawa: Canadian Centre for Policy Alternatives.

Raghu, Pratik. 2018. "The Prism of Expanding Peasants' Rights: A Critical Investigation of Diverse Frames Applied to La Vía Campesina's Human Rights Engagements." *Perspectives on Global Development and Technology* 17 (3): 327–340. https://doi.org /10.1163/15691497-12341481.

Rajagopal, Balakrishnan. 2005. *International Law from Below: Development, Social Movements, and Third World Resistance*. Cambridge: Cambridge University Press.

Ramanujam, T. C. A, and T. C. A Sangeetha. 2001. "New IPR Regime–Protection for Indian Patents." *Hindu Business Line*, April 24.

Rappaport, Joanne. 2005. *Intercultural Utopias: Public Intellectuals, Cultural Experimentation, and Ethnic Pluralism in Colombia*. Durham, NC: Duke University Press.

Rapport, Nigel. 2006. "Anthropology as Cosmopolitan Study." *Anthropology Today* 22 (1): 23–24. https://doi.org/10.1111/j.1467-8322.2006.00415.x.

Razavi, Shahra. 2009. "Engendering the Political Economy of Agrarian Change." *Journal of Peasant Studies* 36 (1): 197–226. http://dx.doi.org/10.1080/03066150902 820412.

Rede Social, GRAIN, Inter Pares, and Solidarity Sweden-Latin America. 2015. "Foreign Pension Funds and Land Grabbing in Brazil." *GRAIN.org*, November 16. https:// grain.org/article/entries/5336-foreign-pension-funds-and-land-grabbing-in-brazil.

Reed, Roger. 2005. "La promotion des droits humains." In *ONU: droits pour tous ou loi du plus fort? Regards militants sur les Nations Unies*, edited by Julie Duchatel and Florian Rochat, 232–246. Geneva: CETIM.

Reuben Soto, William. 1991. "El papel de las ONG en la cooperación europea hacia Centroamérica." In *Más allá del ajuste: La contribución europea al desarrollo democrático y duradero de las economías centroamericanas*, edited by Raúl Ruben and Govert Van Oord, 337–369. San José, Costa Rica: DEI.

Reyes Caballero, Marcial. 1994. Interview with the author. Tegucigalpa, Honduras, July 27.

Riddell, J. 1998. "Contemporary Thinking on Land Reforms." Rome: FAO.

Riding, Alan. 1986. *Distant Neighbors: A Portrait of the Mexicans*. New York: Vintage.

Riechmann, Jorge, and Francisco Fernández Buey. 1994. *Redes que dan libertad: Introducción a los nuevos movimientos sociales*. Barcelona: Paidós.

Riles, Annelise. 2000. *The Network Inside Out*. Ann Arbor: University of Michigan Press.

Risse-Kappen, Thomas, ed. 1995. "Bringing Transnational Relations Back In: Introduction." In *Bringing Transnational Relations Back In: Non-State Actors, Domestic Structures, and International Institutions*, 3–33. Cambridge: Cambridge University Press.

Ritchie, Mark. 1996. "Cross-Border Organizing." In *The Case against the Global Economy and for a Turn toward the Local*, edited by Jerry Mander and Edward Goldsmith, 494–500. San Francisco: Sierra Club.

——. 2001. "From Seattle to Doha: The Role of Agrarian Movements in Shaping the Post-Bretton Woods World Order." Paper presented at Yale Agrarian Studies Seminar, New Haven, CT, September 21.

Rivera Cusicanqui, Silvia. 1985. "Apuntes para una historia de las luchas campesinas en Bolivia (1900–1978)." In *Historia política de los campesinos latinoamericanos: Colombia, Venezuela, Ecuador, Perú, Bolivia, Paraguay*, edited by Pablo González Casanova, 3:146–207. México, DF: Siglo Veintiuno.

Rivera, José Adán. 1994. Interview with author. Managua, Nicaragua, June 29.

Robotham, Don. 2005. *Culture, Society, and Economy: Bringing Production Back In.* Thousand Oaks, CA: Sage.

Rochat, Florian. 2012. Interview with the author. Geneva, March 7.

Roederer-Rynning, Christilla. 2002. "Farm Conflict in France and the Europeanisation of Agricultural Policy." *West European Politics* 25 (3): 105–125.

Rohde, David. 2007. "Army Enlists Anthropology in War Zones." *New York Times*, October 5. https://www.nytimes.com/2007/10/05/world/asia/05afghan.html.

Román Vega, Isabel. 1994. "Costa Rica: los campesinos también quieren futuro." In *Alternativas campesinas: modernización en el agro y movimiento campesino en Centroamérica*, edited by Klaus-Dieter Tangermann and Ivana Ríos Valdés, 71–94. Managua: CRIES.

Ronfeldt, David F., and John Arquilla. 2001. "What Next for Networks and Netwars?" In *Networks and Netwars: The Future of Terror, Crime, and Militancy*, edited by John Arquilla and David F. Ronfeldt, 311–361. Santa Monica, CA: Rand.

Rosa, Herman. 1993. *AID y las transformaciones globales en El Salvador.* Managua: CRIES.

Roseberry, William. 1993. "Beyond the Agrarian Question in Latin America." In *Confronting Historical Paradigms: Peasants, Labor, and the Capitalist World System in Africa and Latin America*, edited by Frederick Cooper, Allen F. Isaacman, Florencia E. Mallon, William Roseberry, and Steve J. Stern, 318–368. Madison: University of Wisconsin Press.

——. 1995. "Latin American Peasant Studies in a 'Postcolonial' Era." *Journal of Latin American Anthropology* 1 (1): 150–177.

——. 1996. "The Rise of Yuppie Coffees and the Reimagination of Class in the United States." *American Anthropologist* 98 (4): 762–775.

Rosenberg, Daniel. 2013. "Data before the Fact." In *"Raw Data" Is an Oxymoron*, edited by Lisa Gitelman, 15–40. Cambridge, MA: MIT Press.

Rosset, Peter M. 2003. "Food Sovereignty: Global Rallying Cry of Farmer Movements." *Institute for Food and Development Policy Backgrounder* 9 (4). https://archive.foodfirst.org/wp-content/uploads/2013/12/BK9_4-Fall-2003-Vol-9-4-Food-Sovereignty.pdf.

——. 2006. *Food Is Different: Why We Must Get the WTO Out of Agriculture.* Halifax, Nova Scotia: Fernwood.

Rosset, Peter M., and Miguel A. Altieri. 2017. *Agroecology: Science and Politics.* Rugby, Warwickshire: Practical Action.

Rosset, Peter M., and Lia Pinheiro Barbosa. 2021. "Autonomía y los movimientos sociales del campo en América Latina: un debate urgente." *Aposta: Revista de Ciencias Sociales* 89:8–31.

Rosset, Peter M., and María Elena Martínez-Torres. 2013. "Rural Social Movements and Diálogo de Saberes: Territories, Food Sovereignty, and Agroecology." Conference presentation, Yale University, September 14–15. http://www.schoolsforchiapas.org/wp-content/uploads/2014/06/4_Rosset_Torres_2013.pdf.

Rosset, Peter M., Valentín Val, Lia Pinheiro Barbosa, and Nils McCune. 2019. "Agroecology and La Via Campesina II. Peasant Agroecology Schools and the Formation of a Sociohistorical and Political Subject." *Agroecology and Sustainable Food Systems* 43 (7–8): 895–914. https://doi.org/10.1080/21683565.2019.1617222.

Ros-Tonen, Mirjam A. F., Yves-Pierre Benoît Van Leynseele, Anna Laven, and Terry Sunderland. 2015. "Landscapes of Social Inclusion: Inclusive Value-Chain Collaboration Through the Lenses of Food Sovereignty and Landscape Governance." *European Journal of Development Research* 27 (4): 523–540. https://doi.org/10.1057/ejdr.2015.50.

Roy, Joaquín. 1992. *The Reconstruction of Central America: The Role of the European Community.* Miami: University of Miami.

Rubin, Jeffrey W., and Emma Sokoloff-Rubin. 2013. *Sustaining Activism: A Brazilian Women's Movement and a Father-Daughter Collaboration.* Durham, NC: Duke University Press.

Rupp, Leila J. 1997. *Worlds of Women: The Making of an International Women's Movement.* Princeton, NJ: Princeton University Press.

Rural Coalition. 1994. *Building the Movement for Community Based Development: Rural Coalition 1994 Annual Assembly.* Arlington, VA: Rural Coalition.

Sahlins, Marshall. 1972. *Stone Age Economics.* Chicago: Aldine.

Saldomando, Ángel. 1992. *El retorno de la AID: El caso de Nicaragua.* Managua: CRIES.

Salemink, Oscar. 2003. "Science Intervention: Moral versus Political Economy and the Vietnam War." In *A Moral Critique of Development: In Search of Global Responsibilities*, edited by Philip Ufford Quarles van and Ananta Kumar Giri, 169–193. London: Routledge.

Salomon, Margot E. 2018. "Nihilists, Pragmatists and Peasants: A Dispatch on Contradiction in International Human Rights Law." IILJ Working Paper 2018/5. New York University Law School. https://www.iilj.org/wp-content/uploads/2018/11/Salomon-IILJ_2018_5-Megareg.pdf.

Salomón, Thomas. 1993. *El chinapopo, compañero del maíz.* Tegucigalpa: COMUNICA-CIDICCO.

Sampat, Preeti. 2015. "The 'Goan Impasse': Land Rights and Resistance to SEZs in Goa, India." *Journal of Peasant Studies* 42 (3–4): 765–790. https://doi.org/10.1080/03066150.2015.1013098.

Sanahuja, José Antonio. 1994. *Relaciones Europa Centroamérica: ¿Continuidad o cambio?* San José, Costa Rica: FLACSO.

——. 1996. "América Central y la Unión Europea: En busca de nuevas formas de cooperación." In *Unión Europea Centroamérica: Cambio de escenarios*, edited by Abelardo Morales, 117–158. San José, Costa Rica: FLACSO.

Sandbrook, Richard, Marc Edelman, Patrick Heller, and Judith Teichman. 2007. *Social Democracy in the Global Periphery: Origins, Challenges, Prospects.* Cambridge: Cambridge University Press.

Sanderson, Steven E. 1986. *The Transformation of Mexican Agriculture: International Structure and the Politics of Rural Change.* Princeton, NJ: Princeton University Press.

Santos, Boaventura de Sousa. 2008. "The World Social Forum and the Global Left." *Politics & Society* 36 (2): 247–270. https://doi.org/10.1177/0032329208316571.

——. 2009. *Sociología jurídica crítica: para un nuevo sentido común en el derecho.* Madrid: Trotta.

Santos, Eduardo A. 1988. "La seguridad alimentaria mundial y el proteccionismo agrícola." *Comercio Exterior* 38:635–644.

Saragih, Henry. 2009. Statement by Mr. Henry Saragih, General Coordinator of La Via Campesina at the UN General Assembly, April 6. https://viacampesina.org/en/via

-campesina-statement-at-the-un-general-assembly-on-the-global-food-crisis-and-the-right-to-food/.

———. 2011. Interview with the author. Jakarta, October 25.

Sassen, Saskia. 2000. "The State and the New Geography of Power." In *The Ends of Globalization: Bringing Society Back In*, edited by Don Kalb, Marco van der Land, and Richard Staring, 49–65. Lanham, MD: Rowman & Littlefield.

Saul, John S., and Roger Woods. 1971. "African Peasantries." In *Peasants and Peasant Societies*, edited by Teodor Shanin, 103–114. Harmondsworth: Penguin.

Schachet, Carol. 2009. "Interview with Diamantino Nhampossa of UNAC." Grassroots International, February 27. https://grassrootsonline.org/blog/newsbloginterview-diamantino-nhampossa-unac/.

Schanbacher, William D. 2010. *The Politics of Food: The Global Conflict between Food Security and Food Sovereignty*. Santa Barbara, CA: Praeger.

Schein, Louisa. 2002. "Mapping Hmong Media in Diasporic Space." In *Media Worlds: Anthropology on New Terrain*, edited by Faye D. Ginsburg, Lila Abu-Lughod, and Brian Larkin, 229–45. Berkeley: University of California Press.

Scheper-Hughes, Nancy. 1995. "Objectivity and Militancy: A Debate. The Primacy of the Ethical: Propositions for a Militant Anthropology." *Current Anthropology* 36 (3): 409–440.

Schiller, Nina Glick, Linda Basch, and Cristina Blanc Szanton. 1992. "Transnationalism, a New Analytic Framework for Understanding Migration." *Annals of the New York Academy of Sciences* 645:1–24.

Schmitt, Carl. 2005 (1922). *Political Theology: Four Chapters on the Concept of Sovereignty*. Chicago: University of Chicago Press.

Schoneveld, George Christoffel. 2014. "The Geographic and Sectoral Patterns of Large-Scale Farmland Investments in Sub-Saharan Africa." *Food Policy* 48:34–50. https://doi.org/10.1016/j.foodpol.2014.03.007.

Schori, Pierre. 1981. *El desafío europeo en Centroamérica*. San José, Costa Rica: EDUCA.

Scott, James C. 1976. *The Moral Economy of the Peasant: Rebellion and Subsistence in Southeast Asia*. New Haven, CT: Yale University Press.

———. 1985. *Weapons of the Weak: Everyday Forms of Peasant Resistance*. New Haven, CT: Yale University Press.

———. 1990. *Domination and the Arts of Resistance: Hidden Transcripts*. New Haven, CT: Yale University Press.

———. 2011. *The Art of Not Being Governed: An Anarchist History of Upland Southeast Asia*. New Haven, CT: Yale University Press.

Seattle Government. 2001. "Seattle's Racial Diversity in 2000."

Second European Forum. 2007. "Diamantino Leopoldo Nhampossa." Second European Forum on Sustainable Rural Development.

Segovia, Alexander. 1993. "Mercado de alimentos y sistema de banda de precios en Centroamérica." *Cuadernos de Investigación* [Centro de Investigaciones Tecnológicas y Científicas, Dirección de Investigaciones Económicas y Sociales, El Salvador] 4 (17): 1–20.

Seidman, Gay W. 2007. *Beyond the Boycott: Labor Rights, Human Rights, and Transnational Activism*. New York: Russell Sage Foundation.

Sen, Amartya. 1981. *Poverty and Famines: An Essay on Entitlement and Deprivation*. Oxford: Oxford University Press.

Seoane, José, and Emilio Taddei, eds. 2001a. "De Seattle a Porto Alegre: Pasado, presente y futuro del movimiento anti-mundialización neoliberal." In *Resistencias mundiales: De Seattle a Porto Alegre*, 105–129. Buenos Aires: CLACSO.

——, eds. 2001b. *Resistencias mundiales: De Seattle a Porto Alegre*. Buenos Aires: CLACSO.

Shanin, Teodor. 1971. "Introduction." In *Peasants and Peasant Societies*, edited by Teodor Shanin, 11–19. Harmondsworth: Penguin.

——. 1972. *The Awkward Class. Political Sociology of Peasantry in a Developing Society: Russia 1910–1925*. Oxford: Clarendon.

——. 1973. "The Nature and Logic of the Peasant Economy 1: A Generalisation." *Journal of Peasant Studies* 1 (1): 63–80.

——. 1990a. *Defining Peasants: Essays Concerning Rural Societies, Expolary Economies, and Learning from Them in the Contemporary World*. Oxford: Blackwell.

——. 1990b. "The Question of Socialism: A Development Failure or an Ethical Defeat?" *History Workshop* 30: 68–74.

Sharp, Gene, and Joshua Paulson. 2005. *Waging Nonviolent Struggle: 20th Century Practice and 21st Century Potential*. Boston: Extending Horizons Books.

Shaw, D. John. 2007. *World Food Security: A History since 1945*. New York: Palgrave Macmillan.

Shaw, Randy. 2008. *Beyond the Fields: Cesar Chavez, the UFW, and the Struggle for Justice in the 21st Century*. Berkeley: University of California Press.

Sheingate, Adam D. 2001. *The Rise of the Agricultural Welfare State: Institutions and Interest Group Power in the United States, France, and Japan*. Princeton, NJ: Princeton University Press.

Shiva, Vandana. 1998. "Dr Shiva's Reply to Prof. Nanjundaswamy's Letter." *Flora.Mai-Not*, December. https://groups.google.com/forum/#!topic/flora.mai-not/oon4Kv E5bAg.

——. 2001. *Yoked to Death: Globalisation and Corporate Control of Agriculture*. New Delhi: Research Foundation for Science, Technology, and Ecology.

Shiva, Vandana, and Radha Holla-Bhar. 1996. "Piracy by Patent: The Case of the Neem Tree." In *The Case Against the Global Economy and for a Turn toward the Local*, edited by Jerry Mander and Edward Goldsmith, 146–159. San Francisco: Sierra Club.

Shukaitis, Stevphen, and David Graeber. 2007. "Introduction." In *Constituent Imagination: Militant Investigations/Collective Theorization*, edited by Stevphen Shukaitis, David Graeber, and Erika Biddle, 11–34. Oakland, CA: AK Press.

Shukaitis, Stevphen, David Graeber, and Erika Biddle, eds. 2007. *Constituent Imagination: Militant Investigations//Collective Theorization*. Oakland, CA: AK Press.

Sierra Mejía, Marció, and Manuel Ramírez Mejía. 1994. "El papel del Estado en el desarrollo del sector rural de Honduras hacia el año 2000." In *¿Estado o mercado? Perspectivas para el desarrollo agrícola centroamericano hacia el año 2000*, edited by Hugo Noé Pino, Pedro Jiménez, and Andy Thorpe. Tegucigalpa: POSCAE-UNAH.

Sikkink, Kathryn. 1993. "Human Rights, Principled Issue-Networks, and Sovereignty in Latin America." *International Organization* 47:411–441.

Silber, Irene Carlota. 2007. "Local Capacity Building in 'Dysfunctional' Times: Internationals, Revolutionaries, and Activism in Postwar El Salvador." *Women's Studies Quarterly* 35 (3–4): 167–183.

Silverman, Sydel. 1979. "The Peasant Concept in Anthropology." *Journal of Peasant Studies* 7 (1): 49–69.

Simpson, Alan. 2004. "Letter from Alan Simpson, MP, 69 Other Parliamentarians, 47 Organizations, and Seven Individuals to Ambassador Tim Groser, Chairperson, WTO Committee on Agriculture, Geneva." Distributed by Aksel Naerstad to agri-trade@yahoogroups.com, July 14.

Simpson, Bradley. 2008. *Economists with Guns: Authoritarian Development and U.S.-Indonesian Relations, 1960–1968.* Stanford, CA: Stanford University Press.

Sinclair, Minor. 1995. *The New Politics of Survival: Grassroots Movements in Central America.* New York: Monthly Review Press.

Singh, Navsharan. 2021. "Agrarian Crisis and the Longest Farmers' Protest in Indian History." *New Labor Forum* 30 (3): 66–75. https://doi.org/10.1177/10957960211036016.

SIPA. 2000. "No to WTO/Seattle International People's Assembly Contribution to Shutting Down the World Trade Organization (WTO)." Secretariat, International People's Assembly. http://www.oocities.org/capitolhill/lobby/4677/sipa-pa.htm.

Sippel, Sarah Ruth, Nicolette Larder, and Geoffrey Lawrence. 2017. "Grounding the Financialization of Farmland: Perspectives on Financial Actors as New Land Owners in Rural Australia." *Agriculture and Human Values* 34:251–265. https://doi.org/10.1007/s10460-016-9707-2.

Smith, Alistair. 1997. "Moving beyond Banana Trade Wars, 1993–96." In *Mediating Sustainability: Practice to Policy for Sustainable Agricultural and Rural Development in Latin America*, edited by Jutta Blauert and Simon Zadek, 131–162. London: Cassell.

Smith, Jackie. 1997. "Characteristics of the Modern Transnational Social Movement Sector." In *Transnational Social Movements and Global Politics: Solidarity Beyond the State*, edited by Jackie Smith, Charles Chatfield, and Ron Pagnucco, 42–58. Syracuse, NY: Syracuse University Press.

——. 2002. "Globalizing Resistance: The Battle of Seattle and the Future of Social Movements." In *Globalization and Resistance: Transnational Dimensions of Social Movements*, edited by Jackie Smith and Hank Johnston, 207–227. Lanham, MD: Rowman & Littlefield.

Smith, Neil. 1993. "Homeless/Global: Scaling Places." In *Mapping the Futures: Local Cultures, Global Change*, edited by Jon Bird, Barry Curtis, Tim Putnam, George Robertson, and Lisa Tucker, 87–119. London: Routledge.

Sojo, Carlos. 1992. *La mano visible del mercado: la asistencia de Estados Unidos al sector privado costarricense en la década de los ochenta.* Managua: CRIES.

Solnit, Rebecca. 2017. "Protest and Persist: Why Giving up Hope Is Not an Option." *The Guardian*, March 13. https://www.theguardian.com/world/2017/mar/13/protest-persist-hope-trump-activism-anti-nuclear-movement.

Solórzano, Orlando. 1994. *El impacto del Sistema Arancelario Centroamericano (SAC) sobre el sector agropecuario: una aproximación.* San José, Cota Rica: IICA.

Spalding, Rose J. 1994. *Capitalists and Revolution in Nicaragua: Opposition and Accommodation, 1979–1993.* Chapel Hill: University of North Carolina Press.

Speed, Shannon. 2008. "Forged in Dialogue: Toward a Critically Engaged Activist Research." In *Engaging Contradictions: Theory, Politics, and Methods of Activist Scholarship*, edited by Charles R. Hale, 213–236. Berkeley: University of California Press.

Stahler-Sholk, Richard. 1990. "Ajuste y el sector agropecuario en Nicaragua en los 80: una evaluación preliminar." In *Políticas de ajuste en Nicaragua*, edited by Mario Arana, 63–94. Managua: CRIES.

Stalin, J. V. 1955. "Dizzy with Success: Concerning Questions of the Collective-Farm Movement." In *Works.* Vol. 12, 197–205. Moscow: Foreign Languages Publishing House.

Stédile, João Pedro. 2002. "Landless Battalions: The Sem Terra Movement of Brazil." *New Left Review* 15:76–104.

——. 2007. "The Class Struggles in Brazil: The Perspective of the MST. João Pedro Stédile Interviewed by Atilio Boron." In *Global Flashpoints: Reactions to Imperialism and Neoliberalism*, 194–216. Socialist Register 2008. London: Merlin.

Stédile, João Pedro, and Bernardo Mançano Fernandes. 1999. *Brava gente: a trajetória do MST e a luta pela terra no Brasil.* São Paulo: Fundacão Perseu Abramo.

Stein, Eduardo. 1994. Interview with author. Panama City, June 22.

Stein, Eduardo, and Salvador Arias Peñate. 1992. *Democracia sin pobreza: Alternativa de desarrollo para el istmo centroamericano.* San José, Costa Rica: DEI.

Stephen, Lynn. 1997. *Women and Social Movements in Latin America: Power from Below.* Austin: University of Texas Press.

Stichting, Max Havelaar. 1992. *Max Havelaar: un modelo exitoso de comercio justo.* Utrecht: mimeographed.

Stiglitz, Joseph E. 2001. "Foreword." In *The Great Transformation: The Political and Economic Origins of Our Time*, by Karl Polanyi, 2nd ed., vii–xvii. Boston: Beacon.

Stirrat, Roderick. 1996. "The New Orthodoxy and Old Truths: Participation, Empowerment and Other Buzzwords." In *Assessing Participation: A Debate from South Asia*, 67–92. Delhi: Konark Publishers.

Stone, Glenn Davis. 2022a. *The Agricultural Dilemma: How Not to Feed the World.* New York: Routledge.

——. 2022b. "Surveillance Agriculture and Peasant Autonomy." *Journal of Agrarian Change* 22 (3): 608–631. https://doi.org/10.1111/joac.12470.

Storey, Shannon. 2002. Interview with author. Saskatoon, Canada, November 24.

Sullivan, Paul. 1991. *Unfinished Conversations: Mayas and Foreigners between Two Wars.* Berkeley: University of California Press.

Sustainable Cities Collective. 2011. "Maine Town Becomes First in US to Declare Food Sovereignty," March 17. http://sustainablecitiescollective.com/node/22295.

Tangermann, Klaus-Dieter, and Ivana Ríos Valdés, eds. 1994. *Alternativas campesinas: modernización en el agro y movimiento campesino en Centroamérica.* Managua: CRIES.

Tarlau, Rebecca. 2014. "From a Language to a Theory of Resistance: Critical Pedagogy, the Limits of 'Framing,' and Social Change." *Educational Theory* 64 (4): 369–392.

Tarrow, Sidney G. 1994. *Power in Movement: Social Movements, Collective Action, and Politics.* Cambridge: Cambridge University Press.

——. 1995. "The Europeanisation of Conflict: Reflections from a Social Movement Perspective." *West European Politics* 18 (2): 223–251.

——. 2001. "Transnational Politics: Contention and Institutions in International Politics." *Annual Review of Political Science* 4: 1–20.

——. 2005. *The New Transnational Activism.* New York: Cambridge University Press.

Thompson, E. P. 1963. *The Making of the English Working Class.* New York: Random House.

——. 1971. "The Moral Economy of the English Crowd in the Eighteenth Century." *Past & Present* 50:76–136.

——. 1991. "The Moral Economy Reviewed." In *Customs in Common*, 259–351. Pontypool, Wales: Merlin.

Thompson, Robert L. 2001. "Thompson to Rafael Alegría: Your Petition on Land Reform." Washington, DC. Photocopy.

Thorpe, Andy, Hugo Noé Pino, Pedro Jiménez, Ana Lucía Restrepo, Dagoberto Suazo, and Ramón Salgado. 1995. *El impacto del ajuste en el agro hondureño.* Tegucigalpa: POSCAE-UNAH.

Thurston, H. David, Margaret Smith, George Abawi, and Steve Kearl, eds. 1994. *Tapado Slash/Mulch: How Farmers Use It and What Researchers Know about It.* Ithaca, NY: Cornell International Institute for Food, Agriculture, and Development.

Tilley, Virginia Q. 2002. "New Help or New Hegemony? The Transnational Indigenous Peoples' Movement and 'Being Indian' in El Salvador." *Journal of Latin American Studies* 34 (3): 525–554. https://doi.org/10.1017/S0022216X0200651X.

Tilly, Charles. 1984. "Social Movements and National Politics." In *Statemaking and Social Movements*, edited by Charles Bright and Susan Harding, 297–317. Ann Arbor: University of Michigan Press.

———. 2001. "Do unto Others." In *Political Altruism? Solidarity Movements in International Perspective*, edited by Marco Giugni and Florence Passy, 27–47. Lanham, MD: Rowman & Littlefield.

Toensmeier, Eric, Mamta Mehra, Chad Frischmann, and Jonathan Foley. 2020. "Farming Our Way Out of the Climate Crisis." Project Drawdown. https://drawdown.org/sites/default/files/pdfs/DrawdownPrimer_FoodAgLandUse_Dec2020_01c.pdf.

Torres, Oscar, and Hernán Alvarado. 1990. *Política macroeconómica y sus efectos en la agricultura y la seguridad alimentaria. Caso: Costa Rica*. Panama: CADESCA.

Trencher, Susan R. 1998. "Righteous Anthropology." *Society in Transition* 29 (3–4): 118–129.

Trouillot, Michel-Rolphe. 1991. "Anthropology and the Savage Slot: The Poetics and Politics of Otherness." In *Recapturing Anthropology: Working in the Present*, edited by Richard G. Fox, 17–44. Santa Fe: School of American Research.

Trubek, Amy B. 2000. "The Taste of Place." Paper presented at the Conference on Taste, Technology and Terroir. European Union Center, University of Wisconsin, Madison.

Tzib, Rodolfo. 1994. Interview with author. Panama City, June 23.

UN Population Division. 2019. *World Urbanization Prospects: The 2018 Revision*. New York: United Nations.

UNAG. 1988. *El campesino va a saber organizarse: Guía metodológica para la organización del campesinado*. Managua: UNAG.

UNDROP. 2018. "United Nations Declaration on the Rights of Peasants and Other People Working in Rural Areas." A/RES/73/165, December 17. https://digitallibrary.un.org/record/1661560/files/A_RES_73_165-EN.pdf.

UNESCO. 2001. "UNESCO Universal Declaration on Cultural Diversity." http://portal.unesco.org/en/ev.php-URL_ID=13179&URL_DO=DO_TOPIC&URL_SECTION=201.html.

UNHRC Advisory Committee. 2010. "Preliminary Study of the Human Rights Council Advisory Committee on Discrimination in the Context of the Right to Food." A/HRC/13/32, February 22. http://www2.ohchr.org/english/bodies/hrcouncil/docs/13session/A-HRC-13-32.pdf.

———. 2011. "Preliminary Study on the Advancement of the Rights of Peasants and Other People Working in Rural Areas." A/HRC/AC/6/CRP.2, January 17–21. http://www2.ohchr.org/english/bodies/hrcouncil/advisorycommittee/docs/session6/A.HRC.AC.6.CRP.2_en.pdf.

———. 2012. "Final Study of the Human Rights Council Advisory Committee on the Advancement of the Rights of Peasants and Other People Working in Rural Areas." A/HRC/19/75, February 24. http://www.ohchr.org/Documents/HRBodies/HRCouncil/RegularSession/Session19/A-HRC-19-75_en.pdf.

UPANACIONAL. 1989. "Los planteamientos de UPANACIONAL frente a la agricultura de cambio." *Panorama Campesino* 3 (May): 1–17.

Uphoff, Norman. 2003. "Higher Yields with Fewer External Inputs? The System of Rice Intensification and Potential Contributions to Agricultural Sustainability." *International Journal of Agricultural Sustainability* 1 (1): 38–50.

Uprimny, Rodrigo. 2011. "The Recent Transformation of Constitutional Law in Latin America: Trends and Challenges." *Texas Law Review* 89:1587–1609.

——. 2018. "En la ONU los campesinos cuentan, pero aquí ni los cuentan." *El Espectador,* September 30. https://www.elespectador.com/opinion/en-la-onu-los-campesinos -cuentan-pero-aqui-ni-los-cuentan-columna-815164.

Val, Valentín, Peter M. Rosset, Carla Zamora Lomelí, Omar Felipe Giraldo, and Dianne Rocheleau. 2019. "Agroecology and La Via Campesina I: The Symbolic and Material Construction of Agroecology through the Dispositive of 'Peasant-to-Peasant' Processes." *Agroecology and Sustainable Food Systems* 43 (7–8): 872–894. https://doi.org /10.1080/21683565.2019.1600099.

Valente, Flavio Luiz Schieck. 2002. "Um breve histórico do conceito de segurança alimentar no âmbito internacional." Red Interamericana de Agriculturas y Democracia.

Van der Ploeg, Jan Douwe. 2008. *The New Peasantries: Struggles for Autonomy and Sustainability in an Era of Empire and Globalization.* London: Earthscan.

Van Rooy, Alison. 2004. *The Global Legitimacy Game: Civil Society, Globalization, and Protest.* New York: Palgrave Macmillan.

Vandenbogaerde, Arne. 2015. *The Human Rights Council from Below: A Case Study of the Declaration on the Rights of Peasants.* Antwerp: University of Antwerp.

Vargas, João H. Costa. 2008. "Activist Scholarship: Limits and Possibilities in Times of Black Genocide." In *Engaging Contradictions: Theory, Politics, and Methods of Activist Scholarship*, edited by Charles R. Hale, 164–182. Berkeley: University of California Press.

Váscomes, Wladimir. 2004. "Tribunal por la soberanía alimentaria: juicio al Banco Mundial y al Banco Interamericano de Desarrollo por su deuda social y ecológica en la agricultura con los pueblos y países de América Latina." Press release, distributed by Jóvenes Tejiendo un Nuevo País to info-jtnp@lists.riseup.net, July 27.

Verdery, Katherine. 1996. *What Was Socialism, and What Comes Next?* Princeton, NJ: Princeton University Press.

Verhagen, Nico. 1998. Interview with the author. Brussels, April 29.

——. 2004. "Commentary on Land and Rural Development Policies of the World Bank. Vía Campesina."

Vidal, John. 2004. "Obituary: MD Nanjundaswamy." *The Guardian*, February 5. http:// www.theguardian.com/news/2004/feb/06/guardianobituaries.globalisation.

Villatoro, Amanda. 1994. Interview with the author. San Salvador, July 21.

Vine, David. 2007. "Island of Injustice: The U.S. Has a Moral Duty to the People of Diego Garcia." *Washington Post*, January 2. http://www.washingtonpost.com/wp -dyn/content/article/2007/01/01/AR2007010100698.html.

Voz Campesina. 1995. "La Mesa Nacional Campesina." *Voz Campesina* 4 (January– February): 15.

Wakin, Eric. 1992. *Anthropology Goes to War: Professional Ethics & Counterinsurgency in Thailand.* Madison: University of Wisconsin, Center for Southeast Asian Studies.

Walker, Kathy Le Mons. 2002. "'Gangster Capitalism' and Peasant Politics in China." Paper presented at the Workshop on Terror and Violence in State and Institutional Context after September 11, New York Academy of Sciences.

Wallace, Robert G. 2016. *Big Farms Make Big Flu: Dispatches on Infectious Disease, Agribusiness, and the Nature of Science.* New York: Monthly Review Press.

Wallace, Robert G., Alex Liebman, Luis Fernando Chaves, and Rodrick Wallace. 2020. "COVID-19 and Circuits of Capital." *Monthly Review*, March 27, 2020. https:// monthlyreview.org/2020/03/27/covid-19-and-circuits-of-capital/.

Wallerstein, Immanuel Maurice. 1974. *The Modern World-System: Capitalist Agriculture and the Origins of the European World-Economy in the Sixteenth Century*. New York: Academic Press.

Warman, Arturo. 1976. *Y venimos a contradecir: los campesinos de Morelos y el estado nacional*. México, DF: La Casa Chata.

——. 1988. "Los estudios campesinos: veinte años después." *Comercio Exterior* 38 (7): 653–658.

——. 2001. *El campo mexicano en el Siglo XX*. México, DF: Fondo de Cultura Económica.

Warren, Kay B. 2006. "Perils and Promises of Engaged Anthropology: Historical Transitions and Ethnographic Dilemmas." In *Engaged Observer: Anthropology, Advocacy, and Activism*, edited by Victoria Sanford and Asale Angel-Ajani, 213–227. New Brunswick, NJ: Rutgers University Press.

Wasserstrom, Robert. 1975. "Revolution in Guatemala: Peasants and Politics Under the Arbenz Government." *Comparative Studies in Society and History* 17 (4): 443–478. https://doi.org/10.1017/S0010417500007969.

Waterman, Peter. 2001. *Globalization, Social Movements, and the New Internationalism*. London: Continuum.

Waterman, Peter, and Jill Timms. 2005. "Trade Union Internationalism and a Global Civil Society in the Making." In *Global Civil Society 2004/5*, edited by Helmut Anheier, Marlies Glasius, and Mary Kaldor, 178–202. London: Sage.

Watts, Jonathan. 2017. "Brazil Abolishes Huge Amazon Reserve in 'Biggest Attack' in 50 Years." *The Guardian*, August 24. http://www.theguardian.com/environment/2017/aug/24/brazil-abolishes-huge-amazon-reserve-in-biggest-attack-in-50-years.

Weber, Max. 1958. *From Max Weber: Essays in Sociology*, edited by C. Wright Mills and Hans Gerth. New York: Oxford University Press.

Webster, Neil. 2004. *Understanding the Evolving Diversities and Originalities in Rural Social Movements in the Age of Globalization*. Civil Society and Social Movements Programme Paper, No. 7. Geneva: UNRISD.

Weis, Tony. 2007. *The Global Food Economy: The Battle for the Future of Farming*. London: Zed Books.

Weiser, Matt. 2004. "UFW, Affiliates Are a Family Affair." *The Bakersfield Californian*, May 9.

Welch, Cliff. 2000. "Marking Time with the CLOC: International Rural Labor Solidarity in the Americas from World War II to the Third Millennium." Paper presented at the XXII International Congress of the Latin American Studies Association, Miami.

Werbner, Pnina. 2008. "Introduction: Towards a New Cosmopolitan Anthropology." In *Anthropology and the New Cosmopolitanism: Rooted, Feminist and Vernacular Perspectives*, edited by Pnina Werbner, 1–29. New York: Berg.

Wickham-Crowley, Timothy P. 1991. *Exploring Revolution: Essays on Latin American Insurgency and Revolutionary Theory*. Armonk, NY: M.E. Sharpe.

Wiebe, Nettie. 2002. Interview with the author. Saskatoon, Canada, November 22.

——. 2013. "Women of La Via Campesina: Creating and Occupying Our Rightful Spaces." In *La Vía Campesina's Open Book: Celebrating 20 Years of Struggle and Hope*, 1–5. Jakarta: La Via Campesina. https://viacampesina.org/en/wp-content/uploads/sites/2/2013/05/EN-01.pdf.

——. 2017. "Agrarian Feminism in Our Time and Place." Active History. January 24. http://activehistory.ca/2017/01/agrarian-feminism-in-our-time-and-place/.

Wijkman, Per Magnus. 2003. "U.S. Trade Policy: Alternative Tacks or Parallel Tracks?" In *Unilateralism and U.S. Foreign Policy: International Perspectives*, edited by David Malone and Yuen Foong Khong, 251–284. Boulder, CO: Lynne Rienner.

Wilford, Allen. 1985. *Farmgate Defense*. Toronto: New Canada Publications.

Windfuhr, Michael, and Rafael Alegría. 2002. "Global Campaign for Agrarian Reform: Letter to James D. Wolfensohn, the World Bank."

Windfuhr, Michael, and Jennie Jonsén. 2005. *Food Sovereignty: Towards Democracy in Localized Food Systems*. Warwickshire: ITDG Publishing & FIAN. http://www .ukabc.org/foodsovereignty_itdg_fian_print.pdf.

Wittman, Hannah, Annette Desmarais, and Nettie Wiebe. 2010. "The Origins and Potential of Food Sovereignty." In *Food Sovereignty: Reconnecting Food, Nature & Community*, edited by Hannah Wittman, Annette Aurélie Desmarais, and Nettie Wiebe, 1–14. Halifax, Nova Scotia: Fernwood.

Wolf, Eric R. 1955. "Types of Latin American Peasantry: A Preliminary Discussion." *American Anthropologist* 57 (3): 452–471.

——. 1957. "Closed Corporate Peasant Communities in Mesoamerica and Central Java." *Southwestern Journal of Anthropology* 13 (1): 1–18.

——. 1966. *Peasants*. Englewood Cliffs, N.J.: Prentice-Hall.

——. 1969. *Peasant Wars of the Twentieth Century*. New York: Harper & Row.

——. 1986. "The Vicissitudes of the Closed Corporate Peasant Community." *American Ethnologist* 13 (2): 325–329.

Wolf, Eric R., and Joseph G. Jorgensen. 1970. "Anthropology on the Warpath in Thailand." *New York Review of Books* 15 (9): 26–35.

Wolff, Karsten. 2004. "Huge Solidarity for the People's Caravan in France." People's Caravan 2004 for Food Sovereignty. Press release, distributed by Pesticide Action Network (PAN) Asia and the Pacific to agri-trade@yahoogroups.com, September 20.

Wolfwood, Theresa. 2009. "Nettie Wiebe: Agrarian Feminist." Barnard-Boecker Centre Foundation, December 13. http://www.bbcf.ca/_articles/2007/wiebe/wiebe.htm.

Wood, Lesley J. 2004. "Breaking the Bank and Taking to the Streets: How Protesters Target Neoliberalism." *Journal of World-Systems Research* 10 (1): 69–89.

Zamorano Villarreal, Gabriela. 2009. "Reimagining the State: Politics, Video and Indigenous Struggles in Bolivia." PhD diss., City University of New York.

Zavala, Wilbur. 1995. Interview with author. Managua, Nicaragua, August 10.

Zerilli, Filippo M. 2010. "The Rule of Soft Law: An Introduction." *Focaal—Journal of Global and Historical Anthropology* 56: 3–18. https://doi.org/10.3167/fcl.2010 .560101.

Zimerman, Artur. 2010. *Terra manchada de sangue: conflitos agrários e mortes no campo no Brasil democrático*. São Paulo: Humanitas FAPESP.

Zoomers, Annelies, and Gemma van der Haar, eds. 2000. *Current Land Policy in Latin America: Regulating Land Tenure under Neo-Liberalism*. Amsterdam: Royal Tropical Institute—KIT Publishers.

Index

Note: Page numbers followed by letters *b, f,* and *t* refer to boxes, figures, and tables.

AAM. *See* American Agriculture Movement
Aberdeen, Ishbel Gordon, 19
academic journals, 287n13, 288n20
academics, and social movements: areas of
synergy between, 233–34, 241–42, 245,
287n12, 289n31; most valuable contribution to, 4, 241, 245, 289n29; sources of
tension between, 234–38, 244–45. *See also*
researcher(s)
Ackerman, Bruce, 87
Action Group on Erosion, Technology and
Concentration (ETC Group), Canada, 59t
activists: multilingualism of, 89, 91, 268n1;
network, disparate demands on, 137–38;
official narratives of, 243; social energy/
cultural capital of, 98, 264. *See also* peasant
activists; researcher-activist relations
ACWW. *See* Associated Country Women of
the World
Adams, Richard N., 288n22
ADC. *See* Democratic Peasant Alliance, El
Salvador
Advisory Committee of the Human Rights
Council, 285n19; definition of "peasant,"
226, 227
Afghanistan: social scientists and US military
strategy in, 237, 278n1; Soviet invasion of,
and farm crisis of 1980s, 24
AFL-CIO: agricultural workers' unions and,
44; and Iniciativa CID, 143
Africa: land grabbing in, 249, 251, 259; "second
green revolution for," advocates of, 258;
timber exploitation in, investments in, 257;
transnational agrarian movement in, 64, 65,
66, 97–98. *See also specific countries*
African palm production: in Honduras, 211;
land grabbing associated with, 250, 252, 253
African Peasants' Academy (Université
Paysanne Africaine), 65
Agee, Philip, 289n24
agrarian change, field of, 22b
agrarian reform(s): and ceilings on farm size,
184; evisceration and reversal of, 161; global

campaign for, 62–63, 67, 281n23; market-
based, 8, 258; market-based, struggles
against, 170, 281n23; state-led, in 1960s-
1970s, 8
agrarian studies, field of, 22b
Agreement on Agriculture (AoA), WTO, 72,
80, 165
agribusiness corporations: anticorporate
farming laws in US and, 184; and commodity prices, downward trend in, 159; critical
agrarian studies confronting, 9; export-
oriented, push to boost international competitiveness, 43; false marketing by, 50b;
food security concept and, 283; and food
supply, efforts to gain control of, 170; and
genetic material, efforts to monopolize, 55;
global trade liberalization and increased
market control by, 72; GM crops promoted
by, 67; Indian laws opening markets to, 12;
influence of financial capital on, 253; mergers among, 25, 68, 163; moral economy and,
169; and peasant networks, challenges for,
68; and politicians, 258; protests against, 47,
50, 73; size of, concept of food sovereignty
and issue of, 182–86, 189; and subsistence
crisis, 161. *See also specific corporations*
agricultor (term), 22b
agricultural commodities, price of. *See*
commodity prices
Agricultural Missions (organization), 19–20
Agriculture, Peasant and Modernization
Network. *See* APM
Agriterra (organization), 59t; and IFAP's
collapse, 269n5
agroecology, growing importance of, 10–11, 258
Agro-Food Solidarities (SOLAGRAL), France,
61t
Alegría, Rafael, 57, 62, 97, 165–66, 169, 268n20
Alvarez, Sonia, 134
Amador, Jorge, 271n6
American Agriculture Movement (AAM),
38; and North American Farm Alliance
(NAFA), 43; symbolic politics of, 58

Milton Keynes UK
Ingram Content Group UK Ltd.
UKHW040636050124
435429UK00003B/87